# JMX™ Programming

## Mike Jasnowski

**WILEY**

Wiley Publishing, Inc.

Best-Selling Books • Digital Downloads • e-Books • Answer Networks • e-Newsletters
Branded Web Sites • e-Learning

**JMX ™ Programming**

Published by
**Wiley Publishing, Inc.**
909 Third Avenue
New York, NY 10022
www.wiley.com

Copyright © 2002 by Wiley Publishing, Inc., Indianapolis, Indiana

Library of Congress Control Number: 2002107906

ISBN: 0-7645-4957-X

Manufactured in the United States of America

10 9 8 7 6 5 4 3 2 1

1O/QX/RS/QS/IN

Published by Wiley Publishing, Inc., Indianapolis, Indiana
Published simultaneously in Canada

## About the Author

**Mike Jasnowski** is a Senior Software Engineer at eXcelon Corporation in Burlington, MA. He is the project leader for the Web-based tools for administering eXcelon's Business Process Manager. He has been involved with computers and software for over 18 years, dating back to the days before Java and XML, and some of his first programs were written on a TRS-80 and Apple IIe. Mike has worked on a variety of operating systems, including MVS, Linux, Windows, and VM, in addition to a variety of programming languages. He was also employed by Sprint for more than nine years as a systems programmer, working on automation and systems management utilities. While at Sprint he also worked in computer operations and was in the trenches keeping critical systems running, so he knows firsthand the importance of being able to efficiently manage computer systems.

Later, he worked in the health care and finance industries as a software engineer before finally landing at eXcelon. He has been published in *Java Developers Journal* and *XML Journal* and recently contributed material to *Developing Dynamic WAP Applications* from Manning Press. He also contributed his expertise on J2EE transaction management with JTA to the *J2EE Bible* from Hungry Minds. He was the lead author on the *Java, XML and Web Services Bible* from Hungry Minds. He lives in Amherst, NH, with his wife, Tracy; his daughter, Emmeline; and a host of pets.

*This book is dedicated to my daughter, Emmeline.*

# Credits

**Executive Editor**
Chris Webb

**Acquisitions Editor**
Grace Buechlein

**Project Editor**
Sara Shlaer

**Technical Editors**
AdventNet, Inc.
Minnie Tanglao

**Copy Editor**
Luann Rouff

**Editorial Manager**
Mary Beth Wakefield

**Vice President and Executive
Group Publisher**
Richard Swadley

**Vice President and Executive
Publisher**
Bob Ipsen

**Executive Editorial Director**
Mary Bednarek

**Project Coordinator**
Maridee Ennis

**Graphics and Production
Specialists**
Karl Brandt

**Proofreader**
Kim Cofer

**Indexer**
Virginia Bess Munroe

# Acknowledgments

I would first like to thank Grace Buechlein and Wiley Publishing, Inc., for giving me the opportunity to work on another project.

I would also like to thank my editor, Sara Shlaer, and technical reviewer Minnie Tanglao, whose constructive comments and insight have made the book more accessible and understandable. Thanks to Todd Thomas for his help in laying out the structure for the book. I would also like to thank Luann Rouff for her excellent copyediting. And many thanks to the following individuals at AdventNet for their technical review of several chapters: Dr. Giri Giridharan, V. Mathivanan, Hyther Nizam, Dr. Tony Thomas, and Sekar Vembu.

Finally, I would like to thank my wife, Tracy, and my daughter, Emmeline, who gave me the time to work on the book during evenings and weekends.

# Preface

Systems management has been around for decades in many shapes and forms. Until the advent of JMX, however, there were few options for integrating the management of Java-based products into management infrastructures. Individual products often had their own management consoles, requiring time and training. With JMX, a unified view of both Java and other applications can be achieved. JMX can be used to provide a management layer around legacy applications written in non-Java applications as well.

Support for JMX has blossomed over the past few years, and JMX is likely to become a part of the J2SE in release 1.5. The creation of JMX has also spawned a number of associated Java Service Requests (JSR) that address various components of JMX and enable the building of management APIs on top of JMX. This book is based on the latest JMX 1.1 maintenance release.

This book was written to serve as a guide to using the Java Management Extensions (JMX) for writing and implementing management into Java applications. It offers complete coverage of the core components of JMX, and provides practical examples of each component, as well as examples of using several of them together. You'll find practical applications of using JMX in later chapters, where you'll write management applications to monitor a hardware device, monitor a J2EE application server, and finally implement and monitor J2EE application components such as servlets and Message-Driven Beans.

## Who Should Read This Book?

This book is aimed at intermediate to advanced Java developers. It is also helpful for readers to have some background in systems management or administration, but it is not required. The first chapter provides some foundation and serves as a backdrop to understanding how JMX fits into the picture. If you are writing enterprise Java applications using J2EE components such as servlets, JavaServer Pages, or Enterprise JavaBeans (EJBS), you will find useful information about providing a management interface to your application.

## Hardware and Software Requirements

This book utilizes the Sun JMX reference implementation version 1.1 maintenance release. You can download the latest JMX 1.1 maintenance release from java.sun.com/jmx.

The book also uses a number of tools and products in various examples. The following products and tools are used in the examples of this book:

◆ MS Visual Studio v. 5.00 (minimum version)

◆ Sun JDK 1.3.1

◆ Editor/IDE (I used Editpad, which is like Notepad)

◆ Microsoft Platform SDK header (provides winspool.h for later examples)

◆ BEA WebLogic Application Server 7.0 (evaluation copy is okay) available at www.beasys.com

Following are the minimum requirements for running the examples in this book:

- ◆ Intel Pentium processor; 450 MHz or equivalent
- ◆ Microsoft Windows 2000, Windows NT 4.0
- ◆ 128MB of available RAM
- ◆ 2GB of available disk space
- ◆ Color monitor capable of 800 x 600 resolution

# How This Book Is Organized

This book is divided into four parts. The following paragraphs explain what you'll find in each section.

## Part I: Getting Started with JMX Programming

Part I is designed to introduce you to the world of systems management and the challenges it presents. It provides an overview of JMX, explaining its architecture and how it fits into systems management. Chapter 1 begins with a review of systems management, including current standards and how they are used. It finishes with an introduction to JMX. Chapter 2 delves further into JMX, exploring its architecture and major components. Chapter 3 takes the reader through a basic JMX application and discusses problems that may arise while creating and running it.

## Part II: Using the Instrumentation Layer

Part II is designed to introduce you to implementing managed resources using the various types of MBeans defined in the JMX specification. Chapter 4 begins with an introduction to the most basic type of component in the JMX architecture, the MBean, and in particular, the standard MBean. It describes how to create a standard MBean and associate it with a managed resource. Chapter 5 introduces you to another type of MBean, the dynamic MBean, and describes how to create one and dynamically create the management interface of a resource. Chapter 6 introduces you to the two remaining types of MBean: model and open. It provides detailed information about the `ModelMBean` interfaces and associated descriptors, and describes how to use them to create a management interface for a resource. Chapter 7 finishes Part II with a discussion of the relation service that is a part of the JMX specification. Relations enable you to create associations between managed resources using notations and conventions similar to those used in Unified Modeling Language.

## Part III: Implementing the Agent Layer

Part III is designed to introduce you to the agent layer and the components — such as the MBean Server — that exist at this level. Chapter 8 begins with a look at a core component of any JMX implementation, the MBean Server. You learn how to use the MBean Server to register and unregister MBeans, as well as query for MBeans. Chapter 9 looks more closely at the query facilities of the MBean Server, and describes how to construct queries using the Query classes and interfaces in the API. Chapter 10 examines the monitoring services of the JMX specification. This service enables you to watch the value of a managed resource's attribute and generate a notification. Chapter 11 looks at the notification facilities of JMX, which enable you to notify another component when a certain even has occurred. Chapter 12 finishes this part with a section that has no definition in the current JMX specification: protocol adapters and connectors. Here you'll learn how to provide remote access to JMX services and the MBean Server using HTTP, RMI, and SNMP.

## Part IV: Programming JMX

Part IV is where you get to flex the knowledge you gained in prior chapters by writing sample applications that cover three different systems management scenarios. Chapter 13 puts your knowledge to work by building a working JMX application for monitoring the state of a printer. Chapter 14 shows you how you can use JMX to remotely manage an application server. You'll use components of the BEA WebLogic Application Server 7.0 to create a management console for monitoring WebLogic servers, and start and stop instances of them. Chapter 15 takes a closer look at JMX as it is used in application servers, and describes how you might implement support for monitoring servlets and Message-Driven Beans.

### Appendixes

The appendixes of this book provide additional useful information. Appendix A offers a list of JMX and systems management resources, and Appendix B contains a list of JMX exceptions and causes. Appendix C covers using the debugging and tracing facilities that Sun provides with its JMX reference implementation, and Appendix D provides a UML diagram quick reference of many of the JMX interfaces and classes.

## Conventions Used in This Book

The following sections explain the conventions used in this book.

### Menu commands

When you are instructed to select a command from a menu, you see the menu and the command separated by an arrow symbol. For example, when you're asked to choose the Open command from the File menu, the directive will appear as File ⇨ Open.

### Typographical conventions

I use *italic* type to indicate new terms or to provide emphasis. I use **boldface** type to indicate text that you need to type directly from the keyboard.

### Code

I use a special typeface to indicate code, as demonstrated in the following example of Java code:

```
PrinterObject bean = new PrinterObject();
```

This special code font is also used within paragraphs to make elements such as method names, for example, `invoke()`, stand out from the regular text.

# Navigating This Book

This book is designed to be read from beginning to end, although if you have already been introduced to the basics of JMX, you can easily skip over the first set of chapters and return to them at some other time.

Tips, Notes, and Cross-References appear in the text to indicate important or especially helpful items. Following is a list of these items and their functions:

> **TIP:** Tips provide you with extra knowledge that separates the novice from the pro.

> **NOTE:** Notes provide additional or critical information and technical data on the current topic.

> **CROSS-REFERENCE:** Cross-Reference icons indicate other chapters in the book where you can find more information about a particular topic.

# Companion Web Site

This book provides a companion Web site where you can download the code from various chapters. All the code listings reside in a single WinZip file that you can download by going to www.wiley.com/extras and selecting the JMX Programming Guide link. After you download the file (jmx.zip), and if you have WinZip already on your system, you can open it and extract the contents by double-clicking. If you don't currently have WinZip, you can download an evaluation version from www.winzip.com.

When extracting the files, use WinZip's default options (confirm that the Use Folder Names option is checked) and extract the jmx.zip file to a drive on your system that has about 3MB of available space. The extraction process creates a folder called JMX-Wiley. As long as the Use Folder Names option is checked in the Extract dialog box, an entire folder structure is created within the JMX-Wiley folder. You'll see folders arranged by chapter number, and some of those chapter folders contain subfolders. If you'd rather download just the code you need from a particular chapter — when you need it — simply click the separate chapter link on the Web site instead of downloading the entire WinZip file.

# Further Information

You can find more help for specific problems and questions by investigating several Web sites. Appendix A contains a list of resources that you can use for this purpose.

Feel free to contact me with any questions or comments. I greatly appreciate any feedback you have about the book (good or bad). It will enable me to update any future editions to ensure that you have the most current information you need to write the best applications you can.

*Good Luck!*

Mike Jasnowski
boopan@msn.com
May 2002

# Contents

# Part I

# Getting Started with JMX Programming

**Chapter 1: Managing Applications and Networks**

**Chapter 2: Inspecting the JMX Architecture**

**Chapter 3: Writing Your First JMX Application**

# Chapter 1

# Managing Applications and Networks

Computer capabilities today far surpass the computing power of ten years ago. The applications and networks that comprise the foundation of computing also surpass those of the previous decade. Over time, the complexity and magnitude of some applications have created a need for better ways to manage them. Managing them must be done in a way that does not create problems of its own.

System managers must address both network and application resources. Network resources can be file shares, printers, or terminals. Application resources can be simple or complex applications, or individual components in an application.

In this chapter, you learn about system management and some of the challenges of managing networks and applications. You are also introduced to a framework for implementing management capabilities using the Java programming language, the JMX API. The chapter begins by describing what it means to manage networks and applications. If you are comfortable with the concepts of system management, and understand conceptually how SNMP works, you can skip ahead to the "Introducing the JMX API" section of this chapter.

## What Is System Management?

A *system* describes all the resources you have in a computing environment. You could describe your home computer as a system: You have a processing unit, software applications, peripherals such as zip drives, printers, floppy drives, and so forth. All of these elements are considered part of the system.

*System management* is a term used to describe the management of a collection of mixed resources. *Mixed resources* refers to the combination of software and hardware you generally end up with as part of the system you are managing.

Your operating system usually provides the necessary tools for you to manage these applications and hardware. For instance, Windows NT and 2000 include several tools for managing various aspects of the operating system. For example, Windows NT and Windows

2000 have the Windows Task Manager, enabling you to monitor statistics about running programs. These statistics can be monitored for CPU utilization, amount of memory being consumed, or the number of threads currently executing. The same operating systems also have the Services applet that enables you to start, stop, and configure programs running as services. Linux generally provides a linuxconf tool that performs a function similar to its Windows counterpart. The numbers and types of tools vary among operating systems.

## Identifying manageable resources

Managed resources exist in a variety of forms, some complex and some simple. In a large data center, you encounter hardware such as terminals and printers, along with various programs that facilitate communication and data exchange. These products enable jobs to run, different types of devices to communicate with one another, and users to log in and use computer systems. They function much the way that you use a computer monitor to view the applications on your home computer.

Data centers often contain hundreds to thousands of such devices, some physical and some virtual, and managing all these requires the combined skills of teams of operators and technicians. Often, the task of managing large-scale enterprise systems is so daunting that entire departments exist to tackle this task. These departments may be further compartmentalized to administer specific aspects of managing the system. Some may be responsible for managing the hardware, while others are responsible for managing elements of the software.

A good example of a large-scale operation is a stock trading floor such as NASDAQ or the New York Stock Exchange. If you've watched televised trading, you've no doubt noticed the large booths with numerous workstations hanging off of them. All of these workstations are attached to one or more even larger networks that are managed by a staff, either locally or remotely. The staff must be able to manage these workstations with precision and speed, given the nature of the applications that run on them. In the same vein, consider the offices of stock traders: row upon row of workstations and devices used to submit stock orders, check the status of orders, and watch the prices of stocks.

On a smaller scale, consider your typical business office, which often contains a handful of desktop systems, a few shared printers, and perhaps a few servers that act as file servers or application servers. A system administrator in this type of environment may be responsible for managing the security of the desktops as well as the servers. He or she may also be responsible for managing the software and versions that exist on the desktops and servers. Figure 1-1 shows a system using a management software application called Network Node Manager from Hewlett Packard. (You can find out more about Network Node Manager by visiting www.openview.hp.com/nnm.) This figure shows that four nodes are being managed. Two are workstations, one is a mid-range size computer, and one is a printer.

By clicking each of the nodes, the system manager can reveal more information about it. Additionally he or she can change the layout of the nodes as they appear on the screen, change the text that appears in the labels, or toggle them off altogether.

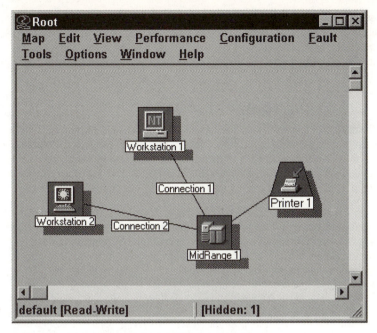

**Figure 1-1:** Using the Hewlett Packard Network Node Manager.

This example represents a complete scenario, but does not represent the details of what is being managed. Consider the layers underneath each device.

Applications have many characteristics that can be measured and monitored, such as the amount of memory being used (main memory and virtual memory), which versions of different system libraries are loaded, and how many transactions are in progress. Application developers also frequently use operating system management software to monitor the system resources that their applications are using; for example, to find bottlenecks, such as how long it takes to read from or write to a disk. If you are a Windows NT user, you can use a tool called PERFMON that enables you to view statistics about both operating system processes and application processes. These are examples of system management software.

Application software is another area in which system management is highly useful. System management tools enable you to install and upgrade software programs, as well as manage components at runtime. Being able to manage software installed on desktops, servers, and notebooks greatly simplifies the tasks of technical staff, who are often responsible for managing hundreds to thousands of computers. With system management tools, they can remotely perform numerous operations, such as selective upgrades or the uniform updating of all machines with the latest virus definitions.

## Distributed applications

You can look further into the challenges of application management by examining distributed applications. Applications that run on a single host are inherently simpler to manage because they don't involve problems such as network traffic, distributed transactions, or clusters. Distributed applications are those that run on multiple hosts, coordinating work between hosts. They may have many databases or servers processing requests, and often the network traffic generated by the application must contend with traffic on the same network, such as intranet, e-mail, or Internet usage.

## Characteristics of a management system

You can also look at the major characteristics of a managed system. What components need to exist in order for a system to be managed? First and foremost, you need resources to manage. Once you have identified the resources you want to manage, you need a way to identify which attributes of each managed resource you want to manage. Managing attributes of a resource can be something as simple as creating new instances of it, changing its name, or removing already existing instances of it.

*Management agents* are components that act as collectors for, or the interface to, the managed resources. Agents are typically small programs that enable management clients to send requests to the agent and retrieve information. Agents typically make requests to managed resources on behalf of management clients.

Management clients can be faceless software components that merely collect management information, or sophisticated graphical clients that present knobs, dials, and gauges. The latter often display management information such as how much CPU is being utilized by a particular computer or how much physical or virtual memory is being used, often in near real time. Management clients that fall into the graphical variety are often written in a programming language like Java, C++, or Visual Basic.

Generally, management systems also incorporate some sort of event management system for collecting events that occur locally or remotely and sending them to interested parties. Protocols such as Simple Network Management Protocol (SNMP) define *traps,* which are used to collect specific occurrences of an event, such as when a device may go offline, when a device comes online, or perhaps when a device receives a specific type of error. Identifying events also suggests the need to let someone know what has happened. This manifests itself as *notifications*. For instance, a help-desk organization may want to receive notifications when printers receive errors that require technical service.

With all these management agents, clients, and systems sending requests and responses back and forth to one another, how are they communicating? They often use protocols such as SNMP, CORBA, or some other proprietary protocol. Typically, TCP/IP is used at the lowest level, and some higher-level protocol is used over TCP/IP. Management tools often utilize multiple protocols because these tools may be used against a variety of devices and applications, each of which may have a different protocol. Figure 1-2 illustrates the relationship between management protocols, clients, agents, and systems.

In Figure 1-2, you can see that management clients utilize protocols such as SNMP and CIM over HTTP to make management requests. The management requests are then picked up by an agent acting on behalf of the managed system, and processed. Processing a management request entails making a request of the managed system and then returning the result of that request to the management client. The response is sent via the same protocol that was used to send the request. In the case of SNMP, the management agent may send a trap to the management client using SNMP.

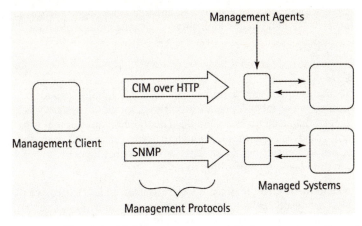

**Figure 1-2:** The relationship between management clients, protocols, agents, and systems.

From the figure, you can also see that management clients gain an advantage by being able to "speak" multiple management protocols. Although most management clients are specific to a single protocol, the possibility of multiple management protocols in a single organization does exist.

# Network and Application Management Challenges

Managing so many different types of resources presents challenges at nearly every turn of the path. Challenges can take the form of personnel, hardware, or software. The following sections describe the major issues in managing networks and applications.

## The division of labor

Network and application management is not a one-person job. Often, organizations subdivide the responsibility for managing different entities into separate groups. For example, some personnel are responsible for monitoring and managing network connections, while others are responsible for monitoring and managing networked devices such as printers and terminals (physical or virtual). Still others may be responsible for monitoring and managing applications or jobs running on multiple operating systems.

This division of personnel and tasks is common throughout many organizations. Two key components to successful management are the ability to effectively and quickly react to situations, and having the right system management tools. Different personnel may have different tools at their disposal, and different hardware on which to run those tools. Some personnel may use "dumb terminals" that have no sophisticated user interfaces and are strictly character-based. A *dumb terminal* refers to a basic piece of hardware that displays screens of text, accepts character input on a command line, and sends that input to the computer. Dumb terminals have no computing power; they simply enable you to access a computer located elsewhere, usually in the same building.

Other personnel may have sophisticated tools for monitoring and managing their systems, including the capability to receive alerts and to use sophisticated graphics to troubleshoot problems from a high level.

## The cost of training

Managing networks and applications effectively requires more than the right tools; it also requires personnel who are trained to use them. Depending on the scope of the system you are managing, you may need a toolset that is complex or simple. The more complex a tool is to use, the longer it takes to learn. A tool may be simple enough that you can quickly learn to accomplish basic procedures, but learning to use all its functions for a high level of productivity may require more time than you are willing to invest.

Training personnel takes time and money, so the easier a tool is to use, the less expensive it will be to train personnel. Costs are associated not only with training personnel to use a tool, but also with integrating the tool into your infrastructure. If a tool uses a proprietary technology, learning to use it may be harder, and it may be more difficult to integrate into your infrastructure.

Costs associated with managing networks can stem not only from the purchase of new software and training, but also from transaction costs associated with improperly managing networks and applications. You want to be able to manage resources efficiently; any hindrance wastes time, which translates into money. Consider what happens if a bank teller's computer terminal goes blank in the middle of a transaction. In a properly managed network, an operator would receive an alert notification. In some cases, the operator may be able to rectify the situation, either locally or remotely, but in other cases, such as a hardware failure, the operator must notify a service technician. The technician receives the notification and heads to the site.

If the software in this example could not send a notification, either because it lacked that capability or was improperly configured, the cost of maintaining the network increases. An operator may not become aware of the problem until some time later, and then must spend time diagnosing the problem. If a problem is not addressed within a reasonable amount of time, more work can back up and further compound the problem. And so the benefit of effective and efficient management software becomes apparent.

If operators can't effectively use their software to do their job, the software may not be worth the investment. You may end up asking yourself, How much work is the software doing and how much work will the user have to do? The software used for system management must be effective and efficient to be worthwhile.

## Vendor tools versus free tools

Should you use vendor-provided tools or free tools? Vendor tools are generally better than free tools in terms of functionality and performance because the vendor knows the product best. However, you can find readily available open-source tools for managing network devices. Some of these tools tend to be specific in nature; that is, they are not the all-encompassing toolsets that professional software companies might produce. This does not mean that tools produced by independent developers are necessarily of lesser quality, but commercial software companies offer technical support, periodic upgrades, and professional documentation. On the other hand, many open-source products reflect the contributions of many individuals, and this joint effort may sometimes produce software of even better quality than commercial products.

In fact, some independent software projects are more up-to-date with regards to standards than some commercial products. Many commercial products are simply newer generations of an earlier software product, and commercial software vendors have less flexibility in changing the way new versions of their software work. This is because of commitments to current customers as well as the demand on resources and the cost that is incurred when developing software. Independent projects can generally produce new versions or releases of a software package or component for less cost and time because the developers are not always bound by the same constraints.

For freely available tools, check sites such as `www.simpleweb.org`, `www.freshmeat.net`, or `www.sourceforge.net`.

## Using standards-based technologies

Which tools and standards do you use? Some tools have been around for a long time, but they may not provide exactly what you want. You want to avoid facing serious integration issues when it comes to using a tool for your particular scenario. This is where standards come into play. Tool vendors that use standards provide easier integration, and ensure that your tool's design is based on the needs of numerous concerned parties. Standards-based technologies tend to change based on widespread need and do so in a logical and controlled fashion. These technologies generally go through a series of reviews, proposals, and drafts before being adopted.

Moreover, a toolset that utilizes standards-based technologies is often easier to learn. Standards-based technologies generally have a plethora of resources you can utilize to learn more about them. Technologies that are not standards-based must rely on the vendor to document them completely and clearly. These technologies may be proprietary and take longer to learn than standards-based technologies because you are relying on a single vendor to provide the information about its technology.

## Managing large amounts of data

Another challenge presented to anyone managing applications and networks is the amount of data that must be managed. Large networks can number in the thousands of nodes (manageable objects). At some point, managers need to decide how to display the information so that an operator or systems administrator is not overwhelmed, and can react quickly to situations that may occur or alerts that are displayed by the system.

Some solutions layer the information displayed, enabling an operator or administrator to drill down into the affected area. Alternatively, the number of nodes may be split into groups, with each group managed by a separate operator. Even with these solutions, the amount of data generated by the system may be enormous. Therefore, it is critical that any management solution be capable of sending alerts and notifications when something goes wrong. Human operators simply cannot watch everything at once, regardless of how many are doing the watching.

## Monitoring and notification

Monitoring network and application resources can also be challenging. How much and which information do you monitor? Most networks and application management tools allow for some degree of configuration. You can often configure or categorize information in a way that is more meaningful to your particular situation. Monitoring requires periodic inquiries into the status of a managed resource, and some management solutions allow managed resources to issue alerts or notifications when something noteworthy occurs.

Monitoring is done using a management console, usually with some graphical display, but not always. Some large IT shops that have been in business for a long time have dumb terminals with simple character displays.

## Security

Security is a big concern in nearly every aspect of computing today. Security is critical, however, when it comes to network and system management. In the past few years, we have seen the tech headlines riddled with accounts of compromised Web sites and networks, often because of improperly configured software and unapplied security patches. Networks devices must be secured against unauthorized access. Systems operators generally have varying levels of access with regards to what they can do to network devices. Operators can take devices offline physically by unplugging them, or by using the facilities of the operating system to remove the device from it.

Applications can also be rendered unusable by operators or attackers who prevent access to the system or crash software applications intentionally. You can see the challenge security poses when it comes to system management. You want only qualified, authorized personnel to perform certain management tasks. Some companies use computer terminals with unrestricted access so that systems operators can gain access quickly and carry out administrative actions as fast as possible. These open terminals are themselves a security risk.

# Currently Available Management Software

Depending on what you want to accomplish, a variety of management software is currently available. Some vendors package management software with their hardware or software. For example, if you have used Microsoft SQL Server or Oracle, you have probably used the database manager consoles to administer databases, users, tables, and data security — sort of an all-in-one. You may, however, have a much broader problem and set of resources that you want to manage; for example, an entire network of printers or Web servers.

Another kind of resource available to you is the new breed of applications that run in application servers. These applications include software components such as Enterprise JavaBeans (EJBs) or Java servlets, and they utilize the resources of Java Virtual Machines (JVM). Application server vendors commonly include management consoles that enable you to deploy and undeploy application resources, or change runtime characteristics such as the amount of heap storage available to a JVM. They also enable you to control where requests run, how many JVMs to make available, and how to pool resources such as EJBs or servlets.

The challenge of managing networks and applications was recognized long ago and continues to be addressed today. Vendors, independent developers, and standards organizations such as the Internet Engineering Task Force (IETF) (`www.ietf.org`) and the Distributed Management Task Force (DMTF) (`www.dmtf.org`) have been instrumental in fostering the development of standards-based management technologies. One of the best-known management technologies is the Simple Network Management Protocol (SNMP). SNMP enables you to collect management information from an SNMP agent using an SNMP manager. The conversation between an agent and a manager takes place using the SNMP protocol. A manager might send a request to get the status of a hard drive, and the agent would respond to the manager with the status report.

Another initiative that is rapidly gaining momentum is the Web Based Enterprise Management (WBEM) initiative. This initiative drives different standards for enterprise management by defining an XML-based representation of manageable resources and protocol bindings.

# Management Protocols

Figuring out exactly what tool to use for each task can sometimes be confusing. Management solutions are generally built from several resources such as protocols, and include software components such as agents and managers. Many times, when you see a software application that supports a specific protocol, it's in the form of an API or software component that can be reused in your own applications or run as a standalone application. The protocols used in most management applications, such as SNMP or WBEM, are standards-based. A management application, on the other hand, is simply an implementation in some programming language. It has the capability to parse and construct messages using a protocol. This way, the program can communicate with managed devices.

Choosing among the various protocols is easy if you have a general understanding of how they work. You don't need to be intimately familiar with each type of protocol, but a broad understanding can show you how they provide the services you require in various management scenarios. This knowledge will also help you to understand how management clients and agents make use of these protocols. When deciding on a protocol, you need to ask questions such as the following:

♦ Does the protocol have the capabilities I require?

♦ How prevalent is the protocol?

♦ How can I implement the protocol? Is an API available?

♦ Will the protocol be easily integrated into an existing infrastructure?

♦ What new requirements will the protocol put on my infrastructure?

The first two points are essential in choosing a management protocol. You want a protocol that can provide you with the capabilities you need, and not one that represents some passing fad. Management protocols have some common characteristics, such as the following:

- A set of ports they use for requests and responses
- A syntax for specifying commands
- A syntax for indicating user-defined objects and commands
- A set of response codes that indicate the success or failure of commands

The next few sections briefly describe a few of the management protocols available. Some extra attention has been given to WBEM and SNMP, given their importance in system management.

## Telnet

Telnet is a protocol that a client can use to gain access to a remote machine. The Telnet specification can be found in Request for Comments (RFC) form at `www.ietf.org/rfc/rfc854.txt`. This specification outlines the conversation that takes place between the Telnet client and a Telnet server. You can also find a host of related Telnet RFCs that further define the Telnet specification, such as how to perform negotiations to log out, or set terminal window size, and what commands need to be exchanged. The Telnet server takes the commands sent by the Telnet client and translates them into commands that are executed locally. In most cases, you can remotely perform all the functions using the Telnet client, just as if you were physically sitting at the same machine. For instance, you could execute commands to list the files in a directory, or if you were accessing a system running a Unix variant, you could mount and unmount drives.

## RAS

Remote Access (RAS) is another method that enables administrators to access a remote computer from another location. Generally the user uses a modem to dial in and access the remote computer. One popular RAS-type tool is PCAnywhere, which enables you to dial into another PC and see its screen. Depending on your network connection, PCAnywhere can be somewhat slow, but it offers a kind of interaction not available with many other tools.

## SNMP primer

SNMP uses the concepts of a management agent, management client, and management protocol. Each object that wishes to be managed is represented in a Management Information Base (MIB) database (covered later in this chapter). There are currently two versions of the SNMP protocol: SNMPv1 and SNMPv2. These two specifications are available as RFC documents from the IETF (Internet Engineering Task Force). You can view the actual specifications at `www.ietf.org/rfc/rfc1157.txt` for SNMPv1. SNMPv1, SNMPv2, and SNMPv3 are comprised of a number of RFCs.

Each specification builds on the preceding one, and provides functionality and specifications for features that were missing or unavailable to previous specifications. These specifications do not cover the entirety of SNMP; there are a number of other related SNMP specifications. In some instances, a specification contains a set of core specifications that collectively form its foundation For instance, RFC 1155 (`www.ietf.org/rfc/rfc1155.txt`) is the specification for describing the structure of management information, and is associated with SNMPv1. In other cases, a single specification defines all the requirements and information. For instance, RFC 768 defines the UDP (Unsigned Datagram Protocol) in a single specification. Appendix A lists a number of SNMP-related resources that provide more information.

If you are using a Windows operating system or a particular Linux distribution, you can probably manage your PC via an SNMP agent.

An SNMP agent can be run virtually anywhere: from part of an application, or embedded in a network device such as a printer. The agent is responsible for receiving requests from the SNMP manager, carrying out the request, and returning the response. If an error or event occurs that is worth noting, the agent can send the manager a trap. The SNMP manager is the application that is interested in what is going on with managed devices. It sends requests and receives responses from the SNMP agents. Managers can also keep track of what agents are available. Managers must also respond to traps sent by SNMP agents.

Like most standards-based protocols, SNMP has standard ports over which managers and agents can communicate. Ports 161 and 162 are the default ports that handle this traffic. Port 161 is for sending requests and receiving responses, and port 162 is for sending asynchronous traps.

## SNMP operations

Four basic types of operations or interactions occur between SNMP agents and SNMP managers. Table 1-1 describes each of these types.

### Table 1-1    SNMP Operations

| SNMP Operation | Description |
|---|---|
| GET | Used to retrieve or read the value of an attribute of a managed object |
| GET NEXT | Used to retrieve the next managed object in a group of managed objects |
| SET | Used to set or write a new value to an attribute of a managed object |
| TRAP | Used to send an asynchronous notification from an agent to a manager |

## Management Information Bases in SNMP

In SNMP, manageable resources are defined using unique identifiers, and groups of managed resources are defined in documents known as Management Information Bases (MIBs). A MIB is written using a syntax defined in the Abstract Syntax Notation (ASN) specification. The actual values you use to write a MIB are defined in various RFCs. Listing 1-1 shows a fictional MIB.

**Listing 1-1: Fictional SNMP MIB**

```
FICTIONAL-MIB DEFINITIONS ::= BEGIN
        sysContact OBJECT-TYPE
            SYNTAX   DisplayString (SIZE (0..255))
            ACCESS   read-write
            STATUS   mandatory
            DESCRIPTION
                    "The textual identification of the contact person
                    for this managed node, together with information
                    on how to contact this person."
            ::= { system 4 }

        sysName OBJECT-TYPE
            SYNTAX   DisplayString (SIZE (0..255))
            ACCESS   read-write
            STATUS   mandatory
            DESCRIPTION
                    "An administratively-assigned name for this
                    managed node.  By convention, this is the node's
                    fully-qualified domain name."
            ::= { system 5 }

        sysLocation OBJECT-TYPE
            SYNTAX   DisplayString (SIZE (0..255))
            ACCESS   read-write
            STATUS   mandatory
            DESCRIPTION
                    "The physical location of this node (e.g.,
                    `telephone closet, 3rd floor')."
            ::= { system 6 }
END
```

This fictional MIB has definitions for three objects: sysContact, sysName, and sysLocation. Each of these objects contains keywords that describe it, such as its type, DisplayString, whether it is read/write, and whether or not the attribute is mandatory. This is a small example of what a MIB might look like. Fully developed MIBs may be many times larger and might import other MIBs as well.

## MIB structure

MIBs have a syntax that enables MIB writers to describe an object, give it a name, and define other attributes, such as whether an attribute is read-only. You create MIBs in a plain text file, and compiled MIBs contain a series of variables, which can also be referred to as attributes. Each variable is given a name and type. The type of variable is specified using a keyword such as INTEGER or DisplayString.

You assign each variable in a MIB a unique identifier called an object identifier (OID). The object identifier is a universally unique attribute. That's right; nowhere in the world should there be the same OID! OIDs can be public or private, and are numerical.

Software and hardware vendors that want to enable SNMP management of their products can register for an enterprise OID. After they receive an enterprise OID, they can define their own OIDs underneath it. Standard MIBs are generally placed under (1.3.6.1.2). (*Standard MIBs* are those that have been agreed upon by the activities board and are generally considered universal, such as those describing an operating system, a printer, or a fax machine.) An OID that is assigned to an enterprise is considered private because each enterprise has its own unique number. Standard OIDs are not considered private and are maintained by the IAB.

So what do you do with an OID? The OID is what agents and managers use to refer to managed objects. When requests get sent back and forth, the OID is sent to tell the recipient to which object the request or response refers. SNMP uses the User Datagram Protocol (UDP)/IP protocol to send requests, unlike other protocols such as HTTP, which use the TCP/IP protocol.

The UDP protocol is a connectionless protocol, meaning that persistent connections are not made to the endpoint while the request or response is being made. An *endpoint* can loosely be defined as a network address that identifies an entity. You can think of the UDP protocol as a kind of "fire-and-forget" protocol, similar to mailing a letter. You put the letter in the mailbox with the recipient's address on it. The letter is then picked up and delivered to the recipient by someone else. It doesn't require any more action on your part.

You can find more information about the User Datagram Protocol by reading the RFC at `www.ietf.org/rfc/rfc768.txt`.

### MIB compiler

Because MIBs are essentially text documents, they must be read and parsed into some meaningful structure that can be manipulated at runtime by an application program, an SNMP agent, or an SNMP manager. In network management toolsets, you'll often see reference to something called a *MIB compiler*. A MIB compiler produces a binary representation of a MIB. This representation can be manipulated, and its values inspected. A number of MIB compilers are floating around, but each one works in essentially the same way. They read in the MIB document, parse each OID, and produce something that can be read by an SNMP agent or manager. Unless you're interested in writing MIB compilers, you don't need to understand how they work in detail. Understanding the format of a MIB document is probably more important.

> **NOTE:** In certain cases, understanding the structure of a MIB document may be unnecessary, as some tools can present a user with a series of options from which they can select or provide information about a managed object. The tool can then produce a MIB document or a compiled version of the MIB. One such tool that you'll see shortly is the Advent Net Toolkit. Another is mibgen, which comes with the Java Dynamic Management Toolkit from Sun Microsystems.

Figure 1-3 shows the MIB compiler from AdventNet (`www.adventnet.com`). The left pane of the screen shows the OID naming hierarchy, and the right pane shows a MIB browser.

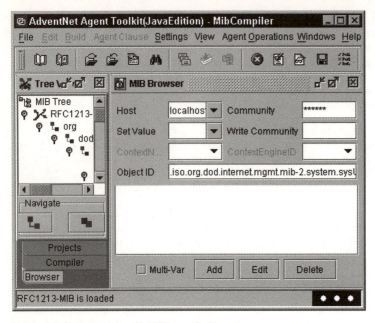

**Figure 1-3:** Using the AdventNet MIB compiler/browser.

MIB compilers also enhance performance because they produce a binary representation. Binary representations generally don't change between invocations of the SNMP agent. Reading the attributes of a binary, in-memory representation of the MIB is faster than reading and parsing it each time a request comes in. The MIB compiler can also catch syntax errors and do type-checking when compilation is done. Type-checking ensures that valid data types are used to represent object values. Valid data types are defined by the various SNMP RFCs.

## WBEM primer

Web Based Enterprise Management (WBEM) is an initiative adopted by the Distributed Management Task Force (DMTF). WBEM defines a series of XML-based schemas that describe managed resources. A number of vendors, including Microsoft and Tivoli, support WBEM in their products. This chapter briefly covers the CIM Schema and CIM operations over HTTP. You can view more information about WBEM at `www.dmtf.org/wbem`.

WBEM makes use of the Common Information Model, (CIM), which is an implementation-neutral representation of manageable resources. The CIM Schema has representations of the following manageable resources:

♦ Systems

♦ Applications

♦ Networks such as a LAN

♦ Devices such as printers and fixed storage

The syntax upon which CIM classes and instances are represented is the Managed Object Format (MOF), which loosely resembles an Interface Definition Language (IDL). You see IDL files used with applications that use Common Object Request Broker Architecture (CORBA) objects. The IDL allows for implementation-neutral representations of a class. The CIM specification defines an XML schema that maps the IDL to an XML document representation of a class. Listing 1-2 shows an IDL, and Listing 1-3 shows the XML representation of that same class.

**Listing 1-2: Fictional IDL for fixed storage device**

```
class FixedStorage
{
  [read]
  string currentDriveLetter;
  sint32 storageUsed;
  sint32 storageAvailable;
  sint32 density;
}
```

From Listing 1-2, you can see that a class named `FixedStorage` has been declared and that it has four readable attributes. The `[read]` notation indicates that these properties are read-only. The first attribute is a string type, and the remaining three are integer types because they store numerical data.

**Listing 1-3: Fictional CIM representation of the IDL in Listing 1-2**

```
<?xml version="1.0"?>
<!DOCTYPE CIM SYSTEM
http://www.dmtf.org/downloads/spec/xmls/CIM_DTD_V20.txt>
<CIM CIMVERSION="2.0" DTDVERSION="2.0">
<CLASS>
<CLASSPATH>
<NAMESPACEPATH>
<HOST>www.dmtf.org</HOST>
<NAMESPACE>
<NAMESPACENODE>ROOT</NAMESPACENODE>
</NAMESPACE>
<NAMESPACE>
<NAMESPACENODE>CIMV2</NAMESPACENODE>
</NAMESPACE>
<CLASSNAME>FixedStorage</CLASSNAME>
</CLASSPATH>
<PROPERTY NAME="currentDriverLetter" CLASSORIGIN="FixedStorage"
LOCAL="true" TYPE="string">
<QUALIFIER NAME="CIMTYPE" LOCAL="true" TYPE="string"
OVERRIDABLE="EnableOverride" TOSUBCLASS="ToSubClass"
TRANSLATEABLE="false">
<VALUE>F</VALUE>
</QUALIFIER>
```

```
<QUALIFIER NAME="read" LOCAL="true" TYPE="boolean"
OVERRIDABLE="EnableOverride" TOSUBCLASS="Restricted"
TRANSLATABLE="false">
<VALUE>TRUE</VALUE>
</QUALIFIER>
</PROPERTY>
<PROPERTY NAME="storageUsed" CLASSORIGIN="FixedStorage" LOCAL="true"
TYPE="string">
<QUALIFIER NAME="CIMTYPE" LOCAL="true" TYPE="sint32"
OVERRIDABLE="Restricted" TOSUBCLASS="Restricted" TRANSLATEABLE="false">
</QUALIFIER>
<QUALIFIER NAME="read" LOCAL="true" TYPE="boolean"
OVERRIDABLE="EnableOverride" TOSUBCLASS="Restricted"
TRANSLATABLE="false">
<VALUE>TRUE</VALUE>
</QUALIFIER>
</PROPERTY>
<PROPERTY NAME="storageAvailable" CLASSORIGIN="FixedStorage"
LOCAL="true" TYPE="string">
<QUALIFIER NAME="CIMTYPE" LOCAL="true" TYPE="sint32"
OVERRIDABLE="Restricted" TOSUBCLASS="Restricted" TRANSLATEABLE="false">
</QUALIFIER>
<QUALIFIER NAME="read" LOCAL="true" TYPE="boolean"
OVERRIDABLE="EnableOverride" TOSUBCLASS="Restricted"
TRANSLATABLE="false">
<VALUE>TRUE</VALUE>
</QUALIFIER>
</PROPERTY>
<PROPERTY NAME="density" CLASSORIGIN="FixedStorage" LOCAL="true"
TYPE="string">
<QUALIFIER NAME="CIMTYPE" LOCAL="true" TYPE="sint32"
OVERRIDABLE="Restricted" TOSUBCLASS="Restricted" TRANSLATEABLE="false">
<VALUE>320</VALUE>
</QUALIFIER>
<QUALIFIER NAME="read" LOCAL="true" TYPE="boolean"
OVERRIDABLE="EnableOverride" TOSUBCLASS="Restricted"
TRANSLATABLE="false">
<VALUE>TRUE</VALUE>
</QUALIFIER>
</PROPERTY>
</CLASS>
</CIM>
```

Listing 1-3 is certainly more verbose than Listing 1-2, due to the nature of XML and the way in which XML documents are constructed. Reading either listing gives you an idea of the type of information about the class being described. Listing 1-3 contains the same information as Listing 1-2, but in a much different syntax, using XML elements and attributes to represent the same information. The <PROPERTY> elements describe each of the properties and the

<QUALIFIER> elements describe the type information about the behavior of each property, such as whether it is read or updated.

## CIM

Formally, CIM provides a set of building blocks upon which management applications can be built. The CIM Schema provides the necessary representations of various manageable objects, as well as ways to extend the schema for other purposes. The CIM specification defines three layers that comprise the model:

♦ The *Core Model* is comprised of information that is common to and applicable to all areas of system or application management.

♦ The next layer is the *Common Model*, which is slightly more specific to an area of management but still implementation-neutral. The common areas are categorized as system, applications, networks, and devices. The Common Model and Core Model together are collectively known as the *CIM Schema*.

♦ The last layer is the *Extension Schemas* layer, which allows for specific extensions to a particular technology, such as an operating system.

You can find more information about CIM by reading the specification at www.dmtf.org/standards/cim_spec_v22/index.php. This is the current specification as of June 14, 1999.

CIM also defines a mapping of CIM operations over HTTP. You can view this specification at www.dmtf.org/download/spec/xmls/CIM_HTTP_Mapping10.php. This specification defines an XML encoding schema that you can use to encode CIM operations, such as retrieving an instance of a CIM class, or setting the value of a CIM class attribute. The CIM operations are held in an HTTP message, sometimes called a *payload*. The CIM specification not only defines a way for you to call your own methods, but also defines a set of "built-in" operations that can be used.

## Choosing your protocols

Once you have a general understanding of the protocols and tools available, choosing the tool that's right for you is next. Refer to the bulleted list of questions in "Management Protocols" to guide you in selecting a protocol. Keep in mind that not all of the questions posed in the list may apply to your situation.

If you compare the protocols presented here, you will notice that SNMP has a long history in system management. It has a small set of easy-to-understand commands, a syntax for defining a set of managed resources, and is supported in a wide variety of management applications as well as hardware devices. On the other hand, the "Simple" in SNMP has been mocked by some, because, while easy to learn, SNMP is difficult (but not impossible) to master.

WBEM, on the other hand, is not as mature as SNMP, but bases its set of commands and syntax for managed resources on CIM. CIM uses XML-based schemas for defining commands and managed resources, making it more extensible than SNMP. Like SNMP, some toolkits are available for generating CIM Schemas from application source code, making the adoption of WBEM and CIM easier.

Most, if not all, management solutions support SNMP, and a growing number support WBEM, but it is nowhere near as prevalent as SNMP. Many vendors of application servers, such as BEA, provide SNMP agents and MIBs with their products. Hands down, SNMP is a sure-fire choice for first-timers, and is likely to meet your needs now and well into the future.

## Introducing the JMX API

The Java Management Extensions (JMX) API provides an architecture and API for use as a standard management infrastructure for your resources. There is also a specification for JMX that details the architecture in which JMX-compliant resources must be structured. In later chapters, you will look at the specific details and layers of the JMX architecture. You can view the JMX JSR003: Java Management Extensions at the Java Community Process site at `www.jcp.org/aboutJava/communityprocess/final/jsr003.jsp`. The site offers background information such as the companies involved, along with various links to related Java Specification Requests (JSRs).

> **NOTE:** For those unfamiliar with JSRs, they are requests made by one or more interested parties to collectively develop a specification around some technology. Formally, this process is referred to as the Java Community Process (JCP). The JCP was created to enable participants from the software and hardware industries to play a part in the development of Java-related standards.

Along with JSR003, there are a host of related JSRs that either provide additional functionality to the JMX core or define new applications of JMX. These related JSRs are worth note:

- JSR – 77 J2EE Management Specification — `www.jcp.org/jsr/detail/077.jsp`
- JSR – 160 JMX 1.5 / Remoting — `www.jcp.org/jsr/detail/160.jsp`

JSR – 77 brings JMX into the J2EE realm by defining the management interfaces for the entire range of J2EE components, including EJBs, servlets, and JSPs. It also defines a set of management interfaces for obtaining performance metrics for various components. JSR – 160 addresses, among other things, the client APIs for accessing remote JMX agents, and receiving notifications from remote MBeans. In a nutshell, it defines some of the undefined distributed features of JMX that are mentioned in the specification, but are not yet fully defined or implemented. As you read Chapter 2, you'll see where the currently undefined distributed features fit into the whole.

JMX provides a Java-based, standards-based, low-cost solution for building management into your applications. JMX is not limited to managing applications and their components; you can also use it to write management agents for managing the physical devices in a network.

Java applications must be able to integrate and interoperate in existing environments with little or no effort. JMX reflects the efforts of many different vendors; and given its extensible nature, it presents a means of instrument management that can interoperate in a variety of environments. Chapter 2 provides a more detailed look at the JMX architecture and the components that are defined in the specification. The JMX architecture does not define a specific management protocol; rather, it allows different management protocols to be plugged into a management agent at runtime.

JMX can be used as the infrastructure for management consoles, to allow remote management as well as management of J2EE environments. The following section describes a few specific advantages the JMX provides.

## Advantages of JMX

By using JMX, you can realize several benefits, including the following:

- ♦ A small footprint enables the scaling of management solutions based on JMX.
- ♦ A modular design allows for easy implementation and management of resources.
- ♦ The Java-based implementation ensures that management solutions can run on multiple platforms.
- ♦ Protocol-neutral design enables a wide variety of management clients, such as Web browsers for SNMP managers.
- ♦ The Java-based implementation also ensures integration into J2EE and enterprise applications.
- ♦ JMX design patterns ensure standard, predictable access to manageable resources.

These benefits are what make JMX so attractive, not only as a solution for developers who want to make their components manageable, but also for vendors who want to provide an extensible management API for their products.

The design of JMX makes it easier to accomplish your applications-management tasks. The JMX architecture follows an architecture similar to that of other management solutions, such as SNMP. It defines a set of key components: managers, agents, and managed resources. Enabling management using JMX involves embedding an object server known as an MBean Server into the application or device you want to manage. Because the MBean Server is often a small-footprint application (in that it doesn't require much memory), it can often be embedded in small network appliances or handheld devices with limited resources. (You'll find out more about the MBean Server in Chapter 8.) The MBean Server enables management clients to access managed resources, acting like a registry of managed objects. All of the implementation of the managed resources is done in the managed resources themselves.

Managed resources can be loaded and unloaded dynamically, which means that your management applications can range from small devices to large devices with little or no rework on your part. Managed resources can be loaded and unloaded at the request of a human operator if desired. For instance, suppose a technician receives an e-mail or page indicating that a network router is having a problem. The technician could log in to the managed resource using a Web browser running on a laptop or on a Web-enabled cell phone and take the router offline.

JMX integrates well into existing infrastructures. JMX agents can utilize common protocols such as SNMP, HTTP, or WAP, enabling a variety of management clients to access and manage components. In addition, given the open, standards-based nature of these technologies,

you don't even have to worry about writing your own management clients in order for people to access your components. You just need to write the interface or let someone else write the HTML pages, JavaServer Pages, or SNMP agents to do the work.

Because JMX is Java-based, it is designed to leverage existing and future Java technologies, such as the Java Database Connectivity (JDBC), Java Naming and Directory Interface (JNDI), and Java Transaction Service (JTS). This means that JMX encompasses a rich and mature set of technologies that cover some major problem domains, including transaction management, naming services, and database connectivity. Again, because Java is standards-based, you can choose from a number of vendor, commercial, or open-source implementations of these technologies.

The JMX specification also defines a set of design patterns that makes the instrumentation of managed resources easy. These design patterns set standards for the naming of accessor methods as well as the name of managed resources. With all of these decisions made for you, it takes less time to instrument your own components and make them manageable, as well as to take existing components and retrofit them to be manageable. Additionally, the MBean specification defines several helper classes that enable application clients to find information about MBeans.

Given the importance and proliferation of J2EE components, tools, and application development, it will become increasingly important to ensure that enterprise class applications can coexist in a management infrastructure with little or no effort on the part of the implementor or purchaser. JMX provides a way to easily implement a management interface to your enterprise application, and can even be extended to allow for customization of management interfaces.

## The audience for JMX

JMX can participate in a variety of scenarios. JMX isn't just for implementing management solutions in your own applications. Vendors can use JMX to provide the infrastructure necessary to manage your applications for you. You write these applications to run in their application server environment. Anything from Java servlets, to Enterprise Java Beans, to ordinary Java classes could be instrumented and managed using the vendor's framework.

Vendors can also provide ways to integrate management of the application server into an existing management infrastructure. Large IT shops probably have preexisting management solutions in place, and extensive, rapid shifts in the way they monitor their systems are economically unfeasible. Therefore, the easier it is to integrate and monitor an application or piece of hardware, the more easily accepted it will be.

JMX is also targeted at another category of users: tool vendors. Tool vendors write protocol adapters and connectors for management frameworks that provide you with out-of-the-box support for using SNMP, WBEM, or RMI. Given the "pluggable" nature of the JMX architecture, these tools offer considerable savings in time and resources applied.

Of course, application component vendors can instrument or provide management interfaces to their own components. Imagine if Web sites such as Flashline.com (`www.flashline.com`) or Component Source (`www.componentsource.com`) presented an icon indicating that the component complied with JMX standards. This would make the component more attractive to customers looking for JMX-compliant products.

# Building solutions with JMX

You can use JMX as little or as much as you want. There is no limit to what you can manage, except perhaps for physical resources such as CPU, disk storage, and display. You can use JMX to manage a single application module, a collection of modules, a single network connection, or a pool of connections. Most commonly, though, you will see JMX used as the basis for application server vendors to provide a management interface to their product.

## Management consoles

A management console can be as simple as a Telnet session with command-line interaction, or as complex as a Web-based or Java Client (Swing) application with dials and meters that enable a user to administer a system. With JMX, management consoles can even be written in languages other than Java because all interaction between management agents is done using standards-based protocols such as RMI, SNMP, RMI, or CORBA. You can even write a Microsoft Windows Foundation Classes (MFC) application in C++ to manage your Java applications.

## Application management

You can use JMX to manage entire applications or individual components of applications. Some J2EE application server vendors now provide JMX interfaces to their products to enable management of the application outside of the tools they provide. You can use these interfaces to write custom management applications or integrate management of the application server into your existing network.

You could also conceivably reuse only parts of the JMX architecture for purposes other than management. As you become more familiar with the JMX architecture, you will come across management agent services such as notification. This service could be used to send an e-mail or set a flag in a software component.

Services like notification can also be used for other purposes, such as distributed messaging or logging. Different management agents can send logging information to a central logging server that collects all the messages and stores them in one place. This type of use gives you an idea of the possibilities and extensibility that JMX provides. Don't misunderstand, however; JMX was not designed as a general-purpose API for tasks other than system management. It just so happens that its design lends itself to solving some other problem domains.

## Remote management

Given the architecture that JMX provides, it's easy to enable remote management of a resource. Because JMX defines protocol adapters and connectors that use standard protocols such as HTTP, you can easily envision pointing your Web browser at a URL and displaying some information about which Java servlets are running on a particular application server. You can also use a management console with a sophisticated Java GUI or simple command-line interface to remotely connect and manage a resource.

Remote management isn't limited to Web-based application consoles. It can also be available using RMI, CORBA, or potentially XML-RPC. Some of the technologies and applications mentioned previously in this chapter, such as RAS or PCAnywhere, enable you to remotely access a computer system and manage it as if you were sitting in front of it.

JMX enables the remote management of resources using protocol adapters and connectors. These protocol adapters and connectors use the protocols to enable clients to connect to a system and manage it. Because protocol adapters and connectors are implemented as MBeans themselves, you can easily add or remove support for a protocol at runtime. You'll learn more about protocol adapters in Chapter 12.

JMX provides the foundation for a wide variety of system management solutions in Java. It enables management clients to access information about resources in a standard way, and provides developers with a standard way to expose their applications for management. Because JMX is Java-based, you can easily integrate it into your new Java applications or add new management capabilities to an existing application.

JMX also alleviates the potential burden of providing a management client for your application by enabling you to focus on exposing attributes and operations for management. You can rely on third-party tools such as HP OpenView or Tivoli NetCenter to monitor your application using management protocols such as SNMP. Its pluggable architecture also enables you to make changes at runtime with little or no interruption of service. In addition, it enables you to integrate the latest Java applications with legacy management solutions.

## Summary

In this chapter, you've looked at the role of system management, and some of its challenges. You looked specifically at some components of system management, such as protocols and software. You also examined the human factor, and how the selection of management tools can affect personnel's ability to effectively manage a system. In the next chapter, you'll begin looking more closely at JMX and its architecture and components.

*Chapter 2*

# Inspecting the JMX Architecture

Chapter 1 briefly introduced you to JMX and some of its benefits. This chapter takes a closer look at JMX, including its architecture and API. It briefly introduces the various components of JMX and the different features that, as a whole, enable you to implement management and build management applications. This chapter serves as a high-level overview of the JMX architecture and packages. The rest of the book provides details about the components described in this chapter.

## The JMX Architecture

One of the first questions that comes to mind when working with a new technology is "How does it work?" The second question is "How can I use it?" To answer these questions, you must understand the architecture and design of the technology.

Because JMX is designed to solve problems that arise in managing systems, it's more than just an API. JMX defines an architecture in which the JMX API can be used. When you look at the diagram of the JMX architecture in Figure 2-1, you'll notice several components, and more important, three layers. Application architectures often span multiple tiers or layers, with each layer providing some key facet of functionality and purpose. An architecture designed in layers provides a way not only to logically separate problem domains, but also to change one of these levels, if desired, without affecting the other levels.

The JMX architecture is represented as a set of three layers:

- Distributed services level
- Instrumentation level
- Agent level

Each layer solves specific problems. The *distributed services level* solves the problem of remote management and how management clients will access your managed resources. It also solves the problem of how managed resources can communicate with one another. This layer defines the components and requirements that must exist at this level in order to make remote management possible.

> **NOTE:** The distributed services level is not completely defined in the JMX specification. There is nothing in the JMX API for building components that exist in the distributed services level, or anything specifying how these components are supposed to interact with the other levels. However, in Chapter 12 you'll learn how to accomplish remote management despite the lack of definition for the distributed services level.

The second layer, the *instrumentation level*, solves the problem of implementing management interfaces and provides a way to access the managed resources. It also defines a mechanism for managed resources to emit events to one another or to other recipients, and to notify a management agent of events.

The *agent level* solves the problem of making the other two levels available by hosting them in a Java Virtual Machine (JVM). It also defines a set of support services for use by implementors and management clients.

Figure 2-1 illustrates the JMX architecture and shows each of the levels. A set of components provides the functionality for each level.

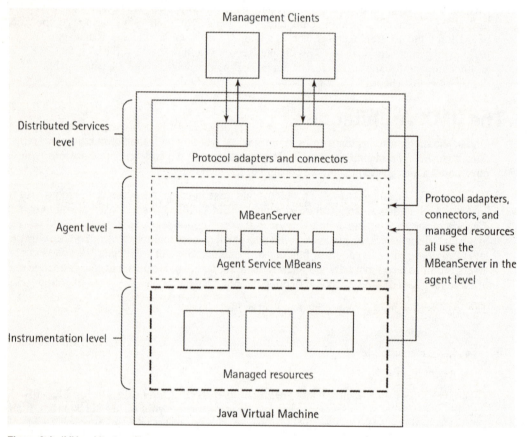

**Figure 2-1:** JMX architecture diagram.

Figure 2-1 illustrates the JMX architecture by showing you where each layer resides. From this figure, you can see that management clients converse with protocol adapters and connectors in the distributed services level. MBeans are resources for which you implement a management interface, and they are defined in the instrumentation level. This level is where application developers work most often, implementing management interfaces for their components. The instrumentation level works in conjunction with the agent level, whose responsibility is to provide a container of sorts for the instrumentation level. The agent level is where the MBean Server resides, and is used as a repository for managed resources. It also defines a set of supporting services known as *agent services*.

Currently, the JMX specification v1.0 includes a description of the distributed services level, but does not define any of its properties or attributes. The distributed services level is supposed to encompass the interaction between management agents, and may describe how notifications are sent between management agents. (A new JSR – 160 will define the distributed aspects of the JMX specification, but there is currently no date set for this specification to become final.)

It may appear as if protocol adapters and connectors seem to cross the boundary between the distributed services and instrumentation levels. This is because protocol adapters and connectors are often implemented as managed resources themselves. This affords them the same benefits that other managed resources have, and they can be managed in the same fashion as other managed resources.

## The instrumentation level

The instrumentation level is where managed resources reside. This is where a software developer or system administrator can provide an interface to a resource so that it can be managed. The instrumentation level defines an entity known as an *MBean*, which represents the managed resource. There are four basic types of MBeans: *standard, dynamic, model, and open*. Standard MBeans present their management interface using a well-established set of methods and properties. The other types present their management interface dynamically at runtime.

When a management client wants to manage a particular resource, it asks the MBean Server for information about the managed resource. You indicate which managed resource, or MBean, you're interested in by using an object name. (You can read more about the object name in the "Metadata and foundation classes" section of this chapter.) Using the object name, the MBean Server finds the managed resource and returns a construct called the `MBeanInfo` structure, which contains a set of methods for retrieving information about the MBean. The `MBeanInfo` structure can provide information about which methods and attributes are available for management. These methods and attributes can change during the life cycle of the MBean.

### Managed resources

Managed beans (which represent managed resources) come in four basic varieties. The design of each type enables you to implement a management interface that appears relatively the same to management applications. However, as you progress from standard MBeans to model MBeans, the advantages that each type provides over the last become more apparent. A management interface for a resource includes not only the attributes and operations of the resource, but information about how to construct instances of it. It also includes notifications that a resource might emit to signify important events in the resource's life cycle.

The various types of MBeans provide developers with options for deciding how they want to implement a managed resource, and possibly how much time they want to devote to maintenance. To choose the right type of MBean implementation, you need to weigh various factors, including available resources, whether you're wrapping legacy management applications or implementing a management interface for a new resource, and the amount of time you have to accomplish the task.

As an application developer, you will work in the instrumentation level, defining interfaces to application components so that they can be managed. You will then utilize features of the agent level to make your components available to management clients.

### Standard MBeans

The first and easiest type of MBean to implement is the standard MBean. The *standard MBean* represents a Java class with a well-known interface. This interface represents accessor methods that enable management applications to manipulate the attributes or fields of an object. The interface also includes methods or operations that represent functions of the MBean. The standard MBean represents a managed resource whose management interface is not expected to change frequently. It exposes the management interface via a standard method, similar to the way in which JavaBeans expose information about themselves. Standard MBeans have a concrete implementation of their management interface in the form of a Java interface named after the implementation class. For example, if you wanted to define the management interface for a class named `Foo`, you would name the interface `FooMBean`. Chapter 4 provides more detail on standard MBeans.

### Dynamic MBeans

The *dynamic MBean* is the next step up. It provides a management interface for managed resources whose interface may change over time. The management interface is represented using the same structure as a standard MBean; however, the dynamic MBean is responsible for building the management interface at runtime. This can be done using a variety of methods, but the point is that the management interface can be different each time the MBean is instantiated, and possibly each time the management interface is queried.

For example, the first time you access a managed resource that represents an application component, it may have an operation called `getActiveThreads()`. The second time you inspect the managed resource, this operation may not be available. This scenario is not unique to dynamic MBeans, but it's more apt to happen than with standard MBeans because the dynamic nature of the interface allows for this type of flexibility. In Chapter 5 you'll see how to create dynamic MBeans and how to construct the management interface at runtime.

### Open MBeans

The *open MBean* is a managed resource that is implemented so that it can be managed by the widest variety of clients. JMX agents and MBean Servers are not required to support open MBeans, however the JMX API documentation includes information about them and they are included in the Sun reference implementation.

Open MBeans present their management interface as fully configured, fully described structures that provide a complete description of the capabilities of the MBean. Other types of managed beans, such as standard and dynamic MBeans, can sometimes return partial information about their managed resources, but open MBeans are required to have all descriptions and names supplied as non-empty values. Open MBeans must implement the same interface as dynamic MBeans, which affords them the same benefits that dynamic MBeans have with regards to a changing management interface. The open MBean also provides a complete picture about the constructors, notifications, attributes, and operations that it exposes, as well as a good indication of the consequences of executing one of its operations.

In order to ensure the most extensive compatibility, open MBeans make use of a small set of standard Java data types. These data types include the object representations of primitive types such as `java.lang.Boolean`, `java.lang.String`, and `java.lang.Float`, to name a few. Two other JMX defined data types are also used to represent more complex data types using an aggregate of the simpler types. Open MBeans are required to use these data types for the return values of all operations, the values of attributes, and method argument types. The complex data types defined for open MBeans are represented by the `CompositeData` and `TabularData` interfaces. The `CompositeData` interface is used to represent a hashtable of data, and the `TabularData` interface is used to represent collections of `CompositeData` interfaces. Together, the two complex data types allow you to build aggregate collections of the other standard Java data types.

### Model MBeans

*Model MBeans* represent yet another mechanism for implementing managed resources. Model MBeans are similar to dynamic MBeans but they have defined interfaces, which enable developers to configure default behaviors when the MBean is instantiated. The model MBean interfaces extend other JMX interfaces, such as the `javax.management.DynamicMBean` interface, and provide descriptors that allow for an extensible and configurable management interface. The descriptors for a model MBean are considered a form of metadata, along with the normal MBean metadata classes described in the next section. Model MBeans also define a set of policies that enable you to control the behavior of features such as persistence, logging, notifications, and attribute value caching.

### Metadata and foundation classes

Information about MBeans is exposed using a common set of classes known as the *MBean metadata classes*. These classes represent information about an MBean, but exclude any data that the MBean wraps. If an MBean representing a printer has an attribute that represents the last print job printed, for example, the metadata classes do not contain information about that attribute.

The metadata classes enable you to retrieve information about the management interface of an MBean. The metadata classes represent the notifications, constructors, operations or methods, and attributes of an MBean. This enables management classes to inspect MBeans at runtime and use this information to perform tasks. Such tasks might include building a visual representation of the managed resource, or in the case of a dynamic MBean, dynamically building the management interface. The metadata classes also enable management clients to obtain sufficient information about a managed resource to construct an instance of it.

Along with the metadata classes, the JMX specification defines two key classes that you can use to work with managed resources. These are the `javax.management.ObjectName` and `javax.management.ObjectInstance` classes. The `javax.management.ObjectName` class is used extensively in this book in a variety of scenarios, from creating instances of MBeans to querying the MBean Server to find an MBean.

The `ObjectName` class represents the name of an MBean. The `ObjectName` is used as an identifying token for a managed resource. As an application developer, you need to determine the object name for a managed resource when you deploy it into an agent. You might decide to take a simple approach to naming MBeans, or adopt a stricter model and enforce a specific syntax. The JMX specification defines a core syntax that object names must follow, but does not specify any values that must appear in an object name. For example, you may want to enforce the rule that object names always contain a key named `location`. To accomplish this, you could extend the `ObjectName` class and check the value passed into the constructor.

An object name can be published for management clients to use, or you can rely on the query facilities in the MBean Server to locate an MBean. You publish an object name by registering an MBean with that name. In the architecture diagram shown in Figure 2-1, the object name would be used in the instrumentation and agent levels. You would define it in the instrumentation level and use it in the agent level with the MBean Server.

In Chapter 8, you'll learn more about the `ObjectName` class and how to use it to find MBeans, set and get attribute values, and invoke methods of managed resources. You'll also learn about the use of syntax and how to construct an `ObjectName` class instance.

## Notification model

The instrumentation level also includes the definition for sending notifications between managed resources and management clients. *Notifications* are messages that can include user-specific data that you want sent to a recipient. The JMX specification defines a set of notifications that are specific to core JMX functions such as registering and unregistering managed resources. You can also define your own notification types for use in your managed resources.

A message can be sent to a single recipient or to multiple recipients, as the notification model is very similar to other Java event listener interfaces. Interested recipients register their interest in receiving notifications. Interested listeners can also indicate which notifications they want to receive and those they don't through the use of filters. Notifications can be sent one time, or periodically at set intervals.

A notification travels between managed resources in a JMX agent. You define a notification type in the instrumentation level, and then transmit it to a recipient in the agent level. A notification can also be emitted by the MBean Server in the agent level. These notifications cover cases such as registering MBeans and the notifications emitted by agent services. In Chapter 11, you'll learn more about notifications and how to construct and send them. You'll also learn how to create a piece of code to listen for notifications.

When the distributed services part of the JMX specification is completely defined, you will be able to send notifications beyond the boundary of a single agent to a recipient in another agent.

# The agent level

The *agent level* is where agents reside. An *agent* is a term used to describe the host of managed resources and supporting services; however, it does not represent a concrete class or an interface. An agent represents a single JVM, and can take the form of a Java application that you write, or it can be an application server. Without an agent, you have no means to use the facilities of JMX. The agent's purpose is to provide access to the MBean Server and agent services through components called *protocol adapters* and *connectors*. The JMX specification defines a list of mandatory components in order for a JMX agent to be considered JMX-compliant. A JMX agent must consist of the following:

♦ An MBean Server

♦ At least one protocol adapter or connector

♦ One or more MBeans representing managed resources

♦ A minimum set of agent services, including monitoring, timer, dynamic loading, and relation

From the preceding list, you can see that it takes only a small amount of code and resources to implement a JMX agent. If you write the agent yourself, you can implement an agent in under twelve lines of code in a simple Java application. If you use an application server or another JMX agent, the amount of code might even be less. You might see the initialization of the MBean Server and agent services in a startup class or Java servlet that loads at startup. You might be responsible only for specifying the names of the managed resources, and the JMX agent would take care of creating and registering them. You will find numerous examples of JMX agents throughout this book. In Chapters 14 and 15, you'll learn how to use an application server as the JMX agent.

There is no implementation or interface that comprises an agent. You must start the MBean Server and various protocol adapters, as well as load references to the managed resources. The MBean Server is the interface to the managed resources; you never directly manipulate a reference to a managed resource. The JMX agent is a collection of components and can take the form of a Java application or class, or you might use the facilities of an application server to contain the components.

## The MBean Server

The MBean Server is the entity responsible for providing access to managed resources in an agent. An MBean Server is responsible for loading and unloading managed resources; for providing access to various agent services such as querying for managed resources; and for retrieving instances of managed resources, and handing those references over to a management client. It is also responsible for enabling management clients and JMX agents to execute methods of a managed resource. In Figure 2-1, the architecture diagram, the MBean Server is part of the agent level. As an application developer, you use the MBean Server to register your managed resources, making them available to management clients.

You use an MBean Server by creating an instance of the `MBeanServer` interface using the `MBeanServerFactory` class. When you start an agent, you must first create an MBean Server. You typically create an MBean Server instance during application startup, so that manageable resources and agent services can be available. These supporting services and the MBean Server are often created during agent startup. You can think of this process as initializing a set of required services; if one of these services fails to initialize, the agent cannot be expected to continue initializing. In the case of an application server acting as an agent, you might see the initialization of the MBean Server and agent services in a startup class or Java servlet that loads at startup.

There is no limit to how many MBean Servers can exist in an agent, but there is usually just one. The MBeanSeverFactory is a factory class provided with the Sun JMX reference implementation that enables you to construct instances of MBean Servers. It also exposes some functionality for finding and removing MBean Servers from memory.

The MBean Server exposes a number of different methods for instantiating and registering MBeans in an MBean Server. It also provides methods for finding MBeans, based on a pattern that identifies an MBean. This is done by querying for certain values that appear in the name of a managed resource.

The MBean Server enables managed resources to be statically and dynamically unloaded, and enables them to override the behavior of the class loader used to load managed resources. This allows you to modify the managed environment at runtime with little effort on your part.

## Protocol adapters and connectors

Protocol adapters provide the necessary network transport, or requests and responses, between a management client and an agent. There is no current specification for protocol adapters and connectors in the JMX specification. However, with a little know-how, you can discern the necessary interaction. The difference between an adapter and a connector is reflected not only by how a managed client interacts with the agent, but by how the management client interacts with the connector. You may also be able to use a third-party reference implementation that provides protocol adapters. A protocol adapter called the HtmlAdapterServer that comes with the Sun JMX reference implementation enables you to manage resources with a Web browser. (You will learn how to use the HtmlAdapterServer protocol adapter in Chapter 3 when you write your first JMX application.)

Connectors are generally used for heavier clients such as Java or WIN32 clients, or by management agents such as other JMX agents. Connectors usually expose their functionality using Remote Method Invocation (RMI), CORBA, or some other remote procedure call–oriented service. Managed resources can be located using the RMI registry or through the Java Naming and Directory Interface (JNDI). This does not prevent other types of management clients from utilizing connectors. For instance, you could have a JavaServer Page that accesses a connector and retrieves management information, which is then presented in a markup language such as HTML or WML.

A protocol adapter can be a single class or a collection of classes. Keep in mind that given the pluggable nature of the JMX agent layer, you need to be able to load and unload the protocol adapters and connectors at runtime.

At least one protocol adapter or connector must be used per JMX agent so that the agent can be managed. You can, of course, use more than one protocol adapter or connector, with each using a different protocol, such as HTTP, SMTP, or SNMP.

Because protocol adapters are often implemented as managed resources themselves, they can be managed in the same fashion as other managed resources. Support for new protocols can be added dynamically, enabling different types of clients to access the managed resources. Another benefit of protocol adapters and connectors is that because protocols are programming language–neutral, you automatically gain another benefit: Clients written in different programming languages can access your management infrastructure.

The Sun JMX reference implementation includes a sample HTML adapter that presents management information using an HTML form, and uses HTTP. In Chapter 12, you'll learn how to construct such a protocol adapter. The JMX specification has spawned several other protocol adapter efforts for protocols such as SNMP, WBEM, and TMN.

## Agent services

In management solutions, many types of activities are occurring at once. In addition to communication between managed resources and agents, and managers and agents, other support activities are present, such as notification attempts to find managed resources, and querying managed resources for the values of their attributes. These types of activities are provided by the agent or manager in management solutions, often in some extensible fashion so that they can be extended to meet some specific need.

A JMX agent provides a set of services known as *agent services*. Agent services are generally implemented as managed resources themselves, meaning there is an MBean for each major agent service. This is actually not a requirement, but implementing the agent service can provide benefits such as dynamically removing and adding new agent services, building relations between managed resources, querying for managed resources, sending notifications at intervals, and monitoring attributes of managed resources. Most often, agents and the resources they manage exist on the same host in a JVM, but this is not always the case. Agents can manage resources residing on a different host.

The framework for adding and removing managed resources enables you to re-use the framework for this purpose. This way, managed resources and the infrastructure for a management agent or system are handled the same way. In the architecture diagram presented in Figure 2-1, agent services would exist in the agent level; however, they are implemented as MBeans, so they have some things in common with the instrumentation level. As an application developer you are not responsible for creating these services, but would need to understand how to locate and use them.

Agent services are categorized into the following groups:

- ◆ Dynamic Loading — The dynamic loading service enables you to load MBeans and other resources dynamically by using the M-Let service. (You can find more information about the M-Let service in Chapter 8.) Dynamically loading a class involves establishing a network connection to a resource, much like requesting a Web page with your Web browser. The Web server sends back the Web page and other related resources, which are then displayed in your browser. MBeans can be loaded the same way by requesting a file containing descriptions of various MBeans, which are then loaded and registered in an MBean Server.

♦ Monitoring — The monitoring service enables management clients and agents to establish traps or monitors for specific pieces of data about a managed resource. For instance, if you have a managed resource representing the amount of free space on a fixed storage device, you may want to establish a monitor for the amount of free storage. Then, when the free storage falls below a certain threshold, the managed resource could make use of the notification facilities in the instrumentation level to send an e-mail, or perhaps to page a system administrator.

Management clients can use the monitoring service to build dashboard-type applications that feature gauges and dials. The gauges and dials show different readings based on the values of the attributes of a managed resource. For instance, an MBean could use the monitoring service to watch the amount of fixed storage available, which could then be represented as a bar graph in a management console.

♦ Timer — Sometimes, you want certain events to happen periodically. The timer service enables you to send out notifications either repeatedly or at specified intervals. This enables you to trigger other events in a managed system. The notifications can be picked up by MBean Servers and other MBeans running in a JMX agent.

♦ Relation — The relation service enables you to establish logical relationships between managed resources. The relation service is also responsible for maintaining the consistency of the relationships. The relation model defined in the JMX specification enables you to establish some sort of loose object model between different MBeans.

To use the agent services, you must register the MBeans representing each service in an MBean Server, and then perform any necessary initialization of each service. There is no implementation or interface that comprises an agent. You must create the MBean Server and start various protocol adapters, as well as load references to the managed resources. The MBean Server is the interface to the managed resources; you never directly manipulate a reference to a managed resource.

Chapter 8 shows you how to use the dynamic loading service. In Chapter 7, you learn how to use the relation service, and Chapter 10 walks you through the process of using the monitoring and timer services. The JMX specification indicates that each of these services is required in a JMX agent, but that doesn't mean you will always make use of them. You'll find that in some cases, the monitoring service is the only one you use. However, you can easily make the other services available at runtime by loading them into an MBean Server without interrupting processing.

## The JMX API Packages

Because architectures often begin as diagrams and concepts, at some point they must be made tangible. The JMX specification not only provides the designs around the architecture, but the implementation of the architectural components in the form of the JMX API. The API is what application developers and vendors work with to implement management of their applications and products according to the JMX specification. When you download the JMX specification, you can download the Sun JMX reference implementation, which enables you to start writing JMX applications right away.

The Sun JMX reference implementation, upon which many of the examples in this book are based, is spread across several Java packages, each of which provides a set of requisite functionality. The `javax.management` package contains many of the core classes and interfaces, such as the `MBeanServer` interface, and the `ObjectName` and `ObjectInstance` classes. It also contains the `NotificationBroadcaster` and `NotificationListener` interfaces, as well as all of the MBean metadata classes.

The `javax.management.loading` package contains the classes that can be used for dynamic loading, such as `MLet` and `DefaultLoaderRepository`. These provide access to the class loaders that an MBean Server knows about at runtime.

The `javax.management.modelmbean` contains all the classes to support the instrumentation of model MBeans. The `javax.management.monitor`, `javax.management.relation`, and `javax.management.timer` contain the necessary classes for providing the agent services: monitoring, relation, and timer. The `javax.management.loading` package previously mentioned provides a fourth agent service: dynamic loading.

As you read through this book and work through the examples, you'll become acquainted with the different packages and the classes and interfaces they contain. The most important package is the `javax.management` package, because it contains the classes and interfaces that you will use most often when writing managed resources. It also contains the classes and interfaces that are used to provide the core functionality of a JMX agent. The other packages provide additional functionality, including the agent support services as well as support for model MBeans.

## Summary

This chapter introduced you to the JMX architecture and its core components, including the MBean Server and MBeans. You were introduced to the agent services — timer, monitoring, dynamic loading, and relation — and where these core components fit in the JMX architecture. As an application developer, you should now begin to see where management of your application fits in. You should also have some understanding of the services an agent makes available to you.

The next chapter will further acquaint you with JMX by demonstrating how to write a simple JMX application. Then, beginning with Chapter 4, you take a closer look at the core components and how to implement them.

# Chapter 3

# Writing Your First JMX Application

The previous two chapters gave you a tour of system management and the JMX architecture, including some key components such as the MBean, the agent, and protocol adapters. In this chapter, you'll create a simple JMX application using the Sun JMX reference implementation. It contains the necessary documentation and includes some pre-built components to get you up and running quickly.

Chapter 2 described the architecture of JMX and how the different components interface. It also covered the role of each component and its basic capabilities. In this chapter, you'll take a short detour to write a simple JMX application, which will further familiarize you with the components and how to use them. The remaining chapters of the book focus on the major component areas of JMX, and every chapter includes many examples of how to use them. Later examples employ the knowledge gained from earlier chapters to write real managed objects.

You're not expected to fully understand the components at this point, but seeing them used in a real application and familiarizing yourself with some of the packages before diving in can be useful. However, if you're anxious to learn more about a key component, feel free to skip ahead.

## Setting up JMX

The first and most obvious thing you need before writing a JMX application is an implementation of the JMX specification. The examples in this book are based on the Sun Microsystems JMX reference implementation, which is also distributed with the JMX specification. You can download the Sun JMX reference implementation from `http://java.sun.com/jmx`.

You can install the API as you would virtually any other Java library. You need to have the JMX libraries in the CLASSPATH of any JMX code that you write. The JMX reference implementation by Sun includes the following JAR files:

◆ `jmxri.jar` — This is the reference implementation; it contains all the core interfaces and classes. This JAR must be included in your CLASSPATH.

♦ `jmxgrinder.jar` — This JAR contains the classes for the JMX Grinder applications, which can be used to check MBean compliancy. It has both command-line mode and GUI mode, which enable you to look at MBeans of different types. The JMX Grinder is covered in detail later in this chapter.

♦ `jmxtools.jar` — This JAR contains classes that are not considered part of the JMX reference implementation but are included by Sun. It contains the classes for debugging and the code for the HTML adapter that is used in some of their examples.

# Identifying the Common JMX Components

An important part of writing any application is an understanding of exactly what you need to do to get started. This chapter serves as a good introduction to where the major components sit in relation to their respective Java packages.

Depending on what part of a management application you are writing, you need to decide which components you are going to use. The example application in this chapter uses many of the major components in a hypothetical JMX application. You will write a JMX agent that includes the necessary components to load a managed object and present its management interface. The example also teaches you how to define the management interface for a managed object, then write the code that implements that interface. Although JMX agents must have certain required components in order to be considered compliant with the JMX specification, this application doesn't include some of the agent services, such as the timer, monitor, and relation services.

## The javax.management package

The Sun JMX reference implementation is spread across several packages. The core interfaces and classes are in the `javax.management` package. This package contains the interfaces for components such as the MBean Server, which enables you to load and unload MBeans as well as execute the methods of MBeans. It also has the `MBeanServerFactory` class, which is used to create instances of the `MBeanServer` interface. The `javax.management` package also includes the classes used to represent metadata about an MBean management interface. It includes classes such as `MBeanAttributeInfo`, `MBeanOperationInfo`, `MBeanConstructorInfo`, `MBeanParameterInfo`, and `MBeanNotificationInfo`, which describe attributes, operations, constructors, parameters, and notifications, respectively. Not all of the classes used for describing MBean metadata are in this package, as other types of MBeans, such as the model MBean, have their own packages. Figure 3-1 shows a diagram of the relationships among these various classes.

> **CROSS-REFERENCE:** Appendix D contains numerous Unified Modeling Language (UML) diagrams that show the relationships between key JMX components in the `javax.management` package. You can review these diagrams before continuing or refer to them at your convenience. Figure D-6 in Appendix D shows the relationships among the metadata classes described in the preceding paragraph.

The `javax.management` package also contains the definitions of the core classes and interfaces that comprise the notification model. It includes the classes that define how a notification is constructed and how to broadcast and listen for notifications. The package contains many of the exception classes that you'll see most often. These exception classes cover cases such as referencing managed resources that don't exist and referencing an attribute of a managed resource that doesn't exist, along with some more general exceptions such as the `javax.management.JMException`.

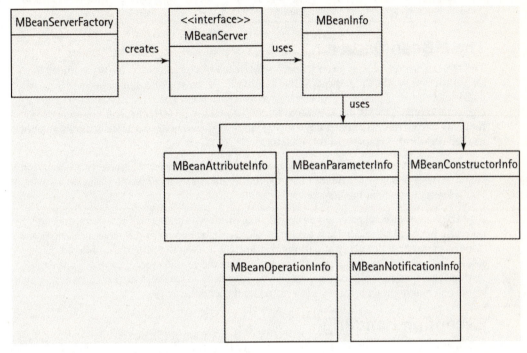

**Figure 3-1:** MBean core classes, interfaces and metadata classes.

Let's talk a little more about some of the common JMX components. You were introduced to the MBean and the MBean Server in Chapter 2; now you'll see how these components are used for this example.

## The MBean

As you have already learned, an MBean represents a managed resource. An MBean has methods and attributes that enable you to access information about — and control the behavior of — the MBean at runtime. There are two basic approaches to creating an MBean: You can implement an interface, or you can register a handle to the managed object. Most of the examples in this book use the former method. In Chapter 6, you'll see an example of the latter method.

In practice, an MBean is represented by an interface and a class that implements that interface. The interface defines the attributes and methods that represent its management information. You'll create a standard MBean for the example in this chapter. The standard MBean is the easiest type of MBean to create because of its straightforward design and implementation. In the JMX API, there are no classes that represent standard MBeans. The other three types of

MBeans — dynamic, open, and model — have a specific interface you must implement called `DynamicMBean`.

> **CROSS-REFERENCE:** Standard MBeans are covered in detail in Chapter 4, dynamic MBeans in Chapter 5, and open and model MBeans in Chapter 6.

## The MBean Server

The MBean Server acts as a repository for MBeans. As a repository, it also includes the means for you to add and remove MBeans from it. When you add and remove MBeans from an MBean Server, you use a process known as *registration* and *unregistration.* The registration process adds the MBean to the registered list of MBeans, and unregistration removes it from the list. You'll use the MBean Server to register an MBean and invoke one of its methods for the example in this chapter.

Along with the registration facilities, the MBean Server provides methods for finding either a single MBean or a set of MBeans. This capability manifests itself as query facilities, which you'll learn more about in Chapter 9.

An MBean Server is represented as an instance of the `MBeanServer` interface, and you normally have only one per JMX agent. In some instances, you might have more than one `MBeanServer`, but not many situations warrant this. Given the importance placed on the `MBeanServer`, it is most commonly created during the initialization phase of application startup. This phase usually encompasses activities used to establish access to critical system resources, making it an ideal phase to initialize the `MBeanServer`.

## Exception handling

When writing JMX applications, you will eventually encounter exceptions. These exceptions take the form of checked exceptions or runtime exceptions. You might need to respond to an exception that occurs somewhere in the JMX API, or it could occur in the managed object itself. When an exception occurs in the API, this usually indicates some syntactical error or procedural error. When an exception occurs in the managed object, it can mean just about anything. These types of exceptions are usually named *user-defined exceptions.* When you write your managed object, you should wrap user-defined exceptions in more general JMX-defined exceptions such as `MBeanExceptions`. This enables management clients to respond to exceptions in a standard way. If a client needs more detail about what has happened, it can examine the underlying exception.

When handling exceptions, you need to determine how the exception affects the availability of the managed resource. The exception may be the result of improper configuration, in which case the offending attribute can be reconfigured to correct the situation. On the other hand, an exception may be the result of a bug in the software, in which case the managed object may be unusable. You might correct this type of problem by unregistering the managed object, thus making it unavailable.

# Writing Your First JMX Application

Now that you've had a brief overview of some of the packages, classes, and interfaces, you can work through a simple application that uses them. You'll write a simple MBean with some attributes and operations, and utilize the MBeanServer to load the MBean. You'll also use the MBeanServer to invoke operations and print the results. Finally you'll use the HtmlAdapterServer protocol adapter to access the MBean remotely and view its attributes. This exercise will acquaint you with these elements and prepare you for later chapters with similar examples.

The first thing you'll do is create a managed resource. For simplicity, this managed resource won't connect to any type of real resource such as a printer or an application, but it demonstrates the concepts nonetheless. Later chapters provide more detail about the components covered in this chapter.

The managed resource in JMX is represented as an MBean. The type of MBean you'll create here is the standard MBean, which presents its management interface using a well-known set of attributes and methods. (Standard MBeans were introduced in Chapter 2 and are discussed in detail in Chapter 4.) The attributes and methods are well known because they are implemented as a Java interface and in a concrete class. The interface does not change frequently, so it can be implemented as an interface. You create the interface first.

The naming convention for interfaces for standard MBeans is the name of the implementation class followed by the letters MBean. (Other types of MBeans in the JMX specification do not have a similar convention.) This convention can be tested using a tool that is distributed with Sun's JMX reference implementation. Listing 3-1 shows the source code for the interface you use for this example.

**Listing 3-1: ManagedObjectMBean interface**

```
public interface ManagedObjectMBean {

    // Accessor for name attribute//
    public String getName();

    // Accessor for name attribute //
    public void setName(String newName);

    // Accessor for description attribute //
    public String getDescription();

    // Accessor for description attribute //
    public void setDescription(String newDescription);

    // An operation //
    public void doSomething();
}
```

The interface named ManagedObjectMBean in Listing 3-1 defines four methods. One unique thing about the names of these methods is that they must comply with the names of defined attributes in the implementation of the interface. For example, the getName() and setName() methods correspond to the name attribute. When you create MBeans, you must follow this convention of naming accessor methods after the attributes they access. If this convention is not followed, the methods will be treated as normal methods and not accessors of the attributes.

The doSomething() method is known as an *operation* in JMX lingo. An operation refers to a method that you can invoke. However, as you'll see shortly, methods of MBeans or managed resources in JMX are not invoked directly, as you might assume. They are invoked using another JMX component, the MBean Server.

To utilize the ManagedObjectMBean interface, you must create an implementation of it that returns actual values for the attributes, and does something when the doSomething() method is invoked. Listing 3-2 shows the source of the ManagedObject class that implements the ManagedObjectMBean interface.

**Listing 3-2: ManagedObjectMBean implementation**

```
public class ManagedObject implements ManagedObjectMBean{

        private String name = "";
        private String description = "";

        public String getName(){
                return name;
        }

        public void setName(String newName){
                name = newName;
        }

        public String getDescription(){
                return description;
        }

        public void setDescription(String newDescription){
                description = newDescription;
        }

        public void doSomething(){

                System.out.println("Printing Something");
        }

}
```

The ManagedObject class implements all the methods of the ManagedObjectMBean interface as required. The doSomething() method prints a simple message, which for management clients is not useful. In Chapter 5, you'll see implementations of MBeans that return actual data.

In addition, you might have noticed that the constructor is omitted from the `ManagedObject` class. This is done so that the compiler will insert a public default constructor. An MBean can have any number of public constructors.

## Running the JMX agent

Now that you essentially have an MBean that can be used, you can write an application that will load it and execute its methods. Chapter 2 described the JMX architecture and the part played by the MBean Server. The MBean Server acts as a repository for MBeans, and provides access to their operations and attributes. By providing access to the attributes and operations, the MBean Server also prevents management clients from directly accessing the managed object.

Managed objects can be loaded and registered both dynamically and statically. You can use the `MBeanServer` interface to create an instance of an MBean and register it dynamically. Alternatively, you can create your own instance of an MBean and then use methods of the `MBeanServer` interface to register the MBean. In both cases, the MBean must be registered in the MBeanServer in order for it to be used by management clients. How do management clients find MBeans in the MBean Server? And how does the MBean Server keep track of its MBeans?

Each MBean in an MBean Server is associated with something called an *object name*. The object name is essentially the handle to the object, but not a direct object reference to it. The MBean Server uses the ObjectName to find and register an MBean, as well as to remove MBeans or invoke methods of MBeans. When a management client or JMX agent wants to interact with an MBean, it needs to have the ObjectName.

The object name is essentially a string that follows a defined syntax consisting of a domain name and a set of key/value pairs. The actual syntax of the object name is discussed in Chapter 8. Once you have an object name, you can use it in operations that require retrieving or setting attributes of MBeans, as well as invoking their methods. The object name is represented by instances of the `ObjectName` class and resides in the `javax.management` package. You will see the `ObjectName` class referred to in the JMX specification as a *foundation class*. A foundation class is one which is used as argument types or return values in methods of the JMX API.

To utilize your MBean, you need to write an application that will start an MBean Server and then instruct it to load an MBean. The MBean Server is not a traditional server such as a Web server or e-mail server; rather, it serves MBeans and keeps track of them. The application that loads the MBean Server can be a simple Java application or it can be any class. The application or code that hosts the MBean Server and MBeans is referred to as the JMX agent, although the application in this example should not be considered a full-fledged JMX agent, as it does not support all the required agent services.

**CROSS-REFERENCE:** See Chapter 2 for a discussion of JMX agents and agent services.

Listing 3-3 shows the source code of the Java application that will load the MBean Server and your MBean.

**Listing 3-3: JMX agent application**

```java
import javax.management.Attribute;
import javax.management.AttributeNotFoundException;
import javax.management.InstanceNotFoundException;
import javax.management.InvalidAttributeValueException;
import javax.management.MBeanException;
import javax.management.MalformedObjectNameException;
import javax.management.ObjectName;
import javax.management.MBeanServer;
import javax.management.MBeanServerFactory;
import javax.management.ReflectionException;


public class ExampleJMXAgent {

    private static MBeanServer server = null;

    public ExampleJMXAgent() {
        server = MBeanServerFactory.createMBeanServer();
    }

    public static void main(String[] args) {

        try {

            ExampleJMXAgent agent = new ExampleJMXAgent();

            ObjectName mngObject = agent.loadBean("ManagedObject",
                                "ManagedObject:name=simple");

            server.setAttribute(mngObject,
                        new Attribute("Name","ManagedObject"));

            String name =
                (String)server.getAttribute(mngObject,"Name");

            System.out.println("Name: " + name);

            server.invoke(mngObject,
                        "doSomething",
                        new Object[]{},
                        new String[]{});


        } catch (MBeanException ex){
            System.out.println(ex);
        } catch (AttributeNotFoundException ex){
            System.out.println(ex);
```

```
        } catch (InstanceNotFoundException ex){
            System.out.println(ex);
        } catch (ReflectionException ex){
            System.out.println(ex);
        } catch (InvalidAttributeValueException ex){
            System.out.println(ex);
        }

    }

    private ObjectName loadBean(String className,String objectName) {

        ObjectName mbeanObjectName = null;
        String domain = server.getDefaultDomain();
        String mbeanName = className;
        try {
            mbeanObjectName = new ObjectName(objectName);
        } catch(MalformedObjectNameException e) {
          e.printStackTrace();
          System.exit(1);
        }
          // Create our simple object to manage //
          try {
            server.createMBean(mbeanName,mbeanObjectName);
          }catch(Exception ex){
              ex.printStackTrace();
              System.exit(1);
          }

        return mbeanObjectName;
    }
}
```

The `ExampleJMXAgent` application loads an MBean, sets the value of an attribute, and then invokes one of the operations of the MBean. The `ExampleJMXAgent` creates a reference to the MBean Server in the constructor using the following line of code:

```
server = MBeanServerFactory.createMBeanServer();
```

In the `main()` method, the `ManagedObject` MBean is created and registered in the `loadBean()` method. This method does two things. It first creates the `ObjectName` reference that you'll use later with the following line of code:

```
mbeanObjectName = new ObjectName(objectName);
```

It also uses the `createMBean()` method of the `MBeanServer` interface to create and register an instance of the MBean using this line of code:

```
server.createMBean(mbeanName,mbeanObjectName);
```

The value returned from the `loadBean()` method is an instance of the `ObjectName` class that can be used to access the managed bean. The class name and `ObjectName` instance are used as arguments to the `createMBean()` method.

After the `loadBean()` method returns, the `main()` method continues by setting the value of the name attribute. It uses the `setAttribute()` method of the `MBeanServer` interface with the following line of code:

```
server.setAttribute(mngObject,new Attribute("Name","ManagedObject"));
```

The `setAttribute()` method takes the `ObjectName` instance, so that the `MBeanServer` can identify the correct MBean, and an instance of the `javax.management.Attribute` class that identifies which attribute to set. This class encapsulates the name and value of an attribute. This line of code sets the value of the name attribute to the value of `ManagedObject`. After the attribute value has been set, the application retrieves and prints the value of the attribute. To retrieve the value of the attribute, you use the `getAttribute()` method of the `MBeanServer` interface with the following line of code:

```
String name = (String)server.getAttribute(mngObject,"Name");
```

The `getAttribute()` method returns a `java.lang.Object` type, so you must cast the return of the `getAttribute()` method to the desired type. You can set attribute values to many types of values, such as `java.lang.Integer`, `java.util.Vector` or some custom type of your own design. Why use "Name" instead of "name" for the attribute? The reason is that the MBean Server uses the name to determine if an attribute value has accessor methods, and which accessor methods to use. Recall from earlier in the chapter that the `ManagedObject` MBean defined a `getName()` and `setName()` method for accessing the name attribute. The name of the attribute is used by the MBean Server to form the name of the accessor method to execute.

After manipulating the name attribute, you invoke the `doSomething()` operation, which prints a simple message. To invoke an operation, you use the `invoke()` method of the `MBeanServer` interface. If you've ever used the Java Reflection API, the usage of this method will look familiar, but not exactly the same. The `invoke()` method takes an ObjectName of the MBean containing the operation, a `java.lang.String` representing the name of the operation, and two arrays. The first array is an array of `java.lang.Object` representing the values of the arguments to the operation, and the second array represents a `java.lang.String` array of the Java types of the arguments to the operation:

```
server.invoke(mngObject,"doSomething",new Object[]{},new String[]{});
```

Because the `doSomething()` operation takes no arguments, both arrays are empty. Once you create the application and compile it, you can execute it. You should see output that looks like the following:

```
Name: ManagedObject
Printing Something
```

# Using the HtmlAdaptorServer

One of the required components of a JMX agent is the protocol adapter. In Chapter 2, you learned the purpose of the protocol adapter and how it fits into the JMX architecture. In Chapter 12, you'll learn how to build protocol adapters, but in the meantime, you can make use of the HTTP-based protocol adapter that comes with the Sun JMX reference implementation. With this protocol adapter, you can add the capability to remotely access your example MBean.

In the example in this chapter, your JMX agent loaded the ManagedObject MBean, manipulated the Name attribute, and invoked the doSomething() operation. This all occurred from within the agent itself. In practice, though, a JMX agent would load the managed resource, load a protocol adapter, and then wait until some action caused the agent to exit. The protocol adapter listens for requests, passes them to the MBean Server, and then returns the result to the client.

The protocol adapter used here is HtmlAdaptorServer, an MBean that enables Web browsers to access managed resources. It presents information about managed resources in HTML and enables you to change attributes and invoke operations using HTML forms. Because the HtmlAdaptorServer is an MBean, you can load it using the same code used for the ManagedObject MBean. Listing 3-4 shows the ExampleJMXAgent class, updated to load the HtmlAdaptorServer MBean. The lines in bold indicate the code added to support using the HtmlAdaptorServer MBean.

**Listing 3-4: The ExampleJMXAgent application**

```
import javax.management.Attribute;
import javax.management.AttributeNotFoundException;
import javax.management.InstanceNotFoundException;
import javax.management.InvalidAttributeValueException;
import javax.management.MBeanException;
import javax.management.MalformedObjectNameException;
import javax.management.ObjectName;
import javax.management.MBeanServer;
import javax.management.MBeanServerFactory;
import javax.management.ReflectionException;

// Sun HTMLAdapter
import com.sun.jdmk.comm.HtmlAdaptorServer;


public class ExampleJMXAgent {

    private static MBeanServer server = null;

    public ExampleJMXAgent() {
        server = MBeanServerFactory.createMBeanServer();
    }

    public static void main(String[] args) {
```

```
        try {

    ExampleJMXAgent agent = new ExampleJMXAgent();

    ObjectName mngObject = agent.loadBean("ManagedObject",
                            "ManagedObject:name=simple");

    // Register HtmlAdaptorServer
    ObjectName adapterObject =
agent.loadBean("com.sun.jdmk.comm.HtmlAdaptorServer",
        "HtmlAdaptorServer:name=HtmlAdapter");

        server.setAttribute(mngObject,new
Attribute("Name","ManagedObject"));

        String name =
(String)server.getAttribute(mngObject,"Name");

        System.out.println("Name: " + name);

        server.invoke(mngObject,
                "doSomething",
                new Object[]{},
                new String[]{});

        // Start the HtmlAdaptorServer
        server.invoke(adapterObject,
                "start",
                new Object[]{},
                new String[]{});

    } catch (MBeanException ex){
        System.out.println(ex);
    } catch (AttributeNotFoundException ex){
        System.out.println(ex);
    } catch (InstanceNotFoundException ex){
        System.out.println(ex);
    } catch (ReflectionException ex){
        System.out.println(ex);
    } catch (InvalidAttributeValueException ex){
        System.out.println(ex);
    }

  }

  private ObjectName loadBean(String className,String objectName) {

    ObjectName mbeanObjectName = null;
```

```
        String domain = server.getDefaultDomain();
        String mbeanName = className;
        try {
             mbeanObjectName = new ObjectName(objectName);
        } catch(MalformedObjectNameException e) {
          e.printStackTrace();
          System.exit(1);
        }
          // Create our simple object to manage //
          try {
             server.createMBean(mbeanName,mbeanObjectName);
          }catch(Exception ex){
                ex.printStackTrace();
                System.exit(1);
          }

          return mbeanObjectName;
     }
}
```

The first change imported the class `HtmlAdaptorServer`, which is in the
`com.sun.jdmk.comm` package. This is a Sun implementation class and not part of the JMX
API. Next, you simply use the `loadBean()` method used in the first example. This method
takes the name of the `HtmlAdaptorServer` class and a string that will be used to form the
`ObjectName` class instance for the MBean.

Loading the MBean makes it available as a registered MBean, but not as a protocol adaptor.
You need to call the `start()` method, which causes the `HtmlAdaptorServer` MBean to
listen on port `8082`, the default, for HTTP requests.

When you start the `ExampleJMXAgent`, you will see the same output as before, but the agent
will not exit as before. Instead, it will pause, because the `HtmlAdaptorServer` has started a
thread to listen for HTTP requests. Only when all threads have terminated will the agent be
able to exit.

You can experiment with the protocol adapter by starting your Web browser and navigating to
the address `http://localhost:8082`. When the page loads, you should see something
similar to what is shown in Figure 3-2.

This figure represents the agent view that the `HtmlAdaptorServer` displays by default. By
scrolling down, you can see the MBeans currently registered in the MBean Server. One of
these is the `ManagedObject` MBean created for this example.

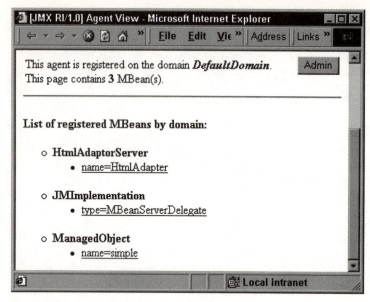

**Figure 3-2:** Using the HtmlAdaptorServer protocol adapter.

Clicking the hyperlink under the `ManagedObject` entry displays the MBean view for that bean, as shown in Figure 3-3.

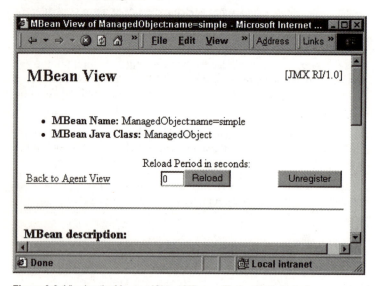

**Figure 3-3:** Viewing the ManagedObject MBean with the HtmlAdaptorServer protocol adapter.

In the MBean view, you can see information about the management interface for the MBean. If you scroll down, you can see the attributes `Description` and `Name`, as well as a button that enables you to invoke the `doSomething()` operation.

If you don't see this output, you can recheck your listing or read the following section on troubleshooting. It describes the causes of some common exceptions that can result from this simple JMX application.

## Troubleshooting

Beyond the simple `ClassNotFoundException` that can result from not having the appropriate JAR in your `CLASSPATH`, some JMX-specific exceptions can result from trying to run the `ExampleJMXAgent` application in Listing 3-3.

Common exceptions you might encounter in the sample JMX application are listed in Table 3-1. Some of these exceptions are caused by simple typographical errors, and others are procedural.

### Table 3-1     Exceptions and Causes

| Exception and Message | Cause |
|---|---|
| `javax.management.Reflection Exception: The MBean class could not be loaded by the default loader repository.` | This exception is caused by not compiling the `ManagedObject` class. In the `ExampleJMXAgent`, the MBean is not referenced by name and is loaded dynamically, so when the `ExampleJMXAgent` is compiled, the `ManagedObject` class is not automatically compiled. |
| `javax.management.Malformed ObjectNameException: ObjectName: domain part must be specified` | The string you pass to the constructor of the ObjectName must include a colon, which separates the domain part from the key/value part. You may have accidentally typed a semicolon. |
| `javax.management.AttributeNot FoundException: name not accessible` | This exception indicates that an accessor method could not be found for the attribute in question. This can be caused by typing in a non-existent attribute name or by using the wrong case. The first letter of the attribute name must be uppercase, such as `Name`. |
| `javax.management.Reflection Exception: The operation with name doSomething could not be found` | This indicates that the operation was not found either because you mistyped the name of the operation or an overloading of the operation that matched the arguments could not be found. The `doSomething()` method in this example takes no arguments. |

| Exception and Message | Cause |
|---|---|
| `javax.management.NotCompliant MBeanException: ManagedObject does not implement the ManagedObjectMBean interface or the DynamicMBean interface` | This indicates that the MBean is not compliant with the JMX specification. This can be caused by not following the naming convention for standard MBean interfaces or by forgetting to implement the MBean interface in the `ManagedObject` class. |

In Table 3-1, the exception `javax.management.NotCompliantMBeanException` indicates that there is something fundamentally wrong with the implementation of the MBean. In that example, the "implements" keyword was excluded, thus the `ManagedObjectMBean` interface was not implemented as required. Given the complexity of an MBean, it is easy to forget some seemingly minor detail; if you're writing MBeans that other developers will use, make sure that they are compliant with the spec.

> **CROSS-REFERENCE:** These exceptions represent the most common cases that you are likely to encounter with this example. You can also find a list of exceptions in Appendix B.

# The JMX Grinder

The Sun JMX reference implementation includes a tool called the JMX Grinder, which enables you to test whether an MBean complies with the JMX spec. You can load different types of MBeans — such as standard, dynamic, and model — into the tool and browse them. It includes a command-line version as well as a GUI version.

This section does not cover all the details about the JMX Grinder tool, as the tool is relatively self-explanatory, and the Sun JMX reference implementation contains detailed instructions on its use. It does, however, show basic usage in command-line mode and GUI mode for testing compliance of the `ManagedObject` MBean created for the example in this chapter.

Whether you're launching the JMX Grinder utility in command-line or GUI mode, make sure that the `jmxgrinder.jar` is in your `CLASSPATH`. Once you're sure it is, you can execute the following command to use the tool in command-line mode:

```
java JMXGrinder ManagedObject
```

You can provide more than one MBean as arguments to the JMXGrinder application, but only one is used for this example. The output from running the JMXGrinder in command-line mode for the `ManagedObject` MBean is as follows:

```
ManagedObject - JMX Standard MBean compliant
Summary:
  JMX Standard MBean compliant : 1
  JMX Dynamic MBean compliant : 0
  Not JMX MBean compliant : 0
  Could not resolve class : 0
-------------------------------------
```

```
Total checked : 1
```

This output indicates that one standard MBean was found as compliant. You could use this utility to find some of the errors that cause the exceptions listed in Table 3-1 before trying to execute the `ExampleJMXAgent` application.

To run the JMXGrinder in GUI mode, you simply omit any arguments:

```
java JMXGrinder
```

This launches the GUI, which does not immediately return any results, as the command-line version did. Figure 3-4 shows how the JMXGrinder GUI looks upon launch. Notice that in the left pane there is a tree view with a  single node labeled `No classes loaded`.

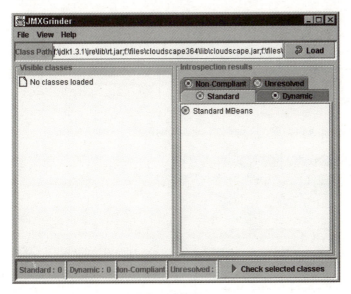

**Figure 3-4:** Launching the JMXGrinder GUI.

Click the button in the upper-left labeled  Load; this causes the left pane to be filled with all the classes found. The `CLASSPATH` is searched, and all classes — whether MBeans or not — are listed. After you've done this, you should have a view that looks like the one shown in Figure 3-5. In Figure 3-5, you can see that the `ManagedObject` MBean is selected.

You can do a variety of things in the JMXGrinder GUI, such as view the properties and operations of an MBean. To view the properties of the `ManagedObject` MBean, use the menu bar and select View ⇨View Properties Window, or double-click the name of the MBean in the Introspection Results pane on the right.

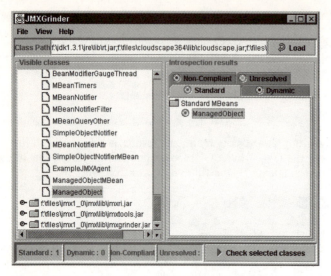

**Figure 3-5:** Selecting the ManagedObject MBean in the GUI.

Viewing the properties brings up a dialog box like the one shown in Figure 3-6.

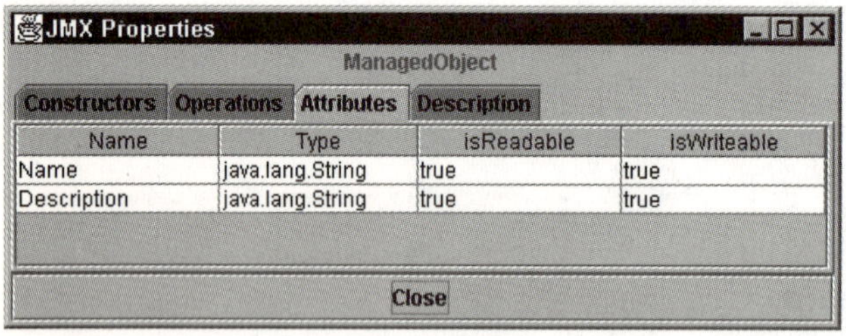

| Name | Type | isReadable | isWriteable |
|---|---|---|---|
| Name | java.lang.String | true | true |
| Description | java.lang.String | true | true |

**Figure 3-6:** Viewing the properties of the ManagedObject MBean.

From this dialog box, you can also view the MBean's constructors and operations, as well as a description of the MBean.

## Summary

This chapter served as a quick introduction to writing a JMX application. You created a simple, standard MBean and changed the value of the Name attribute. You also invoked a method of the MBean. The example doesn't indicate how all JMX applications are written, but it gives you an idea of how to use some of the major components such as the MBean Server and MBeans.

In the next chapter, you'll look more closely at standard MBeans and how to get more information about them at runtime.

# Part II

# Using the Instrumentation Layer

# Chapter 4

# Working with Standard MBeans

You've already looked at the JMX architecture in some detail, and learned how to create a simple JMX application. Now it's time to take a detailed tour of some of the key components. You have seen numerous references to *managed resources,* manageable objects that include applications, application components, and physical devices such as disk drives, printers, network switches, and routers.

In this chapter, you take a closer look at how to create a managed object from scratch. You'll take a closer look at the construct known as the MBean. Before you're done, you'll code one, construct one, and execute one, and build a tool for browsing them and displaying them graphically.

You'll examine the rules for creating an MBean, learning how to define what its management interface looks like to tools and JMX agents. You'll learn how MBeans can inherit their management interface from a parent class, and how attributes and accessor methods for an MBean are constructed. By the end of this chapter, you should be able to build the management interface for a standard MBean.

## What Is an MBean?

An entity or resource that you wish to manage is called a *managed bean*, or *MBean*. You'll see the latter term in the JMX specification and in documentation about JMX. A managed bean falls into one of four basic types:

- Standard MBean
- Dynamic MBean
- Open MBean
- Model MBean

This chapter focuses on the first type, the standard MBean. In subsequent chapters, you look at the other types of MBeans. (Open and model MBeans are types of dynamic MBeans.)

Remember that managed resources can represent almost anything you want, and there are no rules about the scope of a single MBean. An MBean can represent a single EJB, or it can represent a group of EJBs. It can also, of course, be used to represent a physical device such as a network appliance, a fax machine, or a printer. Each of the MBeans mentioned above, however, conform to certain design patterns that define their look and behavior. This definition for look and behavior results in the management interface of the object.

Managed beans can represent real-life objects or virtual objects, just as other Java classes can. However, each must adhere to a set of guidelines developed for that given MBean. The basic rules, those that apply to all MBeans, are covered here. These basic rules provide you with necessary information about how MBeans must be coded in order to be considered MBeans, and in order to work in any MBean-compliant management solution.

You can also use managed beans as wrappers around legacy management solutions. This way, you protect your investment in existing infrastructure and code, even as you put a new face on them. Managed beans can act as proxies between the new and the old, and they can access relational databases, sockets, and more or less anything else. For example, you could have a set of managed beans representing network connections that you manage from a central console. You could monitor traffic on the connections, possibly looking at IP packets. You could, for example, use one managed bean for each major protocol, such as TCP/IP, HTTP, FTP, or SMTP.

## Understanding the MBean design pattern

When writing software that you intend for use as a general framework for accomplishing some task or solving some problem, you want to make design choices that follow certain principles. The JMX specification defines *design patterns* that ensure the consistent use and creation of software components based on your framework for the different types of MBeans. These patterns enable you to easily create MBeans, thus saving you time. They also ensure that your managed resources can be easily plugged in and used in applications that you may not write yourself. If you are writing software components to be sold, for instance, you may want to make them JMX-compliant, particularly if they are intended for use in an application server. The JMX design patterns were inspired by the JavaBeans design patterns, but they deviate in some respects and are considered somewhat unique in that they allow for things such as inheritance of their management interface.

Formally, an MBean is defined as a public Java class that implements a specific interface and conforms to certain design patterns. The interface and design patterns help to define the management interface of the managed resource, which can include the following items:

- ◆ Attributes that can be read or write in nature
- ◆ Operations or methods that can be invoked and may return a value
- ◆ Optional notifications
- ◆ The constructors for the MBean

The attributes and data of an MBean are encapsulated, and are only accessible via `get` or `set` methods. Listing 4-1 illustrates a simple Java class with getter and setter methods, also collectively known as *accessor* methods. You should note that this listing illustrates a class that is not an MBean.

**Listing 4-1: ManageablePrinterResource class with access methods**

```
import java.util.Vector;

public class ManageablePrinterResource {

        private String name = "";
        private Vector jobs = null;
        private int sheetsPaper = 0;

        public ManageablePrinterResource(){}

        public void setName(String newName){
                name = newName;
        }
        public String getName(){
                return name;
        }
        public void setJobs(Vector newJobs){
                if (jobs == null)
                    jobs = new Vector();
                else
                    jobs = newJobs;
        }
        public Vector getJobs(){
                return jobs;
        }
        public int getSheetsPaper(){
                return sheetsPaper;
        }
}
```

Listing 4-1 shows the source of a class called ManageablePrinterResource with accessor methods for each of its three private variables. The ManageablePrinterResource class has methods named getName(), setName(), setJobs(), getJobs(), and getSheetsPaper(), which set the values of the name, jobs, and sheetsPaper variables, respectively. The accessor methods use a naming scheme that adds the prefix *get* to a method that reads a value, and the prefix *set* to a method that updates a value. Some variables may only have a *get* or *set* method; they are not required to have both. In cases where a variable has one or the other, the method determines the read or write properties of the variable. Encapsulating data and using accessor methods ensures data integrity, and that only valid data types are used to set the values of variables.

In addition to get and set methods, MBeans may also implement other methods, called *operations* in the JMX specification. Some MBeans may simply contain data that can be manipulated via the accessor methods, but in many cases, actual operations need to be carried out by the MBean. Consider the ManageablePrinterResource class from Listing 4-1. A class representing a printer probably needs methods to initiate certain actions such as resetting the printer after it receives an error, or perhaps killing a print job or changing its priority.

Extending the `ManageablePrinterResource` from Listing 4-1 yields the code shown in Listing 4-2, which shows the `ManageablePrinterResource` with methods added to perform the operations needed.

**Listing 4-2: ManageablePrinterResource class with operation methods added**

```
import java.util.Vector;

public class ManageablePrinterResource {

        private String name = "";
        private Vector jobs = null;
        private int sheetsPaper = 0;

        public ManageablePrinterResource(){}

        public void setName(String newName){
            name = newName;
        }
        public String getName(){
            return name;
        }
        public void setJobs(Vector newJobs){
            if (jobs == null)
                jobs = new Vector();
            else
                jobs = newJobs;
        }
        public Vector getJobs(){
            return jobs;
        }
        public int getSheetsPaper(){
            return sheetsPaper;
        }
        public void resetPrinter(){
            // Implement printer reset here //
        }
        public void killJob(String jobName){
}
```

The operators or methods that have been added are `resetPrinter()`, `killJob()`, and `changePriority()`. The `ManageablePrinterResource` class is declared public, which is another requirement of any type of MBean. The class cannot have package-only visibility or be an abstract class. This ensures that the MBean Server can easily and legally construct an instance of the class. The same is true for its methods — they must have access modifiers that do not restrict the functions of the MBean Server.

MBeans, dynamic or standard, can optionally have a public constructor. You can take advantage of the Java compiler's behavior and not explicitly declare any constructor. In this case, the compiler generates a default constructor (that is, a constructor with no arguments).

Note that this does not mean the MBean is limited to only one public constructor. You can also have multiple public constructors, but the MBean Server will only use the public versions. A public version is needed so that instances of the MBean can be instantiated without any problems and are always accessible. Classes that are instantiated by a string name or dynamically, such as with the `Class.forName()`, often have default constructors, although this is not a requirement. Listing 4-3 shows a class with several constructors.

**Listing 4-3: Class with multiple constructors**

```
public class ManageableSoftwareComponent{

    public ManageableSoftwareComponent(){}

    public ManageableSoftwareComponent(String name){}

    public ManageableSoftwareComponent(int printerID){}
}
```

## Defining an interface

Standard MBeans conform to a well-known interface, meaning that the interface is defined at design time. The actual method names and accessor methods are defined, and only change with subsequent design changes, not at runtime. The developer of the management interface publishes this interface, probably using Javadoc, describing the methods and attributes of the managed resource. The examples you've seen so far don't use an interface and thus don't qualify as MBeans, although they define public constructors and contain accessor methods for their attributes.

Interfaces for standard MBeans, once initially designed, are not often changed subsequently. This means that the management interface is intended to be static for a long time, or perhaps the interface never needs to change. Interfaces for standard MBeans do represent a slight increase in development time, as they have to be recompiled each time a new attribute or operation is added, which means any subclasses need to change as well. This could become an unacceptable burden, depending on the number of managed resources you have.

## Introspection: Discovering the management interface

A management client may have no information about what resources can be managed in a system. Once it has enough information about the resources that are available, it needs to find out what attributes each resource has so that they can be monitored, or changed if needed. Because of the lack of knowledge about a resource, the management client needs to be able to dynamically find out about the management interface for a resource. Being able to dynamically find out about the management interface also saves time-consuming configuration of the client about what resources can be managed.

Discovering the management interface for an MBean varies depending on the type of MBean you are working with. The management interface for a standard MBean is defined by a public interface that describes its attributes and operations. To determine the management interface for a concrete class at runtime, the MBean Server must inspect the MBean using a process known as *introspection*. Introspection is based on Java reflection and enables you to retrieve information about a class at runtime. The Java Reflection API enables you to inspect a Java class at runtime and find information including the methods, fields, and constructors of the class. Listing 4-4 shows a simple Java application that prints out information about itself.

**Listing 4-4: Simple Java application that uses reflection**

```
import java.lang.reflect.*;


public class SimpleClass {

        public SimpleClass(){}

        public static void main(String args[]) {

                SimpleClass sc = new SimpleClass();

                try {

                Class theClass = sc.getClass();

                // Print Constructor Info //
                Constructor cons[] = theClass.getConstructors();
                for (int i=0;i<cons.length;i++)
                    System.out.println(cons[i]);
                Method methods[] = theClass.getMethods();
                for (int j=0;j<methods.length;j++)
                    System.out.println(methods[j]);

                } catch (Exception ex) {

                  System.out.println(ex);

                }

        }

}
```

The application in Listing 4-4 prints out the methods and constructors of the class. You will also see information about inherited methods. The printout from running this application should look similar to the following:

```
public SimpleClass()
public static void SimpleClass.main(java.lang.String[])
public native int java.lang.Object.hashCode()
public final void java.lang.Object.wait() throws
java.lang.InterruptedException
public final void java.lang.Object.wait(long,int) throws
java.lang.InterruptedEx
```

```
ception
public final native void java.lang.Object.wait(long) throws
java.lang.Interrupte
dException
public final native java.lang.Class java.lang.Object.getClass()
public boolean java.lang.Object.equals(java.lang.Object)
public java.lang.String java.lang.Object.toString()
public final native void java.lang.Object.notify()
public final native void java.lang.Object.notifyAll()
```

The top two lines in boldface highlight the two methods that were explicitly defined in the source code for the `SimpleClass` class. The remaining methods listed are inherited methods from the `java.lang.Object` class. The output produced by Listing 4-4 prints all methods and constructors available for the class.

## MBean metadata

The JMX specification includes several classes designed to provide the information about an MBean at runtime. These classes are said to provide "meta" information about the attributes, operations, constructors, and notifications. JMX agents expose all the management information about a bean, regardless of type, by using metadata classes. The meta information about an MBean can be constructed using introspection, or programmatically in the case of a dynamic MBean.

Accessing the metadata enables JMX agents to manipulate the MBeans in a standard fashion. Being able to access the metadata allows for the construction of tools that visually represent an MBean. You're probably familiar with tools such as Visual Age for Java, JBuilder, or Forte, which display Java classes in a tree view, showing the methods and fields of a Java class. You do this by using metadata about the classes, and introspection of the classes themselves. This introspection method also enables the manipulation of MBeans at runtime, with no prior knowledge of what the class looks like. Of course, when you want to invoke a particular method or read an attribute, you have an actual method or attribute in mind. In this case, you need some kind of check to ensure that the attribute or method exists, and that it takes the arguments, if any, that you are trying to supply to it.

As you will see in Chapter 5, the metadata for a dynamic MBean can be constructed at runtime, whereas standard MBeans use a well-known interface. The management interface for a standard MBean does not change unless you change it at design time and recompile it. A change to the interface might entail adding or removing an attribute or operation.

Table 4-1 describes each of the MBean metadata classes.

## Table 4-1    MBean Metadata Classes

| Class Name | Description |
|---|---|
| MBeanInfo | Provides a list of the attributes, operations, constructors, and notifications for an MBean |
| MBeanFeatureInfo | Provides a superclass for other metadata classes, and provides two inherited methods: getName() and getDescription() |
| MBeanAttributeInfo | Provides information about a particular attribute, such as its name; whether its read- or write-only; and its Java type |
| MBeanConstructorInfo | Provides information about a particular constructor of an MBean and how to get the constructor's signature |
| MBeanOperationInfo | Provides information about a particular operation, including its return type and method signature |
| MBeanParameterInfo | Provides information about an argument to an MBean operation |
| MBeanNotificationInfo | Provides information about a notification emitted by an MBean |

Figure 4-1 illustrates the relationship between the MBeanInfo and the other metadata classes such as MBeanParameterInfo and MBeanOperationInfo, and a ficticious Java class.

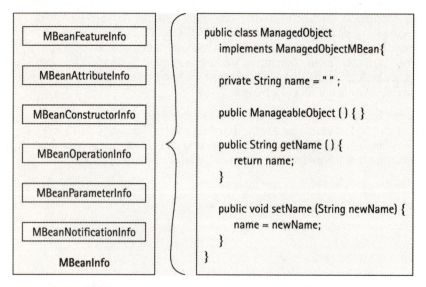

**Figure 4-1:** The MBean metadata classes and their relationship to an MBean.

In this figure, the box on the left displays the MBean metadata classes that represent the MBean in the box on the right. The MBean has attributes, a constructor, and two accessor methods. This information would be represented in the `MBeanAttributeInfo` and `MBeanConstructorInfo` classes. In addition, if the constructor for the `ManagedObject` class in this figure had arguments, this would be represented by an instance of the `MBeanParameterInfo` class.

Now you'll examine each metadata class and write a short application for each one. You start with a skeleton application that provides some basic capabilities for loading MBeans. Some components, such as the MBean Server, are used but are not covered in this chapter. (The MBean Server and facilities are covered in Chapter 8.) For now, you can safely ignore the code related to the MBean Server, and focus on the code that provides the metadata. In addition, if you haven't already, you may want to skim Chapter 3, which explains how to write a simple JMX application and describes the required libraries you will need to have in your `CLASSPATH`.

Before getting into the application and metadata classes, you need to define a resource for which you can gather metadata. The first thing you do is define the interface for the resource. Listing 4-5 shows the source of the `ManageableObjectMBean` interface.

**Listing 4-5: ManageableObjectMBean interface**

```
public interface ManageableObjectMBean{

        public String getName();

        public void setName(String newName);

        public String getDescription();

        public void setDescription(String newDescription);

        public void changeAttributes(){}

        public void changeOperations(){}
}
```

This interface defines accessor methods for two attributes: `Name` and `Description`. It also defines two operations: `changeAttributes()` and `changeOperations()`. Now you need to implement the interface in a class. Listing 4-6 shows the source of a class named `ManageableObject`.

**Listing 4-6: ManageableObject class**

```
public class ManageableObject implements ManageableObjectMBean{

        private String name = "";
        private String description = "";

        public ManageableObject(){}
```

```
public ManageableObject(String iName){
    name = iName;
}

public ManageableObject(String iName,String iDescription){
    name = iName;
    description = iDescription;
}

public String getName(){
    return name;
}

public void setName(String newName){
    name = newName;
}

public String getDescription(){
    return description;
}

public void setDescription(String newDescription){
    description = newDescription;
}

public void changeAttributes(){}

public void changeOperations(){}

}
```

The `ManageableObject` class is simple; it implements the accessor method for each field. It
also provides three different constructors. This should provide enough information to begin
writing the application that will print out the metadata. Listing 4-7 shows the source code for a
class called `MBeanUtils`, which is a Java application that prints out several pieces of
information about an MBean using the MBean metadata classes.

**Listing 4-7: Creating an instance of the MBeanInfo class**

```
import javax.management.MalformedObjectNameException;
import javax.management.ObjectName;
import javax.management.MBeanServer;
import javax.management.MBeanServerFactory;
import javax.management.MBeanInfo;
import javax.management.MBeanAttributeInfo;
import javax.management.MBeanConstructorInfo;
import javax.management.MBeanNotificationInfo;
import javax.management.MBeanOperationInfo;
import javax.management.MBeanParameterInfo;
```

```java
import javax.management.InstanceNotFoundException;
import javax.management.IntrospectionException;
import javax.management.ReflectionException;

public class MBeanUtils {

    private static MBeanServer server = null;

    public MBeanUtils() {
        server = MBeanServerFactory.createMBeanServer();
    }

    public static void main(String[] args) {
 String beanClass = (args.length > 0) ? args[0] : null;
        if (beanClass == null || beanClass.equals(" ")) {
            System.out.println("Please provide the name of the MBean");
            System.exit(0);
        }
        MBeanUtils agent = new MBeanUtils();
        ObjectName simpleObject =
agent.loadBean(beanClass,"MBeanUtils:name="+beanClass);

            try {

                listBeanInfo(simpleObject);

            } catch (Exception ex){}

        System.exit(0);
    }

    private ObjectName loadBean(String className,String objectName) {

        ObjectName mbeanObjectName = null;
        String domain = server.getDefaultDomain();
        String mbeanName = className;
        try {
            mbeanObjectName = new ObjectName(objectName);
        } catch(MalformedObjectNameException e) {
          e.printStackTrace();
          System.exit(1);
        }
          // Create our simple object to manage //
          try {
             server.createMBean(mbeanName,mbeanObjectName);
          }catch(Exception ex){
               ex.printStackTrace();
               System.exit(1);
```

```
            }

            return mbeanObjectName;
    }

    private static void listBeanInfo(ObjectName obj)
    throws InstanceNotFoundException, IntrospectionException,
ReflectionException {
            MBeanInfo beanInfo = server.getMBeanInfo(obj);
            System.out.println("Class: " + beanInfo.getClassName());
    }

}
```

> **CROSS-REFERENCE:** Chapter 8 provides more detailed information about using the MBean Server.

An MBeanServer instance is first created using a factory method with the following line of code:

```
server = MBeanServerFactory.createMBeanServer();
```

Next, a javax.management.ObjectName instance representing the MBean, in this case ManageableObject, is loaded using the following line of code:

```
mbeanObjectName = new ObjectName(objectName);
```

This is the reference that the utility will use during the execution of the application. Creating this handle does not create an instance of the MBean; that's the function of the following line of code in the loadBean() method:

```
server.createMBean(mbeanName,mbeanObjectName);
```

This creates an instance of the MBean and assigns it to the handle represented by the mbeanObjectName variable.

All of the metadata classes inherit from the same class, the superclass MBeanFeatureInfo. It only provides two methods that are common among MBean metadata classes. Table 4-2 describes these methods.

### Table 4-2    MBeanFeatureInfo Class Methods

| Method Name | Description |
|---|---|
| getName() | Returns a java.lang.String type representing the name of the feature |
| getDescription() | Returns a java.lang.String type representing the description of the feature |

In the case of the MBeanInfo class, you start with the listBeanInfo() method, which takes a javax.management.ObjectName type. You use the getClassName() method, which prints the class name of the MBean. Table 4-3 shows the different methods of the MBeanInfo class.

## Table 4-3    MBeanInfo Class Methods

| Method Name | Description |
|---|---|
| clone() | Creates and returns a new copy of this MBeanInfo object |
| getAttributes() | Returns an array of MBeanAttributeInfo objects representing the attributes of this MBean |
| getClassName() | Returns a java.lang.String type representing the class name of this MBean |
| getConstructors() | Returns an array of MBeanConstructorInfo objects representing the constructors for this MBean |
| getDescription() | Returns a java.lang.String type representing the description of this MBean |
| getNotifications() | Returns an array of MBeanNotificationInfo objects representing the notifications this MBean can emit |
| getOperations() | Returns an array of MBeanParameterInfo objects representing the operations or methods that can be executed for this MBean |

Now you can print information about all of the attributes using the metadata contained in the MBeanAttributeInfo class. Listing 4-8 shows the source of the listBeanInfo() method, updated to print information about each attribute of the MBean. Only the updates to the listBeanInfo() method are shown, as the rest of the MBeanUtils class is unchanged at this point.

**Listing 4-8: Getting the attributes of an MBean**

```
private static void listBeanInfo(ObjectName obj)
                throws InstanceNotFoundException,
                    IntrospectionException,
                    ReflectionException {
        MBeanInfo beanInfo = server.getMBeanInfo(obj);
        System.out.println("Class: " + beanInfo.getClassName());
        MBeanAttributeInfo attrInfo[] = beanInfo.getAttributes();
        for (int i=0;i<attrInfo.length;i++) {
            MBeanAttributeInfo anAttr = attrInfo[i];
            System.out.println("Attribute Name: " +
anAttr.getName());
            System.out.println("Attribute Description: " +
                            anAttr.getDescription());
```

```
                    System.out.println("Attribute Type: " +
anAttr.getType());
                System.out.println("Attribute has \"is\" method: " +
                                    anAttr.isIs());
                System.out.println("Attribute is readable: " +
                                    anAttr.isReadable());
                System.out.println("Attribute is writable: " +
                                    anAttr.isWritable());
        }
    }
```

The attribute information is retrieved using the `getAttributes()` method of the `MBeanInfo` class, which returns an array of `MBeanAttributeInfo` objects. The method then uses a simple `for` loop to process each `MBeanAttributeInfo` object in the array. Each time through the array, the following information is printed: the name, the description, the type, whether there is an `is` getter method, and whether the attribute is read/writable. Table 4-4 describes the different methods of the `MBeanAttributeInfo` class.

### Table 4-4    MBeanAttributeInfo Class Methods

| Method Name | Description |
|---|---|
| `clone()` | Creates and returns a new copy of this `MBeanInfo` object |
| `getType()` | Returns a `java.lang.String` type representing the Java type of this attribute |
| `isIs()` | Returns a primitive Java `boolean` indicating whether this attribute has an "is" method to retrieve its value |
| `isReadable()` | Returns a primitive Java `boolean` indicating whether the attribute can be read |
| `isWritable()` | Returns a primitive Java `boolean` indicating whether the attribute can be written or updated |

You may notice that if you run the `MBeanUtils` Java application to print information about the MBean's attributes, you see attribute names that are of a different case. In the preceding example, the attribute `name` appears as `Name` when printed via the `MBeanAttributeInfo` class. This is because the introspection process is using the accessor methods to determine the name of the field, so its case matches that of the accessor method. This does not mean that you need to change the name of the field to match the case.

Many of the MBean metadata classes inherit from the `MBeanFeatureInfo` class and, consequently, have the `getName()` and `getDescription()` methods available to them. However, with standard MBeans, the description will be the same for each bean because it cannot be determined or set by the MBean developer. You'll see this value used to represent the description of an MBean attribute.

> **CROSS-REFERENCE:** In Chapter 5, you'll see how the description can be set by the MBean developer.

Now you'll print information about all of the constructors using the metadata contained in the `MBeanConstructorInfo` class. Listing 4-9 shows the source of the `listBeanInfo()` method, updated to print information about each attribute of the MBean. This time, in addition to the changes to the `listBeanInfo()` method, there is a new method, `listParms()`, whose job is to display information about parameters.

**Listing 4-9: Getting the constructors of an MBean**

```
private static void listBeanInfo(ObjectName obj)
                 throws InstanceNotFoundException,
                        IntrospectionException,
                        ReflectionException {
        MBeanInfo beanInfo = server.getMBeanInfo(obj);
        System.out.println("Class: " + beanInfo.getClassName());
        // Get Attributes of an MBean //
        MBeanAttributeInfo attrInfo[] = beanInfo.getAttributes();
        for (int i=0;i<attrInfo.length;i++) {
            MBeanAttributeInfo anAttr = attrInfo[i];
            System.out.println("Attribute Name: " +
anAttr.getName());
            System.out.println("Attribute Description: " +
                                anAttr.getDescription());
            System.out.println("Attribute Type: " +
anAttr.getType());
            System.out.println("Attribute has \"is\" method: " +
                                anAttr.isIs());
            System.out.println("Attribute is readable: " +
                                anAttr.isReadable());
            System.out.println("Attribute is writable: " +
                                anAttr.isWritable());
        }

        // Get Constructors of an MBean //
        MBeanConstructorInfo constrInfo[] =
beanInfo.getConstructors();
        for (int j=0;j<constrInfo.length;j++) {
            MBeanConstructorInfo anConstr = constrInfo[j];
            System.out.println("Constructor name: " +
anConstr.getName());
            MBeanParameterInfo[] parms = anConstr.getSignature();
            listParms(parms);
        }
    }
    private static void listParms(MBeanParameterInfo parms[]){
        for (int j=0;j<parms.length;j++) {
```

```
                System.out.println("Parameter name: " +
parms[j].getName());
                System.out.println("Parameter type: " +
parms[j].getType());
            }
    }
```

The constructor information is retrieved using the `getConstructors()` method of the `MBeanInfo` class, which returns an array of `MBeanConstructorInfo` objects. The method then uses a simple `for` loop to process each `MBeanConstructorInfo` object in the array. Each time through the array, the name is printed. Then, all of the parameters to the particular constructor are retrieved using the `getSignature()` method of the `MBeanConstructorInfo` class. Remember that a class can have multiple constructors.

The array of parameters returned is passed to the `listParms()` method, which uses a simple `for` loop to print the name and type of each parameter. Table 4-5 describes the different methods of the `MBeanConstructorInfo` class.

### Table 4-5    MBeanConstructorInfo Class Methods

| Method Name | Description |
|---|---|
| clone() | Creates and returns a new copy of this MBeanInfo object |
| getSignature() | Returns an array of MBeanParameterInfo objects representing the arguments to this method |

Recall from earlier in the chapter that MBeans must have at least one public constructor, and they can have any number of public constructors. What if you have a non-public constructor? Does it still show up in the list of constructors generated? Listing 4-10 shows the source of the `ManageableObject` class with a protected constructor added.

**Listing 4-10: ManageableObject with protected constructor**

```
public class ManageableObject implements ManageableObjectMBean{

        private String name = "";
        private String description = "";
        private String foobar = "";

        public ManageableObject(){}

        public ManageableObject(String n){
                name = n;
        }

        public ManageableObject(String n,String d){
                name = n;
                description = d;
```

```
        }

        protected ManageableObject(String n,String y,String z){
                name = n;
        }

        public String getName(){
                return name;
        }

        public void setName(String n){
                name = n;
        }

        public String getDescription(){
                return description;
        }

        public void setDescription(String d){
                description = d;
        }

        public void changeAttributes(){}

        public void changeOperations(){}

        public String getFoobar(){return foobar;}

}
```

You can run the MBeanUtils application against the ManageableObject using this command-line. (You must have the appropriate JMX jars in your CLASSPATH.)

```
java MBeanUtils ManageableObject
```

Running the MBeanUtils application against the ManageableObject class results in output that looks like the following:

```
Class: ManageableObject
Attribute Name: Name
Attribute Description: Attribute exposed for management
Attribute Type: java.lang.String
Attribute has "is" method: false
Attribute is readable: true
Attribute is writable: true
Attribute Name: Description
Attribute Description: Attribute exposed for management
Attribute Type: java.lang.String
Attribute has "is" method: false
Attribute is readable: true
```

```
Attribute is writable: true
Attribute Name: Foobar
Attribute Description: Attribute exposed for management
Attribute Type: java.lang.String
Attribute has "is" method: false
Attribute is readable: true
Attribute is writable: false
Constructor name: ManageableObject
Parameter name:
Parameter type: java.lang.String
Constructor name: ManageableObject
Parameter name:
Parameter type: java.lang.String
Parameter name:
Parameter type: java.lang.String
Constructor name: ManageableObject
```

Notice that only three constructors are shown, although four are specified in the actual `ManageableObject` class. This is how the management interface keeps you compliant, by ignoring constructors that are not allowed.

Now you print information about all of the operators using the metadata contained in the `MBeanOperatorInfo` class. Listing 4-11 shows the source of the `listBeanInfo()` method, updated to print information about each operator or method of the MBean. You can reuse the `listParms()` method in the last section to print the argument information for each operator.

**Listing 4-11: Getting the operators or methods of an MBean**

```
private static void listBeanInfo(ObjectName obj)
                throws InstanceNotFoundException,
                    IntrospectionException,
                    ReflectionException {
        MBeanInfo beanInfo = server.getMBeanInfo(obj);
        System.out.println("Class: " + beanInfo.getClassName());
        // Get Attributes of an MBean //
        MBeanAttributeInfo attrInfo[] = beanInfo.getAttributes();
        for (int i=0;i<attrInfo.length;i++) {
            MBeanAttributeInfo anAttr = attrInfo[i];
            System.out.println("Attribute Name: " +
anAttr.getName());
            System.out.println("Attribute Description: " +
                            anAttr.getDescription());
            System.out.println("Attribute Type: " +
anAttr.getType());
            System.out.println("Attribute has \"is\" method: " +
                            anAttr.isIs());
            System.out.println("Attribute is readable: " +
                            anAttr.isReadable());
            System.out.println("Attribute is writable: " +
                            anAttr.isWritable());
```

```
            }

            // Get Constructors of an MBean //
            MBeanConstructorInfo constrInfo[] =
beanInfo.getConstructors();
            for (int j=0;j<constrInfo.length;j++) {
                MBeanConstructorInfo anConstr = constrInfo[j];
                System.out.println("Constructor name: " +
anConstr.getName());
                MBeanParameterInfo[] parms = anConstr.getSignature();
                listParms(parms);
            }

            // Get the methods of an MBean //
            MBeanOperationInfo opInfo[] = beanInfo.getOperations();
            for (int k=0;k<opInfo.length;k++) {
                MBeanOperationInfo anOp = opInfo[k];
                System.out.println("Operation name: " +
anOp.getName());
                System.out.println("Operation description: " +
                                    anOp.getDescription());
                System.out.println("Operation return type: " +
                                    anOp.getReturnType());
                MBeanParameterInfo parms[] = anOp.getSignature();
                listParms(parms);
                System.out.println("Operation impact: " +
                                    mapImpact(anOp.getImpact()));
            }
    }
    private static void listParms(MBeanParameterInfo parms[]){
            for (int j=0;j<parms.length;j++) {
                System.out.println("Parameter name: " +
parms[j].getName());
                System.out.println("Parameter type: " +
parms[j].getType());
            }
    }
    private static String mapImpact(int impactInt){

            String strImpact = "";

            switch (impactInt) {
                    case MBeanOperationInfo.ACTION:
                        strImpact = "MBeanOperationInfo.ACTION";
                        break;
                    case MBeanOperationInfo.ACTION_INFO:
                        strImpact = "MBeanOperationIfno.ACTION_INFO";
                        break;
                    case MBeanOperationInfo.INFO:
```

```
                    strImpact = "MBeanOperationInfo.INFO";
                    break;
          default:
                    strImpact = "MBeanOperationInfo.UNKNOWN";
                    break;
    }

        return strImpact;
}
```

The constructor information is retrieved using the `getOperators()` method of the `MBeanInfo` class, which returns an array of `MBeanOperationInfo` objects. The method then uses a simple `for` loop to process each `MBeanOperationInfo` object in the array. Each time through the array, the name, the description, and the return type of the operation are printed. Then, all of the parameters to the particular constructor are retrieved using the `getSignature()` method of the `MBeanConstructorInfo` class.

You may be wondering why the methods for getting and setting the values of the name and description are not printed as operations if you run this code. This is because the JMX design patterns state that methods that follow the `get/set` pattern are attribute accessor methods, and can only be used for that purpose. Therefore, they are not included in the printed list. Likewise, if you have an accessor method such as `getFoobar()` and no field named `foobar` in the class, the method is treated as an operation and not an accessor.

The last thing printed is the impact of the method. The `MBeanOperationInfo` class defines four fields, which describe the management impact of executing that method. These do not define any sort of locking, synchronization, or other implementation-specific behavior. Rather, they are used to give management clients and agents an idea of what this method can do. Because the fields are defined as integers, you need to map them to a string representation so they can be printed. The `mapImpact()` method was created to handle this.

The `mapImpact()` method uses the Java `switch` statement to pick between one of four possible values. The value of `MBeanOperationInfo.UNKNOWN` is actually defined as a field, but it's used here as the default value also because if it is not one of the other three, it must be unknown. The method just sets the value of the `strImpact` variable to the appropriate impact value and returns it. Table 4-6 shows the methods of the `MBeanOperationInfo` class.

### Table 4-6    MBeanOperationInfo Class Methods

| Method Name | Description |
| --- | --- |
| `clone()` | Creates and returns a new copy of this `MBeanInfo` object |
| `getImpact()` | Returns a primitive Java `int` representing one of four values that describe the effect of using this operation |
| `getReturnType()` | Returns a `java.lang.String` type representing the Java type that this operation returns |

| Method Name | Description |
|---|---|
| getSignature() | Returns an array of MBeanParameterInfo objects representing the arguments to this method |

The four possible values returned by the getImpact() method are defined as follows:

♦ *ACTION* — Indicates that the method performs some action that would modify the state of the MBean in some way

♦ *ACTION_INFO* — Indicates that the method may modify the state of the MBean, but also could be just a read operation

♦ *INFO* — Indicates that the method is a read-only operation

♦ *UNKNOWN* — Indicates that the nature of the operation cannot be determined

The impact returned does not imply any sort of real behavior; it is merely designed to give management applications an idea of what may happen if they invoke the management method of this bean. The MBean developer should try to ensure that these values are accurate for each method that can be invoked.

I have already touched briefly upon getting parameters, but it is covered here more formally. The MBeanParameterInfo class represents the arguments to a particular MBean operation. Listing 4-12 shows an excerpt of the sample illustrating the use of the MBeanParameterInfo class.

**Listing 4-12: Getting the parameters of an operation or method**

```
            MBeanParameterInfo parms[] = anOp.getSignature();
                listParms(parms);
                System.out.println("Operation impact: " +
                                    mapImpact(anOp.getImpact()));

        }
    }
    private static void listParms(MBeanParameterInfo parms[]){
            for (int j=0;j<parms.length;j++) {
                System.out.println("Parameter name: " +
parms[j].getName());
                System.out.println("Parameter type: " +
parms[j].getType());
            }
    }
```

The parameters represented by the MBeanParameterInfo class are retrieved using the getSignature() method of the MBeanInfo class. This returns an array of MBeanParameterInfo objects. Table 4-7 describes the methods of the MBeanParameterInfo class.

### Table 4-7    MBeanParameterInfo Class Methods

| Method Name | Description |
|---|---|
| clone() | Creates and returns a new copy of this MBeanInfo object |
| getType() | Returns a java.lang.String representing the Java type of this parameter |

The last thing you are going to do is print information about all of the notifications using the metadata contained in the MBeanNotificationInfo class. Listing 4-13 shows the source of the listBeanInfo() method, updated to print information about each notification the MBean can emit.

**Listing 4-13: Getting the notifications of an MBean**

```
private static void listBeanInfo(ObjectName obj)
                  throws InstanceNotFoundException,
                      IntrospectionException,
                      ReflectionException {
          MBeanInfo beanInfo = server.getMBeanInfo(obj);
          System.out.println("Class: " + beanInfo.getClassName());
          // Get Attributes of an MBean //
          MBeanAttributeInfo attrInfo[] = beanInfo.getAttributes();
          for (int i=0;i<attrInfo.length;i++) {
              MBeanAttributeInfo anAttr = attrInfo[i];
              System.out.println("Attribute Name: " +
anAttr.getName());
              System.out.println("Attribute Description: " +
                                  anAttr.getDescription());
              System.out.println("Attribute Type: " +
anAttr.getType());
              System.out.println("Attribute has \"is\" method: " +
                                  anAttr.isIs());
              System.out.println("Attribute is readable: " +
                                  anAttr.isReadable());
              System.out.println("Attribute is writable: " +
                                  anAttr.isWritable());
          }

          // Get Constructors of an MBean //
          MBeanConstructorInfo constrInfo[] =
beanInfo.getConstructors();
          for (int j=0;j<constrInfo.length;j++) {
              MBeanConstructorInfo anConstr = constrInfo[j];
              System.out.println("Constructor name: " +
anConstr.getName());
              MBeanParameterInfo[] parms = anConstr.getSignature();
```

```
                    listParms(parms);
            }

            // Get the methods of an MBean //
            MBeanOperationInfo opInfo[] = beanInfo.getOperations();
            for (int k=0;k<opInfo.length;k++) {
                MBeanOperationInfo anOp = opInfo[k];
                System.out.println("Operation name: " +
anOp.getName());
                System.out.println("Operation description: " +
                                anOp.getDescription());
                System.out.println("Operation return type: " +
                                anOp.getReturnType());
                MBeanParameterInfo parms[] = anOp.getSignature();
                listParms(parms);
                System.out.println("Operation impact: " +
                                mapImpact(anOp.getImpact()));
            }

            // Get the Notifications of an MBean //
            MBeanNotificationInfo notifInfo[] =
beanInfo.getNotifications();
            for (int l=0;l<notifInfo.length;l++) {
                MBeanNotificationInfo anNotify = notifInfo[l];
                String notificationTypes[] = anNotify.getNotifTypes();
                for (int m=0;m<notificationTypes.length;m++)
                    System.out.println("Notification: " +
                                    notificationTypes[m]);
            }
    }
```

The notification information is retrieved using the getNotifications() method of the MBeanInfo class, which returns an array of MBeanNotificationInfo objects. The method then uses a simple for loop to process each MBeanNotificationInfo object in the array. Each time through the array, the getNotifTypes() method is called, which is then looped through using another for loop.

Each time through the array, the notification type is printed. Table 4-8 describes the methods of the MBeanNotificationInfo class.

### Table 4-8    MBeanNotificationInfo Class Methods

| Method Name | Description |
| --- | --- |
| clone() | Creates and returns a new copy of this MBeanInfo object |
| getNotifTypes() | Returns an array of java.lang.String types, which represent the different notifications that this MBean can emit |

> **CROSS-REFERENCE:** Chapter 11 covers the details of JMX notifications.

Now that you have a Java application that can provide quite a bit of information about an MBean, you can execute the application. The output from the application should look similar to the following:

```
Class: ManageableObject
Attribute Name: Name
Attribute Description: Attribute exposed for management
Attribute Type: java.lang.String
Attribute has "is" method: false
Attribute is readable: true
Attribute is writable: true
Attribute Name: Description
Attribute Description: Attribute exposed for management
Attribute Type: java.lang.String
Attribute has "is" method: false
Attribute is readable: true
Attribute is writable: true
Constructor name: ManageableObject
Parameter name:
Parameter type: java.lang.String
Constructor name: ManageableObject
Parameter name:
Parameter type: java.lang.String
Parameter name:
Parameter type: java.lang.String
Constructor name: ManageableObject
Operation name: changeAttributes
Operation description: Operation exposed for management
Operation return type: void
Operation impact: MBeanOperationInfo.UNKNOWN
Operation name: changeOperations
Operation description: Operation exposed for management
Operation return type: void
Operation impact: MBeanOperationInfo.UNKNOWN
```

# Creating the Standard MBean

To be a standard MBean, a class must implement an interface that is named after the class. This interface defines the methods and accessor methods used to manage the bean. Methods that appear in the same class but do not appear in the interface are not considered part of the management interface. The interface name is formed by adding the suffix `MBean` to the class name. Listing 4-14 shows an example interface for the `ManageablePrinterResource` class shown earlier in this chapter.

**Listing 4-14: ManageablePrinterResource MBean interface**

```
import java.util.Vector;

public interface ManageablePrinterResourceMBean {

       public String getName();
       public void setName(String newName);
       public Vector getJobs();
       public void setJobs(Vector newJobs);
       public int getSheetsPaper();
}
```

Here, the ManageablePrinterResourceMBean defines all of the methods you've seen
implemented in the class previously. Listing 4-15 shows the changes to the implementation of
the ManageablePrinterResource to make it use this interface.

**Listing 4-15: ManageablePrinterResource implementing its MBean interface**

```
import java.util.Vector;

public class ManageablePrinterResource
           implements ManageablePrinterResourceMBean {

       private String name = "";
       private Vector jobs = null;
       private int sheetsPaper = 0;

       public ManageablePrinterResource(){}

       public void setName(String newName){
             name = newName;
       }
       public String getName(){
             return name;
       }
       public void setJobs(Vector newJobs){
             jobs = newJobs;
       }
       public Vector getJobs(){
             return jobs;
       }
       public int getSheetsPaper(){
             return sheetsPaper;
       }

       // These two methods are not part of the management interface //
       public void pauseJob(String jobName){
             System.out.println("Pausing " + jobName);
       }
```

```
        public void resumeJob(String jobName){
                System.out.println("Resuming " + jobName);
        }
}
```

As noted in the class comments, this class includes two methods, `pauseJob()` and `resumeJob()`, that are not exposed via the management interface.

## Management interface inheritance

You can also specify management interfaces via parent-class inheritance. You might define a parent class that includes all the management characteristics of a class of objects you want to manage. Then you just need to extend the class to receive the management benefits.

Of course, the parent interface must follow the same guidelines as the subclass would for defining the name of the MBean interface. Subclasses can also override this behavior by implementing their own management interface. In fact, this not only overrides the parent class behavior, the parent class management interface is ignored completely. Take a look at a few examples.

The first example defines a superclass called `ManageableResource`, which has a management interface defined by the `ManageableResourceMBean` interface. Listing 4-16 shows the source of the `ManageableResourceMBean` interface.

**Listing 4-16: ManageableResourceMBean interface**

```
public interface ManageableResourceMBean {

        public String getName();
        public void setName(String name);
        public int getReferenceCount();
        public void setReferenceCount(int cnt);
        public String getDescription();
        public void setDescription(String d);
}
```

Listing 4-17 shows the source code for the `ManageableResource` class that implements its MBean interface.

**Listing 4-17: ManageableResource class that implements ManageableResourceMBean interface**

```
public class ManageableResource implements ManageableResourceMBean {

        private String name = "";
        private String description = "";
        private int referenceCount = 0;

        public String getName(){
                return name;
        }
```

```
        public void setName(String n){
            name = n;
        }
        public String getDescription(){
            return description;
        }
        public void setDescription(String d){
            description = d;
        }
        public int getReferenceCount(){
            return referenceCount;
        }
        public void setReferenceCount(int r){
            referenceCount = r;
        }
}
```

If you run the MBeanUtils application against this MBean, you see three attributes printed, along with their names and types. The focus of this exercise, however, is the behavior of inherited management interfaces. Listing 4-18 shows the source of a class that extends the ManageableResource class.

**Listing 4-18: ApplicationComponent class that extends the ManageableResource class**

```
public class ApplicationComponent extends ManageableResource{

    public ApplicationComponent(){
        setName("ApplicationComponent");
    }
}
```

Running the MBeanUtils Java application against the ApplicationComponent MBean yields results that look like the following:

```
Class: ApplicationComponent
Attribute Name: Name
Attribute Description: Attribute exposed for management
Attribute Type: java.lang.String
Attribute has "is" method: false
Attribute is readable: true
Attribute is writable: true
Attribute Name: Description
Attribute Description: Attribute exposed for management
Attribute Type: java.lang.String
Attribute has "is" method: false
Attribute is readable: true
Attribute is writable: true
Attribute Name: ReferenceCount
Attribute Description: Attribute exposed for management
Attribute Type: int
```

```
Attribute has "is" method: false
Attribute is readable: true
Attribute is writable: true
Constructor name: ApplicationComponent
```

From these results, you can see that ApplicationComponent has inherited all the fields and methods of its parent, ManageableResource. This is not something unique to MBeans; it is just plain old Java inheritance at work. However, ApplicationComponent can now be considered a compliant MBean because it has inherited its management interface in the form of the ManageableResourceMBean interface. This gives developers another way to implement management into their components. Instead of writing the management interfaces themselves, they can simply extend a parent class that has the appropriate interface.

Now see how the behavior changes when the ApplicationComponent class implements its own management interface in addition to extending the parent class ManageableResource. Listing 4-19 shows the source of the ApplicationComponentMBean interface that the ApplicationComponent class will now implement.

**Listing 4-19: ApplicationComponentMBean interface**

```
import java.util.Vector;

public interface ApplicationComponentMBean {

        public void setChildProcesses(Vector p);
        public Vector getChildProcesses();
        public long getWorkingStorage();
        public long getPageSize();

}
```

Listing 4-20 shows the changes to the ApplicationComponent class, highlighted in boldface type.

**Listing 4-20: ApplicationComponent updated to use the ApplicationComponentMBean interface**

```
import java.util.Vector;

public class ApplicationComponent extends ManageableResource
        implements ApplicationComponentMBean{

        public ApplicationComponent(){
                setName("ApplicationComponent");
        }

        public void setChildProcesses(Vector p){
        }
        public Vector getChildProcesses(){
                return new Vector();
```

```
        }
        public long getWorkingStorage(){
                return 0;
        }
        public long getPageSize(){
                return 0;
        }
}
```

If you run the MBeanUtils Java application against the newly changed
ApplicationComponent class, you'll see results that look like the following:

```
Class: ApplicationComponent
Attribute Name: ChildProcesses
Attribute Description: Attribute exposed for management
Attribute Type: java.util.Vector
Attribute has "is" method: false
Attribute is readable: true
Attribute is writable: true
Attribute Name: WorkingStorage
Attribute Description: Attribute exposed for management
Attribute Type: long
Attribute has "is" method: false
Attribute is readable: true
Attribute is writable: false
Attribute Name: PageSize
Attribute Description: Attribute exposed for management
Attribute Type: long
Attribute has "is" method: false
Attribute is readable: true
Attribute is writable: false
Constructor name: ApplicationComponent
```

None of the management methods present in the ManageableResourceMBean interface are
shown in the list. The ApplicationComponentMBean interface is the management interface
for this MBean, although it inherits its methods from its parents. This does not mean that the
methods can no longer be used under normal circumstances. Normal Java inheritance rules
apply, so methods such as setName(), getName(), and setDescription() can all be
used. They just won't be directly available to JMX agents or to tools such as MBeanUtils.
And, of course, the ApplicationComponent class is considered a compliant MBean,
although the management interface of its parent is ignored.

> **CROSS-REFERENCE:** In Chapter 5, you learn how the inheritance of management interfaces differs
> for dynamic MBeans.

The inheritance of management interfaces is not limited to a direct parent. When determining
the management interface for an MBean, the inheritance tree is searched during the
introspection process to locate any compliant management interface. Note another requirement
that applies to MBeans: MBeans can implement only one type of management interface,

meaning that compliant MBeans cannot implement their own MBean interface and the `DynamicMBean` interface. The `DynamicMBean` interface is covered in detail in Chapter 5.

## Attributes

Attributes represent the MBean's fields or properties, which you can manipulate or query the value of. Attributes in MBeans are always accessed via method calls using accessor methods. For attributes that can be read, there is a corresponding `get` method; for attributes that can be updated, there is a corresponding `set` method.

The MBean specification defines a design pattern that is used to identify attributes of an MBean:

```
public AttributeType getAttributeName();
public void setAttributeName(AttributeType newValue);
```

If the MBean contains only the `get` method for an attribute, then this attribute is considered read-only. If the MBean contains only the `set` method for an attribute, then this attribute is considered write-only. And if the MBean has both get and set methods, then the attribute is considered read/write. Accessor methods cannot be overloaded to take different types. Using overloaded accessor methods negates the compliance of the MBean with the MBean specification. Any valid Java types are allowed for the accessor methods, and arrays are operated on as a whole; there is no design pattern for accessor methods that access individual elements of an array.

In addition to the accessor method design pattern, the design pattern allows `get` methods to define an `is` method for retrieving the value of Boolean attributes:

```
public boolean isAttributeName();
```

> **NOTE:** Although the `is` and `get` versions of the accessor method are defined, only one or the other is allowed in a given MBean.

## Case sensitivity

All operations, method names, and attribute names that are formed using the MBean design patterns, are case-sensitive. For example, the methods `getname()` and `getName()` manipulate the attributes `name` and `Name`, respectively. In other words, each manipulates a different attribute, and each will compile cleanly and be recognized differently in a JMX management interface.

# Building an MBean browser

The remainder of this chapter entails beginning a project that will be modified as you work through the book. You are going to build an MBean browser that will enable you to view various pieces of information about a particular MBean, such as its attributes, operations, and notifications. Because this chapter is about standard MBeans, the application will initially only support viewing information about standard MBeans. As you progress through the book, additional functionality will be added, such as viewing dynamic MBeans.

Note that although this MBean browser looks directly at MBean instances, it should not be classified as a management client. That is because, as you learned in Chapter 2, management clients do not directly interact with MBeans.

## The MBean Browser

The application consists of a simple Swing user interface, which consists of a `javax.swing` `.JFrame` that holds a `javax.swing.JTree` that takes up the entire frame. The `javax` `.swing.JTree` represents the various attributes, operations, notifications, and constructors of the MBean you are constructing. The second part of the browser consists of a utility class called `MBeanUtils`. This is the same class you saw in the MBean metadata section, but it has been updated to act in a more generic fashion.

If you are not familiar with Swing, you can find more information by looking at *The JFC Swing Tutorial: A Guide to Constructing GUIs,* by Kathy Walrath and Mary Campione, Addison-Wesley Publishing Company (1999), or the online Java Tutorial at `http://java.sun.com/tutorial`. The tutorial provides information about using all the major Swing components, and includes information about Swing architecture, event handling, and graphics. Listing 4-21 shows the source code for the Swing client.

> **NOTE:** Before you can compile this class, you will need to make the changes to the `MBeanUtils` class detailed in the next section, "MBeanUtils class updated."

**Listing 4-21: The MBeanBrowser application**

```
import javax.swing.*;
import javax.swing.tree.*;
import java.awt.BorderLayout;
import java.awt.event.*;
import java.awt.Event.*;
import javax.management.ObjectName;

public class MBeanBrowser {

        static String beanClass = "";

        public static void main(String args[]){

  beanClass = (args.length > 0) ? args[0] : null;
                if (beanClass == null || beanClass.equals(" ")) {
                        System.out.println("Please provide the name of the
MBean");
                        System.exit(1);
                }

                JFrame frame = new JFrame("MBean Browser");

                frame.setSize(400,400);

                frame.addWindowListener(new WindowAdapter(){
```

```
                     public void windowClosing(WindowEvent ev){
                           System.exit(0);
                     }
               });

               new MBeanBrowser(frame);
       }

       public MBeanBrowser(JFrame frame){

               frame.getContentPane().setLayout(new BorderLayout());

               DefaultMutableTreeNode top = new
DefaultMutableTreeNode("MBean");

               // New instance of MBean Utils //
               MBeanUtils beanUtils = new MBeanUtils();

               ObjectName simpleObject = null;
               try {
                   simpleObject = beanUtils.loadBean(beanClass,
"MBeanBrowser:name="+beanClass);

                   beanUtils.buildBeanInfoTree(top,simpleObject);

               } catch (Exception ex) {
                 System.out.println(ex);
               }
               JTree tree = new JTree(top);

               JScrollPane scrollPane = new JScrollPane(tree);

               frame.getContentPane().add("Center",scrollPane);

               frame.setVisible(true);
       }
}
```

The code begins by creating a javax.swing.JFrame object and setting its title to MBean Browser. This JFrame is passed to the constructor of the MBeanBrowser class.

Next, an instance of the javax.swing.tree.DefaultMutableTreeNode class is created with a name of MBean. This node will serve as the root of the information tree you will display about an MBean. Next, an instance of the MBeanUtils class is created. You will see the changes to the MBeanUtils class to support building a tree in Listing 4-22.

Next, a variable named simpleObject is defined, which is then set to the value of the MBeanUtils loadBean() method. You use the loadBean() method to load the MBean into the MBean Server and return an instance of the `javax.management.Objectname` class representing the MBean. Then you pass the instance of the `javax.management.Objectname` class into the `buildBeanInfoTree()` method of the `MBeanUtils` class. You also pass in the instance of the `javax.swing.tree.DefaultMutableTreeNode` class you created a few lines above. This way, the `buildBeanInfoTree()` method can access the nodes to add new nodes of information.

Assuming that no exceptions have occurred, the tree node represented by the top variable is passed to the constructor of a `javax.swing.JTree` class. The `javax.swing.JTree` class is then passed to the constructor of a `javax.swing.JScrollPane` class, which enables you to scroll the contents of the tree both horizontally and vertically.

Finally, the `javax.swing.JScrollPane` is added to the `javax.swing.JFrame` that was passed in and placed in the center of the frame. It's been added using the value `Center`, which is the `java.awt.BorderLayout` value that tells the container to make the component use all of its available space. Then, the visible property of the frame is set to `true`, causing the `JFrame` to be rendered on the screen.

## MBeanUtils class updated

The `MBeanUtils` class underwent some changes to make it a little more generic and able to support updating the `javax.swing.JTree` presented in the `MBeanBrowser` application. Listing 4-22 shows the source for the updated `MBeanUtils` class.

**Listing 4-22: The MBeanUtils class updated**

```
import javax.management.InstanceNotFoundException;
import javax.management.IntrospectionException;
import javax.management.MalformedObjectNameException;
import javax.management.ReflectionException;
import javax.management.ObjectName;
import javax.management.MBeanServer;
import javax.management.MBeanServerFactory;
import javax.management.MBeanInfo;
import javax.management.MBeanAttributeInfo;
import javax.management.MBeanConstructorInfo;
import javax.management.MBeanOperationInfo;
import javax.management.MBeanParameterInfo;
import javax.management.MBeanNotificationInfo;
import javax.swing.tree.DefaultMutableTreeNode;

public class MBeanUtils {

    private static MBeanServer server = null;

    public MBeanUtils() {
        server = MBeanServerFactory.createMBeanServer();
    }

    public ObjectName loadBean(String className,String objectName) {
```

```
        ObjectName mbeanObjectName = null;

        String domain = server.getDefaultDomain();

        String mbeanName = className;
        try {

            mbeanObjectName = new ObjectName(objectName);

    } catch(MalformedObjectNameException e) {
        e.printStackTrace();
        System.exit(1);
    }
        // Create our simple object to manage //
        try {
            server.createMBean(mbeanName,mbeanObjectName);
        }catch(Exception ex){
            ex.printStackTrace();
            System.exit(1);
        }

        return mbeanObjectName;
    }

    public static void buildBeanInfoTree(DefaultMutableTreeNode node,
                                ObjectName obj)
            throws InstanceNotFoundException,
                    IntrospectionException,
                    ReflectionException {
        MBeanInfo beanInfo = server.getMBeanInfo(obj);
        node.add(new
DefaultMutableTreeNode(beanInfo.getClassName()));
        // Get Attributes of an MBean //
        DefaultMutableTreeNode attrNode =
                new DefaultMutableTreeNode("Attributes");
        MBeanAttributeInfo attrInfo[] = beanInfo.getAttributes();
        for (int i=0;i<attrInfo.length;i++) {
            MBeanAttributeInfo anAttr = attrInfo[i];
            attrNode.add(new DefaultMutableTreeNode("Name: " +
                    anAttr.getName()));
            attrNode.add(new DefaultMutableTreeNode("Description: "

                    anAttr.getDescription()));
            attrNode.add(new DefaultMutableTreeNode("Type: " +
                    anAttr.getType()));
            attrNode.add(new DefaultMutableTreeNode("isMethod: " +
                    anAttr.isIs()));
            attrNode.add(new DefaultMutableTreeNode("readable: " +
```

```
                                  anAttr.isReadable()));
                      attrNode.add(new DefaultMutableTreeNode("writable: " +
                                  anAttr.isWritable()));
              }
            node.add(attrNode);

            // Get Constructors of an MBean //
            DefaultMutableTreeNode conNode =
                    new DefaultMutableTreeNode("Constructors");
            MBeanConstructorInfo constrInfo[] =
beanInfo.getConstructors();
            for (int j=0;j<constrInfo.length;j++) {
                MBeanConstructorInfo anConstr = constrInfo[j];
                MBeanParameterInfo[] parms = anConstr.getSignature();
                conNode.add(new DefaultMutableTreeNode("Name: " +
                        anConstr.getName()));
                listParms(conNode,parms);
            }
            node.add(conNode);

            // Get the methods of an MBean //
            DefaultMutableTreeNode opNode =
                    new DefaultMutableTreeNode("Operations");
            MBeanOperationInfo opInfo[] = beanInfo.getOperations();
            for (int k=0;k<opInfo.length;k++) {
                MBeanOperationInfo anOp = opInfo[k];
                opNode.add(new DefaultMutableTreeNode("Name: " +
                        anOp.getName()));
                opNode.add(new DefaultMutableTreeNode("Description: "
                        anOp.getDescription()));
                opNode.add(new DefaultMutableTreeNode("Return Type: "
                        anOp.getReturnType()));
                opNode.add(new DefaultMutableTreeNode("Impact: " +
                        mapImpact(anOp.getImpact())));
                MBeanParameterInfo parms[] = anOp.getSignature();
                listParms(opNode,parms);
            }
            node.add(opNode);

             // Get the Notifications of an MBean //
            DefaultMutableTreeNode notifNode =
                    new DefaultMutableTreeNode("Notifications");
            //MBeanNotificationInfo notifInfo[] =
beanInfo.getNotifications();
            //for (int l=0;l<notifInfo.length;l++) {
            //     MBeanNotificationInfo anNotify = notifInfo[l];
            //     String notificationTypes[] = anNotify.getNotifTypes();
            //     for (int m=0;m<notificationTypes.length;m++)
            //         System.out.println("Notification: " +
```

```
                                          notificationTypes[m]);
        //}
        node.add(notifNode);
    }
    private static void listParms(DefaultMutableTreeNode node,
                              MBeanParameterInfo parms[]){
        for (int j=0;j<parms.length;j++) {
            node.add(new DefaultMutableTreeNode("Name: " +
                    parms[j].getName()));
            node.add(new DefaultMutableTreeNode("Type: " +
                    parms[j].getType()));
        }
    }
    private static String mapImpact(int impactInt){

        String strImpact = "";

        switch (impactInt) {

            case MBeanOperationInfo.ACTION:
                strImpact = "MBeanOperationInfo.ACTION";
                break;
            case MBeanOperationInfo.ACTION_INFO:
                strImpact = "MBeanOperationIfno.ACTION_INFO";
                break;
            case MBeanOperationInfo.INFO:
                strImpact = "MBeanOperationInfo.INFO";
                break;
            default:
                strImpact = "MBeanOperationInfo.UNKNOWN";
                break;
        }

        return strImpact;
    }
}
```

The primary changes to the MBeanUtils class reflect the fact that it can no longer be considered a Java application. The main() method has been removed. The loadBean() method is still there, but the listBeanInfo() method has been renamed to the buildBeanInfoTree() method.

Still remaining are sections of code that build different parts of the display: information about the MBean class name, the constructors, the operators, and so on. Instead of using the System.out.println() method to print the values to standard output, the sections of code now first create an instance of the javax.swing.tree.DefaultMutableTreeNode class for each major category of information, and then proceed to add new javax.swing.tree .DefaultMutableTreeNode classes for each child of the nodes. For example, consider the following excerpt from the buildBeanInfoTree() method, which handles operations:

```
        // Get the methods of an MBean //
        DefaultMutableTreeNode opNode =
              new DefaultMutableTreeNode("Operations");
        MBeanOperationInfo opInfo[] = beanInfo.getOperations();
        for (int k=0;k<opInfo.length;k++) {
              MBeanOperationInfo anOp = opInfo[k];
              opNode.add(new DefaultMutableTreeNode("Name: " +
                    anOp.getName()));
              opNode.add(new DefaultMutableTreeNode("Description: " +
                    anOp.getDescription()));
              opNode.add(new DefaultMutableTreeNode("Return Type: " +
                    anOp.getReturnType()));
              opNode.add(new DefaultMutableTreeNode("Impact: " +
                    mapImpact(anOp.getImpact())));
              MBeanParameterInfo parms[] = anOp.getSignature();
              listParms(opNode,parms);
        }
        node.add(opNode);
```

In this example, an instance of the `javax.swing.tree.DefaultMutableTreeNode` is created and assigned to the variable `opNode`. Then, in the `for` loop, each time an `MBeanOperationInfo` instance is retrieved, the `add()` method of the `javax.swing` `.tree.DefaultMutableTreeNode` is called, and a new tree node is created. In the case of the operations, a node is added for the name, the description, the return type, and the impact; and a node is added for each argument to the operation.

Finally, after the `for` loop has completed, the set of tree nodes represented by the `opNode` variable is added to the main tree node represented by the `node` variable. This same pattern is repeated for each major piece of information about the MBean.

To run this application, you first need to compile it, if you haven't already. (See Chapter 3 for instructions about how to obtain the Sun JMX reference implementation and the libraries you will need in your CLASSPATH to compile and execute the `MBeanBrowser` application.) You can execute the `MBeanBrowser` application using the following command line, which assumes that the appropriate libraries are in your CLASSPATH:

```
java MBeanBrowser ManageableObject
```

Figure 4-2 shows the output of running the `MBeanBrowser`. Initially, the tree will be in a collapsed state except for the root node. The tree shows the name of the MBean as the first child of the tree root node. The first child node is followed by nodes representing the attributes, constructors, operations, and notifications, if any. Some of the nodes in Figure 4-2 are shown in an expanded state.

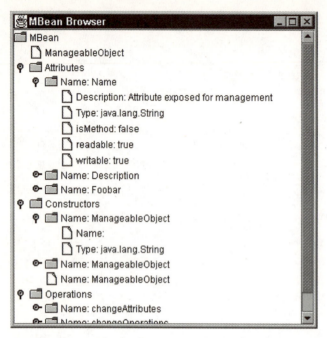

**Figure 4-2:** Running the MBeanBrowser against the ManageableObjectMBean.

Looking at Figure 4-2, you can see that information about the constructors, operations, and attributes have been added.

## Summary

In this chapter you were introduced to standard MBeans. Standard MBeans represent one type of MBean you can use to implement a management interface for a resource. A standard MBean uses a concrete interface that you define and implement. This interface enables management clients to manipulate attributes of a resource and invoke operations against it.

In the next chapter you'll look at dynamic MBeans, and how they differ from standard MBeans. You'll see how to dynamically construct the management interface using the MBeanInfo, MBeanAttributeInfo, and other classes that represent metadata about a managed object.

# Chapter 5

# Using Dynamic MBeans

Chapter 4 introduced you to the standard MBean, which can be used to provide a well-known, infrequently changing interface to a resource you want to manage. In many cases, the standard MBean will provide all that you need. However, in some cases, your components may require a more dynamic approach. In addition, you may want to make your beans more manageable by adding attributes and methods to them — with little impact on the clients or other applications. This is where the dynamic MBean comes in. The dynamic MBean uses a well-known access point for obtaining information about the attributes and methods available for an MBean. This list could be generated at runtime or created using reflection, but there is a standard class, the MBeanInfo class, that is available for retrieving such information.

In this chapter, you will learn how to code, compile, and execute dynamic MBeans. You'll also learn how dynamic MBeans present their management interface, and how it differs from the management interface of standard MBeans. If you've used Java Beans before, the design patterns for obtaining information about dynamic MBeans will look similar to the BeanInfo interface.

By the end of this chapter, you should have an understanding of how dynamic MBeans differ from standard MBeans. You will also learn how to construct the management interface for a dynamic MBean, and how to manipulate a dynamic MBean using the public methods of the DynamicMBean interface.

## What Is a Dynamic MBean?

A dynamic MBean is an MBean that presents its management information at runtime; subsequent queries about the management interface could change with each query. An initial query might contain a method named getName(), whereas a second query might not. The term *querying the management interface* refers to the process by which tools and JMX agents query the MBean about its management interface.

If you recall from Chapter 4, the method that is used to discover the management interface of a standard MBean is called introspection. With dynamic MBeans, the JMX agent or tool calls a method of the dynamic MBean, which returns an MBeanInfo object, just as the getMBeanInfo() method of the MBeanServer class does. The implementation of the dynamic MBean fills out this structure, possibly by using a process similar to introspection.

When you code a dynamic MBean, the steps that you take to fill out the `MBeanInfo` structure are up to you. You will learn a few different ways to construct the `MBeanInfo` structure for a dynamic MBean in this chapter.

Dynamic MBeans provide a quick way to build the management interface for MBeans, and they provide a flexible solution for management interfaces that may change over time. They differ from standard MBeans, which are designed to reflect management interfaces that change infrequently.

Although dynamic MBeans do not have the same type of design pattern as standard MBeans, they do conform to a specific interface, the `DynamicMBean` interface. This interface also defines a well-known method for accessing the operators and attributes of a dynamic MBean. It also includes a method to retrieve the metadata about the bean. Table 5-1 describes the methods of the `DynamicMBean` interface.

### Table 5-1    DynamicMBean Interface Methods

| Method Name | Description |
|---|---|
| `getAttribute(java.lang.String attrName)` | Returns a `java.lang.Object` representing an attribute of the MBean |
| `getAttributes(java.lang.String [] attrNames)` | Returns a `javax.management.AttributeList` of several attributes of the MBean. It takes a single argument representing an array of `java.lang.String` objects representing the names of the attributes. |
| `getMBeanInfo()` | Returns the `javax.management.MBeanInfo` object for this MBean |
| `invoke(java.lang.String opName,java.lang.Object[] parms,java.lang.String[] signature)` | Invokes the specified method of the MBean. It takes a `java.lang.String` representing the name of the operation to invoke; an array of `java.lang.Object` objects representing the parameters to the operation; and an array of `java.lang.String` objects representing the signature of the method. It returns a `java.lang.Object` representing the result of executing the operation. |
| `setAttribute(javax.management .Attribute)` | Sets the value of the specified attribute. A `javax.management.Attribute` object is the single argument representing the attribute to set. |
| `setAttributes(javax.management .AttributeList)` | Sets the value of several attributes. A `javax.management.AttributeList` is passed in representing the attributes to set. |

This chapter describes each of these methods in detail, and explains how to create the `MBeanInfo` object for a dynamic MBean.

## Management interface inheritance

In Chapter 4, you learned how inheritance plays a part in defining the management interface for a standard MBean. Dynamic MBeans have special rules regarding inheritance and how it affects the management interface for the bean.

With dynamic MBeans, inheritance is exposed via the getMBeanInfo() method. This means that a class that extends from a parent that implements the DynamicMBean interface will have its management interface defined by the value returned from the getMBeanInfo() method of the parent.

If the MBean class also implements its own MBean interface as standard MBeans do, then this behavior overrides the behavior of inheriting the management interface from the parent. This is the same behavior that occurs when a standard MBean implements its own MBean interface while extending from a parent that also implements an MBean interface.

## MBean attributes

Attributes of a dynamic MBean are accessed via a set of well-known accessor methods. Accessor methods in dynamic MBeans are not required to follow the same design patterns as standard MBeans. You may not see get and set methods in a dynamic MBean at all. It is the responsibility of the dynamic MBean implementation to map the values passed into the well-known accessor methods to the attributes of the MBean so that they may be properly exposed to JMX agents and tools.

The first attribute-related methods you'll examine are those responsible for retrieving the values of a particular attribute or set of attributes (Listing 5-1).

**Listing 5-1: Updating the DynamicManageableObject to return attribute values**

```
import javax.management.Attribute;
import javax.management.AttributeList;
import javax.management.DynamicMBean;
import javax.management.MBeanInfo;
import javax.management.MBeanAttributeInfo;
import javax.management.MBeanConstructorInfo;
import javax.management.MBeanOperationInfo;
import javax.management.MBeanNotificationInfo;


public class DynamicManageableObject implements DynamicMBean {

        private MBeanInfo beanInfo = null;
        private String name = "DynamicManageableObject";
        private String description = "It's dynamic!";

        public Object getAttribute(String name){
                if (name.equals("name"))
                        return getName();
                else if (name.equals("description"))
```

```
                    return getDescription();
            else
                    return null;
      }

      public String getName(){
            return name;
      }

      public String getDescription(){
            return description;
      }

      public AttributeList getAttributes(String attributes[]){
            return null;
      }

      public MBeanInfo getMBeanInfo(){

            MBeanInfo beanInfo =
                new MBeanInfo("DynamicManageableObject",
                              "DynamicObject",
                              new MBeanAttributeInfo[]{},
                              new MBeanConstructorInfo[]{},
                              new MBeanOperationInfo[]{},
                              new MBeanNotificationInfo[]{});

            return beanInfo;
      }

      public Object invoke(String operationName,
                           Object parameters[],
                           String signature[]){
            return null;
      }

      public void setAttribute(Attribute attribute){
      }

      public AttributeList setAttributes(AttributeList attributes){
            return null;
      }
}
```

The DynamicMBean interface uses the getAttribute() and getAttributes() methods to retrieve the value of one or multiple attributes from a dynamic MBean. Refer to Table 5-1 for a description of the arguments to each method. Listing 5-2 uses the getAttribute() method in a simple application that resembles the MBeanUtils Java application from Chapter 4. This method illustrates all four attribute-related methods of the DynamicMBean interface.

**Listing 5-2: Using the getAttribute method to retrieve the values of attributes**

```java
import javax.management.Attribute;
import javax.management.AttributeList;
import javax.management.DynamicMBean;
import javax.management.InstanceNotFoundException;
import javax.management.IntrospectionException;
import javax.management.MalformedObjectNameException;
import javax.management.ReflectionException;
import javax.management.ObjectName;
import javax.management.MBeanServer;
import javax.management.MBeanServerFactory;
import javax.management.MBeanInfo;
import javax.management.MBeanAttributeInfo;
import javax.management.MBeanConstructorInfo;
import javax.management.MBeanOperationInfo;
import javax.management.MBeanParameterInfo;
import javax.management.MBeanNotificationInfo;

public class DynamicMBeanUtil {

    private static MBeanServer server = null;

    public DynamicMBeanUtil() {
        server = MBeanServerFactory.createMBeanServer();
    }

    public static void main(String[] args) {

        DynamicMBeanUtil agent = new DynamicMBeanUtil();
        ObjectName simpleObject =
agent.loadBean("DynamicManageableObject",

"DynamicManageableObject:name=simple");

        try {

            String value =
(String)server.getAttribute(simpleObject,"name");
            System.out.println("Value is: " + value);
            value =
(String)server.getAttribute(simpleObject,"description");
            System.out.println("Value is: " + value);

        } catch (Exception ex){System.out.println(ex);}
```

```
        System.exit(0);
    }

    private ObjectName loadBean(String className,String objectName) {

        ObjectName mbeanObjectName = null;
        String domain = server.getDefaultDomain();
        String mbeanName = className;
        try {
            mbeanObjectName = new ObjectName(objectName);
        } catch(MalformedObjectNameException e) {
          e.printStackTrace();
          System.exit(1);
        }
          // Create our simple object to manage //
          try {
              server.createMBean(mbeanName,mbeanObjectName);
          }catch(Exception ex){
              ex.printStackTrace();
              System.exit(1);
          }

          return mbeanObjectName;
    }
}
```

The output from running the `DynamicMBeanUtil` Java application looks like the following:

```
Value is: DynamicManageableObject
Value is: It's dynamic!
```

The last set of attribute-related methods we'll look at are those that enable you to set the value of a particular attribute or set of attributes. Listing 5-3 shows the updates to the `DynamicManageableObject` that allow you to set the value of a particular attribute.

**Listing 5-3: Updating the DynamicManageableObject to set the values of attributes**

```
import javax.management.Attribute;
import javax.management.AttributeList;
import javax.management.DynamicMBean;
import javax.management.MBeanInfo;
import javax.management.MBeanAttributeInfo;
import javax.management.MBeanConstructorInfo;
import javax.management.MBeanOperationInfo;
import javax.management.MBeanNotificationInfo;


public class DynamicManageableObject implements DynamicMBean {

        private MBeanInfo beanInfo = null;
```

```
private String name = "DynamicManageableObject";
private String description = "It's dynamic!";

public Object getAttribute(String name){
        if (name.equals("name"))
            return getName();
        else if (name.equals("description"))
            return getDescription();
        else
            return null;
}

public String getName(){
        return name;
}
public void setName(String n){
        name = n;
}

public String getDescription(){
        return description;
}

public void setDescription(String d){
        description = d;
}

public AttributeList getAttributes(String attributes[]){
        return null;
}

public MBeanInfo getMBeanInfo(){

        MBeanInfo beanInfo =
            new MBeanInfo("DynamicManageableObject",
                        "DynamicObject",
                        new MBeanAttributeInfo[]{},
                        new MBeanConstructorInfo[]{},
                        new MBeanOperationInfo[]{},
                        new MBeanNotificationInfo[]{});

        return beanInfo;
}

public Object invoke(String operationName,
                    Object parameters[],
                    String signature[]){
        return null;
}
```

```
        public void setAttribute(Attribute attribute){
            if (attribute.getName().equals("name"))
                setName((String)attribute.getValue());
            else if (attribute.getName().equals("description"))
                setDescription((String)attribute.getValue());
        }

        public AttributeList setAttributes(AttributeList attributes){
            return null;
        }

}
```

Next, to use the attributes, you can update the `main()` method of the `DynamicMBeanUtil` class you created in Listing 5-2 to set the values and print them. Listing 5-4 shows the updates to the `main()` method you need to make.

**Listing 5-4: Updating the main() method to set the attribute values**

```
public static void main(String[] args) {

        DynamicMBeanUtil agent = new DynamicMBeanUtil();
        ObjectName simpleObject =
agent.loadBean("DynamicManageableObject","DynamicManageableObject:name=s
imple");

            try {

                System.out.println("Getting the values >>>>>>>>>>>>>>>");
                String value =
(String)server.getAttribute(simpleObject,"name");
                System.out.println("Value is: " + value);
                value =
(String)server.getAttribute(simpleObject,"description");
                System.out.println("Value is: " + value);
                System.out.println("Setting the values >>>>>>>>>>>>>>>");
                Attribute attr1 = new Attribute("name","HungryMinds
Inc.");
                server.setAttribute(simpleObject,attr1);
                Attribute attr2 = new Attribute("description","Publishing
Company");
                server.setAttribute(simpleObject,attr2);
                System.out.println("Getting the values again >>>>>>>>>");
                value = (String)server.getAttribute(simpleObject,"name");
                System.out.println("Value is: " + value);
                value =
(String)server.getAttribute(simpleObject,"description");
                System.out.println("Value is: " + value);
```

```
          } catch (Exception ex){System.out.println(ex);}

       System.exit(0);
   }
```

After making the updates to the `DynamicMBeanUtil` Java application and running it, the output should look like the following:

```
Getting the values >>>>>>>>>>>>>>
Value is: DynamicManageableObject
Value is: It's dynamic!
Setting the values >>>>>>>>>>>>>
Getting the values again >>>>>>>>
Value is: HungryMinds Inc.
Value is: Publishing Company
```

You may be confused about how the values of the attributes are actually getting changed. As a Java programmer, you are undoubtedly familiar with fields and accessor methods. You may also be familiar with *delegation,* in which one object performs an action for another. Such is the case with dynamic MBeans. With standard MBeans, the actual methods of the class are called directly by the MBean Server, using reflection. With dynamic MBeans, the same process occurs, but you use the well-known methods of the dynamic MBean interface to carry them out. In Chapter 8, you'll see in detail how the MBean Server does this delegation for the dynamic MBean.

You call the `setAttribute()` method of the `MBeanServer interface`, which in turn calls the `setAttribute()` method of the `DynamicMBean`. This is where you take over; you are responsible for setting the value or retrieving the value depending on whether you're reading or writing the attribute value. If you want to set or get more than one attribute at a time, there is the `AttributeList` class. Table 5-2 shows the methods of the `AttributeList` class and a brief description of each.

The `AttributeList` class extends from the `java.util.ArrayList` class from the JDK 1.3. Therefore, it also inherits some methods from that class, as well as from the `java.util.AbstractList` from which the `java.util.ArrayList` class inherits. You can view the actual inherited methods by viewing the JMX API documentation.

### Table 5-2    AttributeList Class Methods

| Method Name | Description |
| --- | --- |
| add(javax.management .Attribute attr) | Takes a single `javax.management.Attribute` object and adds it to the list of attributes |
| add(int index,javax.management .Attribute attr) | Inserts the `javax.management.Attribute` in the list of attributes at the index specified by the first argument |

| Method Name | Description |
|---|---|
| addAll(javax.management.AttributeList) | Appends all the attributes specified in the javax.management.AttributeList object passed to the end of the list of attributes |
| addAll(int index,javax.management.AttributeList) | Inserts all the attributes specified in the javax.management.AttributeList object at the point specified by the index passed in as the first argument |
| set(int index,javax.management.Attribute attr) | Sets the element in the list to be the javax.management.Attribute specified using the index passed in |

You can get the values from the javax.management.AttributeList object in a couple of ways. Because it extends the java.util.ArrayList class, it has the capability to use the get() method to retrieve a single element of the list using an index to identify the element. It also inherits the java.util.Iterator, which can be used to access the attributes in the list.

Getting or setting the values of several attributes at once is also quite easy using the getAttributes() and setAttribute() methods, respectively. Listing 5-5 shows the updates to the DynamicManageableObject to support setting and getting the values of more than one attribute at a time.

**Listing 5-5: Updating DynamicManageableObject to set or get multiple attributes**

```
import javax.management.Attribute;
import javax.management.AttributeList;
import javax.management.DynamicMBean;
import javax.management.MBeanInfo;
import javax.management.MBeanAttributeInfo;
import javax.management.MBeanConstructorInfo;
import javax.management.MBeanOperationInfo;
import javax.management.MBeanNotificationInfo;


public class DynamicManageableObject implements DynamicMBean {

        private MBeanInfo beanInfo = null;
        private String name = "DynamicManageableObject";
        private String description = "It's dynamic!";

        public Object getAttribute(String name){
                if (name.equals("name"))
                        return getName();
                else if (name.equals("description"))
                        return getDescription();
                else
                        return null;
        }
```

```java
    public String getName(){
        return name;
    }
    public void setName(String n){
        name = n;
    }

    public String getDescription(){
        return description;
    }

    public void setDescription(String d){
        description = d;
    }

    public AttributeList getAttributes(String attributes[]){

        AttributeList list = new AttributeList();
        for (int i=0;i<attributes.length;i++) {
            if (attributes[i].equals("name"))
                list.add(new Attribute("name",getName()));
            if (attributes[i].equals("description"))
                list.add(new
Attribute("description",getDescription()));
        }
        return list;
    }

    public MBeanInfo getMBeanInfo(){

        MBeanInfo beanInfo =
            new MBeanInfo("DynamicManageableObject",
                          "DynamicObject",
                          new MBeanAttributeInfo[]{},
                          new MBeanConstructorInfo[]{},
                          new MBeanOperationInfo[]{},
                          new MBeanNotificationInfo[]{});

        return beanInfo;
    }

    public Object invoke(String operationName,
                    Object parameters[],
                    String signature[]){
        return null;
    }

    public void setAttribute(Attribute attribute){
        if (attribute.getName().equals("name"))
```

```
                    setName((String)attribute.getValue());
            else if (attribute.getName().equals("description"))
                    setDescription((String)attribute.getValue());
    }

    public AttributeList setAttributes(AttributeList attributes){

        AttributeList list = new AttributeList();

        for (int i=0;i<attributes.size();i++) {

            Attribute attr = (Attribute)attributes.get(i);

            if (attr.getName().equals("name")){
                setName((String)attr.getValue());
                list.add(new Attribute("name",getName()));
            }
            if (attr.getName().equals("description")){
                setDescription((String)attr.getValue());
                list.add(new
Attribute("description",getDescription()));
            }
        }

        return list;
    }

}
```

Next, you can update the DynamicMBeanUtil class to use the new setAttributes() and getAttributes() methods. Listing 5-6 shows the updates to the main() method of the DynamicMBeanUtil class to exercise the new methods.

**Listing 5-6: Updating DynamicMBeanUtil main() method to get and set multiple attribute values**

```
public static void main(String[] args) {

        DynamicMBeanUtil agent = new DynamicMBeanUtil();
        ObjectName simpleObject =
agent.loadBean("DynamicManageableObject","DynamicManageableObject:name=s
imple");

        try {

            System.out.println("Getting the values >>>>>>>>>>>>>>>");
            String value =
(String)server.getAttribute(simpleObject,"name");
            System.out.println("Value is: " + value);
```

```
              value =
(String)server.getAttribute(simpleObject,"description");
              System.out.println("Value is: " + value);
              System.out.println("Setting the values >>>>>>>>>>>>>");
              Attribute attr1 = new Attribute("name","HungryMinds
Inc.");
              server.setAttribute(simpleObject,attr1);
              Attribute attr2 = new Attribute("description","Publishing
Company");
              server.setAttribute(simpleObject,attr2);
              System.out.println("Getting the values again >>>>>>>>");
              value = (String)server.getAttribute(simpleObject,"name");
              System.out.println("Value is: " + value);
              value =
(String)server.getAttribute(simpleObject,"description");
              System.out.println("Value is: " + value);

              // Set multiple attribute values //
              System.out.println("Setting multiple attribute values");
              AttributeList atts = new AttributeList();
              atts.add(new Attribute("name","BeeBop Inc."));
              atts.add(new Attribute("description","Makes Bee Bop
Transports"));

              AttributeList newAtts =
server.setAttributes(simpleObject,atts);

              // Display new Attributes values //
              System.out.println("Getting new values from MBean using
getAttribute >>>>>");
             value = (String)server.getAttribute(simpleObject,"name");
              System.out.println("Value is: " + value);
              value =
(String)server.getAttribute(simpleObject,"description");
              System.out.println("Value is: " + value);

              // Showing values using returned AttributeList //
              System.out.println("Getting values from returned
AttributeList
                                  object>>>>>");
              for (int i=0;i<newAtts.size();i++){
                  Attribute att = (Attribute)newAtts.get(i);
                  System.out.println("Value is: " +
(String)att.getValue());
                  }

              // Get Multiple Attribute Values //
              System.out.println("Getting multiple attributes
>>>>>>>>>>>>");
```

```
            String attsArray[] = new String[]{"name","description"};
            newAtts = server.getAttributes(simpleObject,attsArray);
            for (int i=0;i<newAtts.size();i++) {
                Attribute att = (Attribute)newAtts.get(i);
                System.out.println("Value is: " +
(String)att.getValue());
                }


        } catch (Exception ex){System.out.println(ex);}

    System.exit(0);
}
```

The output of running the `DynamicMBeanUtil` Java application with the new updates will yield the output shown in Listing 5-7.

**Listing 5-7: Output from getting and setting attribute values**

```
Getting the values >>>>>>>>>>>>>>
Value is: DynamicManageableObject
Value is: It's dynamic!
Setting the values >>>>>>>>>>>>>>
Getting the values again >>>>>>>>
Value is: HungryMinds Inc.
Value is: Publishing Company
Setting multiple attribute values
Getting new values from MBean using getAttribute >>>>>
Value is: BeeBop Inc.
Value is: Makes Bee Bop Transports
Getting values from returned AttributeList object>>>>>
Value is: BeeBop Inc.
Value is: Makes Bee Bop Transports
Getting multiple attributes >>>>>>>>>>>>>
Value is: BeeBop Inc.
Value is: Makes Bee Bop Transports
```

As you can see from the output, the values change correctly from calls to `getAttribute()` and `setAttribute()` as expected. Similarly, the new `setAttributes()` and `getAttributes()` methods print the correct results. The methods shown in Listings 5-3 and 5-4 used static means to determine the names of attributes that you could access. For this example, that is fine; however, in real implementations, which attribute to get or set would probably be determined dynamically, which would make the MBean even more extensible. If you use the static method, each time you add a new field you have to add a new if/then construct to handle it. Using the reflection API, you can update the `setAttributes()` and `getAttributes()` methods to dynamically find the proper attributes.

Listing 5-8 shows the source of a class named `DynamicManageableObjectRef`. Instead of updating the `DynamicManageableObject` class to use reflection, I've subclassed it and overridden the `setAttribute()` and `getAttribute()` methods to use reflection. For purposes of focusing on the reflection pieces, I have foregone any sort of real error handling, and simply printed the exception. Many of the reflection methods throw exceptions, as do many of the JMX API methods. In real practice, you should handle and throw exceptions as necessary.

**Listing 5-8: DynamicManageableObjectRef class**

```java
import javax.management.Attribute;
import java.lang.reflect.*;


public class DynamicManageableObjectRef extends DynamicManageableObject
{

        public Object getAttribute(String name){

                Object value = null;

                // Make sure the field exists //

                if (hasField(name))
                    value = getFieldValue(name);

                return value;
        }

        public void setAttribute(Attribute attribute){

                String attrName = attribute.getName();
                Object attrValue = attribute.getValue();

                if (hasField(attrName))
                    setFieldValue(attrName,attrValue);
        }

        // Use accessors to set values //

        private void setFieldValue(String name,Object fieldValue){

                try {

                    String methodName = "set"+
name.substring(0,1).toUpperCase()+
                                            name.substring(1,name.length());

                    System.out.println("Using Method: " + methodName);

                    Class args[] = new Class[]{fieldValue.getClass()};
```

```
                         Method method =
this.getClass().getSuperclass().getMethod(methodName,args);

                    Object parms[] = new Object[]{fieldValue};

                    method.invoke(this,parms);

               } catch (Exception ex){

                    System.out.println(ex);
               }
          }

     // Use accessors to get values //

     private Object getFieldValue(String name){

               Object value = null;

               try {

                    String methodName = "get"+
name.substring(0,1).toUpperCase()+
                                   name.substring(1,name.length());

                    System.out.println("Using Method: " + methodName);

                    Method method =
this.getClass().getSuperclass().getMethod(methodName,new Class[]{});

                    value = method.invoke(this,new Object[]{});

               } catch (Exception ex){

                    System.out.println(ex);
               }

               return value;
          }

     private boolean hasField(String name){

               boolean exists = false;

               try {
```

```
            Field fld =
this.getClass().getSuperclass().getDeclaredField(name);

          exists = true;

        } catch (NoSuchFieldException ex){

          System.out.println(ex);
        }

        return exists;


    }

}
```

The methods getAttribute() and setAttribute() delegate the actual retrieval or setting of the value to the private methods getFieldValue() and setFieldValue(), respectively. Each method ensures that the field exists before trying the action. In the event that the field does not exist, the getAttribute() method returns null; the setAttribute() method does nothing.

If the field does exist, the getAttribute() method passes the name of the value into the getFieldValue() method. The getFieldValue() first attempts to construct the name of the accessor method, much in the spirit of the MBean design pattern. It adds the prefix get to an uppercase version of the name of the attribute passed in. For example, name becomes getName().

After printing the name of the method, you need to determine if the method actually exists in the class. To do this, you need to use the getMethod() method of the java.lang.Class class. This method takes two arguments. The first is the name of the method, and the second is an array of java.lang.Class types representing the Java types used as arguments to the method.

In the preceding example, I've made an educated assumption that the DynamicManageableObjectRef does not have other methods to just pass an empty array of java.lang.Class objects to the method. In real practice, you would probably want to examine the types and build the array appropriately.

If no exceptions have occurred, I now have a reference to the method that I need to execute. Note that I have retrieved a reference to a method that does not exist in the DynamicManageableObjectRef. This is because normal Java inheritance rules are at work, and the getMethod() method searches the hierarchy of classes and finds the method in the parent. Before I can execute the method, I need to build another array of java.lang.Object types, which are the actual object references to the values I would use to execute the method. Again, in this case, the get methods do not take arguments, so I can safely pass in an empty array of objects.

The `invoke()` method of the `java.lang.reflect.Method` class is used to execute the method, and it returns a `java.lang.Object` representing the result. This result is then passed back to the caller; in this case, the `getAttribute()` method, which then passes it back out. This value then shows up in the `DynamicMBeanUtils` Java application.

### Setting the values using reflection

The process for setting the values using reflection are quite similar to getting them, although you need to take a couple of extra steps. The `setAttribute()` method ensures that the field exists, and then passes the name of the attribute at its desired value as a `java.lang.Object` to the private method `setFieldValue()`.

The `setFieldValue()` method then proceeds to determine the name of the accessor method using the same process as the `getFieldValue()` method described earlier. Next, you need to make sure that the method exists, just as the `getFieldValue()` method does. In this case, you know that the `set` methods take an argument, so you need to build the array of `java.lang.Class` objects to represent the Java class names of the arguments you are passing in:

```
Class args[] = new Class[]{fieldValue.getClass()};
```

This line of code creates an array of `java.lang.Class` types with a single element. This array is then passed to the `getMethod()` method along with the method name. Assuming no exceptions occur, you have a reference to the method. Normal Java inheritance rules apply and the method is located in the parent class.

Now that you have a reference to the method, you can build the necessary arguments to the `invoke()` method. Because you are passing in arguments this time, you need to build an array of `java.lang.Object` types to pass in:

```
Object parms[] = new Object[]{fieldValue};
```

This line of code builds an array of `java.lang.Object` types with a single element representing the value you want to pass to the method. This array is passed into the `invoke` method, along with a reference to the class in which this method is supposed to exist. (I say "supposed to" because it's always possible that while coding you could have used the wrong reference.) In this example, you know that the method should exist in the parent class, so pass in a value using the Java `this` keyword (which means the current caller of this method — in this case, the `DynamicManageableObjectRef` class). Although the `invoke()` method returns a value, discard it because the `set` methods are not supposed to return anything. In other cases of using reflection, you may be returning an actual value.

Once you have coded and compiled the `DynamicManageableObjectRef` class, you can update the `MBeanUtils` class to use this class. The output from the class should look identical to Listing 5-7.

### Using complex types for attribute values

The examples shown so far have only used `java.lang.String` values to illustrate the use of attributes. However, you may have noticed that the `javax.management.Attribute` class actually stores the value as a `java.lang.Object` type (because it wouldn't make sense to assume that attributes' values would always be of `java.lang.String` type). This means, of course, that you can use other types to represent attribute values, such as `java.util.Vector`, `java.util.Date`, or custom types that you define yourself.

# Invoking Operations of the DynamicMBean

One method of the `DynamicMBean` interface that hasn't been covered yet is the `invoke()` method. Unlike standard MBeans, which have well-known interfaces and methods, the dynamic MBean has a dynamic management interface, as you have seen demonstrated. This means that a method or operation that you want to execute may not be present the next time you look at the management interface.

To enable callers such as JMX agents and management clients to execute the methods of a dynamic MBean, the `DynamicMBean` method includes the `invoke()` method. Table 5-1 shows the signature of the method, which includes the following elements:

- A `java.lang.String` representing the name of the operation or method
- An array of `java.lang.Object` objects representing the arguments to the method
- An array of `java.lang.String` objects representing the method signature

With these pieces of information, you should be able to execute any public method of a dynamic MBean. Using the `invoke()` method does not guarantee anything; rather, it executes a method via reflection, instead of against a concrete interface.

As with standard MBeans, you don't actually call the `invoke()` method of the `DynamicMBean` itself; rather, you call the `invoke()` method of the `MBeanServer` interface, which in turn calls the method.

> **CROSS-REFERENCE:** Chapter 8 provides more details about the `MBeanServer` interface.

Up to this point, you've seen a few examples of constructing parameters for using in reflection API calls. Calling a method of a `DynamicMBean` is quite similar. You must build two arrays containing information about the operation you want to execute. The value returned from the `invoke()` method is a `java.lang.Object` that you must cast to the value you expect to be returned. Listing 5-9 shows the source of a class that uses the `invoke()` method. You should note that the `invoke()` method of the `MBeanServer` is slightly different than the `invoke()` method of the `DynamicMBean` itself. The `invoke()` method of the `MBeanServer` takes an additional argument representing the object name of the MBean that contains the method to execute.

**Listing 5-9: Using the invoke() method**

```
import java.util.ArrayList;
import java.util.Arrays;
import java.lang.reflect.Method;
import javax.management.Attribute;
import javax.management.AttributeList;
import javax.management.DynamicMBean;
import javax.management.MBeanInfo;
```

```java
import javax.management.MBeanAttributeInfo;
import javax.management.MBeanConstructorInfo;
import javax.management.MBeanOperationInfo;
import javax.management.MBeanNotificationInfo;


public class DynamicInvocationObject implements DynamicMBean {

        private MBeanInfo beanInfo = null;
        private String name = "DynamicInvocationObject";
        private String description = "It's dynamic!";

        public Object getAttribute(String name){

                  return null;
        }

        public String getName(){
              return name;
        }
        public void setName(String n){
              name = n;
        }

        public String getDescription(){
              return description;
        }

        public void setDescription(String d){
              description = d;
        }

        public AttributeList getAttributes(String attributes[]){

              return null;
        }

        public MBeanInfo getMBeanInfo(){

              MBeanInfo beanInfo =
                 new MBeanInfo("DynamicManageableObject",
                              "DynamicObject",
                              new MBeanAttributeInfo[]{},
                              new MBeanConstructorInfo[]{},
                              new MBeanOperationInfo[]{},
                              new MBeanNotificationInfo[]{});

              return beanInfo;
        }
```

```
public Object invoke(String operationName,
                     Object parameters[],
                     String signature[]){

    Object value = null;

    try {

      ArrayList al = new ArrayList();

      for (int i=0;i<parameters.length;i++)
         al.add((Class)parameters[i].getClass());

      Class args[] = new Class[al.size()];

      for (int j=0;j<al.size();j++)
         args[j] = (Class)al.get(j);

      Method method =
           this.getClass().getMethod(operationName,args);

      value = method.invoke(this,parameters);

    } catch (Exception ex) {

      System.out.println(ex);

    }

    return value;
}

public void setAttribute(Attribute att){}

public AttributeList setAttributes(AttributeList atts){

    return null;

}

public String getFoobar(){

    return "FooBar";

}

public String concat(String str1,String str2){
```

```
                return str1+str2;

    }

}
```

Listing 5-10 shows the source for a Java application named MBeanInvokeUtil that will
execute the getFoobar() and concat() methods of the DynamicInvocationObject
class.

### Listing 5-10: The MBeanInvokeUtil class

```
import javax.management.InstanceNotFoundException;
import javax.management.IntrospectionException;
import javax.management.MalformedObjectNameException;
import javax.management.ReflectionException;
import javax.management.ObjectName;
import javax.management.MBeanServer;
import javax.management.MBeanServerFactory;
import javax.management.MBeanInfo;
import javax.management.MBeanAttributeInfo;
import javax.management.MBeanConstructorInfo;
import javax.management.MBeanOperationInfo;
import javax.management.MBeanParameterInfo;
import javax.management.MBeanNotificationInfo;
import javax.swing.tree.DefaultMutableTreeNode;

public class MBeanInvokeUtil {

    private static MBeanServer server = null;

    public MBeanInvokeUtil() {
        server = MBeanServerFactory.createMBeanServer();
    }

    public static void main(String args[]) {

            MBeanInvokeUtil agent = new MBeanInvokeUtil();
        ObjectName simpleObject =
agent.loadBean("DynamicInvocationObject",

"DynamicInvocationObject:name=simple");

            try {

                String str = (String)server.invoke(simpleObject,
                                        "getFoobar",
                                        new Object[]{},
                                        new String[]{});
```

```
                System.out.println("Value is: " + str);

            str = (String)server.invoke(simpleObject,
                                        "concat",
                                        new Object[]{"JMX
","Programming"},
                                        new
String[]{"java.lang.String",

"java.lang.String"});

                System.out.println("Value is: " + str);

        } catch (Exception ex) {

            System.out.println(ex);

        }

    }

    public ObjectName loadBean(String className,String objectName) {

        ObjectName mbeanObjectName = null;
        String domain = server.getDefaultDomain();
        String mbeanName = className;
        try {
            mbeanObjectName = new ObjectName(objectName);
        } catch(MalformedObjectNameException e) {
          e.printStackTrace();
          System.exit(1);
        }
          // Create our simple object to manage //
          try {
              server.createMBean(mbeanName,mbeanObjectName);
          }catch(Exception ex){
              ex.printStackTrace();
              System.exit(1);
          }

        return mbeanObjectName;
    }
}
```

The first invocation is on the getFoobar() method, which uses the name of the method, an empty array of java.lang.Object objects, and an empty array of java.lang.String objects. The method takes no arguments, so constructing the arrays is easy.

The second invocation is on the `concat()` method. The steps you take to execute the `concat()` method are similar to those followed for the `getFoobar()` method. However, you need to construct the arguments that will be passed to the `concat()` method. The output from running the `MBeanInvokeUtil` class should look like the following:

```
Value is: FooBar
Value is: JMX Programming
```

From this example, it should be easy to see how other sets of arguments can be constructed in the same way. Obviously, operations with more complex method signatures require more code to properly construct the appropriate arrays.

## Creating the MBeanInfo Class

Because the management interface of a dynamic MBean can change frequently, though it's certainly not required to, the dynamic MBean is responsible for creating its own `MBeanInfo` class. This offers the added benefit of providing a lot of flexibility for the dynamic MBean developer.

As you saw in Chapter 4, the `MBeanInfo` class is comprised of many pieces of information about an MBean, such as the constructors, attributes, and operations. You learned how to extract this information by using the `getMBeanInfo()` method of the `MBeanServer` class. Collectively, this information is known as the *metadata* of the MBean.

With dynamic MBeans, the `getMBeanInfo()` method is part of the `DynamicMBean` interface. This enables you, the MBean developer, to create this structure yourself. The structure is composed of a series of related classes that represent each major type of information. Chapter 4 provided you with the information; now you will create them from scratch. In the following sections, you'll learn how to create this information statically and dynamically from an external source. Because the `MBeanInfo` class was covered in Chapter 4, its methods are not covered here. Instead, you will learn how to create the different structures representing the attributes, operations, and constructors.

Before getting into how to create each metadata class, you'll create a simple dynamic MBean to which you'll add the code for creating each piece of information. Listing 5-11 shows the source for a dynamic MBean.

**Listing 5-11: Source for a simple dynamic MBean**

```java
import javax.management.Attribute;
import javax.management.AttributeList;
import javax.management.DynamicMBean;
import javax.management.MBeanInfo;


public class SimpleDynamicObject implements DynamicMBean {

    private MBeanInfo beanInfo = null;

    public Object getAttribute(String name){
```

```
            return null;
    }

    public AttributeList getAttributes(String attributes[]){
            return null;
    }

    public MBeanInfo getMBeanInfo(){
            return null;
    }

    public Object invoke(String operationName,
                         Object parameters[],
                         String signature[]){
            return null;
    }

    public void setAttribute(Attribute attribute){
    }

    public AttributeList setAttributes(AttributeList attributes){
            return null;
    }

}
```

Listing 5-12 shows the source of the MBeanInfoBuilder class. This class will be responsible for building the MBeanInfo structure for the SimpleDynamicObject. As you move through an example of constructing each type of structure, the example code will grow until it becomes fully functional. Then you'll update the SimpleDynamicObject class to make use of it.

**Listing 5-12: The MBeanInfoBuilder class**

```
import javax.management.MBeanAttributeInfo;
import javax.management.MBeanParameterInfo;
import javax.management.MBeanNotificationInfo;
import javax.management.MBeanOperationInfo;
import javax.management.MBeanConstructorInfo;
import javax.management.Attribute;
import javax.management.AttributeList;
import javax.management.MBeanInfo;
import javax.management.DynamicMBean;
import java.util.List;
import java.util.Arrays;
import java.lang.reflect.Method;
import java.lang.reflect.Field;


public class MBeanInfoBuilder {
```

```
        public MBeanAttributeInfo getAttributeInfo(){
            return null;
        }

        public MBeanParameterInfo getParameterInfo(){
            return null;
        }

        public MBeanOperationInfo getOperationInfo(){
            return null;
        }

        public MBeanConstructorInfo getConstructorInfo(){
            return null;
        }

        public MBeanNotificationInfo getNotificationInfo(){
            return null;
        }

}
```

## Creating the MBeanAttributeInfo class

The `MBeanAttributeInfo` class represents the attributes or fields of an MBean. The bullet list shows the two constructors you can use to build an instance of the `MBeanAttributeInfo` class.

♦ **MBeanAttributeInfo**(String name, String type, String description, boolean isRead, boolean isWrite, boolean isIs)

♦ **MBeanAttributeInfo**(String name, String description, java.lang.reflect.Method get, java.lang.reflect.Method write)

Listing 5-13 shows the source code for the updates to the `getAttributeInfo()` method.

**Listing 5-13: The updated getAttributeInfo method of the MBeanInfoBuilder class**

```
public MBeanAttributeInfo getAttributeInfo(String name,
                                           String type,
                                           String desc,
                                           boolean read,
                                           boolean write,
                                           boolean hasIs){

        MBeanAttributeInfo attrInfo =
            new MBeanAttributeInfo(name,type,desc,
                                   read,write,hasIs);
        return attrInfo;
}
```

This method takes an argument representing the name of the attribute, the Java type, the description, and three `boolean` arguments indicating that the attribute is readable, writeable, and has an `is` method, respectively. (Chapter 4 explains what the "is" method is for an attribute.) These arguments are then passed to the constructor of the `MBeanAttributeInfo` class. This `MBeanAttributeInfo` object instance is then returned.

## Creating the MBeanParameterInfo class

The `MBeanParameterInfo` class is used to construct meta information about a parameter, which may appear as an argument to an operation or constructor. The bullet shows the constructor for the `MBeanParameterInfo` class.

♦ **MBeanParameterInfo**`(String name, String type, String description)`

Listing 5-14 shows the source code for the updates to the `getParameterInfo()` method.

**Listing 5-14: The updated getParameterInfo method of the MBeanInfoBuilder class**

```
public MBeanParameterInfo getParameterInfo(String name,
                                           String type,
                                           String desc){


        MBeanParameterInfo parmInfo =
            new MBeanParameterInfo(name,type,desc);

        return parmInfo;
}
```

The method takes an argument representing the name of the parameter, the Java type of the parameter, and the description of the parameter. These arguments are then passed to the constructor of the `MBeanParameterInfo` class. This `MBeanParameterInfo` object instance is then returned.

## Creating the MBeanConstructorInfo class

The `MBeanConstructorInfo` class is used to construct meta information about a constructor for an MBean. The bullet list describes the constructors for the `MBeanConstructorInfo` class.

♦ **MBeanConstructorInfo**`(String name,java.lang.reflect.Constructor)`
♦ **MBeanConstructorInfo**`(String name, String description, MBeanParameterInfo[] signature)`

Listing 5-15 shows the source code for the updates to the `getConstructorInfo()` method.

**Listing 5-15: The updated getConstructorInfo method of the MBeanInfoBuilder class**

```
public MBeanConstructorInfo getConstructorInfo(String name,
                                               String desc,
                                               MBeanParameterInfo[]
                                                   sig){
```

```
        MBeanConstructorInfo constrInfo =
            new MBeanConstructorInfo(name,desc,sig);

        return constrInfo;
}
```

This method takes an argument representing the name of the constructor, and an array of
`MBeanParameterInfo` objects representing the arguments to the constructor. These
arguments are then passed to the constructor of the `MBeanConstructorInfo` class. This
`MBeanConstructorInfo` object instance is then returned.

## Creating the MBeanOperationInfo class

The `MBeanOperationInfo` class is used to construct meta information about an operation or
method in an MBean. The bullet list shows the constructors for the `MBeanOperationInfo`
class.

♦ **MBeanOperationInfo**(String description, java.lang.reflect.Method
   operation)

♦ **MBeanOperationInfo**(String name, String description,
   MBeanParameterInfo[] signature, String returnType, int impact)

Listing 5-16 shows the source code for the updates to the `getOperationInfo()` method.

**Listing 5-16: The updated getOperationInfo method of the MBeanInfoBuilder class**

```
public MBeanOperationInfo getOperationInfo(String name,
                                           String desc,
                                           MBeanParameterInfo[] sig,
                                           String type,
                                           int impact){

        MBeanOperationInfo opInfo =
            new MBeanOperationInfo(name,desc,sig,
                                   type,impact);
        return opInfo;
}
```

The method takes an argument representing the name of the operation, the description of the
operation, an array of `MBeanParameterInfo` objects representing the arguments to the
operation, a string representing the Java type returned by the operation, and finally, a Java
primitive `int` representing the potential impact of executing the method. (Chapter 4 describes
the values represented by the `impact` argument.) These arguments are then passed to the
constructor of the `MBeanAttributeInfo` class. This `MBeanAttributeInfo` object instance
is then returned.

## Creating the MBeanNotificationInfo class

The MBeanNotificationInfo class is used to construct meta information about the notifications emitted by an MBean. The bullet shows the constructor for the MBeanNotificationInfo class.

♦ **MBeanNotificationInfo**(String notifTypes[], String name, String description)

> **CROSS-REFERENCE:** Chapter 11 covers the topic of notifications in detail.

Listing 5-17 shows the code updates for the getNotificationInfo() method.

**Listing 5-17: The updated getNotificationInfo method of the MBeanInfoBuilder class**

```
public MBeanNotificationInfo getNotificationInfo(String notifications[],
                                                 String name,
                                                 String description){

        MBeanNotificationInfo opInfo =
             new
MBeanNotificationInfo(notifications,name,description);
        return opInfo;
}
```

This method takes an array of java.lang.String types representing the names of the notifications that the MBean can emit, an argument representing the name, and the description of the notification. These arguments are then passed to the constructor of the MBeanAttributeInfo class. This MBeanAttributeInfo object instance is then returned. The actual syntax and API for working with notifications is covered in Chapter 11.

## Creating the MBeanFeatureInfo class

The MbeanFeatureInfo class is the superclass of all the metadata classes, except for the MBeanInfo class. The MBeanFeatureInfo class has two methods, getName() and getDescription(), that many of the metadata classes use to provide a name and description for certain pieces of meta information, such as the name of an attribute or operation. The constructor for the MBeanFeatureInfo class is MBeanFeatureInfo(String name, String description). This method takes an argument representing the name of the feature and the description. The MBeanInfoBuilder class does not include a wrapper method for the MBeanFeatureInfo class.

Now that you have examined how to build each of the metadata classes, you can put this knowledge to use. You are going to add a method to the MBeanInfoBuilder class that builds an MBeanInfo object using the other methods in the class. These other methods will act as wrappers around code that creates the different metadata classes. This way, you can change the implementation of how you create instances of the different metadata classes without changing the callers of the MBeanInfoBuilder class.

Listing 5-18 shows the source code for the getMBeanInfo() method added to the MBeanInfoBuilder class. The rest of the class has been omitted for brevity.

**Listing 5-18: Adding the getMBeanInfo method to the MBeanInfoBuilder class**

```
public MBeanInfo getMBeanInfo(DynamicMBean bean,
                              String name,
                              String description){


        MBeanAttributeInfo attrInfo[] =
            new MBeanAttributeInfo[]{
                        getAttributeInfo("Name",
                                         "java.lang.String",
                                         "The name of the MBean",
                                         true,
                                         true,
                                         false),
                        getAttributeInfo("Description",
                                         "java.lang.String",
                                         "The description of the
MBean",

                                         true,
                                         true,
                                         false)};

        MBeanOperationInfo opInfo[] =
            new MBeanOperationInfo[]{};

        MBeanConstructorInfo conInfo[] =
            new MBeanConstructorInfo[]{};

        MBeanNotificationInfo notifInfo[] =
            new MBeanNotificationInfo[]{};

        MBeanInfo beanInfo = new MBeanInfo(name,
                                           description,
                                           attrInfo,
                                           conInfo,
                                           opInfo,
                                           notifInfo);

        return beanInfo;

    }
```

This class builds an MBeanInfo object with a name, a description, and an array of MBeanAttributeInfo objects. Each MBeanAttributeInfo object represents a field in the ManageableDynamicMBean class. This example only provides information about the attributes of the MBean. No other information is currently provided. Remember, with dynamic MBeans you can control the management interface and what information is available to tools and JMX agents. The remaining arrays for the constructors, operations, and notifications are empty at this point.

After you've added the `getMBeanInfo()` method to the `MBeanInfoBuilder` class, you need to update the `SimpleDynamicObject` class to use it. To accomplish this task, change the `getMBeanInfo()` method of the `SimpleDynamicObject` to look like this:

```
public MBeanInfo getMBeanInfo(){
       MBeanInfoBuilder beanBld = new MBeanInfoBuilder();

       MBeanInfo beanInfo = beanBld.getMBeanInfo(this,
                                        "SimpleDynamicObject",
                                        "A Simple Object");

       return beanInfo;
}
```

The updates will cause the `getMBeanInfo()` method of the `MBeanInfoBuilder` class to be called when information about the management interface is needed.

In Chapter 4, you wrote a utility called `MBeanUtils` that printed information about an MBean. You can re-use this class to print information about the `SimpleDynamicObject` MBean class that you created earlier. You just need to execute the following command:

```
java MBeanUtils SimpleDynamicObject
```

The name of the MBean that will be loaded is changed to reflect the name of the MBean from this chapter. After running the `MBeanUtils` Java application, you should see output that looks like the following:

```
Class: SimpleDynamicObject
Attribute Name: Name
Attribute Description: The name of the MBean
Attribute Type: java.lang.String
Attribute has "is" method: false
Attribute is readable: true
Attribute is writeable: true
Attribute Name: Description
Attribute Description: The description of the MBean
Attribute Type: java.lang.String
Attribute has "is" method: false
Attribute is readable: true
Attribute is writeable: true
```

Information about the two attributes, `name` and `description`, is displayed in the output. The difference between this output and that from the `MBeanUtils` application from Chapter 4 is that the descriptions now reflect what you provided, instead of the value `Attribute exposed for management` value.

## Using static values versus reflection

The JMX API contains two versions of each of the constructors for the metadata classes, as you probably noted as you went through the previous section. Both versions of each method take the same number of arguments in most cases. Some of the versions of the methods take Java types that belong to the `java.lang.reflect` package in the Java API.

These types are used to represent values that are generally determined at runtime using the reflection API. Using the version that takes a Java type from the reflection API ensures that the method exists in the MBean. The other versions, which do not take Java types from the reflection API, will work just as well, but an exception will be thrown down the line if this method does not exist. This would happen, for example, if you misspelled the name of the method when building the `MBeanInfo` object for the MBean.

The methods you've seen so far for building the management interface for the `DynamicManageableObject` MBean are static. By static I mean that you can only change the management interface by updating the source code of the interface and class, and then recompiling them both. This might be acceptable in some cases, but it's entirely possible that the management interface could be loaded from an external source.

# Building the Management Interface Dynamically

The capability to build the management interface dynamically from an external source provides for a great degree of flexibility. The management interface could be stored in a database, a flat-file, or an XML document, for example. The management interface could also be built at runtime by the dynamic MBean itself using introspection. This is similar to what occurs when using standard MBeans. In this case, however, the management interface could later be appended to if need be by adding new methods and attributes from an external source.

Dynamically built attributes and operations of an MBean run a slight risk because no compile-time checking or type checking of operation arguments is performed. Standard MBeans have an advantage in this regard, and will quickly notify you up front if you have an error in the management interface. That said, it is feasible that you could provide a similar checking method against a dynamic MBean given a management interface.

In this section, you will examine providing a management interface using the reflection API. First consider building the management interface using the reflection API. The following example shows you how to build a list of attributes. These will be accessible via the `getAttributes()` method of the `MBeanInfo` class. Listing 5-19 shows the dynamic MBean you'll use for this example. The first step is to add a new main entry point to the `MBeanInfoBuilder` called `getMBeanInfoRef()`, indicating that this method is for using reflection to build the `MBeanInfo` object.

**Listing 5-19: The ReflectiveManagementObject**

```
import javax.management.Attribute;
import javax.management.AttributeList;
import javax.management.DynamicMBean;
import javax.management.MBeanInfo;
```

```
public class ReflectiveManagementObject implements DynamicMBean {

        private MBeanInfo beanInfo = null;
        private String name = "ReflectiveManagementObject";
        private String description = "It's dynamically reflective";

        public Object getAttribute(String name){
                return null;
        }

        public String getName(){
            return name;
        }
        public void setName(String n){
            name = n;
        }

        public String getDescription(){
            return description;
        }

        public void setDescription(String d){
            description = d;
        }

        public AttributeList getAttributes(String attributes[]){
            return null;
        }

        public MBeanInfo getMBeanInfo(){

            MBeanInfoBuilder beanBld =
                new MBeanInfoBuilder();

            MBeanInfo beanInfo =
                beanBld.getMBeanInfoRef(this,
                                        name,
                                        description);

            return beanInfo;
        }

        public Object invoke(String operationName,
                        Object parameters[],
                        String signature[]){
            return null;
        }
```

```
        public void setAttribute(Attribute attribute){

        }

        public AttributeList setAttributes(AttributeList attributes){
                return null;
        }

}
```

The getMBeanInfo() method makes use of several other methods to build the various metadata classes that comprise the MBeanInfo object. The getMBeanInfo() method body looks similar to the getMBeanInfo() method used previously. It does not include the calls to getAttributeInfo() though; rather, it defines a new method called getAccessors(), which returns an array of MBeanAttributeInfo objects. Listing 5-20 shows the source code that must be added to the MBeanInfoBuilder class.

### Listing 5-20: Methods added to the MBeanInfoBuilder class

```
public MBeanInfo getMBeanInfoRef(DynamicMBean bean,
                                 String name,
                                 String description){

        MBeanInfo beanInfo = null;

        MBeanAttributeInfo attrInfo[] = getAccessors(bean);

        MBeanOperationInfo opInfo[] =
            new MBeanOperationInfo[]{};

        MBeanConstructorInfo conInfo[] =
            new MBeanConstructorInfo[]{};

        MBeanNotificationInfo notifInfo[] =
            new MBeanNotificationInfo[]{};

        beanInfo = new MBeanInfo(name,
                                 description,
                                 attrInfo,
                                 conInfo,
                                 opInfo,
                                 notifInfo);

        return beanInfo;
}

        private MBeanAttributeInfo[] getAccessors(DynamicMBean bean){

                AttributeList list = new AttributeList();
```

```
              MBeanAttributeInfo info[] = null;

              Class beanClass = bean.getClass();

              Method methods[] = beanClass.getMethods();

              for (int i=0;i<methods.length;i++) {

                  String methodName = methods[i].getName();

                  if (methodName.startsWith("get")) {

                      String attrName =
                          methodName.substring(3,4).toLowerCase() +
                          methodName.substring(4,methodName.length());

                      String methodClassStr =
                          methods[i].getDeclaringClass().getName();
                      String beanClassStr = bean.getClass().getName();
                      if (methodClassStr.equals(beanClassStr) &&
                          !isReservedMethod(methods[i].getName()) &&
                          hasField(bean.getClass(),
                                  attrName)){

                          // Create MBeanAttributeInfo here //
                          list.add(new MBeanAttributeInfo(attrName,
                              "java.lang.String",
                              "Reflective Attribute for
Management",

                              true,
                              isWriteable(bean.getClass(),
                              methodName),
                              false));

                      }

                  }
              }


              info = new MBeanAttributeInfo[list.size()];
              for (int i=0;i<list.size();i++)
                  info[i] = (MBeanAttributeInfo)list.get(i);

              return info;

      }

  private boolean isWriteable(Class owner,String getter){
```

```java
                  String methodName = "set"+
                                getter.substring(3,4).toUpperCase()+
                                getter.substring(4,getter.length());

            List methods =
                Arrays.asList(methodsToArray(owner.getMethods()));

            return (methods.contains(methodName))? true: false;
    }

    private String[] methodsToArray(Method m[]){

            String[] methods = new String[m.length];
            for (int i=0;i<m.length;i++)
                methods[i] = m[i].getName();

            return methods;
    }

    private boolean isReservedMethod(String name){

            // Could also check to see if declaring class is //
            // DynamicMBean interface                        //

            List keywords =
                Arrays.asList(new String[]{"getMBeanInfo",
                                            "getAttribute",
                                            "getAttributes",
                                            "setAttribute",
                                            "setAttributes",
                                            "invoke"});

            return (keywords.contains(name))? true: false;
    }

    private boolean hasField(Class owner, String name){

        boolean exists = false;

        try {

            Field fld = owner.getDeclaredField(name);

            exists = true;

        } catch (NoSuchFieldException ex){
```

```
        System.out.println(ex);
    }

    return exists;

}
```

The `MBeanInfoBuilder` class has had four new methods added to it to support building the `MBeanInfo` object using reflection. The `getAccessors()` method takes an instance of the `DynamicMBean` interface. This means that any class implementing this interface can be supplied as a parameter to this method. When the `ReflectiveManagementObject` runs, it passes a reference to itself using the `this` keyword.

The approach taken here follows the MBean design pattern by only creating `MBeanAttributeInfo` objects for fields that have accessors of the get/set pattern. You could have simply created one for each method that appears in the class. However, when you list the methods, every method that the class implements is listed, including those it inherits. You don't want everything showing up in the management interface, so you need some way to filter the list.

The first filter that is applied specifies that the method must start with the letters `get`. If this is satisfied, the `getAccessors()` method proceeds to construct the attribute name by stripping off the `get` letters and using the rest of the method name; for example, `getName()` becomes `name`. Then, make sure that the method belongs to the same class as the MBean class by comparing the declaring class of the method to the class that the bean belongs to. In cases where inheritance is involved, this could cause some methods to be missed, but for the purposes of this example this ensures that only methods in the MBean class pass through. Alternatively, you could use the `getDeclaredMethods()` method to return only the methods that appear in the `ReflectiveManagementObject` class.

Once you're sure that this method belongs to the MBean class, you need to make sure it's not one of the `DynamicMBean` interface methods. You do this by passing the method name to the `isReservedMethod()` method, which returns a `boolean` indicating that it is not. Alternatively, you could check to see if the method appeared in the `DynamicMBean` interface using reflection. Lastly, you need to check whether a field by that name actually appears in the `ReflectiveManagementObject` class, using the `hasField()` method. This method is identical to the one shown in Listing 5-8.

Assuming the method passes the test, create a new `MBeanAttributeInfo` object using the attribute name, a hard-coded value of `java.lang.String`, a hard-coded description of `Reflective Attribute for Management`, and a `boolean` of true indicating that the attribute can be read. (You know it can from the earlier check for the value of `get`.) You then pass in the return value of calling the `isWriteable()` method. This method checks to see whether a corresponding `set` method appears in the class. Finally, pass in a `boolean` value of false indicating that no `is` method exists. Once this is done, the `MBeanAttributeInfo` array is constructed by retrieving all the elements from the `javax.management.AttributeList` object that was used to temporarily hold the objects.

Running the `ReflectiveManagementObject` through the `MBeanUtils` Java application should yield output that looks like the following:

```
Class: ReflectiveManagementObject
Attribute Name: name
Attribute Description: Reflective Attribute for Management
Attribute Type: java.lang.String
Attribute has "is" method: false
Attribute is readable: true
Attribute is writeable: true
Attribute Name: description
Attribute Description: Reflective Attribute for Management
Attribute Type: java.lang.String
Attribute has "is" method: false
Attribute is readable: true
Attribute is writeable: true
```

Using reflection to do runtime discovery can be a useful tool when creating dynamic MBean interfaces. However, take care that the performance penalty doesn't outweigh the benefits. Reflection can be a costly performance hit depending on the size of the objects you're working with. The examples shown here work on small classes, some of which have no arguments, so there is not as much work going on.

Larger classes with methods that have complex arguments can possibly be a detriment to the performance of the MBean. Still, if you only initialize the management interface during construction of the MBean, and cache the `MBeanInfo` object in the MBean itself, you only incur the performance penalty during initialization. At the same time, by caching the reference to the `MBeanInfo` object, you lose some flexibility if you want to be able to change the interface at runtime.

Caching the `MBeanInfo` object simply means keeping a copy of it in an instance variable defined to be private to the class. When a caller attempts to access it, you can check for a cached copy and return it if you need to.

Another thing to keep in mind about using reflection is access to attributes and operations. Remember that modifiers such as `public`, `private`, and `protected` are used on attributes and operations to control scope and visibility. Rather than using reflection to access attributes directly, you can use the accessor methods, if they exist, to retrieve or set the values of variables. If you try to access the fields directly using reflection, you will receive an exception indicating that the variables could not be directly accessed.

# Summary

In this chapter you've looked at dynamic MBeans, how to construct and use them, and how they differ from standard MBeans. Unlike the standard MBean, the dynamic MBean places the responsibility of creating the management interface on the implementor. As the implementor, you must create the `MBeanInfo` class, fill it out, and return it when the `getMBeanInfo()` method is called.

In the next chapter you'll take a look at model and open MBeans, types of dynamic MBeans that provide extensible and configurable behavior.

## Chapter 6

# Open and Model MBeans

The MBeans you've seen so far, standard and dynamic, are only two of the types of MBeans defined in the JMX specification. Chapter 2 briefly introduced you to the other two types, open and model.

Open and model MBeans are designed to be even more flexible and easier to use than standard and dynamic MBeans. This is due in part to the way their management interface is presented and the level of default behavior and configuration you can implement with them. The following analogy summarizes the benefit that model MBeans provide. If a standard MBean is a compact car and a dynamic MBean is a mid-size car, then model MBeans are luxury automobiles. They have many features and are quite easy to use. You can also configure their behavior through a common interface and customize them as well.

In this chapter, you will learn how to use model MBeans and learn a bit about programming open MBeans. The information provided about open MBeans is limited because they are not yet considered mandatory per the JMX specification.

## What Is a Model MBean?

Model MBeans use the MBean design patterns and extend them further to enable more flexibility and extensibility in implementing managed resources. The JMX specification defines an interface named ModelMBean just as with DynamicMBean, but model MBeans also define an implementation class named javax.management.modelmbean .RequiredModelMBean. This class is a required component of any JMX implementation, just as model MBeans in general are. The RequiredModelMBean class enables you to take advantage of the model MBean design with very little work on your part. You can, of course, build your own implementation by implementing the ModelMBean interface.

Model MBeans differ somewhat in how their management interface is presented. The ModelMBean interface extends the DynamicMBean interface and provides the standard getMBeanInfo() method that the DynamicMBean interface defines. This gives you the advantages of the dynamic management interface described in Chapter 5. A model MBean also uses an interface named ModelMBeanInfo that describes the management interface. An instance of the ModelMBeanInfo interface can be retrieved using the getMBeanInfo() method. This is similar to the MBeanInfo class that is used with standard and dynamic MBeans. Figure 6-1 shows the relationship between the ModelMBean interface and related classes and interfaces.

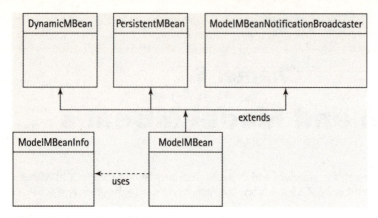

**Figure 6-1:** The relationship between the ModelMBean and related classes.

Figure 6-2 illustrates the concept of a model MBean in the JMX architecture.

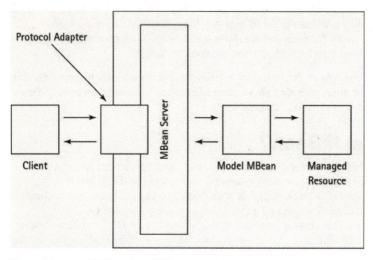

**Figure 6-2:** A model MBean in a JMX agent

The diagram in Figure 6-2 illustrates how a model MBean is used in a JMX agent. However, as you'll shortly see, model MBeans can be configured quite differently than other MBeans, and their interaction with a managed resource can be specified differently. Model MBeans can be implemented to contain all the attributes and operations directly, or the model MBeans can delegate these to a managed resource.

Model MBeans also make use of *descriptors,* which are metadata for describing the attributes and behaviors of a model MBean and its managed resource. Descriptors are not required for a model MBean, although default descriptors are created. This is in addition to the regular host of classes such as MBeanOperationInfo or MBeanAttributeInfo. Descriptors are accessible via the `ModelMBeanInfo` interface, which contains both the descriptors and the information classes just described. The information classes, such as `MBeanOperationInfo`, have been slightly modified to enable a descriptor to be associated with each of them. This means that there can be a descriptor for each `MBeanAttributeInfo` class that a model MBean might have. Figure 6-3 illustrates the relationship between the various model MBean metadata classes and interfaces.

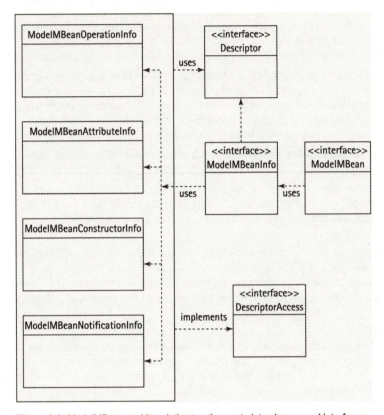

**Figure 6-3:** ModelMBean and its relation to other metadata classes and interfaces.

## Configurable behavior

What does it mean to say that model MBeans have configurable behavior? Operations of a class are commonly termed as the behavior of an object, and the values of attributes can be used to control the behavior of an object. For example, a timer class may signal an alarm when the value of a field becomes set. Model MBeans behave similarly.

Model MBean behavior can be affected by the values of fields in a descriptor. As you will see in this chapter, you can use pre-defined descriptor fields to affect the behavior of a model MBean. For example, you can use a series of pre-defined fields to control the persistence of an MBean and its attributes. If these fields are set to certain values, the persistence of an MBean and its attributes can be turned on and off. Not all of the behaviors are mandatory, and they may not be implemented in a particular JMX reference implementation.

The `RequiredModelMBean` class that is part of the JMX API implements default behaviors that cover the following areas:

♦ Persistence — Persistence is not turned on by default. Normally, model MBeans are transient in nature, which means that all state, settings, and configuration are lost when the model MBean instance is destroyed. A model MBean instance may be destroyed as part of a controlled procedure such as system shutdown of a managed resource, or perhaps when an exception is thrown, which makes the model MBean instance unusable.

Before the MBean instance is completely removed from the JVM it is running in it may be desirable to store the state, settings, or configuration. If you want to be able to persist the state of a model MBean, you must implement the `PersistentMBean` interface. There are other ways you could implement persistence, but the `PersistentMBean` interface enables you to implement this persistence using the standard JMX interface.

Persistence can be specified using pre-defined fields at either the MBean level or the attribute level.

♦ Caching and default values — When you access an attribute of a managed resource, in most scenarios you call the `getAttribute()` method of the model MBean, which in turn invokes the accessor method of the managed resource. The value is then returned to the calling application.

With model MBeans, the descriptor contains the last value retrieved plus a default value of the attribute. If the descriptor for an attribute contains no accessor methods, the descriptor will always contain the value you get and set. If there are accessor methods, you can make use of some other fields that control whether or not you get a cached value or a new value.

The fields `currencyTimeLimit` and `lastUpdatedTimeStamp` work together to enable a model MBean to determine whether or not an attribute value is stale. If the value contained in the descriptor is stale, the attribute value is retrieved from the managed resource; otherwise, the value in the descriptor is returned to the caller. This type of behavior enables faster access and minimal disruption to the managed resource.

♦ Notification Logging — With respect to model MBeans, logging behavior controls whether or not notifications that the model MBean sends and receives are logged. This feature is controlled by the `log` and `logFile` fields, both of which must be present for logging to work. The fields controlling logging can be specified at both the `MBean` and `ModelMBeanNotificationInfo` level. The `log` field is a Boolean indicating whether to log, and the `logFile` field is a fully qualified path to a filename where notifications are stored.

♦ Protocolmap — This field is designed to enable you to map the attributes of a model MBean and its managed resource to other management schemas. The value of this field is a descriptor that also has fields mapping this field to other management schema representations, such as the Common Information Model (CIM) or an SNMP MIB Object Identifier. This enables a single model MBean to be exposed to many different types of management agents and management applications.

♦ Visibility — Managed resources can be simple or complex. A single managed object might have three or four attributes, and so representing this in a user interface or to other management applications would be relatively simple. However, if you multiply this simple object by a factor of a thousand and add several other managed resources into the mix, the picture becomes quite complex. At this point, you have to start asking yourself what level of detail you need to present to a management application.

The `visibility` field enables you to assign a level of granularity to a managed resource at the attribute and MBean level. The values you can assign range from one (1) to four (4), with 1 indicating that the component in question should always be visible. This assignment enables management applications to make decisions about what they want to work with at runtime. Some user interfaces for management applications might present a high-level view of the managed resources and then provide ways to drill down into lower levels of the resource. The `visibility` field provides hints to the management applications, enabling them to decide whether or not to include a component in a high-level view or a detailed view. Of course, this is completely up to the management application, and the `visibility` field does not in any way restrict access to a component or MBean based on its value.

♦ Presentation – The JMX specification defines the `presentation` field to be a pre-defined view of a management component, such as a model MBean or one of its attributes. The idea behind this field is to give management user interfaces some idea of how to present the component.

The fields and definitions of this view have not been defined, although you'll see the acronym XML used throughout the descriptions of this field, and the JMX reference implementation mentions it. Any output from the `toString()` methods of the various model MBean components should not be relied upon at this point, as they may change in future releases.

♦ Export policy – In multi-JMX agent environments, you might need to access an MBean from various locations. To be able to access an MBean, its agent must export the management interface in such a way that it can be remotely accessed, and the agent must know how to export it. The export may be done using Remote Method Invocation (RMI), in which case the export policy and field might define a name that will be bound into the RMI registry, and which can be looked up using the MBean Server.

The configuration of fields in a descriptor, and the expected resulting behavior is commonly referred to as a *policy*. The policies for a model MBean define the contract between the fields and the behavior. In other words, if you set a field to a specific value, and its policy states that the bean will perform some action based on that value, the bean will perform that value. There is no implementation or definition of a policy; rather, it's a conceptual entity used to describe the relationship between fields and the model MBean behavior.

When you create your own model MBean implementation, it is up to you to define its behaviors and policies. Each of these policies is enforced and controlled by the values of the fields found in the descriptors. The `RequiredModelMBean` implements a series of policies that control the behaviors described in the preceding list.

## Attribute policy

You access the attributes of a model MBean using the normal methods of `getAttribute()` and `setAttribute()`. This results in a call being made to the managed resource where the attribute actually resides, but it could also exist in the MBean itself.

With model MBeans, you can specify attributes that exist only in the descriptors (also called fields). All access to this data will be to and from a descriptor. However, you can also specify the attributes that exist in your managed resource using a descriptor. Attributes you specify using the `ModelMBeanAttributeInfo` will make the attribute appear in the model MBean itself unless you associate a descriptor for the attribute with the `ModelMBeanAttributeInfo` class.

When you create an attribute descriptor, you indicate the accessor methods using the `getMethod` and `setMethod` fields, and provide the operation name that will be used to access the value of the attribute. You then need to provide an operation descriptor that indicates the class name of the object where the operation exists; otherwise, the MBean Server will attempt to find the `get` and `set` methods in the model MBean itself. You'll learn how to build attribute descriptors and operation descriptors in the "Descriptors" section of this chapter.

As mentioned previously in the "What Is a Model MBean?" section, the `ModelMBean` interface extends the `NotificationBroadcaster` interface, which can be used by JMX components to send notifications. The `RequiredModelMBean` class inherits this functionality and emits notifications automatically for things such as attribute value changes.

Before looking at the rest of the classes and interfaces for model MBeans, let's take a tour of descriptors. Descriptors are one of the primary differences between model MBeans and standard or dynamic MBeans.

# Descriptors

You might be wondering why model MBeans represent metadata using two types of classes. Descriptors and the MBean information classes both represent meta information about a model MBean. Descriptors provide additional information, and they are extensible in that they can represent arbitrary information that can be associated with each of the different types of meta information classes. For example, the JMX specification reference implementation defines a `ModelMBeanAttributeInfo` class that has a descriptor. Model MBeans also have a descriptor at the MBean level. If no descriptor is explicitly specified, one is created for each component type.

Descriptors can be easily changed at runtime using the methods of the `Descriptor` interface. They are comprised of fields, each of which has a value. You can name the fields in a descriptor anything you want, and they don't have to represent actual fields in an MBean.

Descriptors can represent attributes, operations, constructors, and notifications of a model MBean, but they can also represent this type of information about the managed resource itself. In Chapter 4, the distinction between the MBean and its managed resource was minimal because the standard MBean interface directly represented the information about the managed resource. With model MBeans, it's somewhat different because of the managed resource and the way that a model MBean interacts with this resource.

You can construct a descriptor using an implementation of the `Descriptor` interface. Table 6-1 shows the methods of the `Descriptor` interface and a description of each.

### Table 6-1    Descriptor Interface Methods

| Method Name | Description |
|---|---|
| `clone()` | Returns a copy of this descriptor |
| `getFieldNames()` | Returns an array of `java.lang.String` objects representing the names of the fields in a descriptor |
| `getFields()` | Returns an array of `java.lang.String` representing the fields in the descriptor, in the format "fieldName=fieldValue" |
| `getFieldValue()` | Returns a `java.lang.Object` that represents the value of a field in the descriptor |
| `getFieldValues()` | Returns an array of `java.lang.Object` that represents the values of the fields in a descriptor |
| `isValid()` | Returns a primitive Java Boolean indicating whether the descriptor is valid |
| `removeField(java.lang.String fieldName)` | Removes a field from a descriptor |
| `setField(java.lang.String fieldName, java.lang.Object fieldValue)` | Sets the value of a field in a descriptor |
| `setFields(java.lang.String[] fieldNames, java.lang.Object[] fieldValues)` | Sets the values of several fields in a descriptor |

The fields and values can be arbitrary, but some default fields are defined by the JMX specification for each major component of information about an MBean. If you don't specify a descriptor for one of the components, a default descriptor will be created and the pre-defined fields will be filled out with default values.

## Creating a descriptor

If you choose to create a descriptor, you can do one of two things. You can create your own class to implement the `Descriptor` interface, or you can use the `DescriptorSupport` class found in the `javax.management.modelmbean` package. I recommend the latter option, as it is much easier and there is no real benefit to implementing your own.

The `DescriptorSupport` class implements the `Descriptor` interface and, therefore, inherits all of the methods listed in Table 6-1. Because the descriptor itself is abstract, the fields you add may not mean anything until you try to use the descriptor along with a real MBean. The fields that comprise a descriptor can be specified in the constructor of a descriptor, or afterward by using one of the methods listed in Table 6-1. You can construct a `DescriptorSupport` object using the following methods:

- ♦ Use the default constructor with no arguments.

- ♦ Pass in an instance of another `DescriptorSupport` object.

- ♦ Pass in an integer representing the number of fields.

- ♦ Pass in an XML string representing the fields and values. The schema of the XML is currently undefined.

- ♦ Pass in an array of `java.lang.String` objects with each element set to a field=value pair. This obviously only works for fields with string values.

- ♦ Pass in an array of `java.lang.String` objects representing field names, and an array of `java.lang.Object` objects representing the field values.

Some examples use the first method in this list and then use the `setField()` method to add field/value pairs to the descriptor, resulting in something like the following:

```
Descriptor desc = new DescriptorSupport();
desc.setField("name","foobar");
desc.setField("descriptortype","attribute");
```

However, you could also do this same example using code that looks like this:

```
String fields[] = new String[]{"name=foobar",
"descriptortype=attribute"};
Descriptor desc = new DescriptorSupport(fields);
```

The preceding example uses an array of string/value pairs to initialize the descriptor, which is functionally equivalent to the previous example.

The values that you use for fields can be arbitrary or they can represent real attributes of a managed object. Some of the fields, though, are pre-defined and mandatory for a model MBean. The pre-defined fields help to define the behavior of the various policies described previously for a model MBean.

## Pre-defined descriptor fields

The `RequiredModelMBean` class uses some pre-defined descriptor fields. These pre-defined fields control aspects of the `RequiredModelMBean`, such as persistence and logging. The `RequiredModelMBean` is packaged with a set of default descriptor fields that correspond to the policies of behavior described earlier. These fields control display information about the MBean, logging, persistence, and attribute value caching. The `RequiredModelMBean` implementation understands these default descriptor fields and how they affect the behavior of the MBean.

For example, with respect to persistence, changing certain fields controls whether or not the RequiredModelMBean will attempt to initialize itself with data from a persistent store, or will attempt to store internal state in a persistent store. Because major components of an MBean, such as operations and attributes, can have a descriptor, there are pre-defined descriptor fields for each of the major types. Many of these fields are for use by the RequiredModelMBean itself, but others — such as those controlling persistence and logging — can be manipulated by management applications.

Before examining each of the pre-defined descriptor fields, you'll write a simple application that lists each of the descriptor fields. You use the familiar code that you've seen used throughout the book, which loads an MBean. Then you extract each descriptor of the RequiredModelMBean. Listing 6-1 shows the source of the application.

**Listing 6-1: Displaying the pre-defined descriptor fields of the RequiredModelMBean**

```
import javax.management.InstanceNotFoundException;
import javax.management.IntrospectionException;
import javax.management.MalformedObjectNameException;
import javax.management.ReflectionException;
import javax.management.ObjectName;
import javax.management.MBeanServer;
import javax.management.MBeanServerFactory;
import javax.management.Descriptor;
import javax.management.modelmbean.ModelMBeanInfo;
import javax.management.modelmbean.RequiredModelMBean;

public class ModelMBeanJMXAgent {

    private static MBeanServer server = null;

    public ModelMBeanJMXAgent() {
        server = MBeanServerFactory.createMBeanServer();
    }

    public static void main(String[] args) {

        ModelMBeanJMXAgent agent = new ModelMBeanJMXAgent();
        ObjectName simpleObject =

agent.loadBean("javax.management.modelmbean.RequiredModelMBean",
                        "ModelMBean:type=model");

            try {

                ModelMBeanInfo mldBeanInfo =
                    (ModelMBeanInfo)server.getMBeanInfo(simpleObject);

                Descriptor beanDescriptor =
                        mldBeanInfo.getMBeanDescriptor();
```

```
                    agent.printDescriptor(beanDescriptor);

                    Descriptor desc[] = mldBeanInfo.getDescriptors(null);

                    System.out.println("Descriptors found: " +
                                    desc.length);

                    for (int i=0;i<desc.length;i++)
                        agent.printDescriptor(desc[i]);

                } catch (Exception ex){
                        System.out.println(ex);
                }

        }

    private void printDescriptor(Descriptor desc) {

System.out.println(">>>>>>>>>>>>>>>>>>>>>>>>>>>>>>>>>>>>>>>>>>>>>>>>>>>
>>>>");
            System.out.println("Descriptor type: " +
                                desc.getFieldValue("descriptortype"));
            String fieldNames[] = desc.getFieldNames();
            Object fieldValues[] = desc.getFieldValues(fieldNames);
            for (int i=0;i<fieldValues.length;i++) {
                System.out.println("Field Name: " + fieldNames[i] +
                                ", Field Value: " + fieldValues[i]);
            }


        }

    private ObjectName loadBean(String className,String objectName) {

            ObjectName mbeanObjectName = null;
            String domain = server.getDefaultDomain();
            String mbeanName = className;
            try {
                mbeanObjectName = new ObjectName(objectName);
            } catch(MalformedObjectNameException e) {
                e.printStackTrace();
                System.exit(1);
            }
            // Create our simple object to manage //
            try {
            server.createMBean(mbeanName,mbeanObjectName);
            }catch(Exception ex){
                ex.printStackTrace();
                System.exit(1);
```

```
        }

        return mbeanObjectName;
    }
}
```

The application creates and registers an instance of the `RequiredModelMBean` model MBean and then uses the `getMBeanInfo()` method to get an instance of the `ModelMBeanInfo` class. You need to cast this to `ModelMBeanInfo` because `getMBeanInfo()` returns `MBeanInfo`. You then call the `getMBeanDescriptor()` method of the `ModelMBeanInfo` class to get the descriptor for the MBean itself.

The output from running the `ModelMBeanJMXAgent` application looks like the following:

```
>>>>>>>>>>>>>>>>>>>>>>>>>>>>>>>>>>>>>>>>>>>>>>>>>>>>>>>>
Descriptor type: mbean
Field Name: persistpolicy, Field Value: never
Field Name: descriptortype, Field Value: mbean
Field Name: log, Field Value: F
Field Name: export, Field Value: F
Field Name: visibility, Field Value: 1
Field Name: displayname, Field Value:
javax.management.modelmbean.RequiredModelMBean
Field Name: name, Field Value:
javax.management.modelmbean.RequiredModelMBean
Descriptors found: 0
```

The pre-defined fields shown in this example are `persistPolicy`, `descriptortype`, `log`, `export`, `visibility`, `displayname`, and `name`. Each of these fields was given a value determined by the `RequiredModelMBean`. Not all of these fields are required, although they are defined, meaning that the `log` field does not have to be set and given a value in order for the descriptor to be considered valid.

Any remaining descriptors are printed by first using the `getDescriptors()` method to retrieve all remaining descriptors for the major components. You can pass a value of null to this method to retrieve all descriptors. The output from this is nothing at all, which means that although there are pre-defined fields, these must be set manually for the `RequiredModelMBean`. There is also an overloading of the `getDescriptors()` method that takes a string argument that represents the descriptor type. This string argument must be one of these values:

♦ `mbean`

♦ `attribute`

♦ `operation`

♦ `constructor`

♦ `notification`

The `RequiredModelMBean` class will check the validity of the descriptor type against the value you are trying to use. If you try to set a descriptor type as something other than one of the pre-defined types or if you forget to set the value of a required field of a particular descriptor, the descriptor will be considered invalid. You can check the validity of a descriptor using the `isValid()` method of the `Descriptor` interface. Listing 6-2 shows an application that creates an invalid MBean descriptor.

**Listing 6-2: Invalid MBean descriptor**

```
import javax.management.ObjectName;
import javax.management.MBeanServer;
import javax.management.MBeanServerFactory;
import javax.management.Descriptor;
import javax.management.modelmbean.DescriptorSupport;
import javax.management.modelmbean.ModelMBeanInfo;
import javax.management.modelmbean.ModelMBeanInfoSupport;
import javax.management.modelmbean.RequiredModelMBean;

public class ModelMBeanJMXAgentBadDescriptor {

    private static MBeanServer server = null;

    public ModelMBeanJMXAgentBadDescriptor() {
        server = MBeanServerFactory.createMBeanServer();
    }

    public static void main(String[] args) {

        ModelMBeanJMXAgentBadDescriptor agent =
            new ModelMBeanJMXAgentBadDescriptor();

            try {

                ObjectName simpleObject =
                    new ObjectName("ModelMBean:type=model");

                RequiredModelMBean bean = new RequiredModelMBean();

                DescriptorSupport desc = new DescriptorSupport();
                desc.setField("descriptortype","mbean");
                desc.setField("displayName","Foobar");

                System.out.println("Descriptor is valid: " +
                                    desc.isValid());

                ModelMBeanInfoSupport mldInfo =
                    new
ModelMBeanInfoSupport(agent.getClass().getName(),
                    "RequiredModelMBean",
```

```
                            null,null,null,null,desc);

                bean.setModelMBeanInfo(mldInfo);

                ModelMBeanInfo beanInfo =
                    (ModelMBeanInfo)bean.getMBeanInfo();

                agent.printDescriptor(beanInfo.getMBeanDescriptor());

            } catch (Exception ex){
                ex.printStackTrace();
            }
    }

    private void printDescriptor(Descriptor desc) {
        System.out.println("Descriptor type: " +
                            desc.getFieldValue("descriptortype"));
        String fieldNames[] = desc.getFieldNames();
        Object fieldValues[] = desc.getFieldValues(fieldNames);
        for (int i=0;i<fieldValues.length;i++) {
            System.out.println("Field Name: " + fieldNames[i] +
                            ", Field Value: " + fieldValues[i]);
        }

    }

}
```

The `ModelMBeanJMXAgent` creates an instance of the `RequiredModelMBean` class and then creates a descriptor. Two fields are added using the `setField()` method, one for the `descriptortype` descriptor field and one for the `displayName` descriptor field. It then creates a `ModelMBeanInfoSupport` object and passes the descriptor as the last parameter. This `ModelMBeanInfoSupport` object is then used as the argument to the `setModelMBeanInfo()` method, setting the management interface for this model MBean. It prints the result of the `isValid()` method of the `DescriptorSupport` class, which in this case is `false`.

It then continues by retrieving the `ModelMBeanInfo` object for the `RequiredModelMBean` and prints the descriptor for the MBean. The output from the application looks like the following:

```
Descriptor is valid: false
Descriptor type: mbean
Field Name: persistpolicy, Field Value: never
Field Name: descriptortype, Field Value: mbean
Field Name: log, Field Value: F
Field Name: export, Field Value: F
Field Name: visibility, Field Value: 1
Field Name: displayname, Field Value: ModelMBeanJMXAgentBadDescriptor
Field Name: name, Field Value: ModelMBeanJMXAgentBadDescriptor
```

The result is `false` for the descriptor because the `name` pre-defined field was not defined for the descriptor. The remaining fields are printed but the `displayname` field has a different value than the one you specified! This is because when an invalid descriptor is detected, a default descriptor replaces it with values determined by the `RequiredModelMBean`. This is the same result as if no descriptor were explicitly specified.

You can change line of the `ModelMBeanJMXAgentBadDescriptor` application's `main()` method as follows:

```
desc.setField("name",bean.getClass().getName());
```

And here is the resulting output:

```
Descriptor is valid: true
Descriptor type: mbean
Field Name: persistpolicy, Field Value: never
Field Name: descriptortype, Field Value: mbean
Field Name: displayname, Field Value: Foobar
Field Name: log, Field Value: F
Field Name: name, Field Value:
javax.management.modelmbean.RequiredModelMBean
Field Name: export, Field Value: F
```

As you can see from the output, the correct values are now set for the `displayname` field, as our descriptor was used as is and not replaced by a default descriptor.

Now that you've taken a brief look at how to create a descriptor and display some pre-defined descriptor fields, take a look at the pre-defined fields for the rest of the information classes. Recall the list of descriptor types presented earlier. These types were string values that correspond to MBean metadata types, such as attribute information, constructor information, and operation information. Each of these metadata information types also has a descriptor associated with it.

The pre-defined fields can be organized under each of the five descriptor types. Table 6-2 lists the descriptors and which information class they relate to, along with pre-defined attributes.

## Table 6-2    Descriptors and Pre-defined Fields

| Descriptor Type | Pre-defined Fields |
| --- | --- |
| mbean | name, descriptortype, displayname, persistPolicy, persistPeriod, persistLocation, log, logFile, currencyTimeLimit, export, visibility, presentationString |
| attribute | name, descriptortype, value, default, displayname, getMethod, setMethod, protocolMap, persistPolicy, persistPeriod, currencyTimeLimit, lastUpdatedTimeStamp, iterable, visibility, presentationString |

| Descriptor Type | Pre-defined Fields |
|---|---|
| operation | name, descriptortype, displayName, lastReturnedValue, currencyTimeLimit, lastReturnedTimeStamp, visibility, presentationString, class, targetObject, targetObjectType |
| notification | name, descriptortype, severity, messageId, log, logFile, presentationString |

Don't be overwhelmed by the number of fields; they are not all required. However, if you decide to use one, the value you give it must fall within the allowed values for that field. All of the descriptor types share some common field names, including the following:

♦ name — This is the name of the entity to which this descriptor belongs. For an attribute, this would be the name of the attribute; for an operation, it would be the name of the operation.

♦ descriptortype — One of the four pre-defined types that the JMX specification allows: mbean, attribute, operation, and notification.

♦ displayname — This field represents the value that GUI applications should use when displaying information about the entity in question. This field could be likened to a description.

> **NOTE:** The descriptor type for a model MBean constructor is operation.

Next you'll examine each of the descriptor types starting with MBean descriptor fields — what their various fields mean and the values you can assign to them. Your eye may be drawn to the presentationString field that accompanies the various descriptors, but the XML representation of the various components is still undefined, so you should not attempt to base any code on the XML representation. This would not, of course, keep you from implementing your own model MBean and devising your own schema if you felt the need.

## MBean descriptor fields

The following fields represent the pre-defined fields that may appear in the descriptor for a model MBean. Some of the fields are optional; these are identified in italics. If one of the fields in the MBean descriptor exists in any of the other component descriptors, they override the values in the MBean descriptor; otherwise, the MBean descriptor values provide a default value for the other component descriptors. For example, by specifying a value of true for the log field, you can turn on logging of notifications.

♦ name — The case-sensitive name of the attribute.

♦ descriptortype — A string representing the type of descriptor; must always be a value of attribute.

♦ displayname — A string representing a name for the attribute. If this value is absent, the value of the name field should be used.

♦ *currencyTimeLimit* — The period of time, in seconds, for which the value last returned is not stale. If the next time the operation is executed the last returned value is not stale, the cached value is returned without actually executing the operation of the managed resource. If the currencyTimeLimit value is zero, the value of the operation is never cached; if currencyTimeLimit is given a value of negative one (–1), the value is never stale and will always be returned from the cache.

♦ *protocolMap* — The value of this field must be a descriptor that contains a set of protocol names and value pairs. These protocol name/value pairs enable an attribute to be associated with an external management protocol identifier, like those used with CIM or an SNMP MIB Object ID. This field should be set by the managed resource to enable adapters to present the management interface to a wide variety of management clients.

♦ *persistPolicy* — The value of this field determines if and when an attribute value should be persisted using the store() method of the PersistentMBean interface. It can have one of the following values:

  • Never — The attribute should never be persisted.

  • OnTimer — The attribute is stored whenever the period specified in the persistPeriod elapses.

  • OnUpdate — The attribute is stored every time it is updated. This would occur when setAttribute() or setAttributes() is called or when an accessor method is called directly.

  • NoMoreOftenThan — The attribute is stored each time it is updated unless the updates occur closer together than the value defined in the persistPeriod field.

♦ *persistPeriod* — The value of this field is the number of seconds that must elapse for persistence of an attribute to occur. This field is only valid if the persistPolicy is OnTimer or NoMoreOftenThan. When the value of persistPolicy is OnTimer, the attribute value is stored whenever the persistPeriod begins after the value of the attribute is first set.

♦ *persistLocation* — This is the fully qualified directory where fields representing the persistent MBean should be stored for the RequiredModelMBean implementation. For other implementations, it can be some other value, such as the name of an LDAP server.

♦ *persistName* — This is the filename into which the persistent representation will be stored. For the RequiredModelMBean implementation, this should be the same name as the MBean itself.

♦ *log* — This is a primitive Java boolean; if true, it will cause this notification to be logged to a file. The values in the MBean for this field can override this value.

♦ *logFile* — This is the fully qualified name of of the location where notifications should be logged. If this field is set but the log field is not, no logging is performed.

♦ *visibility* — This field holds an integer with a range of values from one (1) to four (4) indicating the granularity or use of the MBean. A value of 1 indicates an MBean that is used frequently and viewed often, whereas a value of 4 indicates an MBean that is viewed infrequently. The visibility field can be used by adaptors or GUI applications when rendering a graphical display of a management interface.

♦ *presentationString* — This field holds an XML representation of the MBean.

## Attribute descriptor fields

The following fields represent the pre-defined fields that may appear in the descriptor for a model MBean attribute. Optional fields are identified in italics.

♦ `name` — The case-sensitive name of the attribute.

♦ `descriptortype` — A string representing the type of descriptor; this must always be a value of `attribute`.

♦ `displayname` — A string representing a friendly description of the attribute.

♦ `value` — The value of this field is the object representing the value of the attribute if it has been set. The value of this field will be returned to callers if the value of the `currencyTimeLimit` field is not stale.

♦ `default` — The value that will be returned if the `value` field is not set and no `get` method has been defined.

♦ *`getMethod`* — The operation name specified in an operation descriptor that will be used to retrieve the value of the attribute. The value retrieved is returned and also stored in the `value` field of the attribute descriptor.

♦ *`setMethod`* — The name of the operation specified in an operation descriptor that will be used to set the value of the attribute in the managed resource. The value that is passed to the `set` method is also stored in the `value` field of the attribute descriptor.

♦ *`currencyTimeLimit`* — The period of time, in seconds, for which the value last returned is not stale. If the next time the operation is executed the last returned value is not stale, the cached value is returned without actually executing the operation of the managed resource. If the `currencyTimeLimit` value is zero (0), the value of the operation is never cached; if `currencyTimeLimit` is given a value of negative one (−1), the value is never stale and will always be returned from the cache.

♦ *`protocolMap`* — The value of this field must be a descriptor that contains a set of protocol names and value pairs. These protocol name/value pairs enable an attribute to be associated with an external management protocol identifier like those used with CIM or an SNMP MIB Object ID. This field should be set by the managed resource to enable adapters to present the management interface to a wide variety of management clients

♦ *`persistPolicy`* — The value of this field determines if and when an attribute value should be persisted using the `store()` method of the `PersistentMBean` interface. It can have one of the following values:

   • `Never` — The attribute should never be persisted.

   • `OnTimer` — The attribute is stored whenever the period specified in the `persistPeriod` elapses.

   • `OnUpdate` — The attribute is stored every time it is updated. This would occur when `setAttribute()` or `setAttributes()` is called or when an accessor method is called directly.

   • `NoMoreOftenThan` — The attribute is stored each time it is updated unless the updates occur closer together than the value defined in the `persistPeriod` field.

♦ *persistPeriod* — The value of this field is the number of seconds that must elapse for persistence of an attribute to occur. This field is only valid if the `persistPolicy` is `OnTimer` or `NoMoreOftenThan`. When the value of `persistPolicy` is `OnTimer`, the attribute value is stored whenever the `persistPeriod` begins after the value of the attribute is first set.

♦ `lastUpdatedTimeStamp` — The time stamp of when the `value` field was updated.

♦ `iterable` — A primitive Java `boolean` indicating whether or not a value can be enumerated. A value of `true` indicates that the attribute is enumerable, and a value of `false` indicates it is not.

♦ *visibility* — An integer with a range of values from 1 to 4, indicating the granularity or use of the attribute. A value of 1 indicates an attribute that is used frequently and viewed often, whereas a value of 4 indicates an attribute that is viewed infrequently. The visibility field can be used by adaptors or GUI applications when rendering a graphical display of a management interface.

♦ *presentationString* — An XML representation of this attribute.

## Operation descriptor fields

The following fields represent the pre-defined fields that may appear in the descriptor for a model MBean operation. Optional fields are identified in italics. Field values specified at this level override those that appear at the MBean level.

♦ `name` — The case-sensitive name of the operation.

♦ `descriptortype` — A string representing the type of descriptor; this must always be a value of `operation`.

♦ `displayname` — A string representing a friendly description of the operation.

♦ `classname` — A string representing the name of the class in which the operation resides.

♦ `targetObject` — An object representing the target of the operation or where the operation resides.

♦ `targetObjectType` — A string indicating the Java type of the object in which the operation resides.

♦ *lastReturnedValue* — The value that was returned from the operation the last time the operation was executed. Values from the execution of operations can be cached if the `currencyTimeLimit` field value is greater than zero.

♦ *currencyTimeLimit* — The period of time, in seconds, for which the value last returned is not stale. If the next time the operation is executed the last returned value is not stale, the cached value is returned without actually executing the operation of the managed resource. If the `currencyTimeLimit` value is zero, the value of the operation is never cached; if `currencyTimeLimit` is given a value of −1, the value is never stale and will always be returned from the cache.

♦ `lastReturnedTimeStamp` — The time stamp of when the `lastReturnedValue` field was updated.

♦ *visibility* — An integer with a range of values from 1 to 4, indicating the granularity or use of the operation. A value of 1 indicates an operation that is used frequently and viewed often, whereas a value of 4 indicates an operation that is viewed infrequently. The visibility field can be used by adaptors or GUI applications when rendering a graphical display of a management interface.

♦ *presentationString* — An XML representation of this operation.

## Notification descriptor fields

The following fields represent the pre-defined fields that may appear in the descriptor for a model MBean notification. Optional fields are identified in italics. Field values specified at the notification descriptor level override those that appear at the MBean level.

♦ name — The case-sensitive name of the notification or its type.

♦ descriptortype — A string representing the type of the descriptor; it must always have a value of notification.

♦ severity — An integer with a value of 0 to 6, with each integer value representing one of the following meanings:

  • Unknown, Indeterminate

  • Non recoverable

  • Critical, Failure

  • Major, Severe

  • Minor, Marginal, or Error

  • Warning

  • Normal, Cleared, or Informative

♦ messageId — An ID for the notification.

♦ log — A primitive Java boolean that if true, will cause this notification to be logged to a file. The values in the MBean for this field can override this value.

♦ logFile — The fully qualified name of the location where notifications should be logged. If this field is set but the log field is not, no logging is performed.

♦ *PresentationString* — An XML encoded string that can be used to present the notification.

Although this certainly seems to be a lot of choices to make, keep in mind that if you decide not to set these values, the majority of them are disabled by default. For example, persistence does not occur automatically, and notifications are not logged automatically.

## Using a descriptor

After you have created a descriptor, you need to associate it with the entity that it represents. Because descriptors are not general enough to be applied to any of the different MBean information components, you must assign a type to the descriptor. This means that when you create a descriptor and set its descriptor type to `attribute`, the descriptor has to be associated with a `ModelMBeanAttributeInfo` object.

The way that you associate a descriptor with its related information object is either by specifying the descriptor in the constructor, or by using the `setDescriptor()` method. The `setDescriptor()` method is specified in the `DescriptorAccess` interface, which also defines the `getDescriptor()` method. All the model MBean information classes implement the `DescriptorAccess` interface. If you don't use the `setDescriptor()` method or the constructor, a default descriptor is assigned until replaced.

When you use the `setDescriptor()` method, the descriptor you provide completely replaces any previous descriptor that was specified. Each of the model MBean information classes has a constructor variant that takes a descriptor as its last argument.

A problem with a descriptor can render it invalid. As you saw in an earlier example, the result of an invalid descriptor can be either an exception or a reversion to a default descriptor, which may contain a minimum of values depending on the information component type. The following code snippet shows two variations of how to specify a descriptor for an operation:

```
Descriptor startDesc = new DescriptorSupport();
startDesc .setField("name","start");
startDesc .setField("descriptortype","operation");
startDesc .setField("role","operation");
startDesc .setField("class","PrinterBean");
startDesc .setField("targetObject",prtBean);
startDesc .setField("targetObjectType","ObjectReference");

ModelMBeanOperationInfo opInfo1 =
    new ModelMBeanOperationInfo("start",
                                "Start the printer",
                                null,
                                null,
                                MBeanOperationInfo.INFO,
                                startDesc);

//* The ModelMBeanOperationInfo declaration could be change to this

ModelMBeanOperationInfo opInfo1 =
    new ModelMBeanOperationInfo("start",
                                "Start the printer",
                                null,
                                null,
                                MBeanOperationInfo.INFO);
opInfo1.setDescriptor(startDesc);
```

The two variations of specifying the descriptor for the `ModelMBeanOperationInfo` class are functionally equivalent, although in the second case, the `ModelMBeanOperationInfo` declaration will cause a default descriptor to be assigned until the `setDescriptor()` method is called and it is replaced by the descriptor we created.

Descriptors can easily be changed at runtime, so you can use the `ModelMBeanInfo` class to get a reference to other metadata classes, such as `ModelMBeanAttributeInfo`, and replace its descriptor dynamically. This is done by first getting a reference to the `ModelMBean`. Then, use the `getModelMBeanInfo()` method, get the relevant `ModelMBeanAttributeInfo` object from it, and call the `setDescriptor()` method on the `ModelMBeanAttributeInfo` class. You can either construct a new descriptor or use the `getDescriptor()` method to retrieve the current descriptor. You must then use the `setDescriptor()` method to replace it because the `getDescriptor()` method returns a copy of the descriptor, not a reference to the descriptor.

## Finding attributes and operations

Normally, when you attempt to access an attribute or operation of an MBean, you can determine with certainty whether the attribute or operation exists in the MBean. The management interface supplies you with this information at runtime so you can make decisions about the information you can access.

Model MBeans are somewhat different, because there is some behind-the-scenes sleight of hand going on with respect to where an attribute or operation really exists. This means that you can define a `ModelMBeanAttributeInfo` object that defines an attribute called `Name`. This attribute may not actually exist in the model MBean itself; it may be intended to exist in the managed resource of the model MBean. However, to access this attribute, you must define an operation using the `ModelMBeanOperationInfo` class, as well as a descriptor that indicates the class in which the operation exists.

At runtime, when you invoke the `getAttribute()` method of the `MBeanServer` interface, the MBean Server will first attempt to look for the accessor method in the model MBean class. If it doesn't find the method there, it will then look in the descriptor for an operation by the same name and determine what class that operation is in. If both of those lookups fail, an exception will be thrown. In practice, the second lookup will not fail unless you have not defined the accessor method in your managed resource.

The attribute policy discussed earlier in this chapter can also have an effect on attribute access. If an attribute value caching policy is in effect, the attribute value may be retrieved from the descriptor, and not the managed resource. In any event, the value of an attribute may be cached in the descriptor for faster access.

# ModelMBean Metadata Classes

Descriptors exist only as part of other classes, which also provide meta information about model MBeans. In Chapter 4, you saw classes such as `MBeanAttributeInfo`, `MBeanConstructorInfo`, `MBeanNotificationInfo`, and `MBeanOperationInfo`, which describe the individual components of the management interface of an MBean. Model MBeans are different in that they have similar classes, but the classes are named differently. The model MBean metadata classes are named by prefixing the standard meta information classes with "Model." For example, `ModelMBeanAttributeInfo` is equal in function to `MBeanAttributeInfo`. The model MBean metadata classes are as follows:

- ModelMBeanInfo

- ModelMBeanAttributeInfo

- ModelMBeanConstructorInfo

- ModelMBeanNotificationInfo

- ModelMBeanOperationInfo

The Model MBean meta information classes also have a descriptor, which serves to further describe and extend the management interface of model MBeans. Model MBeans do not define a ModelMBeanParameterInfo class; rather, they use the MBeanParameterInfo class to describe parameters to operations of model MBeans.

The model MBean metadata classes can also specify a descriptor in the constructor, in addition to using the setDescriptor() method of the DescriptorAccess interface. The following code snippet illustrates the similarity between the two sets of meta information classes by constructing ModelMBeanAttributeInfo and MBeanAttributeInfo classes:

```
ModelMBeanAttributeInfo modelAttr =
    new ModelMBeanAttributeInfo("Name",              /* name */
                                "java.lang.String",  /* Java type */
                                "Name of attribute", /* description */
                                true,                /* readable */
                                true,                /* writeable */
                                false);              /* is is     */

MBeanAttributeInfo mbeanAttr =
    new MBeanAttributeInfo("Name",              /* name */
                           "java.lang.String",  /* Java type */
                           "Name of attribute", /* description */
                           true,                /* readable */
                           true,                /* writable */
                           false);              /* is is */
```

Except for the class name, these two lines of code are nearly identical. Therefore, you construct the information classes just as you did for standard and dynamic MBeans. The main difference is that model MBeans have additional constructors that take a descriptor as the last argument. This section does not describe how to construct an instance of each of the model MBean classes because they are nearly identical to those shown in Chapter 5. Any differences regarding descriptors were covered in the "Descriptors" section earlier in this chapter.

Model MBeans use the ModelMBeanInfo interface to serve as the main information class; it is functionally similar to the MBeanInfo class associated with standard and dynamic MBeans. An interesting difference is that ModelMBeanInfo is an interface, whereas MBeanInfo is declared as a class. The ModelMBeanInfo provides additional methods for retrieving specific information classes, in addition to retrieving all the information classes for one of the component types, such as attributes or operations. Table 6-3 describes the methods of the ModelMBeanInfo interface.

**Table 6-3    ModelMBeanInfo Interface**

| Method | Description |
|---|---|
| `clone()` | Returns a copy of the `ModelMBeanInfo` class |
| `getAttribute(java.lang.String attrName)` | Returns a `ModelMBeanAttributeInfo` object for the named attribute |
| `getAttributes()` | Returns an array of `ModelMBeanAttributeInfo` objects |
| `getClassName()` | Returns a `java.lang.String` representing the name of the MBean class |
| `getConstructors()` | Returns an array of `ModelMBeanConstructorInfo` objects |
| `getDescription()` | Returns a `java.lang.String` representing a description of the MBean |
| `getDescriptor(java.lang.String descriptorName,java.lang.String descriptorType)` | Returns a descriptor using the name and type of the descriptor |
| `getDescriptors(java.lang.String descriptorType)` | Returns all descriptors for the MBean |
| `getMBeanDescriptor()` | Returns the descriptor for the ModelMBean |
| `getNotification()` | Returns a single `ModelMBeanNotificationInfo` object using the notification type |
| `getNotifications()` | Returns an array of `ModelMBeanNotificationInfo` objects |
| `getOperation(java.lang.String opName)` | Returns a single `ModelMBeanOperationInfo` object using the operation name specified |
| `getOperations()` | Returns an array of `ModelMBeanOperationInfo` objects |
| `setDescriptor(javax.management .Descriptor desc,java.lang.String descriptorType)` | Sets the descriptor for a specified descriptor type in all info classes |
| `setDescriptors(javax.management .Descriptor[] descriptors)` | Sets all the descriptors for the ModelMBean in all info classes |
| `setMBeanDescriptor(javax .management.Descriptor)` | Sets the descriptor for the model MBean |

When you construct the management interface for a model MBean, you have to create an instance of a class that you can operate on. Standard and dynamic MBeans work with the `MBeanInfo` class, which defines a constructor that takes the various arguments, although you can only define the interface dynamically for dynamic MBeans. Standard MBeans fill out their `MBeanInfo` classes using introspection.

Model MBeans use the `ModelMBeanInfoSupport` class to construct instances of the `ModelMBeanInfo` interface. The `ModelMBeanInfoSupport` class takes arguments that represent the attributes, operations, notifications, and descriptors for a model MBean. This class also extends from the `MBeanInfo` class and inherits the `getClassName()` and `getDescription()` methods from that class. Despite these minor differences and the addition of descriptors, constructing the management interface for a model MBean and a dynamic MBean are very similar.

Once you have created an instance of the `ModelMBeanInfo` class, you need to associate it with the model MBean using the `setModelMBeanInfo()` method of the `ModelMBean` interface.

## Creating a ModelMBean

When you define the management interface for a model MBean, you are defining attributes and operations that exist in either the model MBean or the resource that it manages. The section on descriptors earlier in this chapter describes how the information classes and descriptors work together to associate the management interface with the managed resource.

In Chapter 5, you learned how to construct an `MBeanAttributeInfo` that represents an attribute that may be in the MBean, or in a remote object represented by the MBean. This is not too difficult because the dynamic MBean can in turn access a remote object to retrieve the attribute value. This is the case sometimes with model MBeans as well. If you use the `RequiredModelMBean` implementation, you have no control over what attributes and operations exist in the `RequiredModelMBean` unless you subclass it, which is somewhat self-defeating. The `RequiredModelMBean` is designed to provide you with an out-of-the-box model MBean implementation that you can work with.

Model MBean attributes that are defined via descriptors and associated with a `ModelMBeanAttributeInfo` class are assumed to exist in the managed resource. Therefore, if you skip a step when constructing the interface and the application fails because it says it cannot find the attribute you want, make sure that the proper descriptors have been constructed for your attribute.

Now that you've taken a look at how to build the various information classes, it's time to examine the `ModelMBean` interface that is used to represent an instance of a model MBean.

## The ModelMBean interface

The `ModelMBean` interface is used to implement resources as model MBeans. The `ModelMBean` interface only declares two methods, and it gets the majority of its functionality through inheritance. The `ModelMBean` interface inherits methods from the `DynamicMBean`, `PersistentMBean`, `ModelMBeanNotificationBroadcaster`, and

`NotificationBroadcaster` interfaces. This enables the `ModelMBean` interface to represent an MBean with a lot of built-in functionality. Of course, you must implement a lot of this functionality if you want your own model MBean. The alternative is to use the pre-built functionality of the `RequiredModelMBean` class. Table 6-4 describes the declared methods of the `ModelMBean` interface.

### Table 6-4    ModelMBean Interface Methods

| Method Name | Description |
|---|---|
| `setManagedResource(java.lang.Object mr,java.lang.String mrType)` | Sets the managed resource that this model MBean represents. It takes an object reference and a string indicating the type of managed resource. |
| `setModelMBeanInfo(javax.management .modelmbean.ModelMBeanInfo)` | Sets the `ModelMBeanInfo` class for the model MBean. This essentially sets the management interface for the model MBean. |

### The managed resource

Because the goal of all MBeans is to represent a managed resource, at some point an MBean must become aware of the resource it is managing. This is usually accomplished by the managed resource establishing an MBean representation of itself in the MBean Server, or by an MBean locating the managed resource and establishing a link to it. The former method is probably the easiest because the management system does not have to constantly check whether — or be notified when — the managed resource is present.

You use the `setManagedResource()` method of the `ModelMBean` interface to provide a reference to an object to be managed. The reference you pass to this method could be to an Enterprise JavaBean, a normal Java object, or an RMI remote interface.

> **NOTE:** In the current version of the Sun JMX 1.0 reference implementation, only normal Java object references are supported as arguments.

Because the `ModelMBean` interface has a specific method for associating the MBean with a managed object, model MBeans are somewhat easier to use than other MBean types such as standard or dynamic MBeans. For example, with other types of MBeans, it's up to the MBean developer and application developer to determine how a standard MBean will interact with its managed resource.

The `setManagedResource()` method takes two arguments: The first is the reference to the actual object, and the second is a string representing the class name of the object being managed. In a managed system, you can envision how an application would locate an `MBeanServer`, locate the `ModelMBean` implementation, and then call its `setManagedResource()` method. A `ModelMBean` can only represent a single managed resource, although the managed resource may represent a larger set of managed resources.

The `ModelMBeanInfo` class is set externally to the actual implementation of the MBean, either through the constructor of the `RequiredModelMBean` class or through the `setModelMBeanInfo()` method of the `ModelMBean` interface. This gives you the capability to create the management interface externally in a number of ways. In Chapter 5, you learned how the `MBeanInfo` class is created dynamically, either by executing a set of Java code or by using the Java Reflection API. In either case, the `MBeanInfo` class is set from within the MBean.

## Registering the resource

A managed resource normally seeks out the model MBean that will represent it and then configures the model MBean with information about itself. This information includes the typical things you have seen so far, such as attributes, operations, notifications, and constructors.

Seeking out the model MBean can occur in a variety of ways. For example, a managed resource that runs in the same JVM as the MBean Server might use the static `findMBeanServer()` method of the `MBeanServerFactory` class. This method can be used to return a single instance of the MBean Server. Then, using the MBean Server, you can find the model MBean you want to use. Another possible means of finding the MBean Server uses a remote protocol involving JNDI or RMI. Chapter 12 covers the use of RMI to create a connector that can be attached to a remote MBean Server and interact with MBeans that are registered in a remote JMX agent.

You can also find the model MBean using one of the methods described in Chapter 9, such as `queryMBeans()` or `getObjectInstance()`. These will return either an `ObjectName` or `ObjectInstance` that you can use in subsequent calls to `MBeanServer` methods to configure the model MBean.

You can configure the model MBean using the `setModelMBeanInfo()` and `setManagedResource()` methods of the `ModelMBean` interface. You register the resource the model MBean using the `setManagedResource()` method. The object reference that is passed to this method is what the model MBean will invoke operations against and retrieve the values of attributes from. Setting the managed resource of a model MBean does not expose any sort of management interface about the resource. You must create and set the `ModelMBean` info class for the managed resource and call the `setModelMBeanInfo()` method. Take a look at a simple example that sets the managed resource of a model MBean.

This example uses a class called `PrinterBean`, which is a simple Java class, not an MBean. Recall that the managed resource does not have to be an MBean. Rather, it can be a set of specific types, one of which is a value of `ObjectReference`. Listing 6-3 shows the source of the `PrinterBean`. In later chapters in this book, you'll look at more complicated examples.

**Listing 6-3: PrinterBean class to be managed**

```
public class PrinterBean {

        private String name = "";
        private int jobs = 0;
```

```
        public int getJobs(){
                return jobs;
        }

        public void setJobs(int n){
                jobs = n;
        }

        public String getName(){
                return name;
        }

        public void setName(String n){
                name = n;
        }

        public void start(){
                System.out.println("Starting printer");
        }

        public void stop(){
                System.out.println("Stopping printer");
        }
}
```

This class defines two attributes: `name` and `jobs`, with accessor methods for each. It also defines two operations: `start()` and `stop()`. Although this class looks similar in structure to an MBean, it's only a coincidence. You could just as easily name a couple of the methods something like `getTheName()` and `setTheName()`.

The code to implement management of this class is shown next in Listing 6-4. This application creates a model MBean and then sets its managed resource as an instance of the `PrinterBean`. It then proceeds to define the management interface of the class, as well as some management information about the model MBean itself. It then invokes a couple of management methods to get the `Name` attribute and invoke the `start()` operation.

**Listing 6-4: Managing the PrinterBean**

```
import javax.management.ObjectName;
import javax.management.MBeanServer;
import javax.management.MBeanServerFactory;
import javax.management.Descriptor;
import javax.management.MBeanOperationInfo;
import javax.management.modelmbean.DescriptorSupport;
import javax.management.modelmbean.ModelMBeanInfo;
import javax.management.modelmbean.ModelMBeanAttributeInfo;
import javax.management.modelmbean.ModelMBeanInfoSupport;
import javax.management.modelmbean.ModelMBeanOperationInfo;
import javax.management.modelmbean.RequiredModelMBean;
```

```java
public class ModelMBeanJMXAgentResource {

    private static MBeanServer server = null;

    public ModelMBeanJMXAgentResource() {
        server = MBeanServerFactory.createMBeanServer();
    }

    public static void main(String[] args) {

            PrinterBean prtBean = new PrinterBean();

        ModelMBeanJMXAgentResource agent =
             new ModelMBeanJMXAgentResource();

            //JMXDebug debug = new JMXDebug(agent);

            try {

                ObjectName simpleObject =
                    new ObjectName("ModelMBean:type=model");

                RequiredModelMBean bean = new RequiredModelMBean();

                DescriptorSupport beanDesc = new DescriptorSupport();
                beanDesc.setField("descriptortype","mbean");
                beanDesc.setField("displayName",
                                    bean.getClass().getName());
                beanDesc.setField("name",bean.getClass().getName());

                bean.setManagedResource(prtBean,"ObjectReference");

                // Create the management interface

                Descriptor nameDscr = new DescriptorSupport();
                nameDscr.setField("name","Name");
                nameDscr.setField("getMethod","getName");
                nameDscr.setField("setMethod","setName");
                nameDscr.setField("descriptortype","attribute");

                ModelMBeanAttributeInfo attrInfo1 =
                    new ModelMBeanAttributeInfo("Name",
                                                "java.lang.String",
                                                "Name of attribute",
                                                true,
                                                true,
                                                false,
                                                nameDscr);
```

```
ModelMBeanAttributeInfo attrInfo2 =
    new ModelMBeanAttributeInfo("Jobs",
                                "java.lang.Integer",
                                "Number of jobs",
                                true,
                                true,
                                false);


Descriptor startDesc = new DescriptorSupport();
startDesc .setField("name","start");
startDesc .setField("descriptortype","operation");
startDesc .setField("role","operation");
startDesc .setField("class","PrinterBean");
startDesc .setField("targetObject",prtBean);
startDesc .setField("targetType",
                    "ObjectReference");

ModelMBeanOperationInfo opInfo1 =
    new ModelMBeanOperationInfo("start",
                                "Start the printer",
                                null,
                                null,
                                MBeanOperationInfo.INFO,
                                startDesc);

ModelMBeanOperationInfo opInfo2 =
    new ModelMBeanOperationInfo("stop",
                                "Stop the printer",
                                null,
                                null,
                                MBeanOperationInfo.INFO);

Descriptor nameDesc = new DescriptorSupport();
nameDesc.setField("name","getName");
nameDesc.setField("descriptortype","operation");
nameDesc.setField("role","getter");
nameDesc.setField("class","PrinterBean");
nameDesc.setField("targetObject",prtBean);
nameDesc.setField("targetType",
                  "ObjectReference");

ModelMBeanOperationInfo opInfo3 =
    new ModelMBeanOperationInfo("getName",
                        "Get the name of the printer",
                        null,
                        "java.lang.String",
                        MBeanOperationInfo.INFO,
                        nameDesc);
```

```
                    ModelMBeanInfoSupport mldInfo =
                     new ModelMBeanInfoSupport(agent.getClass().getName(),
                                           "RequiredModelMBean",
                                           new
ModelMBeanAttributeInfo[]{attrInfo1,

attrInfo2} /*attribute*/,

                                                  null /*constructor*/,
                                                  new
ModelMBeanOperationInfo[]{opInfo1,

opInfo2,

opInfo3} /*operations*/,

                                                  null /*notifications*/,
                                                  beanDesc);

                bean.setModelMBeanInfo(mldInfo);

                // Register the MBean

                server.registerMBean(bean,simpleObject);

                // Manage the resource

                String str =
                    (String)server.getAttribute(simpleObject,"Name");

                System.out.println("Str = " + str);

                server.invoke(simpleObject,
                             "start",
                             new Object[]{},
                             new String[]{});

            } catch (Exception ex){
                 ex.printStackTrace();
            }

    }

}
```

That's a lot of code to digest, so let's take it one piece at a time. By the end of the explanation, I hope that you'll understand the sequence of events that takes place when setting up the management interface and setting the managed resource of the model MBean.

The sequence of events shown in Figure 6-4 illustrates the normal mode of operation of a model MBean. In some cases, the attribute `Name` does not exist in the `PrinterBean` class. When the `getAttribute()` method is invoked, the accessor method is looked up in the descriptor and the `getName()` method of the `PrinterBean` class is invoked.

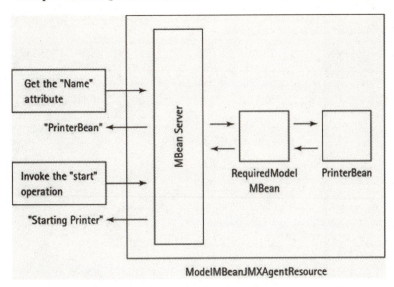

**Figure 6-4:** Using the PrinterBean from the RequiredModelMBean.

The same sequence of lookup occurs when invoking the `start()` operation. The descriptor is checked for the existence of the method that is invoked on the `PrinterBean` by the MBean Server.

## Persistence of model MBeans

The persistence policy described at the beginning of this chapter is implemented using the `PersistentMBean` interface, which defines two methods: `load()` and `store()`. These are called to initialize and save the state of a model MBean, respectively. MBeans of other types, such as standard MBeans, can also make use of the `PersistentMBean` interface. The persistent policy is an optional feature, which means a model MBean does not have to support persistence even though it implements the `PersistentMBean` interface.

The `load()` method is normally called during construction of a model MBean before it has been registered in the MBean Server. The information it loads could be from sources such as a flat file, a database, or an LDAP directory. Under most circumstances, it is the responsibility of the MBean implementing the `PersistentMBean` interface to call this method; but in the case of model MBeans, the MBean Server is supposed to call this method based on the values found in the descriptor of the MBean.

The `store()` method is called on demand or based on the values of the `persistPolicy` descriptor field described in the "Pre-defined descriptor fields" section earlier in this chapter.

The MBean can, of course, store the state using the same destinations that the load() method uses for sources. The RequiredModelMBean uses these fields to determine when to persist its state. When persisting the managed resource, it must implement the java.io .Serializable interface. Listing 6-5 shows the source of the PrinterBean class used for this example.

**Listing 6-5: The PrinterBean managed resource**

```
import java.io.Serializable;

public class PrinterBean implements Serializable {

        private String name = "PrintBean";
        private int jobs = 0;

        public Integer getJobs(){
                return new Integer(jobs);
        }

        public void setJobs(Integer n){
                jobs = n.intValue();
        }

        public String getName(){
                System.out.println("Calling getName()................");
                return name;
        }

        public void setName(String n){
                System.out.println("Calling setName()................");
                name = n;
        }

        public void start(){
                System.out.println("Starting printer");
        }

        public void stop(){
                System.out.println("Stopping printer");
        }

}
```

Take a look at a simple example that illustrates model MBean persistence. This example establishes the descriptor fields for making the model MBean persist when an attribute changes. The MBean is persisted into a file named persistmbean.txt. Listing 6-6 shows the source of the JMX agent that loads the model MBean and the PrinterBean that is the managed resource and then sets an attribute value on the PrinterBean.

**Listing 6-6: Using model MBean persistence**

```
import javax.management.Attribute;
import javax.management.AttributeChangeNotification;
import javax.management.ObjectName;
import javax.management.ObjectInstance;
import javax.management.MBeanServer;
import javax.management.MBeanServerFactory;
import javax.management.Notification;
import javax.management.NotificationListener;
import javax.management.MBeanOperationInfo;
import javax.management.Descriptor;
import javax.management.modelmbean.DescriptorSupport;
import javax.management.modelmbean.ModelMBeanInfo;
import javax.management.modelmbean.ModelMBeanAttributeInfo;
import javax.management.modelmbean.ModelMBeanInfoSupport;
import javax.management.modelmbean.ModelMBeanOperationInfo;
import javax.management.MBeanParameterInfo;
import javax.management.modelmbean.RequiredModelMBean;

public class ModelMBeanJMXAgentPersist
          implements NotificationListener {

    private static MBeanServer server = null;

    public ModelMBeanJMXAgentPersist () {
        server = MBeanServerFactory.createMBeanServer();
    }

    public static void main(String[] args) {

        ModelMBeanJMXAgentPersist agent =
              new ModelMBeanJMXAgentPersist ();

            try {

                ObjectName simpleObject =
                        new ObjectName("ModelMBean:type=model");

                PrinterBean prtBean = new PrinterBean();

                RequiredModelMBean bean = new RequiredModelMBean();

                DescriptorSupport beanDesc = new DescriptorSupport();
                beanDesc.setField("descriptortype","mbean");
                beanDesc.setField("displayName",
                                    bean.getClass().getName());
                beanDesc.setField("name",bean.getClass().getName());
                beanDesc.setField("persistlocation",".");
```

```
            beanDesc.setField("persistname","persistmbean.txt");
            beanDesc.setField("persistpolicy","onupdate");

            // Create the management interface

            Descriptor nameDscr = new DescriptorSupport();
            nameDscr.setField("name","Name");
            nameDscr.setField("getMethod","getName");
            nameDscr.setField("setMethod","setName");
            nameDscr.setField("descriptortype","attribute");
            // Setting the persistpolicy to "update" causes an
exception

            ModelMBeanAttributeInfo attrInfo1 =
                new ModelMBeanAttributeInfo("Name",
                                            "java.lang.String",
                                            "Name of attribute",
                                            true,
                                            true,
                                            false,
                                            nameDscr);

            Descriptor nameDesc = new DescriptorSupport();
            nameDesc.setField("name","setName");
            nameDesc.setField("descriptortype","operation");
            nameDesc.setField("role","setter");
            nameDesc.setField("class","PrinterBean");
            nameDesc.setField("targetObject",prtBean);
            nameDesc.setField("targetType",
                        "ObjectReference");

            MBeanParameterInfo parmInfo =
                new MBeanParameterInfo("Name",
                                        "java.lang.String",
                                        "The name");

            ModelMBeanOperationInfo opInfo3 =
                new ModelMBeanOperationInfo("setName",
                        "Get the name of the printer",
                        new MBeanParameterInfo[]{parmInfo},
                        null,
                        MBeanOperationInfo.INFO,
                        nameDesc);

            Descriptor getDesc = new DescriptorSupport();
            getDesc.setField("name","getName");
            getDesc.setField("descriptortype","operation");
            getDesc.setField("role","getter");
            getDesc.setField("class","PrinterBean");
```

```
                getDesc.setField("targetObject",prtBean);
                getDesc.setField("targetType",
                              "ObjectReference");

                ModelMBeanOperationInfo opInfo4 =
                    new ModelMBeanOperationInfo("getName",
                                "Get the name of the printer",
                                new MBeanParameterInfo[]{},
                                "java.lang.String",
                                MBeanOperationInfo.INFO,
                                getDesc);

                // ModelMBean Info class
        ModelMBeanInfoSupport mldInfo =
                new ModelMBeanInfoSupport(agent.getClass().getName(),
                          "RequiredModelMBean",
                        new ModelMBeanAttributeInfo[]{attrInfo1}
/*attribute*/,
                                          null /*constructor*/,
                                          new
ModelMBeanOperationInfo[]{opInfo3,

opInfo4} /*operations*/,

                                          null /*notifications*/,
                                          beanDesc);


                bean.setModelMBeanInfo(mldInfo);

                bean.setManagedResource(prtBean,"ObjectReference");

                // Add Attribute Notification Listener
                bean.addAttributeChangeNotificationListener(agent,
                                              "Name",
                                              agent);

                // Register the MBean

                ObjectInstance inst =
                        server.registerMBean(bean,simpleObject);

                if (inst != null) {
                    // Change "Name" attribute value so it persists
                    ObjectName objName = inst.getObjectName();
                    if (objName != null) {
                        System.out.println("Setting attribute....on " +
                                        objName.getCanonicalName());
                        server.setAttribute(objName,
                                    new Attribute("Name","foobar"));
```

```
                        }else
                            System.out.println("ObjectName is null");
                    } else {
                        System.out.println("ObjectInstance is null");
                }

            } catch (Exception ex){
                    ex.printStackTrace();
            }


        }

        // Listen for notifications
        public void handleNotification(Notification notif,
                                       Object handBack){
            AttributeChangeNotification attNote =
                        (AttributeChangeNotification)notif;
            System.out.println("Attribute Change for : " +
                            attNote.getAttributeName());
            System.out.println("Attribute Old Value: " +
                            attNote.getOldValue());
            System.out.println("Attribute New Value: " +
                            attNote.getNewValue());

        }

}
```

The application begins by creating an instance of the PrinterBean and the RequiredModelMBean, and then proceeds to build the descriptors and metadata classes that describe the interface. The PrinterBean actually includes some operations that are not listed in this example, such as start() and stop(). The code to build the metaclasses for these operations has been omitted for brevity. At this point, it will be more useful to focus on building the information classes for the attribute you will be working with.

The MBean descriptor has the persistlocation, persistname, and persistpolicy fields set to the values F:/files/JMX-Hungryminds, persistmbean.txt, and always, respectively. This causes the MBean to persist into the file named persistmbean.txt whenever an action occurs that causes persistence, such as an attribute value change.

After all the required information classes have been built, you can proceed to build the ModelMBeanInfo class by adding the information classes for the Name attribute along with the operations used to access this attribute. The ModelMBeanInfo class is then passed to the setModelMBeanInfo() method. The instance of the PrinterBean object created at the beginning of the application is passed to the setManagedResource() method. You finish the process by calling the registerMBean() method, which registers the model MBean in the MBean Server.

To cause the persistence process to occur, you call the `setAttribute()` method of the `MBeanServer` interface. When an attribute change occurs in a model MBean, an `AttributeChangeNotification` notification is sent to registered listeners.

> **CAUTION:** There is a bug in the Sun JMX 1.0 reference implementation that causes an exception in the model MBean implementation when dealing with attribute change notifications. Normally, you do not have to register interest in notifications, but if you do not register as an attribute change listener, an `MBeanException` will occur.

Before you register the model MBean, you add an attribute change listener to the model MBean and have the JMX agent implement the `NotificationListener` interface. When the attribute change occurs, you print the attribute `name`, and its old value and the new value.

When the persistence occurs, you do not receive any indication. If you're interested in seeing the events bouncing around inside the JMX implementation, you can use the `JMXDebug` class introduced in Chapter 8. After you run the application, you should have a file named `persistmbean.txt` in whichever directory you used for this example. The output from running this example looks like the following:

```
Setting attribute....on ModelMBean:type=model
Calling getName()...............
Calling setName()...............
Attribute Change for : Name
Attribute Old Value: PrintBean
Attribute New Value: foobar
```

The messages indicating when `setName()` and `getName()` are being called are printed from the `PrinterBean` class. To reinitialize the model MBean, you need to change the name of the file specified in the `persistname` field to match that of the class name. The model MBean will automatically look for this filename after calling the `load()` method of the `PersistentMBean` interface.

In the "Pre-defined descriptor fields" section earlier in the chapter, you learned about the various descriptor field settings that control persistence, most of which you just saw demonstrated. Another field named `persistperiod` can control whether or not persistence is performed. This field and its value are only applicable when the `persistpolicy` field is set to a value of `ontimer` or `nomoreoftenthan`.

# Open MBeans

In the same spirit of model MBeans, an open MBean presents its information using rich metadata that describes its attributes and operations. It also uses a strongly typed set of classes to represent method return values and arguments to its methods. With a rich description of its management interface and a small set of datatypes, open MBeans are as easy or easier to use than any of the MBeans defined in the JMX specification. Because of their open nature and the small set of datatypes they work with, open MBeans can be easily understood.

Open MBeans are dynamic and implement the `DynamicMBean` interface; there is no `OpenMBean` interface. An open MBean indicates its type by returning an `OpenMBeanInfo` class from the getMBeanInfo() method of the DynamicMBean interface. The OpenMBeanInfo class extends from the MBeanInfo class.

As with the ModelMBeanInfo and MBeanInfo classes, a developer must ensure the integrity of the open MBean classes, given their dynamic nature. The contents of the OpenMBeanInfo class may not represent a real view of the management interface because it's dynamic. Components of the management interface for any MBean include the operations and attributes that define various values of the MBean and its managed resource. The open MBean part of the JMX specification defines a small set of universal datatypes, as well as a requirement that all operations use these types for arguments and return values.

## Open MBean datatypes

The datatypes used as attribute, method return, and argument values must be one of the defined Java wrapper types for primitive values. For example, if a method takes a primitive int as an argument, you must define it as a java.lang.Integer, which is the object type for an integer. If an operation returns a primitive double, it must return a java.lang.Double. The list of wrapper types is as follows:

- ◆ java.lang.void
- ◆ java.lang.Boolean
- ◆ java.lang.Byte
- ◆ java.lang.Character
- ◆ java.lang.String
- ◆ java.lang.Short
- ◆ java.lang.Integer
- ◆ java.lang.Long
- ◆ java.lang.Float
- ◆ java.lang.Double
- ◆ javax.management.ObjectName
- ◆ javax.management.openmbean.CompositeData
- ◆ javax.management.openmbean.TabularData

There is also a defined javax.management.openmbean.ArrayType that is used to represent single or multidimensional arrays.

The last two items in the preceding list, CompositeData and TabularData, are interfaces, which are used to represent aggregates of the other types in the list. These interfaces are used to define complex datatypes that can be of different types and of different levels of containment. For example, an instance of the CompositeData interface can hold a reference to one or more CompositeData interface instances.

An implementation of the CompositeData interface is used to represent a hashtable of values that you can access using an index. The TabularData interface is used to represent a collection of `CompositeData` objects from which items can be retrieved using an index. When you create an instance of the `CompositeData` interface, it is immutable. In other words, it cannot be changed — items cannot be added or removed from it. Instances of the `TabularData` interface can be changed, however, and new rows can be added or removed.

The JMX specification defines a `CompositeDataSupport` class and `TabularDataSupport` class, which serve as implementations of the `CompositeData` and `TabularData` interfaces. You can enumerate items and find items based on keys that are string values. The keys in the set are maintained by the `CompositeDataSupport` class when new items are added to the set.

The `TabularDataSupport` class enables you to construct tables of information from `CompositeData` interface instances. The tables consist of rows and columns, and the columns are comprised of the items in the `CompositeData` interface, which are used as header names.

When working with different types of data in JMX, and specifically open MBeans, it is necessary to indicate the datatype of the data using a string. However, because of the open and general nature of open MBeans, a simple string value does not suffice. The JMX specification defines the `OpenType` superclass; and the `CompositeType`, `TabularType`, `SimpleType`, and `ArrayType` subclasses, which are returned from the `getOpenType()` method. These types provide information at runtime about the universal datatypes used with open MBeans for all except the wrapper datatypes defined in the Java API.

All of these types provide information such as descriptions, number of dimensions, and the type of each element in a dimension. This information assists management applications and user interfaces of management applications about how to treat the data returned to — and passed from — an open MBean. In addition to the set of universal datatypes, the open MBean specification defines a set of meta information interfaces to describe the management interface:

♦ `OpenMBeanInfo` — Represents a collection of the other meta information classes.

♦ `OpenMBeanOperationInfo` — Represents information about an open MBean operation.

♦ `OpenMBeanConstructorInfo` — Represents information about the constructor of an open MBean.

♦ `OpenMBeanParameterInfo` — Represents information about the parameters of an operation.

♦ `OpenMBeanAttributeInfo` — Represents information about an attribute of a model MBean.

The majority of these interfaces extend from the info classes defined for dynamic MBeans, but have some additional requirements specific to open MBeans. One of the methods that exists in the `MBeanFeatureInfo` class is the `getDescription()` method, which all open MBean meta information classes inherit. The return value of this method must not be empty for open MBeans.

Each of the meta information classes defines a support class such as OpenMBeanInfoSupport, which is an implementation of one of the preceding interfaces and inherits the methods of that interface.

> **NOTE:** One exception to open MBeans is that there is no corresponding meta information class for notifications. Open MBeans use the MBeanNotification class to represent notifications.

The meta information classes override various methods to make them compliant with the requirements of open MBeans, and they define new methods that are specific to open MBeans where necessary. The methods that are specific to open MBeans generally deal with determining the datatypes of attributes and operation arguments. Additionally, the OpenMBeanAttributeInfo and OpenMBeanParameterInfo interfaces define the getDefaultValue() and getLegalValues() methods, which provide the default value and an optional list of permissible values. Table 6-5 shows a list of the classes related to open MBeans that are implementations of key open MBean interfaces.

### Table 6-5    Open MBean Related Classes

| Class or Interface | Description |
|---|---|
| ArrayType | This class represents multidimensional arrays of other open types. |
| CompositeDataSupport | This class enables you to construct instances of the CompositeData interface. |
| CompositeType | This class represents instances of CompositeData types. |
| OpenMBeanAttributeInfoSupport | This class enables you to construct meta information about an attribute of an open MBean. |
| OpenMBeanConstructorInfoSupport | This class enables you to construct meta information about an constructor of an open MBean. |
| OpenMBeanInfoSupport | This class enables you to construct meta information about an open MBean. |
| OpenMBeanOperationInfoSupport | This class enables you to construct meta information about an operation of an open MBean. |
| OpenMBeanParameterInfoSupport | This class enables you to construct meta information about an parameter of an open MBean method or constructor. |
| OpenType | The superclass of all open types related to open MBeans. |
| SimpleType | This class represents all open types that are not tabular, composite, or arrays. |

| Class or Interface | Description |
|---|---|
| `TabularDataSupport` | This class enables you to construct instances of the TabularData interface. |
| `TabularType` | This class represents instances of the `TabularData` type. |

Now let's put some of these classes and interfaces to use in an example.

## Creating an open MBean

In this example, you create an open MBean, which is a type of dynamic MBean. You'll also register this MBean in a JMX agent and access its attributes. Listing 6-7 shows the source code for an open MBean named `OpenBean`. This open MBean has a single attribute named `OpenBeanType` that is a `CompositeData` type.

### Listing 6-7: The OpenBean class

```
import javax.management.Attribute;
import javax.management.AttributeList;
import javax.management.AttributeNotFoundException;
import javax.management.DynamicMBean;
import javax.management.MBeanInfo;
import javax.management.MBeanNotificationInfo;
import javax.management.MBeanException;
import javax.management.ReflectionException;
import javax.management.openmbean.OpenDataException;
import javax.management.openmbean.OpenMBeanInfoSupport;
import javax.management.openmbean.OpenMBeanAttributeInfoSupport;
import javax.management.openmbean.OpenMBeanConstructorInfoSupport;
import javax.management.openmbean.OpenMBeanParameterInfoSupport;
import javax.management.openmbean.OpenMBeanConstructorInfoSupport;
import javax.management.openmbean.OpenMBeanOperationInfoSupport;
import javax.management.openmbean.CompositeType;
import javax.management.openmbean.SimpleType;
import javax.management.openmbean.OpenType;


public class OpenBean implements DynamicMBean {

    private OpenMBeanInfoSupport beanInfo;
    private CompositeType compositeType = null;
    private static String[] itemNames = {"Item1", "Item2"};
    private static String[] itemDescriptions = {"Item1 description",
"Item2 description"};
    private static OpenType[] itemTypes = {SimpleType.STRING,
SimpleType.STRING};

    public OpenBean() throws OpenDataException {
    buildBeanInfo();
```

```
    }

    public Object getAttribute(String attrName)
 throws AttributeNotFoundException{

        if (attrName.equals("OpenBeanType"))
           return compositeType;
        else
           return null;

    }
    public void setAttribute(Attribute attr){

        if (attr.getName().equals("OpenBeanType"))
            compositeType = (CompositeType)attr.getValue();

    }

    public AttributeList getAttributes(String[] attributeNames) {
        return new AttributeList(); // unimplemented for this example
    }

    public AttributeList setAttributes(AttributeList attributes) {
    return new AttributeList(); // unimplemented for this example
    }

    public Object invoke(String operationName, Object[] params, String[]
signature)
 throws MBeanException,
        ReflectionException{

        return null; // unimplemented for this example

    }

    public MBeanInfo getMBeanInfo() {
    return beanInfo;
    }

    private void buildBeanInfo() throws OpenDataException  {

 OpenMBeanAttributeInfoSupport[]   attributes    = new
OpenMBeanAttributeInfoSupport[1];
 OpenMBeanConstructorInfoSupport[] constructors  = new
OpenMBeanConstructorInfoSupport[1];
 OpenMBeanOperationInfoSupport[]   operations    = new
OpenMBeanOperationInfoSupport[0];
```

```
 MBeanNotificationInfo          []      notifications = new
MBeanNotificationInfo[0];

        compositeType = new CompositeType("OpenBeanType", /* Type name
*/
        "An OpenBean Type", /* Type description */
        itemNames,/* String[] names */
        itemDescriptions, /* String[] descriptions of items */
        itemTypes);/* String[] data types */

 attributes[0] = new OpenMBeanAttributeInfoSupport("Name", /* Name of
attribute */
            "Name of the OpenMBean", /* description */
            compositeType, /* open type */
            true, /* readable */
            false, /* writable */
            false); /* has "is" */

 // constructor
 constructors[0] = new OpenMBeanConstructorInfoSupport("OpenBean",
            "Constructs a OpenBean.",
            new OpenMBeanParameterInfoSupport[0]);

      // The OpenMBeanInfo
 beanInfo = new OpenMBeanInfoSupport(this.getClass().getName(),
        "Sample Open MBean",
        attributes,
        constructors,
        operations,
        notifications);
    }
}
```

Since open MBeans are a type of dynamic MBean, the implementation of an open MBean looks very similar to that of other dynamic MBean examples you've seen in this book. The primary difference is in the datatypes that an open MBean uses.

The `OpenBean` class implements the `DynamicMBean` interface and all its requisite methods. When the constructor for the `OpenBean` class is called, it calls the `buildBeanInfo()` private method where you construct the `OpenMBeanInfo` object containing the management interface for the MBean. In this example you only provide meta information about one attribute, `OpenBeanType`, and the constructor for the class. The remaining meta information about the class, such as parameters, operations, and notifications, is not present.

**CROSS-REFERENCE:** The `DynamicMBean` interface is covered in Chapter 5.

In this example you only implement the `getAttribute()` and `setAttribute()` methods, which are hardcoded to work only with the `OpenBeanType` attribute. The instance variable `beanInfo` is assigned the value of the `OpenMBeanInfoSupport` object you create at the end of the method. When you call the `getMBeanInfo()` method of the `DynamicMBean` interface, the `beanInfo` variable is returned.

Now that you've constructed the open MBean, you can write a simple JMX agent to use it. Listing 6-8 shows the source for the `OpenBeanAgent` JMX agent application.

**Listing 6-8: The OpenBeanAgent application**

```
import javax.management.ObjectName;
import javax.management.MBeanServer;
import javax.management.MBeanServerFactory;
import javax.management.Attribute;
import javax.management.openmbean.CompositeType;
import java.util.Set;
import java.util.Iterator;

public class OpenBeanAgent {

    private static MBeanServer server = null;

    public OpenBeanAgent() {

    server = MBeanServerFactory.createMBeanServer();
    }

    public static void main(String[] args) {


    OpenBeanAgent agent = new OpenBeanAgent();

            try {

                OpenBean bean = new OpenBean();
                ObjectName openObj = new
ObjectName("OpenBean:type=open");
                server.registerMBean(bean,openObj);

                // Access attributes
                CompositeType type =
(CompositeType)server.getAttribute(openObj,"OpenBeanType");

                System.out.println("Type Name: " + type.getTypeName());
                System.out.println("Type Description: " +
type.getDescription());
                System.out.println("Type Class: " + type.getClassName());

                // Access Composite Type Items
                Set items = type.keySet();
                Iterator itemIter = items.iterator();
                while (itemIter.hasNext()){
```

```
                          String itemName = (String)itemIter.next();
                          System.out.println("Item Name: " + itemName +
                                                      ", Description: " +
type.getType(itemName).getDescription());


                }

        }catch(Exception ex){
                System.out.println(ex);
        }
    }
}
```

The `OpenBeanAgent` application in Listing 6-8 first creates an instance of the `OpenBean` class and creates an object name for it. You then take the object name and the `OpenBean` instance and pass those to the `registerMBean()` method of the `MBeanServer` interface. Next you access the `OpenBeanType` attribute and print out information about the type, such as the name, description, and the class name of the type, and then use a `while` loop to print information about each of the items in the type. The output from the `OpenBeanAgent` application looks like the following:

```
Type Name: OpenBeanType
Type Description: An OpenBean Type
Type Class: javax.management.openmbean.CompositeData
Item Name: Item1, Description: java.lang.String
Item Name: Item2, Description: java.lang.String
```

Open MBeans may one day become a mandatory part of JMX, although standard, dynamic, and model MBeans provide a wide range of options for implementing managed resources. You should not find any real shortcomings in any of these currently available types. Depending on the JMX reference implementation you use, you might find support for open MBeans.

# Summary

In this chapter you examined model MBeans and how they differ from MBeans of other types, such as standard and dynamic. You've seen how the meta information and management interface for model MBeans is specified using descriptors and information classes. Model MBeans utilize a number of policies that enable you to control attribute value caching, notification logging, and persistence. Descriptors can represent transient values or actual values in a managed resource. Managed resources for a model MBean can be specified using the `setManagedResource()` method. In the next chapter you'll take a look at the relation service. The relation service enables you to build relationships and define roles among MBeans.

# Chapter 7

# Building MBean Relations

In large-scale and even some small-scale managed systems, you need to be able to find associated resources quickly. For example, you might receive an alert that a printer has not been printing for over an hour. Using a management console, you check the printer's status and then click on an option to see associated resources such as network connections. This action indicates that the connection leading to the network on which the printer is located is down.

The network connections were located because they were associated with the printer. The capability to make associations between managed resources enables you to set up groupings of like resources, as well as groupings of dependent resources. Being able to associate arbitrary groups of resources enables you to quickly monitor a large number of resources at a glance.

The *relation service* is one of the four agent services that are a described in this book and part of the JMX specification. (The other agent services are *timer, monitor,* and *dynamic loading.)* The relation service enables you to set up associations between MBeans, and define roles for each relation. The relations can include, but are not limited to, information such as the multiplicity and class name of the MBeans. The multiplicity indicates how many times a resource is expected to exist as a child of another resource.

The relation service also provides the capability to maintain the relations and enforce the relations that have been established. Finally, the relation service enables you to search among MBeans to find related MBeans. You might remember the example from Chapter 4 that illustrates a dependent MBean that was loaded inside another MBean. The relation service goes far beyond this simple example, as you will see later in this chapter.

This chapter also covers what relations are and how to construct them. You'll learn how relations are maintained and how to perform queries between related MBeans. The relation service and supporting classes and exceptions are maintained in the `javax.management` `.relation` package defined by the JMX specification.

## Relations and Relation Types

Relations are formally defined as a set of named roles, with each role having a value that is a list of MBeans in that role. Using the printer example described in the opening paragraphs of this chapter, for example, you could have a role named `Printer` for which a number of printer MBeans are defined. The `Printer` role can have any number of printer MBeans defined for it (which you would expect for a resource such as a printer, as companies often have multiple printers). The relation service would maintain the consistency of the `Printer` role and the multiplicity of the associations in that role. For example, if you defined the `Printer` role so that only a single printer MBean could belong to it, and an attempt to add a second printer was made, the relation service would ensure that the addition could not happen. You can represent the relations that you can define with the relation service using a standard Unified Modeling Language (UML) diagram, such as the one shown in Figure 7-1.

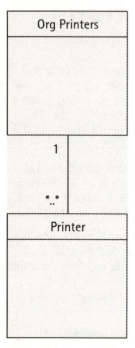

**Figure 7-1:** UML diagram of the Org Printers role.

The diagram in Figure 7-1 shows a role named `Org Printers` that could contain zero or more `Printer` objects. (In the "Defining and Creating Roles" section you'll learn how to construct roles and specify their values. Later, in the "Role metadata: the `RoleInfo` class" section you'll learn how to specify the constraints of a role.) In Figure 7-1, one of the constraints shown is the number of `Printer` objects that can be associated with the `Org Printers` role.

In order for a relation to exist in the relation service, it must define some basic information on which the relation can be based. This information is used to describe relations that are made from it, and provides some loose validation capabilities about which roles can be a part of it.

Relations are defined by a relation type that is a container for MBeans with related roles. The roles in a relation do not have to be in any way directly related but the relation type serves as a loose coupling for them. There must be at least one role in a relation type for the relation type to be created.

Relation types are implementations of the `javax.management.relation.RelationType` interface. The `RelationType` interface has methods that enable you to retrieve the name of the relation type, as well as metadata about a single role or all the roles in a relation. The metadata is represented using a class called `RoleInfo`. You'll learn more about `RoleInfo` later in this chapter. The JMX specification includes a class called `RelationTypeSupport`, which provides a default implementation of the `RelationType` interface for use in your own applications.

Relations can be classified in two broad categories: *internal* and *external*. Internal relation types are created and maintained by the relation service. You can create internal relation types by using the `createRelationType()` method of the `RelationService` class. Internal types are not accessible to applications or other MBeans other than through well-defined accessor methods in the `RelationService` class.

External relations are those that are completely accessible to applications and other MBeans directly. External relation types are defined using the set of classes and interfaces previously described. You can define your own external relation type by implementing the `RelationType` interface or by extending the `RelationTypeSupport` class. An external relation type must manage the roles that are a part of it, and ensure that duplicate roles are not added to the relation.

## Defining and Creating Roles

A role is a set of MBeans in a relation where the MBeans represent the value of the role. Roles in JMX are represented by instances of the `javax.management.relation.Role` class. In the example of the printer and network connections in a managed system, the printers and network connections could be represented as roles, and could be part of a hypothetical relation called `Printer Network`. The `Printer Network` relation can have zero or more printer roles and zero or more network connection roles.

Roles have a name and a value, which is represented by an instance of the `java.util.List` interface. The `List` interface holds the references to the MBeans. The references to the MBeans themselves are performed using the familiar `ObjectName` class.

Normally, when you add a role to a relation, it cannot be updated afterwards. This helps maintain the consistency of the relations in the relation service. You can, however, explicitly specify whether a role can be read from and written to when you are creating the relation.

To create a role, you use a class called `Role`. The `Role` class is a simple class that contains `accessor` methods for getting and setting the name, and `accessor` methods for getting and setting the value. The value, as described in the preceding section, is a `java.util.List` of the `ObjectNames` of the MBeans that are a part of the role.

Table 7-1 describes the methods of the `Role` class.

## Table 7-1    Role Class Methods

| Method Name | Description |
|---|---|
| clone() | Returns a complete copy of the role |
| getRoleName() | Returns a java.lang.String representing the name of the role |
| getRoleValue() | Returns an instance of java.util.List representing the value of the role |
| roleValueToString(java.util. List roleValue) | Returns a java.lang.String representing the value of the role |
| setRoleName(java.lang.String roleName) | Sets the name of the role using a java.lang.String |
| setRoleValue(java.util.List roleValue) | Sets the value of the role using an instance of java.util.List |
| toString() | Returns a java.lang.String describing the role |

Creating roles is a multi-step process because you must first have a relation that is based on a relation type. The role must be constructed within the constraints specified in the RoleInfo class. Before you can continue with the relation service example, you need to define an MBean that you'll use in the relations. Listing 7-1 shows the source of an interface for this example.

**Listing 7-1: The PrintObjectMBean interface**

```
public interface PrintObjectMBean{
}
```

For the relation examples in this chapter, you don't need to define any methods for this interface. As a result, the implementation of this interface will also be sparse. Listing 7-2 shows the source of a class implementing the PrintObjectMBean interface.

**Listing 7-2: The PrintObject class**

```
public class PrintObject implements PrintObjectMBean{
}
```

Now you have an MBean you can use in the subsequent examples. Listing 7-3 shows the source of a class that creates a single relation and role, and adds three MBeans to the role as its value.

**Listing 7-3: Creating roles**

```
import javax.management.MBeanServer;
import javax.management.MBeanServerFactory;
import javax.management.ObjectName;
import javax.management.relation.Role;
```

```
import javax.management.relation.RoleInfo;
import javax.management.relation.RoleList;
import javax.management.relation.RoleResult;
import javax.management.relation.RelationService;
import java.util.ArrayList;
import java.util.Iterator;
import java.util.List;
import java.util.Vector;


public class ExampleJMXAddRoles {

      private static MBeanServer server = null;


      public ExampleJMXAddRoles(){
            server = MBeanServerFactory.createMBeanServer();
      }

      public static void main(String args[]){

            ExampleJMXAddRoles agent = new ExampleJMXAddRoles();

            RelationService relServ = new RelationService(false);

            PrintObject prntObj = new PrintObject();

            try {

                  ObjectName objName =
                      new ObjectName("RelationService:type=relate");

                  server.registerMBean(relServ,objName);

                  ObjectName pObj =
                      new ObjectName("PrinterObject:name=HP Deskjet");
                  ObjectName pObj1 =
                      new ObjectName("PrinterObject:name=HP Laserjet");
                  ObjectName pObj2 =
                      new ObjectName("PrinterObject:name=HP Deskjet
Color");

                  server.registerMBean(prntObj,pObj);
                  server.registerMBean(prntObj,pObj1);
                  server.registerMBean(prntObj,pObj2);

                  // Add Relation Type //

                  String className =
```

```
                    server.getObjectInstance(pObj).getClassName();

        RoleInfo rInfo = new RoleInfo("Printers",
                                      className,
                                      true,
                                      true,
                                      0,
                                      3,
                                      "Printers Role");

        relServ.createRelationType("IT Printers",
                                   new RoleInfo[]{rInfo});

        // Add a relation //
        relServ.createRelation("ID1","IT Printers",
                               new RoleList());

        // Add a Role //
        List roles = new ArrayList();
        roles.add(pObj);
        roles.add(pObj1);
        roles.add(pObj2);

        Role aRole = new Role("Printers",roles);

        // Set the role //
        relServ.setRole("ID1",aRole);

        // Access the Roles //
        RoleResult roleResult = relServ.getAllRoles("ID1");

        // Print Roles Successfully Accessed //
        RoleList roleList = roleResult.getRoles();
        Iterator roleIter = roleList.iterator();
        while (roleIter.hasNext()){
                Role theRole = (Role)roleIter.next();
                System.out.println("Role Name: " +
                                   theRole.getRoleName());
                System.out.println("MBeans in Role: " +
                                   theRole.getRoleValue().size());
        }

    } catch (Exception ex) {
        ex.printStackTrace();
    }
  }

}
```

The `ExampleJMXAddRoles` application in Listing 7-3 creates a role with the name of `Printers Role` and adds it to a relation named `IT Printers`. (Note that to make this example more readable, I've forgone catching all the different exceptions explicitly and simply caught the class `java.lang.Exception`.)

The application begins by creating an instance of the `RelationService` MBean, and another MBean with the class name `PrinterObject`. It then creates three unique object names based on the `PrinterObject` class that will be used in the role you will create. Once you have the necessary MBeans loaded and registered, you can proceed with building your relations and adding roles to it.

## Setting up the relation and adding roles

Begin the process by creating a `RoleInfo` class that will contain the information about the role you will add later. The following code fragment describes the arguments to the `RoleInfo` constructor used:

```
RoleInfo rInfo =
   new RoleInfo("Printers",        // Name of the role
               className,          // Class name of MBeans in role
               true,               // Role is readable
               true,               // Role is writable
               0,                  // Can have zero MBeans in role
               3,                  // Can have max three MBeans in role
               "Printers Role");   // Description of role
```

Once you have information about at least one role, you can create a relation type. The `createRelationType()` method is used, with a name of `IT Printers` and an array of `RoleInfo` objects with a single element of the `RoleInfo` object just created. From this relation type, you create a relation with the `createRelation()` method. Assign the relation an ID of `ID1` and give it the name of the relation type on which it is based: `IT Printers`. Pass in an empty list of Roles with a `RoleList` object. You will add the roles later in the application using another method.

To create the roles, you first define an instance of the `java.util.List` interface and add the three `ObjectNames` representing the three `PrinterObject` MBeans defined previously, and then pass this into the constructor of the `Role` class along with a string identifying the role name. If any mistakes have been made, such as adding four MBeans when the `RoleInfo` dictates a maximum of three, an exception will be thrown.

If no exceptions occur creating the `Role` object, you then use the `setRole()` method of the `RelationService` class and pass it in as an argument along with the ID of the relation to which you want to add this role. To prove that the role exists and contains the correct number of MBeans, you use the `getAllRoles()` method and pass in the ID of the relation, which returns an instance of the `RoleResult` class. This class contains all the `Role` objects, whether they were unresolved or not. You then use the `getRoles()` method of the `RoleResult` class, which returns all unresolved roles. In this case, you will not have any unresolved roles, so calling the `getRolesUnresolved()` method is not necessary. The `getRoles()` method returns an iterator that you can use to access the roles and print their names, as well as the number of MBeans in each role. The output from running the `ExampleJMXAddRoles` application looks like the following:

```
Role Name: Printers
MBeans in Role: 3
```

Note that although the `java.util.List` interface is used to represent a list of role values, the JMX specification defines a `RoleList` class. The `RoleList` class is used to represent a list of roles, and it provides checks that maintain the integrity of the list. It ensures that only non-null `Role` objects are added to the list. The `RoleList` class is also used as the return value for some of the methods of the `RelationService` class and as the argument to several methods of the `RelationService` class, such as `createRelation()`. It is also used in the constructor of the `RoleResult` class.

The `RoleList` class is based on the `java.util.ArrayList` class. It includes methods for adding single `Role` objects, single `Role` objects at an index, a set of `Roles` using another `RoleList` object, and methods for cloning assorted inherited methods .

## Role metadata: the RoleInfo class

Information about a role is represented by an instance of the `RoleInfo` class. The `RoleInfo` class is used in a number of places to represent a set of roles being operated on. For instance, when creating new relation types, an array of `RoleInfo` objects is used to initialize the list of role information for the relation. The `RoleInfo` class also contains the name of the MBean that is referenced by the role, the cardinality of the role, and some additional pieces of information. Table 7-2 describes the methods of the `RoleInfo` class.

### Table 7-2    RoleInfo Class Methods

| Method Name | Description |
| --- | --- |
| `checkMaxDegree(int value)` | Returns a primitive Java boolean indicating that the value passed in is less than or equal to the maximum degree |
| `checkMinDegree(int value)` | Returns a primitive Java boolean indicating that the value passed in is greater than or equal to the minimum degree |
| `getDescription()` | Returns a `java.lang.String` representing the description of the role |
| `getMaxDegree()` | Returns a primitive Java integer representing the maximum degree for the role |
| `getMinDegree()` | Returns a primitive Java integer representing the minimum degree for the role |
| `getName()` | Returns a `java.lang.String` representing the name of the role |
| `getRefMBeanClassName()` | Returns a `java.lang.String` representing the class name of the MBeans in the role. Each class name must be of the same MBean class type. |

| Method Name | Description |
|---|---|
| isReadable() | Returns a primitive Java boolean indicating whether a role is readable |
| isWritable() | Returns a primitive Java boolean indicating whether a role is writable |
| toString() | Returns a `java.lang.String` describing the role |

Although the `Role` class specifies some basic information about the role, it does not specify any of its cardinality requirements. Notice the methods `getMaxDegree()` and `getMinDegree()` in Table 7-2. These two methods provide the values specified when the `RoleInfo` object was created. When role values are updated or created, these values must satisfy the constraints specified in the `RoleInfo` class. These constraints are enforced when the role is set in a relation. Depending on the `RoleInfo` constructor used when creating a `RoleInfo` object, the minimum and maximum cardinality are set to a value of one.

So what happens when the constraints are not satisfied or a problem occurs while working with a role? The JMX specification defines a state called *unresolved,* which you can think of as an error state for a role.

## Unresolved roles

Occasionally, problems occur when using roles, such as access restrictions or an error reading from or writing to the role. Some problems cause the role to enter an unresolved state. The `javax.management.relation.RoleUnresolved` class is used to represent an unresolved role. It looks similar to the `Role` class with one exception: The `RoleUnresolved` class contains a method called `getProblemType()`, which returns an integer representing the error. This integer value maps to one of the static integer fields in the `javax.management.relation.RoleStatus` class. The `RoleUnresolved` class also includes a `setProblemType()` that can be used to set the integer value. Table 7-3 describes the fields of the `RoleStatus` class.

### Table 7-3    RoleStatus Fields

| Field Name | Description |
|---|---|
| LESS_THAN_MIN_ROLE_DEGREE | Indicates a problem when trying to set a role value with a number of `ObjectNames` less than the minimum expected cardinality |
| MORE_THAN_MAX_ROLE_DEGREE | Indicates a problem when trying to set a role value with a number of `ObjectNames` more than the maximum expected cardinality |
| NO_ROLE_WITH_NAME | No role by that name exists |
| REF_MBEAN_NOT_REGISTERED | Indicates a problem when trying to set a role value with an MBean that is not currently registered in the MBean Server |

| Field Name | Description |
|---|---|
| REF_MBEAN_OF_INCORRECT_CLASS | Indicates a problem when trying to set a role value with an MBean of a class not expected for that role |
| ROLE_NOT_READABLE | Indicates a problem when trying to read a nonreadable role |
| ROLE_NOT_WRITABLE | Indicates a problem when trying to write to a nonwritable role |

The Sun JMX reference implementation is relatively good at catching problems with roles at runtime, depending on how you add the roles to a relation. If you use the method shown in Listing 7-1, which uses the setRole() method, a variety of exceptions will be thrown if something is wrong.

The detection of an unresolved role may not occur until runtime in some cases, however. You may configure a role that passes runtime access by some components but later results in an exception when accessed by others. Listing 7-4 shows the source code for an application that demonstrates how an unresolved role can happen.

**Listing 7-4: An unresolved role**

```
import javax.management.MBeanServer;
import javax.management.MBeanServerFactory;
import javax.management.ObjectName;
import javax.management.relation.Role;
import javax.management.relation.RoleInfo;
import javax.management.relation.RoleList;
import javax.management.relation.RoleResult;
import javax.management.relation.RoleStatus;
import javax.management.relation.RoleUnresolved;
import javax.management.relation.RoleUnresolvedList;
import javax.management.relation.RelationService;
import java.util.ArrayList;
import java.util.Iterator;
import java.util.List;


public class ExampleJMXAddRolesUnresolved {

    private static MBeanServer server = null;


    public ExampleJMXAddRolesUnresolved(){
        server = MBeanServerFactory.createMBeanServer();
    }

    public static void main(String args[]){
```

```
ExampleJMXAddRolesUnresolved agent =
     new ExampleJMXAddRolesUnresolved();

RelationService relServ = new RelationService(false);

PrintObject prntObj = new PrintObject();

try {

    ObjectName objName =
         new ObjectName("RelationService:type=relate");

    server.registerMBean(relServ,objName);

    ObjectName pObj =
         new ObjectName("PrinterObject:name=HP Deskjet");
    ObjectName pObj1 =
         new ObjectName("PrinterObject:name=HP Laserjet");
    ObjectName pObj2 =
    new ObjectName("PrinterObject:name=HP Deskjet Color");

    server.registerMBean(prntObj,pObj);
    server.registerMBean(prntObj,pObj1);
    server.registerMBean(prntObj,pObj2);

    // Add Relation Type //

    String className =
       server.getObjectInstance(pObj).getClassName();

    RoleInfo rInfo = new RoleInfo("Printers",
                                   className,
                                   false,
                                   true,
                                   0,
                                   3,
                                   "Printers Role");

    relServ.createRelationType("IT Printers",
                                new RoleInfo[]{rInfo});

    // Add a Role //
    List roles = new ArrayList();
    roles.add(pObj);
    roles.add(pObj1);
    roles.add(pObj2);

    // Add a relation //
    relServ.createRelation("ID1","IT Printers",
```

```
                                        new RoleList());

        Role aRole = new Role("Printers",roles);

        RoleList aRoleList = new RoleList();
        aRoleList.add(aRole);
        relServ.setRoles("ID1",aRoleList);

        // Access the Roles //
        RoleResult roleResult = relServ.getAllRoles("ID1");

        // Print Roles Successfully Accessed //
        RoleList roleList = roleResult.getRoles();
        System.out.println("Resolved roles: " +
                        roleList.size());
        Iterator roleIter = roleList.iterator();
        while (roleIter.hasNext()){
            Role theRole = (Role)roleIter.next();
            System.out.println("Role Name: " +
                                theRole.getRoleName());
            System.out.println("MBeans in Role: " +
                        theRole.getRoleValue().size());
        }

        // Print Roles Unsuccessfully Accessed//
        RoleUnresolvedList roleListBad =
            roleResult.getRolesUnresolved();
        System.out.println("Unresolved roles: " +
            roleListBad.size());
        Iterator roleIterBad = roleListBad.iterator();
        while (roleIterBad.hasNext()){
            RoleUnresolved theRole =
                (RoleUnresolved)roleIterBad.next();
            System.out.println("Unresolved Role Name: " +
                                theRole.getRoleName());
            System.out.println("Reason unresolved: " +
                mapReason(theRole.getProblemType()));
        }

    } catch (Exception ex) {
        ex.printStackTrace();
    }
}

// Map problem type to a string //
private static String mapReason(int problem){
    String reason = "Unknown";
    switch(problem){
        case RoleStatus.LESS_THAN_MIN_ROLE_DEGREE:
```

```
                             reason = "Too few MBeans in role";
                             break;
                   case RoleStatus.MORE_THAN_MAX_ROLE_DEGREE:
                             reason = "Too many MBeans in role";
                             break;
                   case RoleStatus.NO_ROLE_WITH_NAME:
                             reason = "No role with that name found";
                             break;
                   case RoleStatus.REF_MBEAN_NOT_REGISTERED:
                             reason = "No MBean with that classname
registered";

                             break;
                   case RoleStatus.REF_MBEAN_OF_INCORRECT_CLASS:
                             reason = "An MBean of incorrect type is in
role";

                             break;
                   case RoleStatus.ROLE_NOT_READABLE:
                             reason = "The role is not readable";
                             break;
                   case RoleStatus.ROLE_NOT_WRITABLE:
                             reason = "The role is not writable";
                             break;
                   default:
                             reason = "Unknown";


         }

         return reason;
    }

}
```

This listing is quite similar to Listing 7-3, but it has been modified to print unresolved roles and then add the role in a way that defers detection of the unresolved state until the role is accessed. The ways in which this application differs from the one shown in Listing 7-1 begin with the information that is passed to the RoleInfo constructor. The argument representing the read attribute of the role is set to false, which means the role cannot be read. This simply sets up the role but does not cause any unresolved states.

Next, instead of using the setRole() method and passing the java.util.List, you create a RoleList and add the Role object to it. Then pass the RoleList object into the setRoles() method, along with the ID of the relation to which the roles should be added. The application then attempts to print out all resolved and unresolved roles using the getRolesUnresolved() method of the RoleResult class. The integer values have been mapped to descriptive strings of what the problem was or why an unresolved state resulted.

The output from running the ExampleJMXAddRolesUnresolved application looks like the following:

```
Resolved roles: 0
```

```
Unresolved roles: 1
Unresolved Role Name: Printers
Reason unresolved: The role is not readable
```

Other unresolved values can result at later points of access and may not immediately appear as they did in this example. For example, if the role were updated after it was created by the addition of another MBean of a different type, the role would become unresolved.

The examples provided so far in this chapter illustrate the core components of building roles and relations. They have also utilized the relation service MBean, which is the subject of the following section.

# Using the Relation Service

The classes and interfaces you have seen so far in this chapter enable you to define the relations and roles for MBeans, but taken alone, they don't enable you to do anything. The relation service itself is what brings all of these classes and interfaces together, enabling you to utilize the relations you have built. The relation service is implemented as an MBean, and can be loaded, registered, and unregistered just like any ordinary MBean.

The relation service is implemented as the `javax.management.relation` `.RelationService` class and extends the `NotificationBroadcasterSupport` class so that it can send notifications. The types of notifications that are sent reflect when relations are added or removed, or when MBeans become eligible or ineligible to be part of a relation. The `RelationService` class also implements the `MBeanRegistration interface`, the `NotificationListener interface`, and the `RegistrationServiceMBean` interface. You learn more about the `MBeanRegistration` interface in Chapter 8; basically, it enables MBeans to receive notifications about registration events in the MBean Server. The `NotificationListener` interface is covered in Chapter 11; it enables an MBean to receive notifications from a class implementing the `NotificationBroadcaster` interface.

The relation service itself enables you to add and remove relation types, add and remove relations, and retrieve lists of relation types and relations by ID. In the "Finding MBeans in the relation service" section in this chapter, you will also see three methods that can be used to perform queries based on those two types of information.

## Instantiating the relation service

The relation service can be instantiated using either static or dynamic registration, both of which you have seen in this book. The constructor of the `RelationService` class takes a single primitive Java `boolean` argument. This argument indicates whether notifications will be sent when an MBean that was part of a relation becomes unregistered or is removed from the relation. If you pass a value of false, notifications will not be sent automatically unless you call the purgeRelations() method of the RelationService class.

Listing 7-5 illustrates how to create an instance of the registration service in an MBean Server.

**Listing 7-5: Instantiating the relation service**

```
import javax.management.InstanceAlreadyExistsException;
import javax.management.MalformedObjectNameException;
import javax.management.MBeanRegistrationException;
import javax.management.MBeanServer;
import javax.management.MBeanServerFactory;
import javax.management.NotCompliantMBeanException;
import javax.management.ObjectName;
import javax.management.relation.RelationService;


public class ExampleJMXRelations {

      private static MBeanServer server = null;


      public ExampleJMXRelations(){
            server = MBeanServerFactory.createMBeanServer();
      }

      public static void main(String args[]){

            ExampleJMXRelations agent = new ExampleJMXRelations();

            RelationService relServ = new RelationService(false);

            try {

                ObjectName objName =
                    new ObjectName("RelationService:type=relate");

                server.registerMBean(relServ,objName);

            } catch (MalformedObjectNameException ex){
                System.out.println(ex);
            } catch (InstanceAlreadyExistsException ex){
                System.out.println(ex);
            } catch (MBeanRegistrationException ex){
                System.out.println(ex);
            } catch (NotCompliantMBeanException ex){
                System.out.println(ex);
            }
      }
```

```
}
```

In the `ExampleJMXRelations` application in Listing 7-5 you instantiate the
`RelationService` class using the `new` operator. Next, you need to register this class in the
MBean Server by creating the object name, and then use the `registerMBean()` method of
the `MBeanServer` interface. Once you have performed these steps the relation service is
available for use.

## Adding relation types

Before you can define a relation in the relation service, you must define at least one relation
type. As you saw earlier in the chapter, relation types serve as a sort of template from which
relations can be created. Relation types can be added to the relation service in one of two
ways. The first way creates an internal relation type; the second way creates an external
relation type.

Internal relation types are created using the `createRelationType()` method of the
`RelationServiceMBean` interface. This method takes two arguments: The first argument is
a `java.lang.String` representing the name you want to give to the relation type. The
second argument is an array of `javax.management.relation.RoleInfo` classes, which
describe the roles that participate in relations of that type. The array of `RoleInfo` objects
must contain at least one instance of the `RoleInfo` class or else an exception of type
`InvalidRelationTypeException` will be thrown.

Listing 7-6 shows the source code for an application that creates a relation of type
`Organizational Printers` and adds a single `RoleInfo` class with the name `Printers`.

**Listing 7-6: Using createRelationType to create a relation**

```
import javax.management.InstanceAlreadyExistsException;
import javax.management.InstanceNotFoundException;
import javax.management.MalformedObjectNameException;
import javax.management.MBeanRegistrationException;
import javax.management.MBeanServer;
import javax.management.MBeanServerFactory;
import javax.management.NotCompliantMBeanException;
import javax.management.ObjectName;
import javax.management.relation.InvalidRelationTypeException;
import javax.management.relation.RoleInfo;
import javax.management.relation.RelationService;
import java.util.Iterator;
import java.util.List;

public class ExampleJMXAddRelationTypes {

        private static MBeanServer server = null;


        public ExampleJMXAddRelationTypes(){
```

```
                    server = MBeanServerFactory.createMBeanServer();
        }

        public static void main(String args[]){

                ExampleJMXAddRelationTypes agent =
                        new ExampleJMXAddRelationTypes();

                RelationService relServ = new RelationService(false);

                PrintObject prntObj = new PrintObject();

                try {

                    ObjectName objName =
                            new
ObjectName("RelationService:type=relate");

                        server.registerMBean(relServ,objName);

                    ObjectName pObj =
                            new ObjectName("PrinterObject:name=HP
Deskjet");

                        server.registerMBean(prntObj,pObj);

                        // Add Relations //

                        String className =
server.getObjectInstance(pObj).getClassName();

                        RoleInfo rInfo = new RoleInfo("Printers",className);

                        relServ.createRelationType("Organization Printers",
                                            new RoleInfo[]{rInfo});

                        // List all internal relations //
                        List relations = relServ.getAllRelationTypeNames();

                        Iterator iter = relations.iterator();
                        while (iter.hasNext())
                            System.out.println("Relation Type: " +
                                            (String)iter.next());

                } catch (MalformedObjectNameException ex){
                        System.out.println(ex);
                } catch (InstanceAlreadyExistsException ex){
                        System.out.println(ex);
```

```
                    } catch (MBeanRegistrationException ex){
                        System.out.println(ex);
                    } catch (NotCompliantMBeanException ex){
                        System.out.println(ex);
                    } catch (InvalidRelationTypeException ex){
                        System.out.println(ex);
                    } catch (InstanceNotFoundException ex){
                        System.out.println(ex);
                    } catch (ClassNotFoundException ex){
                        System.out.println(ex);
                    }
            }
    }

}
```

The `ExampleJMXAddRelationTypes` application in Listing 7-6 creates an instance of the `RelationService` MBean, as well as an MBean called `PrinterObject`. Once both of the MBeans have been registered, you create a new relation type. You need at least one instance of the `RoleInfo` class to pass to the `createRelationType()` method of the `RelationServiceMBean` interface. The `RoleInfo` class you create will represent the `PrinterObject` MBean, but you need the class name of the MBean. You use the `getObjectInstance()` method of the `MBeanServer` interface to retrieve an `ObjectInstance` object from which you can retrieve the class name of the MBean. You could also use the `getClass()` method that the `PrinterObject` class would have inherited, but using the methods of the `MBeanServer` interface and the `ObjectInstance` class is more portable.

Once you have the class name and instance of the `RoleInfo` class, you call the `createRelationType()` method of the `RelationServiceMBean` interface with the name `Organizational Printers` and an array containing the single `RoleInfo` object you created previously.

To show that the relation has indeed been added, you use the `getAllRelationTypeNames()` method of the `RelationServiceMBean` interface. This method returns a `java.util.List` instance containing the single relation type name that was created using the `createRelationType()` method. Once you have the list, you use the iterator from it to loop through the list and print each type. The output from the `ExampleJMXAddRelationTypes` application looks like the following:

```
Relation Type: Organization Printers
```

The second type of relation is considered an external relation type in that it is created and added manually by an application. As you saw earlier in the chapter, external relation types are represented using a set of classes and interfaces that enable you to specify and control the information about the type. You can create an external type by implementing the `javax.management.relation.RelationType` interface or you can extend the `javax.management.relation.RelationTypeSupport` class. This class implements the `RelationType` interface and provides the necessary infrastructure for adding `RoleInfo` classes, in addition to providing accessors to the `RoleInfo` objects and the name of the type.

Listing 7-7 provides the source code of an external relation type named `HMIRelationType`, which extends the `RelationTypeSupport` class. You might have noticed a pattern with classes that end in the suffix `Support`. The JMX specification uses these to provide implementation classes you can extend from to create your own relation types, notification broadcasters, descriptors, or notification filters. You do not have to use these support classes, but they do expedite implementation if you're in a hurry.

**Listing 7-7: The HMIRelationType class**

```
import javax.management.relation.InvalidRelationTypeException;
import javax.management.relation.RelationTypeSupport;
import javax.management.relation.RoleInfo;


public class HMIRelationType extends RelationTypeSupport{

        public HMIRelationType(String relationName, RoleInfo roles[])
                throws InvalidRelationTypeException{
                super(relationName,roles);
        }
}
```

If you were to implement the `RelationTypeSupport` interface instead of using the `RelationTypeSupport` class, the `HMIRelationType` class might look like the one shown in Listing 7-8.

**Listing 7-8: HMIRelationType directly implementing the RelationType interface**

```
import javax.management.relation.InvalidRelationTypeException;
import javax.management.relation.RelationType;
import javax.management.relation.RoleInfo;
import java.util.Arrays;
import java.util.Iterator;
import java.util.List;


public class HMIRelationTypeDirect implements RelationType{

        private String relationTypeName = "";
        private List roleInfos = null;

        public HMIRelationTypeDirect(String relationName){
                relationTypeName = relationName;
        }

        public HMIRelationTypeDirect(String relationName, RoleInfo
rInfos[]){
                relationTypeName = relationName;
                roleInfos = Arrays.asList(rInfos);
        }
```

```
    public void addRoleInfo(RoleInfo roleInfo)
            throws InvalidRelationTypeException{
        if (roleInfos.contains(roleInfo))
            throw new InvalidRelationTypeException("Role already
exists");
        else
            roleInfos.add(roleInfo);
    }

    public String getRelationTypeName(){
        return relationTypeName;
    }

    public RoleInfo getRoleInfo(String roleInfoName){
        RoleInfo foundRoleInfo = null;
        Iterator iter = roleInfos.iterator();
        while (iter.hasNext()) {
            RoleInfo rInfo = (RoleInfo)iter.next();
            if (rInfo.getName().equals(roleInfoName)){
                foundRoleInfo = rInfo;
                break;
            }
        }
        return foundRoleInfo;
    }

    public List getRoleInfos(){
        return roleInfos;
    }
}
```

The `HMIRelationTypeDirect` class implements all the methods as required by the `RelationTypeSupport` interface. The class maintains two private instance variables to hold the name of the relation type and the list of `RoleInfo` objects. The second constructor, which takes two arguments, uses the `Arrays.asList()` static method to set the list of `RoleInfo` objects that were passed in. The class also implements the necessary methods to retrieve all the `RoleInfo` objects, a single `RoleInfo`, as well as the `addRoleInfo()` method for adding new `RoleInfo` objects to the relation type. The `addRoleInfo()` method throws an `InvalidRelationTypeException` if a `RoleInfo` object passed in contains a role that already exists for that relation.

Using the `HIMRelationType` and `HMIRelationTypeDirect` classes is the same. You can construct instances of each and use the methods of each exactly the same way. The only real difference is how much work you are willing to do to implement your own relation type or utilize the `RelationTypeSupport` class. Listing 7-9 shows the source of a class that uses both of the relation types you've just created and then prints out information about them.

**Listing 7-9: Using external relation types**

```java
import javax.management.InstanceAlreadyExistsException;
import javax.management.InstanceNotFoundException;
import javax.management.MalformedObjectNameException;
import javax.management.MBeanRegistrationException;
import javax.management.MBeanServer;
import javax.management.MBeanServerFactory;
import javax.management.NotCompliantMBeanException;
import javax.management.ObjectName;
import javax.management.relation.InvalidRelationTypeException;
import javax.management.relation.RoleInfo;
import javax.management.relation.RelationService;
import java.util.Iterator;
import java.util.List;


public class ExampleJMXAddRelationTypesExternal {

        private static MBeanServer server = null;


        public ExampleJMXAddRelationTypesExternal(){
                server = MBeanServerFactory.createMBeanServer();
        }

        public static void main(String args[]){

                ExampleJMXAddRelationTypesExternal agent =
                        new ExampleJMXAddRelationTypesExternal();

                RelationService relServ = new RelationService(false);

                PrintObject prntObj = new PrintObject();

                try {

                    ObjectName objName =
                            new ObjectName("RelationService:type=relate");

                    server.registerMBean(relServ,objName);

                    ObjectName pObj =
                            new ObjectName("PrinterObject:name=HP Deskjet");

                    server.registerMBean(prntObj,pObj);

                    // Add Relations //
```

```
                String className =

server.getObjectInstance(pObj).getClassName();

            RoleInfo rInfo = new RoleInfo("Printers",className);

            HMIRelationType hmiRelType =
                    new HMIRelationType("Organization Printers",
                                        new RoleInfo[]{rInfo});

            relServ.addRelationType(hmiRelType);

            // Use our homegrown relation type //
            HMIRelationTypeDirect hmiRelTypeDirect =
                new HMIRelationTypeDirect("IT Printers",
                                        new RoleInfo[]{rInfo});

            relServ.addRelationType(hmiRelTypeDirect);

            // List all internal relations //
            List relations = relServ.getAllRelationTypeNames();

            Iterator iter = relations.iterator();
            while (iter.hasNext())
                System.out.println("Relation Type: " +
                                   (String)iter.next());

        } catch (MalformedObjectNameException ex){
            System.out.println(ex);
        } catch (InstanceAlreadyExistsException ex){
            System.out.println(ex);
        } catch (MBeanRegistrationException ex){
            System.out.println(ex);
        } catch (NotCompliantMBeanException ex){
            System.out.println(ex);
        } catch (InvalidRelationTypeException ex){
            System.out.println(ex);
        } catch (InstanceNotFoundException ex){
            System.out.println(ex);
        } catch (ClassNotFoundException ex){
            System.out.println(ex);
        }
    }
}
```

The ExampleJMXAddRelationTypesExternal application in Listing 7-9 works very similarly to the ExampleJMXAddRelationTypes application in Listing 7-6. The primary difference between the two applications, of course, is the method used to create the relation type in the relation service. This example also utilizes relation types that I have defined myself.

The first relation type is the `HMIRelationType`, which extends the `RelationTypeSupport` class. This class is then added as a relation using the `addRelationType()` method. The constructor of the `HMIRelationType` class takes the name of the relation type and an array of `RoleInfo` objects. This is the same way it was done in Listing 7-6, but you could also use the `addInfo()` method to add a new `RoleInfo` object to the array. The second relation type, `HMIRelationTypeDirect`, implements the `RelationType` directly and is added exactly the same as `HMIRelationType`, using the `addRelationType()` method.

Once the two types have been added, they are treated the same and can be retrieved using the same `getAllRelationTypeNames()` method. The output from running this example looks like the following:

```
Relation Type: Organization Printers
Relation Type: IT Printers
```

The two relation types from this example can now be used to create relations. In the "Adding relation types" section earlier in the chapter I covered creating relation types and relations from those types.

## Finding MBeans in the relation service

At some point, you may need to use some sort of query operation to find a set of information, such as finding all relation IDs for a given relation type or all MBeans in a role. The `RelationService` class includes three methods that enable you to query for MBeans and relation IDs, as well as find relations in which a particular MBean is referenced. The latter is particularly useful because there is no restriction on how many times an MBean can appear in relations, only that it cannot appear more than once in the same role. The methods that you can use to perform queries are as follows:

- findAssociateMBeans
- findReferencingRelations
- findRelationsOfType

Listing 7-10 illustrates the use of the `findReferencingRelations()` method to find all the relations in which an MBean appears.

**Listing 7-10: Using the findReferencingRelations method**

```
import javax.management.MBeanServer;
import javax.management.MBeanServerFactory;
import javax.management.ObjectName;
import javax.management.relation.Role;
import javax.management.relation.RoleInfo;
import javax.management.relation.RoleList;
import javax.management.relation.RoleResult;
import javax.management.relation.RelationNotification;
import javax.management.relation.RelationService;
```

```
import java.util.ArrayList;
import java.util.Map;
import java.util.Iterator;
import java.util.List;
import java.util.Vector;


public class ExampleJMXFindMethods{

        private static MBeanServer server = null;


        public ExampleJMXFindMethods(){
                server = MBeanServerFactory.createMBeanServer();
        }

        public static void main(String args[]){

                ExampleJMXFindMethods agent = new ExampleJMXFindMethods();

                RelationService relServ = new RelationService(false);

                PrintObject prntObj = new PrintObject();

                try {

                        ObjectName objName = new
ObjectName("RelationService:type=relate");

                        server.registerMBean(relServ,objName);

                        ObjectName pObj = new
ObjectName("PrinterObject:name=HP Deskjet");
                        ObjectName pObj1 = new
ObjectName("PrinterObject:name=HP Laserjet");
                        ObjectName pObj2 = new
ObjectName("PrinterObject:name=HP Deskjet Color");

                        server.registerMBean(prntObj,pObj);
                        server.registerMBean(prntObj,pObj1);
                        server.registerMBean(prntObj,pObj2);

                        // Add Relation Type //

                        String className =
server.getObjectInstance(pObj).getClassName();

                        RoleInfo rInfo = new RoleInfo("Printers",
                                                className,
```

```
                                                true,
                                                true,
                                                0,
                                                3,
                                                "Printers Role");

                relServ.createRelationType("IT Printers",new
RoleInfo[]{rInfo});
                relServ.createRelationType("HR Printers",new
RoleInfo[]{rInfo});
                relServ.createRelationType("Marketing Printers",new
RoleInfo[]{rInfo});

                // Add a relation //
                relServ.createRelation("IT1","IT Printers",new
RoleList());
                relServ.createRelation("HR1","HR Printers",new
RoleList());
                relServ.createRelation("MK1","Marketing Printers",new
RoleList());

                // Add a Role //
                List roles = new ArrayList();
                roles.add(pObj);
                roles.add(pObj1);
                roles.add(pObj2);

                Role aRole = new Role("Printers",roles);

                // Set the role //
                relServ.setRole("IT1",aRole);
                relServ.setRole("HR1",aRole);
                relServ.setRole("MK1",aRole);

                // Do queries //
                System.out.println("Referencing
relations>>>>>>>>>>>>");
                Map map =
relServ.findReferencingRelations(pObj2,null,null);
                System.out.println("Object: " +
pObj2.getCanonicalName() + " appears in these relations...");
                Iterator iter = map.keySet().iterator();
                while (iter.hasNext()) {
                        String relId = (String)iter.next();
                        System.out.println("Relation: " + relId);
                }

            } catch (Exception ex) {
```

```
                          ex.printStackTrace();
                 }
          }

}
```

The ExampleJMXFindMethods application in Listing 7-10 creates three relations from three relation types and then adds all three PrinterObject MBeans to roles in each using the setRole() method. The same RoleInfo object is used to create each relation type. Next, the findReferencingRelations() method is called with the ObjectName of one of the PrinterObject MBeans and a value of null for the second and third arguments. A value of null to the second and third arguments causes all relation types and roles to be returned in the results. Otherwise, the results are filtered based on the values supplied in the second and third arguments.

The output from running the ExampleJMXFindMethods application looks like the following:

```
Referencing relations>>>>>>>>>>>>
Object: PrinterObject:name=HP Deskjet Color appears in these
relations...
Relation: MK1
Relation: IT1
Relation: HR1
```

The information returned from one of the find methods is useful, but it is also useful to be able to retrieve information about a particular role in a relation. The following section will show you how to do just that.

## Getting role information

At any time, you can obtain information about a particular role by using the getRoleInfo() method of the RelationService MBean. This method can be useful if you're displaying role information in a GUI or if you're trying to determine if a role can be updated by viewing the constraints in the role. Listing 7-11 shows the source code for a small application that prints information about the RoleInfo class.

**Listing 7-11: Printing role information**

```
import javax.management.MBeanServer;
import javax.management.MBeanServerFactory;
import javax.management.ObjectName;
import javax.management.relation.Role;
import javax.management.relation.RoleInfo;
import javax.management.relation.RoleList;
import javax.management.relation.RoleResult;
import javax.management.relation.RoleStatus;
import javax.management.relation.RoleUnresolved;
import javax.management.relation.RoleUnresolvedList;
import javax.management.relation.RelationService;
import java.util.ArrayList;
```

```java
import java.util.Iterator;
import java.util.List;


public class ExampleJMXPrintInfo {

        private static MBeanServer server = null;


        public ExampleJMXPrintInfo(){
                server = MBeanServerFactory.createMBeanServer();
        }

        public static void main(String args[]){

                ExampleJMXPrintInfo agent = new ExampleJMXPrintInfo();

                RelationService relServ = new RelationService(false);

                PrintObject prntObj = new PrintObject();

                try {

                        ObjectName objName =
                            new ObjectName("RelationService:type=relate");

                        server.registerMBean(relServ,objName);

                        ObjectName pObj =
                            new ObjectName("PrinterObject:name=HP Deskjet");
                        ObjectName pObj1 =
                            new ObjectName("PrinterObject:name=HP Laserjet");
                        ObjectName pObj2 =
                         new ObjectName("PrinterObject:name=HP Deskjet
Color");

                        server.registerMBean(prntObj,pObj);
                        server.registerMBean(prntObj,pObj1);
                        server.registerMBean(prntObj,pObj2);

                        // Add Relation Type //

                        String className =
                            server.getObjectInstance(pObj).getClassName();

                        RoleInfo rInfo = new RoleInfo("Printers",
                                                        className,
                                                        true,
                                                        true,
```

```
                                                0,
                                                3,
                                                "Printers Role");

        relServ.createRelationType("IT Printers",
                                    new RoleInfo[]{rInfo});

        RoleInfo rInfoPrint =
            relServ.getRoleInfo("IT Printers","Printers");

        System.out.println("Role Name: " +
                            rInfoPrint.getName());
        System.out.println("Role Description: " +
                            rInfoPrint.getDescription());
        System.out.println("Role Class Name: " +
                            rInfoPrint.getRefMBeanClassName());
        System.out.println("Is Readable: " +
                            rInfoPrint.isReadable());
        System.out.println("Is Writable: " +
                            rInfoPrint.isWritable());
        System.out.println("Min Beans: " +
                            rInfoPrint.getMinDegree());
        System.out.println("Max MBeans: " +
                            rInfoPrint.getMaxDegree());

    } catch (Exception ex) {
        ex.printStackTrace();
    }
  }
}
```

The output from running the `ExampleJMXPrintInfo` application looks like the following:

```
Role Name: Printers
Role Description: Printers Role
Role Class Name: PrinterObject
Is Readable: true
Is Writable: true
Min Beans: 0
Max MBeans: 3
```

As different events occur in the relation service, such as a role being updated or a relation being created, the relation service sends notifications to interested listeners. The notifications take the form of the `javax.management.relation.RelationNotification` class.

## Relation notifications

Recall from the beginning of this chapter that the relation service can send notifications of events, such as a relation being added or an MBean being removed from a relation. The relation service can send notifications of the following events:

♦ A relation is created via the relation service
♦ An MBean is added as a relation
♦ A role is updated in a relation
♦ A relation is removed from the relation service

Like all the other agent services defined in the JMX specification, the notifications emitted from the relation service are based on the notification model for MBeans. Each agent service — timer, monitoring, and dynamic loading — has defined a subclass of the `Notification` class and added methods unique to the service in question. The relation service is no different.

The `javax.management.relation.RelationNotification` class serves as the class for building notifications for relation service events. Table 7-4 describes the declared methods of the `RelationNotification` class.

### Table 7-4    RelationNotification Class Methods

| Method Name | Description |
|---|---|
| `getMBeansToUnRegister()` | Returns a `java.util.List` of MBean `ObjectNames`, which will be unregistered due to the removal of a relation |
| `getNewRoleValue()` | Returns a `java.util.List` of the new value for a role when a role is updated |
| `getObjectName()` | Returns the `ObjectName` of an MBean serving as a relation when it is created, updated, or removed |
| `getOldRoleValue()` | Returns a `java.util.List` of the old value for a role when a role is updated |
| `getRelationId()` | Returns a `java.lang.String` of the relation ID of the relation that was created, updated, or removed |
| `getRelationTypeName()` | Returns a `java.lang.String` of the relation ID of the relation that was created, updated, or removed |
| `getRoleName()` | Returns a `java.lang.String` of the role name that was updated in a relation |

Some of the methods only make sense when the type of relation notification sent matches the method use. For example, if a notification for an update to a relation occurs, then using the `getRoleName()` method would not make sense, as a role is not being updated. I've borrowed Listing 7-3 to demonstrate the types of notifications that are sent during various operations with the relation service. Listing 7-12 shows the source of an application, which will receive notifications of the various activities occurring during the application.

**Listing 7-12: Receiving relation service notifications**

```java
import javax.management.MBeanServer;
import javax.management.MBeanServerFactory;
import javax.management.ObjectName;
import javax.management.Notification;
import javax.management.NotificationListener;
import javax.management.relation.Role;
import javax.management.relation.RoleInfo;
import javax.management.relation.RoleList;
import javax.management.relation.RoleResult;
import javax.management.relation.RelationNotification;
import javax.management.relation.RelationService;
import java.util.ArrayList;
import java.util.Iterator;
import java.util.List;
import java.util.Vector;


public class ExampleJMXAddRolesNotification implements
NotificationListener {

        private static MBeanServer server = null;


        public ExampleJMXAddRolesNotification(){
                server = MBeanServerFactory.createMBeanServer();
        }

        public static void main(String args[]){

                ExampleJMXAddRolesNotification agent =
                        new ExampleJMXAddRolesNotification();

                RelationService relServ = new RelationService(false);

                PrintObject prntObj = new PrintObject();

                try {

                        ObjectName objName = new
ObjectName("RelationService:type=relate");

                        server.registerMBean(relServ,objName);

                        ObjectName pObj =
                            new ObjectName("PrinterObject:name=HP Deskjet");
                        ObjectName pObj1 =
                            new ObjectName("PrinterObject:name=HP Laserjet");
                        ObjectName pObj2 =
```

```
                        new ObjectName("PrinterObject:name=HP Deskjet
Color");

            server.registerMBean(prntObj,pObj);
            server.registerMBean(prntObj,pObj1);
            server.registerMBean(prntObj,pObj2);

            relServ.addNotificationListener(agent,null,null);

            // Add Relation Type //

            String className =
                    server.getObjectInstance(pObj).getClassName();

            RoleInfo rInfo = new RoleInfo("Printers",
                                          className,
                                          true,
                                          true,
                                          0,
                                          3,
                                          "Printers Role");

            relServ.createRelationType("IT Printers",
                            new RoleInfo[]{rInfo});

            // Add a relation //
            relServ.createRelation("ID1","IT Printers",
                            new RoleList());

            // Add a Role //
            List roles = new ArrayList();
            roles.add(pObj);
            roles.add(pObj1);
            roles.add(pObj2);

            Role aRole = new Role("Printers",roles);

            // Set the role //
            relServ.setRole("ID1",aRole);

            // Access the Roles //
            RoleResult roleResult = relServ.getAllRoles("ID1");

            // Print Roles Successfully Accessed //
            RoleList roleList = roleResult.getRoles();
            Iterator roleIter = roleList.iterator();
            while (roleIter.hasNext()){
                    Role theRole = (Role)roleIter.next();
                    System.out.println("Role Name: " +
```

```
                                      theRole.getRoleName());
                   System.out.println("MBeans in Role: " +
                             theRole.getRoleValue().size());
                }

          } catch (Exception ex) {
              ex.printStackTrace();
          }
      }


      // Print Notification //
      public void handleNotification(Notification notif,
                                     Object handBack){
             RelationNotification relNotify =
                             (RelationNotification)notif;
             System.out.println("Relation Type Name: " +
                             relNotify.getRelationTypeName());
             System.out.println("Relation Id: " +
                             relNotify.getRelationId());
             System.out.println("Role Name: " +
                             relNotify.getRoleName());
             System.out.println("New Role Value: " +
                             relNotify.getNewRoleValue());
             System.out.println("Old Role Value: " +
                             relNotify.getOldRoleValue());
      }

}
```

The output from running the `ExampleJMXAddRolesNotification` should look like the following:

```
Relation Type Name: IT Printers
Relation Id: ID1
Role Name: null
New Role Value: []
Old Role Value: []
Relation Type Name: IT Printers
Relation Id: ID1
Role Name: Printers
New Role Value: [PrinterObject:name=HP Deskjet, PrinterObject:name=HP
Laserjet,
PrinterObject:name=HP Deskjet Color]
Old Role Value: []
Role Name: Printers
MBeans in Role: 3
```

The output from this example includes two notifications. The first notification is sent when the relation with ID `ID1` is created for relation type `IT Printers`. The role name and the new and old role values are null because at this point in the application those values are not being used.

The second notification is sent when the role `Printers` is added to the relation with ID `ID1`. The role name of `Printers` is printed and the new role value of the three `PrinterObject` MBeans is printed. The old role value is still null because the role previously had no value. The application finishes by printing some role information for the relation.

# Summary

In this chapter, you examined the relation service and how to use its various components. You learned how to create relation types, relations, and roles, and how these three components interact. Roles can exist in a resolved or unresolved state, the latter indicating a problem related to the cardinality of the role or the read/write access to the role. Information about a role is expressed as an instance of the `RoleInfo` class, which defines the role's constraints.

In the next chapter, you examine the MBean Server, which is responsible for providing access to management clients an applications.

# Part III

# Implementing the Agent Layer

## Chapter 8

# Understanding the MBean Server

Chapters 4 and 5 covered two types of MBeans — standard and dynamic — and described how to construct them and other rules related to their creation. I briefly touched on invoking methods of MBeans, and made many references to something called the *MBean Server*. In Chapter 2, you examined the JMX architecture and the role the MBean Server plays in that architecture.

This chapter goes into more detail about the MBean Server, including how to use it and what its methods do. You'll learn how to interact with MBeans that are registered in the server, as well as dynamically loaded MBeans using an MLet.

This chapter also begins your exploration of the JMX agent layer of the JMX architecture. The MBean Server is a critical and mandatory component of the JMX specification and the JMX agent layer. You'll soon understand how to create an instance of an MBean Server, as well as how to load MBeans into the MBean Server. You'll also perform some new updates to the `MBeanBrowser` that was started in Chapter 4.

## Learning about the MBean Server

The MBean Server acts as a broker between managed beans and JMX agents and management applications. A JMX agent has at least one MBean Server, which contains a registry of MBeans that it knows about. The registry of MBeans can be built using a few different means, which are covered in this chapter. The MBean Server registry can also contain different types of MBeans, such as dynamic and standard MBeans. You can register and unregister MBeans at any time using the MBean Server.

The MBean Server takes requests from clients and passes the request on to the MBean in the form of getting or setting an attribute or invoking an operation. The MBean Server then returns the result to the caller. The MBean Server also has some other capabilities such as searching for MBeans, providing hooks into the MBean registration process, and sending notifications.

Without the MBean Server, management applications cannot interact with managed resources. You may recall from Chapters 4 and 5 the discussions about the `javax.management` `.ObjectName` class, which serves as a reference to a managed bean. This reference is not a direct reference, such as an object handle created by using the `new` operator. The name MBean

Server may suggest something similar to other "server" types of applications, such as Web or FTP servers. While conceptually similar, an MBean Server operates quite differently. The MBean Server does not listen on a network port for requests to come in. However, you'll learn how to use the MBean Server in a distributed environment by using Remote Method Invocation (RMI) and the Java Naming and Directory Interface (JNDI).

The MBean Server is responsible for creating and destroying references to registered MBeans, as well as delivering notifications to MBeans in its registry when MBeans are registered and unregistered. In a nutshell, the MBean Server functionality falls into these categories:

♦ Registering and unregistering MBeans

♦ Providing access to MBeans and their data

♦ Providing means to query for MBeans

♦ Enabling addition of notification listeners to an MBean

# Understanding the MBeanServer Interface

The MBean Server exposes many methods that in turn expose a variety of functionality and interaction with the MBean Server. Before learning how to create an instance of an MBean Server, you should understand the class that enables this. The JMX API defines a class named the MBeanServerFactory that is responsible for managing instances of an MBean Server. With this class, you can create new instances, find an existing instance, or instruct the MBeanServerFactory to release an instance of an MBean Server so that it may be garbage collected. The MBeanServerFactory class contains a small number of methods that enable you to accomplish these things. The methods of the MBeanServerFactory are described in Table 8-1.

### Table 8-1    MBeanServerFactory Methods

| Method Name | Description |
| --- | --- |
| createMBeanServer() | Creates an MBean Server that uses the default domain |
| createMBeanServer(java.lang .String domain) | Takes a java.lang.String and creates an MBean Server using the domain specified by the string |
| findMBeanServer(java.lang.String id) | Takes a java.lang.String representing the ID of an MBean Server to find. The ID of the MBean Server is the value of the MBeanServerId attribute of the MBean Server's delegate MBean. |
| newMBeanServer() | Creates a new MBean Server and returns it without keeping a reference to it |

| Method Name | Description |
|---|---|
| `newMBeanServer(java.lang.String domain)` | Creates a new MBean Server reference in the domain specified by the ID without keeping a reference to it |
| `releaseMBeanServer(javax.management.MBeanServer)` | Takes an MBean Server instance and releases the reference to the MBean Server. You use this method if you used the `createMBeanServer()` method to create an MBean Server instance. |

## MBean Server Permission Checks

The `MBeanServerFactory` class methods are protected against unauthorized access by MBean Server permission checking. When you write a JMX application that utilizes a security manager, each call to the following methods is checked for authorized access:

♦ `createMBeanServer`

♦ `findMBeanServer`

♦ `newMBeanServer`

♦ `releaseMBeanServer`

If you are not utilizing a security manager in your application, you don't need to worry about permission checking. However, if you are writing JMX applications that run in an application server, for example, the likelihood that a security manager is present is greatly increased, in which case you need to be able to enable or disable the permissions needed by your application.

You enable permissions to execute these methods in the same way as other Java permissions, by making an entry in the appropriate security policy file. You can also utilize the new `javax.management.MBeanServerPermission`. The following code snippet is an example of updating a security policy file:

```
// "standard" properties that can be read by anyone
grant {
        permission javax.management.MBeanServerPermission "*";
};
```

This example indicates that all permissions can be executed. If you want to restrict the permissions to a single permission such as creating an MBean Server, you use the value of `createMBeanServer`. The names of the permissions follow the names of the methods listed in the earlier bullet list.

## Instantiating the MBean Server

You have two ways to get an instance of an MBean Server. You can create a new instance of an MBean Server, or you can get an existing instance of an MBean Server. The first method is relatively straightforward; you use class named `javax.management.MBeanServerFactory` to create a new instance of an MBean Server and return it.

You can create a new instance of an `MBeanServer` using the factory class `javax.management.MBeanServerFactory`. Listing 8-1 shows a simple Java application that creates an instance of an `MBeanServer`.

**Listing 8-1: Instantiating an MBeanServer**

```
import javax.management.MBeanServer;
import javax.management.MBeanServerFactory;

public class CreateMBeanServer {

    public static void main(String[] args) {

        MBeanServer server = MBeanServerFactory.createMBeanServer();
    }

}
```

This example presents the simplest scenario of instantiating an `MBeanServer`. The other method requests that the MBean Server use an existing instance. To use an existing instance of an MBean Server, you can do one of two things. The first is to keep a reference to the MBean Server in an instance variable and use the reference whenever you need to. The example shown in Listing 8-2 keeps an instance variable reference to an MBean Server.

**Listing 8-2: Using an instance variable to refer to an MBean Server**

```
import javax.management.MBeanServer;
import javax.management.MBeanServerFactory;

public class CreateMBeanServerRef {

    private static MBeanServer beanServer = null;

    public static void main(String[] args) {

        beanServer = MBeanServerFactory.createMBeanServer();
    }

}
```

Here, the private instance variable `beanServer` is used to provide access to an MBean Server while an instance of the `CreateMBeanServerRef` class is present. If you needed to perform any functions that required the use of an MBean Server, you could use the `beanServer` variable, providing you have proper access to it. You may want to provide an accessor method, such as `getMBeanServerInstance()` or something similar. Later in this section, you'll learn how to ensure that only one instance of an MBean Server is running in an agent. In most cases, unless you're just writing a simple demo application, you'll probably want to store the reference to the MBean Server for later retrieval, or use the next method to get an existing instance of an MBean Server.

The second way to get an instance of an existing MBean Server is to ask the `MBeanServerFactory` class to find an instance of the MBean Server using an identification string. The identification string is specified when the MBean Server instance is created in the `createMBeanServer()` method. This string becomes the default domain when the MBean Server is created. The example shown in Listing 8-3 creates an MBean Server with a default domain of `Foobar`.

**Listing 8-3: Creating an MBean Server with an ID**

```
import javax.management.MBeanServer;
import javax.management.MBeanServerFactory;

public class CreateMBeanServerById {

    public static void main(String[] args) {

        MBeanServer server =
                MBeanServerFactory.createMBeanServer("Foobar");

        System.out.println("Default Domain: " +
                            server.getDefaultDomain());
    }

}
```

The output from the second line of code, which prints the default domain, should look like the following:

```
Default Domain: Foobar
```

As you can see, the value has indeed become the default domain. As indicated, this value can also be used to find an instance of an existing MBean Server. Table 8-1 described the methods of the `MBeanServerFactory()` method, including a method named `findMBeanServer()`, which takes a `java.lang.String` representing the ID used in Listing 8-3. The example shown in Listing 8-4 uses the MBean Server ID to locate an existing MBean Server.

**Listing 8-4: Using the findMBeanServer method to locate an existing MBean Server**

```
import java.util.ArrayList;
import javax.management.ObjectName;
import javax.management.MBeanServer;
import javax.management.MBeanServerFactory;

public class LocateMBeanServerById {

    public static void main(String[] args) {

                LocateMBeanServerById agent =
```

```
                          new LocateMBeanServerById();


        MBeanServer server1 =
MBeanServerFactory.createMBeanServer("MBeanServer1");
                MBeanServer server2 =
MBeanServerFactory.createMBeanServer("MBeanServer2");
                MBeanServer server3 =
MBeanServerFactory.createMBeanServer("MBeanServer3");

                // Find the MBeanServers and try to find one that doesn't
exist //

                findMBeanServer(getMBeanServerId(server1));
                findMBeanServer(getMBeanServerId(server2));
                findMBeanServer(getMBeanServerId(server3));
    }

    private static String getMBeanServerId(MBeanServer server){
                String id = "";
                try{
                    ObjectName name = new
ObjectName("JMImplementation:type=MBeanServerDelegate");
                    id =
(String)server.getAttribute(name,"MBeanServerId");
                }catch(Exception ex){
                    System.out.println(ex);
                }
                return id;
    }

    private static void findMBeanServer(String id){

                ArrayList servers =
MBeanServerFactory.findMBeanServer(id);

                System.out.println("Servers Found: " + servers.size());

                if (servers.size() > 0) {
                    MBeanServer server =
(MBeanServer)servers.iterator().next();
                    System.out.println("MBeanServer with id " + id + "
was found with domain " + server.getDefaultDomain());
                }else
                    System.out.println("MBeanServer with id " + id + "
was not found");
    }

}
```

This example loads three MBean Servers: MBeanServer1, MBeanServer2, and MBeanServer3, respectively. It then uses a private method, findMBeanServer(), to call the findMBeanServer() method of the MBeanServerFactory() class to locate each MBean. If the MBean Server is found, a message indicating such is printed. The value you pass to the findMBeanServer() is the value of the MBeanServerId attribute of the MBean Server's delegate MBean. In this example, you use the getMBeanServerId() private method to lookup the delegate MBean for the MBeanServer instance passed into the getMBeanServerId() method. In the getMBeanServerId() method, you lookup the MBeanServerId attribute using the getAttribute() method and return the string value to the caller.

> **NOTE:** You can create a new MBean Server instance using the createMBeanServer() method that takes a string argument. You should remember, however, that the value you pass to this method is the value that will be used for the default domain, not the ID. When using the findMBeanServer() to find that same MBean Server, you need to use the value of the MBeanServerId attribute of its delegate MBean.

## MBeanServer interface methods

Once you have an MBean Server instantiated, you undoubtedly will want to use it to do something such as load an MBean, query for an MBean, or invoke a method of an MBean. The MBeanServer interface includes several methods that enable you to perform the aforementioned functions. Some of these methods have different overloadings, so only a subset of the methods is described here. Once you are comfortable with these methods, you should have no trouble using the other variants. (You can review the other variants in the JavaDoc for the MBeanServer interface.) Table 8-2 describes this subset of the methods of the MBeanServer interface.

### Table 8-2    Subset of MBeanServer Interface Methods

| Method Name | Description |
| --- | --- |
| addNotificationListener(javax.management.ObjectName name, javax.management.NotificationListener listener, javax.management.NotificationFilter filter, java.lang.Object handBack) | Enables you to add a notification listener that will receive notifications emitted by the MBean represented by the ObjectName "name" |
| createMBean(java.lang.String className, javax.management.ObjectName name) | Creates and registers an MBean in an MBean Server |
| deserialize(javax.management.ObjectName name, byte[] data) | Enables you to deserialize an MBean |
| instantiate(java.lang.String className) | Enables you to instantiate an object without registering it in an MBean Server |

| Method Name | Description |
|---|---|
| `isInstanceOf(javax.management.ObjectName name, java.lang.String className)` | Enables you to check whether an MBean is an instance of a particular class or interface |
| `RegisterMBean(java.lang.Object object, javax.management.ObjectName name)` | Enables you to register an existing object as an MBean in an MBean Server |
| `unregisterMBean(javax.management.Objectname name)` | Enables you to unregister an MBean from an MBean Server |
| `invoke(javax.management.ObjectName name, java.lang.String opName, java.lang.Object[] parms, java.lang.String[] signature)` | Enables you to execute the method of an MBean using the MBean Server |
| `setAttribute(javax.management.ObjectName name,javax.management.Attribute attr)` | Enables you to set the value of an attribute |
| `getAttribute(javax.management.ObjectName name,java.lang.String attr)` | Enables you to retrieve the value of an attribute |
| `getMBeanInfo(javax.management.ObjectName name)` | Enables you to retrieve the `MBeanInfo` object for the name's MBean |
| `getMBeanCount()` | Enables you to return the number of MBeans registered in the MBean Server |

**CROSS-REFERENCE:** The MBeanInfo class returned from the getMBeanInfo() method is covered in Chapter 5.

The `addNotificationListener()` method is covered in detail in Chapter 11. The remaining methods are covered in the rest of this chapter.

## The MBeanServerDelegate MBean

Within the MBean Server you may notice an MBean named `MBeanServerDelegate` with an object name of `JMImplementation:type=MBeanServerDelegate`. The purpose of this MBean is to represent the MBean Server to other MBeans, as well as emit notifications for the MBean Server such as when an MBean is registered and unregistered. You do not explicitly create or register this MBean, and you cannot unregister it from the MBean Server. When you want to register interest in notifications of the MBean Server, you use the `MBeanServerDelegate`.

The `MBeanServerDelegate` MBean has several read-only attributes that provide information about the MBean Server and the implementor of the MBean Server. These attributes are as follows:

♦ `MBeanServerId` — This attribute identifies the agent. Its format is not specified.

♦ `SpecificationName` — This attribute specifies the full name of the JMX specification upon which this MBean Server implementation is based. It must have a value of `Java Management Extensions`.

♦ `SpecificationVersion` — This attribute specifies the version of the JMX specification on which this MBean Server implementation is based. It must have a value of `1.1 Maintenance Release`.

♦ `SpecificationVendor` — This attribute indicates the name of the vendor of the JMX specification on which this MBean Server implemenation is based. It must have a value of `Sun Microsystems`.

♦ `ImplementationName` — This attribute specifies the implementation name of the MBean Server. Its format and content are defined by the implementor.

♦ `ImplementationVersion` — This attribute specifies the version of the MBean Server. Its format and content are defined by the implementor.

♦ `ImplementationVendor` — This attribute specifies the name of the vendor of the MBean Server. The format and content are defined by the implementor.

# Registering an MBean

The registration process of an MBean occurs while creating an instance of the MBean. You can register an MBean dynamically by using the `createMBean()` method of the `MBeanServer` interface, or by using the `registerMBean()` method. To create an instance of the MBean, you need two pieces of information: the class name of the MBean and an instance of the `javax.management.ObjectName` class.

## Creating the ObjectName class

A `javax.management.ObjectName` class identifies an instance of an MBean in an MBean Server. An `ObjectName` instance serves as a reference, which management applications and JMX agents must use when they want to interact with the MBean. This does not mean that management clients, such as Web browsers or management consoles, will use the `ObjectName`. Rather, the application or JMX agent that is working with the MBean in question will work with the `ObjectName`.

The `ObjectName` instance to an MBean does not provide a direct reference to the MBean; rather, it serves as sort of a token that is passed to the MBean Server, which maintains the associations between `ObjectName` instances and the actual MBeans. The `ObjectName` consists of two parts:

♦ A domain name

♦ An unordered set of one or more key properties

You've already seen object names used in Chapters 4 and 5 when you created standard and dynamic MBeans. You used the object name to print information such as operations, attributes, and notifications of each type of MBean. When creating the MBean `ObjectName`, you specified two parameters to a method called `createMBean()`. The first was the class name of the MBean and the second was the `ObjectName` of the MBean, which had been previously created. For reference, Listing 8-5 contains the relevant lines of code.

**Listing 8-5: Creating an ObjectName and the MBean**

```
private ObjectName loadBean(String className,String objectName) {

        ObjectName mbeanObjectName = null;
        String domain = server.getDefaultDomain();
        String mbeanName = className;
        try {
            mbeanObjectName = new ObjectName(objectName);
        } catch(MalformedObjectNameException e) {
          e.printStackTrace();
          System.exit(1);
        }

          // Create our simple object to manage //
                            try {
            server.createMBean(mbeanName,mbeanObjectName);
          }catch(Exception ex){
                ex.printStackTrace();
                System.exit(1);
          }

          return mbeanObjectName;
}
```

The `loadBean()` method takes the class name and `java.lang.String` representing the object name and passes the object name to the constructor of the `javax.management` `.ObjectName` class. The instance of the `javax.management.ObjectName` class is then passed, along with the class name, to the `createMBean()` method, which instructs the MBean Server to create and register an instance of that MBean. The class name argument is self-explanatory, but the string representing the object name deserves more explanation.

As noted at the beginning of this section, the object name is constructed using a string that consists of a domain name and one or more key value pairs, which are used to initialize the MBean. The domain name of an MBean is used to indicate the realm of administration to which an MBean belongs. The domain can also be used to locate an MBean. Any MBean that is created can also belong to a default domain of `com.sun.management.jmx` `.ServiceName.DOMAIN`. You can retrieve the default domain of an MBean by using the `getDefaultDomain()` method of the `javax.management.MBeanServer` interface, as shown in Listing 8-6.

**Listing 8-6: Printing the default domain**

```
import javax.management.MBeanServer;
import javax.management.MBeanServerFactory;

public class MBeanServerDefaultDomain {
```

```
public static void main(String[] args) {

    MBeanServer server = MBeanServerFactory.createMBeanServer();

    System.out.println("Default Domain: " +
                        server.getDefaultDomain());
}
}
```

Running this application with the Sun JMX reference implementation produces the following output:

```
Default Domain: DefaultDomain
```

The domain name can be constructed out of any printable characters other than the colon (`:`), the comma (`,`), the equal sign (`=`), the asterik (`*`), or the question mark (`?`). These characters are considered *separator characters* between the domain name and the list of name/value pairs.

The second part of the `ObjectName` is an unordered list of key/value pairs, also called name/value pairs. These values are used to specify parameters to the initialization of the MBean. In Chapters 4 and 5, you may have noticed a string like the one that follows, which appears when constructing an instance of the `ObjectName`:

```
ObjectName simpleObject = agent.loadBean("DynamicManageableObjectRef",
                        "DynamicManageableObjectRef:name=simple");
```

The second argument to the `loadBean()` method with the `colon` and `name=simple` value is the key/value pair. You can use any number of key/value pairs, although if the number is large you should consider a different means of initializing MBean values. You could, for instance, load a properties file with the MBean inside the constructor. You could also hook into the registration process, which you'll see later in the "The MBeanRegisteration interface" section, and load the properties there as well.

Note that the key/value properties passed in do not need to actually correspond to any attributes of the MBean itself. They are used for identifying a particular MBean, and when performing queries for MBeans in an MBean Server. The `ObjectName` class exposes several methods that enable you to access the properties that were passed in. Table 8-3 describes a subset of the methods of the `javax.management.ObjectName` class that are used for working with key/value properties.

## Table 8-3    Subset of ObjectName Methods

| Method Name | Description |
|---|---|
| getCanonicalKeyPropertyListString() | Retuns a `java.lang.String` representing the properties specified at runtime and sorted in lexographical order |
| getKeyProperty() | Returns a `java.lang.String` representing the value of the property name passed in |
| getKeyPropertyList() | Returns a `java.util.Hashtable` containing the key/value pairs specified at runtime |
| getKeyPropertyListString() | Returns a `java.lang.String` representation of the properties specified at runtime |

The last three methods in Table 8-3 are straightforward in that they retrieve the value of the properties as a single value, a set of values, or a string of the values. The first method, however, manipulates the string and sorts the values before returning them. Listing 8-7 shows the use of the `getCanonicalKeyPropertyListString()` method, followed by some sample output that results from using it. This example uses the `DynamicManageableObjectRef` MBean that was introduced in Chapter 5.

**Listing 8-7: Using the getCanonicalKeyPropertyListString method**

```
import javax.management.ObjectName;
import javax.management.MalformedObjectNameException;
import javax.management.MBeanServer;
import javax.management.MBeanServerFactory;

public class GetKeyProperties {

    private static MBeanServer server = null;

    public static void main(String[] args) {

        server = MBeanServerFactory.createMBeanServer();

        String properties = "port=8000," +
                            "name=DynamicManageableObjectRef," +
                            "ssl=true," +
                            "username=mikej";

        ObjectName simpleObject =
            loadBean("DynamicManageableObjectRef",
```

```
                        "DynamicManageableObjectRef:" + properties);

            // Print out properties //
            System.out.println("Properties: " +
                simpleObject.getCanonicalKeyPropertyListString());

    }

    private static ObjectName loadBean(String className,
                                       String objectName) {

        ObjectName mbeanObjectName = null;
        String domain = server.getDefaultDomain();
        String mbeanName = className;
        try {
            mbeanObjectName = new ObjectName(objectName);
        } catch(MalformedObjectNameException e) {
          e.printStackTrace();
          System.exit(1);
        }
            // Create our simple object to manage //
            try {
                server.createMBean(mbeanName,mbeanObjectName);
            }catch(Exception ex){
                ex.printStackTrace();
                System.exit(1);
            }

            return mbeanObjectName;
    }
}
```

The output from running the GetKeyProperties Java application should look like the
following. As you can see, the properties have been sorted beginning with the name property.

```
Properties:
name=DynamicManageableObjectRef,port=8000,ssl=true,username=mikej
```

Now that you've been exposed to domains and key/value property lists, you should have some
idea of what constitutes a valid ObjectName. If you try to use invalid syntax to construct an
ObjectName, a javax.management.MalformedObjectNameException is thrown. You
should also know that you don't need an actual MBean or MBean Server in order to construct
an ObjectName. Listing 8-8 shows the source code for a sample program that attempts to
construct three different ObjectNames and prints the results and failures of each attempt.

**Listing 8-8: Constructing an ObjectName**

```
import javax.management.ObjectName;
import javax.management.MalformedObjectNameException;
```

```
public class MakeObjectNames {

    public static void main(String args[]) {

        makeObjectName("SimpleObject");

        makeObjectName("SimpleObject:name=simple,port=8000");

        makeObjectName(":");
    }

    private static void makeObjectName(String name) {

        System.out.println("");

        try {

            ObjectName obj = new ObjectName(name);

            System.out.println(name + " was successfully constructed");

        } catch (MalformedObjectNameException mfo) {

            System.out.println(name + " could not be constructed ");
            System.out.println("Reason: " + mfo.getMessage());

        }
    }
}
```

The MakeObjectNames Java application in Listing 8-8 attempts to construct three different ObjectNames using three different names, two of which are invalid, as you'll see next. The output from running the MakeObjectNames Java application should look like the following:

```
SimpleObject could not be constructed
Reason: ObjectName: domain part must be specified

SimpleObject:name=simple,port=8000 was successfully constructed

: could not be constructed
Reason: ObjectName: Key properties cannot be null
```

From the output, you can see that the first attempt failed because the domain part of the object name is missing. The first attempt used only the string SimpleObject in the constructor of the ObjectName. The second attempt was successful because it included the required domain name as well as a list of name/value pairs. The third and last attempt failed because the key/properties value was null. The constructor of the ObjectName expected to see a list of key/value properties because of the constructor used for the ObjectName. The ObjectName class has three constructors, one of which you just saw in Listing 8-8. This constructor takes a single string representing the domain name and one or more key/value pairs to identify the MBean.

The other two constructors take the same types of arguments, but they are handled a little differently. One constructor takes two arguments: the domain name and a `java.util.Hashtable` containing the key/value pairs. The third constructor overloading takes three arguments: the domain name, the name of a key, and value of the key. The third constructor overloading enables you to construct an `ObjectName` with exactly one key/value pair.

## Creating an MBean

After you have created an `ObjectName`, you can use it to create an MBean in one of two ways. The first way involves utilizing the `createMBean()` method of the `MBeanServer` interface. When you use the `createMBean()` method, the MBean Server handles registration of the MBean for you.

The `MBeanServer` interface has four different overloadings for the `createMBean()` method. The overloading you've seen used throughout this book so far is the one that takes two arguments:

- A `java.lang.String` representing the class name of the MBean
- A `javax.management.ObjectName` for the MBean

The other methods are variations that enable you to control which constructor is used to instantiate an MBean or which class loader is used to load the class and create an instance of it. Listing 8-9 shows the source of an interface you'll use for an MBean that you'll later load with the MBean Server.

**Listing 8-9: The SimpleObjectMBean interface**

```
public interface SimpleObjectMBean{

    public String getName();

    public void setName(String newName);

    public String doNothing();

}
```

The implementation of this interface is shown in Listing 8-10.

**Listing 8-10: The SimpleObject class**

```
public class SimpleObject implements SimpleObjectMBean{

    private String name = "Simple Object";

    public SimpleObject(){
    }
```

```
    public SimpleObject(String iName){
        name = iName;
    }

    public String getName(){
        return name;
    }

    public void setName(String newName){
        name = newName;
    }

    public String doNothing(){
        return "Nothing";
    }

}
```

The simple process of loading the `SimpleObjectMBean` is shown in Listing 8-11.

**Listing 8-11: Creating and registering an MBean with the createMBean method**

```
import javax.management.ObjectName;
import javax.management.MBeanServer;
import javax.management.MBeanServerFactory;

public class CreateMBean {

    private static MBeanServer server = null;

    public CreateMBean() {

        server = MBeanServerFactory.createMBeanServer();

    }

    public static void main(String[] args) {

    CreateMBean agent = new CreateMBean();

        ObjectName mbeanObjectName1 = null;
        ObjectName mbeanObjectName2 = null;

        String domain = server.getDefaultDomain();
        String mbeanName = "SimpleObject";
        try {

            mbeanObjectName1 =
                new ObjectName("SimpleObject:name=simple1");
```

```
                    server.createMBean(mbeanName,mbeanObjectName1);

                mbeanObjectName2 =
                    new ObjectName("SimpleObject:name=simple2");

                server.createMBean(mbeanName,
                                mbeanObjectName2,
                                new Object[]{"Simple Object"},
                                new String[]{"java.lang.String"});

        } catch(Exception e) {
            e.printStackTrace();
            System.exit(1);
        }
        }

}
```

This listing constructs an ObjectName using the string SimpleObject:name=simple and then passes this and the string representing the name of the MBean class (SimpleObject) to the createMBean() method. By now, you are probably comfortable creating an MBean this way, as it has been handled like this in other parts of the book.

The second method in this application shows how to use the createMBean() method, which takes the same arguments as the first, but adds the capability to specify constructors, using two arrays. The first array specifies the actual objects representing the arguments, and the second array specifies the class names of each argument passed in.

These two methods represent the easiest and most straightforward ways to create and register MBean instances. You can also load arbitrary classes using the instantiate() method of the MBeanServer interface. The variations of this method enable you to create instances of classes using the class loader that the MBeanServer knows about. You can also use an instance of a javax.management.ObjectName to represent the class loader with which you want to load the class. Using the instantiate() method is quite simple, as shown in Listing 8-12.

**Listing 8-12: Using the instantiate method to load a class**

```
import javax.management.ObjectName;
import javax.management.MBeanServer;
import javax.management.MBeanServerFactory;

public class InstantiateMBean {

    private static MBeanServer server = null;

    public InstantiateMBean() {
        server = MBeanServerFactory.createMBeanServer();
    }
```

```
    public static void main(String[] args) {

      InstantiateMBean agent = new InstantiateMBean();

      try {

        Object obj = server.instantiate("SimpleObject");

        if (obj instanceof SimpleObjectMBean)
                System.out.println("SimpleObject MBean created");

        server.registerMBean(obj,
              new ObjectName("SimpleObject:name=simple"));

    } catch(Exception e) {
      e.printStackTrace();
      System.exit(1);
    }
  }
}
```

Listing 8-12 uses the `instantiate()` method to load the `SimpleObject` class, which happens to be an MBean. This example does not present the most common way to load an MBean; it merely uses the `SimpleObject` class for this example. You would more commonly use the `createMBean()` method of the `MBeanServer` interface or the `new` operator to load an MBean. However, you can use the `instantiate()` method to load an MBean and then use the `registerMBean()` method to register it.

## Statically registering and unregistering MBeans

Sometimes, you may want to unregister an MBean without destroying the instance of it. For example, you may want to unregister an MBean representing a set of socket connections. If you were to destroy the MBean, all of the socket connections would have to be reestablished the next time the MBean was instantiated. If you have an MBean that will perform lengthy operations during initialization you should consider simply unregistering it instead of destroying the MBean altogether.

You can also use this method to register objects loaded using other means, such as with the `instantiate()` method used in Listing 8-12. Likewise, if you want to unregister the MBean, you just pass the `ObjectName` to the `unregisterMBean()` method of the `MBeanServer` interface.

Using the `instantiate()` and `registerMBean()` methods presents a way of statically registering an MBean, whereas using the `createMBean()` enables you to dynamically register an MBean. The `createMBean()` method instructs the MBean Server to register the MBean for you.

### Examining the ObjectInstance class

What is the `javax.management.ObjectInstance` class needed for? The `ObjectInstance` class is the link between the MBean implementation class and the `ObjectName` for the MBean. It does not allow you to access the `MBean` class, but you can get a reference to the `ObjectName` of the MBean.

The `ObjectInstance` class pops up in a few places that you may not immediately notice. For instance, when you construct an MBean using the `createMBean()` method of the `MBeanServer` interface, an `ObjectInstance` is returned from the `createMBean()` method. If you take an existing MBean and register it with an MBean Server, an `ObjectInstance` for the MBean is returned.

## The MBeanRegistration interface

When you work with objects that are managed by a container of sorts, it's often desirable to be able to hook in and see what's going on at certain points of execution. If you've done any Enterprise JavaBean (EJB) development, you have probably seen the `EntityBean` and `SessionBean` interfaces. These interfaces define methods such as `ejbRemove()`, `ejbPassive()`, and `ejbCreate()`, which enable the EJB developer to receive events in the form of a callback when the EJB container is performing certain functions, such as activating an instance of an EJB or removing the EJB from the EJB container.

The MBean Server also provides the same type of callback functionality in the form of the `javax.management.MBeanRegistration` interface. Any type of MBean can implement the `MBeanRegistration` interface and receive notifications of four types of events. Table 8-4 shows the methods of the `MBeanRegistration` interface.

### Table 8-4    The MBeanRegistration Interface

| Method Name | Description |
| --- | --- |
| `postDeregister()` | Called before the MBean is unregistered in the MBean Server |
| `postRegister(java.lang.Boolean registrationDone)` | Called after the MBean has been registered or after registration has failed in the MBean Server |
| `preDeregister()` | Called before the MBean is unregistered in the MBean Server |
| `preRegister(javax.management.MBean Server,javax.management.ObjectName)` | Called before the MBean is registered in the MBean Server |

The capability to receive notifications of these types of events taking place in the MBean Server is useful because it allows the MBean to perform actions that may need to take place at specific points. For example, if you have an MBean that represents a pool of database connections, you could receive a notification when the MBean is registered so that you could initialize the pool; and when the MBean was unregistered, you could destroy the pool. Another example is if the MBean is working with native code. The MBean can load the necessary libraries before registration, and unload them after registration.

Being able to receive notifications before registration can enable you to prevent an MBean from being registered. If a given condition is not met, such as the unavailability of a network address, you could throw an exception, preventing the MBean from initializing. Of course, without the `MBeanRegistration` interface, you could throw an exception in the constructor of an MBean. Listing 8-13 shows the source code for an MBean interface.

**Listing 8-13: The ApplicationComponentMBean interface**

```
import java.util.Vector;

public interface ApplicationComponentMBean {

        public void setChildProcesses(Vector p);
        public Vector getChildProcesses();
        public long getWorkingStorage();
        public long getPageSize();
        public void setName(String newName);
        public String getName();

}
```

Listing 8-14 shows the source of the MBean that implements the `MBeanRegistration` interface and the `ApplicationComponentMBean` interface.

**Listing 8-14: A class that implements the MBeanRegistration interface**

```
import java.util.Vector;
import javax.management.MBeanRegistration;
import javax.management.MBeanServer;
import javax.management.ObjectName;

public class ApplicationComponent implements ApplicationComponentMBean,
                MBeanRegistration{

        private String name = "";

        public ApplicationComponent(){
                setName("ApplicationComponent");

        }

        public void setChildProcesses(Vector p){
        }
        public Vector getChildProcesses(){
                return new Vector();
        }
        public long getWorkingStorage(){
```

```
              return 0;
       }
       public long getPageSize(){
              return 0;
       }

       public void setName(String newName){
              name = newName;
       }

       public String getName(){
              return name;
       }

       // MBeanRegistration interface methods //
       public void postDeregister(){
              System.out.println("postDeregister:: ");
              System.out.println("After deregistering " + getName());
       }

       public void preDeregister(){
              System.out.println("preDeregister:: ");
              System.out.println("Before deregistering " + getName());
       }

       public void postRegister(Boolean ok) {
              System.out.print("postRegister:: ");
              System.out.println("After registring " + getName() +
                                 " successful = " + ok);
       }

       public ObjectName preRegister(MBeanServer server,
                                     ObjectName name){
              System.out.println("preRegister:: ");
              System.out.println("Before registering " + getName());
              System.out.println(getName() + " is in domain: " +
                                 name.getDomain());
              System.out.println("Name: " + name.getCanonicalName());

              return name;
       }
}
```

You can use the `CreateMBean` application from Listing 8-11 and specify the
`ApplicationComponent` class as the MBean to load. When you run the `CreateMBean`
application using the `ApplicationComponentMBean` you will see output that looks like the
following:

```
preRegister::
Before registering ApplicationComponent
ApplicationComponent is in domain: ApplicationComponent
Name: ApplicationComponent:name=simple
postRegister:: After registring ApplicationComponent successful = true
preDeregister::
Before deregistering ApplicationComponent
postDeregister::
After deregistering ApplicationComponent
```

Sometimes MBeans want to find other MBeans or use the query capabilities of the `MBeanServer` to find MBeans. Using the `MBeanRegistration` interface, an MBean can store a copy of the MBean that it was registered into for later use. MBeans can also cause other MBeans to be loaded, but they need the reference to the `MBeanServer` for this.

If an MBean wants to perform some sort of rudimentary dependency checking to ensure that the required MBeans were loaded, it can use the `MBeanRegistration` interface. The MBean would get the `MBeanServer` reference passed into the `preRegister()` method of the `MBeanRegistration` interface to look for other required MBeans. This might be useful, for instance, if you are managing a mixture of network and application components. The network components may need to be loaded before certain application components are allowed to start. Listing 8-15 provides the source for an MBean interface that will be implemented by an MBean that loads two MBeans; the second MBean that is loaded checks for the existence of the first MBean.

**Listing 8-15: The MBeanDependancyMBean interface**

```
public interface MBeanDependancyMBean {}
```

Listing 8-16 shows the source of the `MBeanDependancy` MBean that loads a dependant MBean.

**Listing 8-16: An MBean that loads another dependant MBean**

```
import java.util.Vector;
import javax.management.MBeanRegistration;
import javax.management.MBeanServer;
import javax.management.ObjectName;

public class MBeanDependancy implements MBeanDependancyMBean,
                                        MBeanRegistration{


        // MBeanRegistration interface methods //
        public void postDeregister(){
        }

        public void preDeregister(){
        }
```

```
    public void postRegister(Boolean ok) {
    }

    public ObjectName preRegister(MBeanServer server,
                                  ObjectName name){

        ObjectName depObj =
            getDependantObjectName("SimpleObject:name=simple");

        try {

            if (depObj != null)
                server.createMBean("SimpleObject",depObj);

        } catch (Exception ex) {

            System.out.println("Initialization of dependant MBean
failed " + ex);
        }

        return name;
    }

    private ObjectName getDependantObjectName(String name){

        ObjectName depObj = null;

        try {

            depObj = new ObjectName(name);

        } catch (Exception ex) {
            System.out.println(ex);
        }

        return depObj;

    }
}
```

In the example shown in Listing 8-16, the MBeanDependancy MBean uses the
preRegister() method to load an MBean with the name SimpleObject:name=simple.
The MBeanDependancy MBean uses the reference to the MBeanServer to call the
createMBean() method to load the second, dependant MBean. Using the javax
.management.ObjectName that was passed in, you could pass in the name of the next
MBean to load in the dependancy chain.

Another possible scenario involves having an MBean notify other MBeans if a problem occurs
and the MBean is going to be unregistered. The MBean being unregistered could notify

dependant MBeans that it is going to be unregistered. This scenario delves somewhat into notifications, a topic covered in Chapter 11.

You could even imagine a single MBean loading other dependant MBean instances by overriding the postRegister() method. The postRegister() method passes in a Boolean argument indicating whether the MBean was registered successfully or not. This Boolean argument could allow the MBean to decide whether to let dependant MBeans be loaded. In the case of dependant MBeans, however, it is likely that the dependant MBeans would not be loaded.

The Boolean that is passed in could have a value of true or false, which begs the question of whether the postRegister() method is called if an exception is thrown during construction of the MBean. Let's find out. The following snippet shows the source code for a constructor that answers this question.

```
public ApplicationComponent(){
            setName("ApplicationComponent");
            throws RuntimeException ("Exception in " + getName());
}
```

# Using MLets

MLets are features of JMX MBean Servers that enable you to load an MBean from a remote location (formally referred to as *dynamic loading* in the JMX specification). MBean classes and related resources are often on the same machine in the CLASSPATH of the MBean Server. However, in some cases the MBean may be located on another machine in the same or a different network. The MLet service, which is an abbreviation for Management Applet, enables the MBean Server to load the remote MBean dynamically. The MLet service is implemented as an MBean, which is controlled solely by an instance of the MBean Server.

MLets are specified in external files using syntax similar to Java applets. An MLet file can contain references to several different MBeans that you want the MBean Server to load. The capability to dynamically load MBeans from remote locations provides additional flexibility in how management solutions are constructed, as well as security. With dynamic loading, you can prevent unauthorized MBeans from being loaded into the MBean Server.

Listing 8-17 shows the syntax for the MLet tag.

**Listing 8-17: Syntax for the MLet tag**

```
<MLET
CODE = class | OBJECT = serfile
ARCHIVE = "archivelist"
[CODEBASE = codebaseURL]
[NAME = MBeanName]
[VERSION = version]
>
[arglist]
</MLET>
```

# The MLet tag and attributes

MBeans loaded using the MLet service can be in either Java class form or Java serialized object form and must exist in one of the JAR files listed in the ARCHIVE attribute. Packaging MBeans for use in an MLet tag is similar to packaging code for use with Java applets. You specify the CODE attribute, which must have a value of the fully qualified class name of the MBean, or you can specify the OBJECT attribute, which must have a value of the name of a serialized (.ser) file containing the MBean. If using the OBJECT attribute, you must specify the necessary directory path information reflected in the JAR. In either case, CODE or OBJECT; the MBean class must reside in the JAR file named in the <ARCHIVE> tag.

The <MLET> tag also includes three additional, optional attributes: CODEBASE, NAME, and VERSION. The CODEBASE attribute specifies the directory in which the JAR containing the MBean code is located. If this attribute is missing, the JAR is assumed to be in the same directory as the MLET text file.

The NAME attribute specifies the name of the MBean when the MBean Server registers it. Recall from Chapters 4 and 5 that the MBean Server is given the name of an MBean to use when it registers it. If the name starts with the colon (:) character, the domain part of the name is the domain of the agent into which the MBean is loaded. (Domains were covered earlier in this chapter in the "Creating the ObjectName class" section.)

The optional VERSION attribute can be used to specify the VERSION of the JAR used to load MBeans from. It can be used to update the JAR that was loaded the last time the MLET file was requested.

The last tag, which is also optional, is the <ARG> tag. The <ARG> tag sits in between the opening and closing tags of the <MLET> tag. The <ARG> tag enables you to specify arguments to be passed to the MBean when it is instantiated.

Table 8-5 shows the <MLET> tag and its attributes.

### Table 8-5    The <MLET> Tag and Its Attributes

| Attribute or Tag Name | Description |
|---|---|
| CODE | This mandatory attribute represents the fully qualified Java class name of the MBean. This class must exist in one of the JARs specified with the ARCHIVE attribute. Either the CODE or OBJECT attribute are required. |
| OBJECT | This mandatory attribute represents the name of a serialized Java class (.ser extension) that is the MBean. This class must exist in one of the JARs specified with the ARCHIVE attribute. Either the CODE or OBJECT attribute are required. |
| ARCHIVE | This mandatory attribute specifies one or more JARs containing MBean classes and other resources needed by MBeans. Multiple JARs can be specified using the comma (,) as a delimiter. |

| Attribute or Tag Name | Description |
| --- | --- |
| CODEBASE | This optional attribute specifies a directory to search for MBeans and resources. If not specified, the directory from which the MLet text file was loaded is the code base. |
| NAME | This optional attribute can be used to provide a name to an MBean. This will serve as the string value used to construct an instance of the `javax.management.ObjectName` class. The value you specify is subject to all of the same rules that apply when you directly construct an `ObjectName` instance. |
| VERSION | This optional attribute can be used to specify the version of a JAR so that dynamic replacement and versioning of JARs can be done. The MLet service may have cached JARs, and the VERSION attribute can be used to replace them. |
| ARG | This optional tag can appear between the start and end `<MLET>` tags. It is used to pass arguments to the constructor of the MBean. It has a TYPE attribute, which indicates the Java type that the argument is to be treated as, and a VALUE attribute that provides the actual value for the argument. |

Before looking at an example, you should understand the potential problems that can arise with the `<MLET>` tag. The `<MLET>` tag is parsed in a manner similar to an HTML document in that the case of the attributes does not matter. For example, the attributes `archive` and `ARCHIVE` are treated the same. The `<MLET>` tag must have an end tag `</MLET>`. You cannot use an empty tag such as `<MLET … />` to specify the tag. Other problems that can arise include the possibility that the URL you specified is malformed. The MLet service will notify you about other errors with your `<MLET>` tag, such as a missing mandatory attribute. Be aware, however, that when the MLet service fails because of one of these errors, it is sometimes vague about what has happened. The `getMBeansFromURL()` method, shown in the next example, can throw a `javax.management.ServiceNotFoundException`, whose documentation provides a variety of different causes.

These problems are actually implementation-specific requirements based on the Sun JMX reference implementation. The JMX specification says nothing about rules concerning `<MLET>` document construction. The Sun JMX reference implementation appears to hang when it encounters an empty `<MLET>` tag. While the goal of the JMX API specification is to provide a standard framework for management applications, the MLet service is a mandatory component of the JMX architecture. However, this just means that a compliant JMX reference implementation should provide a way to dynamically load classes. Later in this chapter, you'll build your own MBean, one that enables you to load MBeans dynamically. Before you do that, however, it would be useful to examine some facilities that can help you debug errant `<MLET>` tags. The classes and interfaces mentioned here are covered in more detail in Appendix C, but a brief introduction now may save you some time and trouble.

## Debugging MLet tags

The Sun JMX reference implementation includes some debugging and trace level facilities that enable you to perform debugging. The debugging and trace facilities are not considered part of the JMX specification, although the Sun reference implementation makes use of the debugging and trace facilities in its own reference implementation.

A package called `com.sun.management.jmx` includes four classes for doing debugging, by receiving trace messages about what is going on. These same debugging and trace facilities can be used in your own implementations if you want, and while they do provide useful information about what is going on, they don't provide the fine-grained debugging information you would get from an actual debugger. However, for some problems, just having the messages available can be a big help.

Rather than duplicate all the same information that appears in Appendix C, the following listing presents a Java class that you can extend or modify to suit your own debugging needs. It enables you to perform debugging and print trace messages while using different components of the Sun JMX reference implementation. Listing 8-18 shows the source code for the `JMXDebug` class.

### Listing 8-18: A JMX debugging class

```java
import com.sun.jdmk.Trace;
import com.sun.jdmk.TraceFilter;
import com.sun.jdmk.TraceListener;


public class JMXDebug {

        public JMXDebug(Object callback) {

                TraceFilter filter =

                new TraceFilter(Trace.LEVEL_DEBUG,Trace.INFO_MLET |
Trace.INFO_MISC);

                Trace.addNotificationListener(new TraceListener(),
                                              filter,
                                              callback);
        }

}
```

The `JMXDebug` class, shown in Listing 8-18, takes an instance of the `java.lang.Object` that will be passed to the `addNotificationListener()` method of the `Trace` class. The `Trace` class is used to establish a `TraceListener` that will receive the trace events by using the `addNotificatationListener()` method. The first argument is a new `TraceListener`, constructed using the `TraceListener` constructor with no arguments, which creates a `TraceListener` that sends messages to standard output. The `TraceListener` can also be constructed to send its output to a file or other `java.io.PrintStream` type compatible I/O stream class.

The second argument is a `TraceFilter` that tells the `Trace` class which types of trace events should be captured, as well as what level: `LEVEL_DEBUG` or `LEVEL_TRACE`. These two levels define the amount of detail that is emitted by the `Trace` class during execution of a program. The JMX documentation for the `Trace` class includes all the different types of trace messages that correspond to the different subsystems in the Sun JMX reference implementation. To use the `JMXDebug` class, you must insert a line in the `LoadMBeanWithMLet` application that looks like the following:

```
JMXDebug debug = new JMXDebug(this);
```

The `this` keyword should correspond to the `LoadMBeanWithMLet` class. You can place this line before any JMX-specific code begins to run.

Running the application in Listing 8-19 with the debugging class from Listing 8-18 would produce output similar to the following:

```
(MLet getMBeansFromURL) <URL = file:///f:/files/JMX-Hungryminds/simple-
mlet.txt>

(MLet getMBeansFromURL) MLET TAG     = {name=SimpleObject:name=simple,
archive=m
beans.jar, code=SimpleObject.class}
(MLet getMBeansFromURL) CODEBASE     = file:/f:/files/JMX-Hungryminds/
(MLet getMBeansFromURL) ARCHIVE      = mbeans.jar
(MLet getMBeansFromURL) CODE         = SimpleObject
(MLet getMBeansFromURL) OBJECT       = null
(MLet getMBeansFromURL) NAME         = SimpleObject:name=simple
(MLet getMBeansFromURL) VERSION      = null
(MLet getMBeansFromURL) DOCUMENT URL = file:/f:/files/JMX-
Hungryminds/simple-mle
t.txt
(MLet getMBeansFromURL) Load archive for codebase <file:/f:/files/JMX-
Hungrymind
s/>, file <mbeans.jar>
>Beans Found: 1
Bean Class Name: SimpleObject
Bean Domain: SimpleObject
Done...
```

The output from the trace messages can be interpreted as the name of the MBean, followed by the method that is being executed, followed by the message. Note that this is totally implementation-dependant, and there is no guarantee that the same structure will be followed in other JMX subsystems.

The immediate benefit to tracing is evident in the following example. If you removed the `CODE` attribute from an `<MLET>` tag and then tried to use the MLET text file, using the `JMXDebug` class prints the following output:

```
(MLet getMBeansFromURL) <URL = file:///f:/files/JMX-Hungryminds/simple-
mlet.txt>

(MLetParser parse) <mlet> tag requires either code or object parameter.
```

```
(MLet getMBeansFromURL) Problems while parsing URL file:///f:/files/JMX-
Hungrymi
nds/simple-mlet.txt
Exception javax.management.MBeanException: Exception thrown in operation
getMBea
nsFromURL
javax.management.MBeanException: Exception thrown in operation
getMBeansFromURL
        at
com.sun.management.jmx.MBeanServerImpl.invoke(MBeanServerImpl.java:16
44)
        at
com.sun.management.jmx.MBeanServerImpl.invoke(MBeanServerImpl.java:15
23)
        at LoadMBeanWithMLET.main(LoadMBeanWithMLET.java:37)
```

Here you can see that the <MLET> tag is missing either the CODE or OBJECT attributes. If you
didn't use the JMXDebug class and used the MLET text file with the missing CODE attribute,
the output would look as follows:

```
Exception javax.management.MBeanException: Exception thrown in operation
getMBeansFromURL
javax.management.MBeanException: Exception thrown in operation
getMBeansFromURL
        at
com.sun.management.jmx.MBeanServerImpl.invoke(MBeanServerImpl.java:16
44)
        at
com.sun.management.jmx.MBeanServerImpl.invoke(MBeanServerImpl.java:15
23)
        at LoadMBeanWithMLET.main(LoadMBeanWithMLET.java:37)
```

As you can see, nothing is indicated about the tag at all, which could result in valuable time
lost trying to figure out exactly what is wrong.

Nevertheless, the MLet service does perform as advertised. Listing 8-19 shows a Java
application that uses the MLet service to load an MBean named SimpleObject and then print
some information about the MBean.

**Listing 8-19: Loading an MBean with the MLet service**

```
import java.util.Iterator;
import java.util.Set;
import javax.management.ObjectName;
import javax.management.ObjectInstance;
import javax.management.loading.MLet;
import javax.management.MBeanServer;
import javax.management.MBeanServerFactory;

public class LoadMBeanWithMLET {
```

```
    private static MBeanServer server = null;

    public LoadMBeanWithMLET() {
        server = MBeanServerFactory.createMBeanServer();
    }

    public static void main(String[] args) {

        try {

        LoadMBeanWithMLET agent =
                new LoadMBeanWithMLET();

        ObjectName mletName = new ObjectName("MLet:name=mlet");

        server.createMBean("javax.management.loading.MLet",
                            mletName);

        Set beans =
            (Set)server.invoke(mletName,
                            "getMBeansFromURL",
                            new Object[]{"file:///f:\\files\\JMX-
Hungryminds\\simple-mlet.txt"},
                            new String[]{"java.lang.String"});

        System.out.println(">Beans Found: " + beans.size());

        Iterator beanIter = beans.iterator();

        while (beanIter.hasNext()) {
        Object nextBean = beanIter.next();
        if (nextBean instanceof Throwable) {
            System.out.println(">Set returned contains a throwable");
            System.out.println(">Detail: " + nextBean);
            ((Throwable)nextBean).printStackTrace();
        } else {
            ObjectInstance beanInstance =
                    (ObjectInstance)nextBean;
            System.out.println("Bean Class Name: " +
                            beanInstance.getClassName());

            System.out.println("Bean Domain: " +
                    beanInstance.getObjectName().getDomain());
        }
        }

            System.out.println("Done...");
```

```
      } catch (Exception ex){
            System.out.println("Exception " + ex);
            ex.printStackTrace();
      }

      System.exit(0);
   }

}
```

The first thing to remember when using the MLet service is that it is an MBean. When reading the JMX API documentation, you may be tempted to use the `new` operator and construct an instance of it that way. However, you actually need to treat it like any other MBean and use the MBean Server to create an instance of it, and then invoke the methods you want against it.

As with any MBean you want to work with, you first need to create an `ObjectName`. The `LoadMBeanWithMLET` application creates the `ObjectName` using the following line:

```
ObjectName mletName = new ObjectName("MLet:name=mlet");
```

Next, it creates an instance of the MLet MBean using this line:

```
server.createMBean("javax.management.loading.MLet",mletName);
```

Assuming no exceptions occur while creating the MBean, you are now ready to execute the method you need to load the MBeans from the MLet text file. To do this, you use the `invoke()` method of the `MBeanServer` interface, as shown in the following bit of code from Listing 8-19:

```
Set beans =
     (Set)server.invoke(mletName,
                        "getMBeansFromURL",
                         new Object[]{"file:///f:\\files\\JMX-
Hungryminds\\simple-mlet.txt"},
                         new String[]{"java.lang.String"});
```

The first argument passed to the `invoke()` method is the `ObjectName` instance, and the second argument is the name of the method to invoke: `getMBeansFromURL()`. The third argument is an array of `java.lang.Object` objects representing the arguments to the method. The `getMBeansfromURL()` method takes a single `java.lang.String` argument. The fourth and final argument is an array of `java.lang.String` objects representing the Java types of each of the arguments to the method.

If everything goes okay, the `getMBeansFromURL()` method returns an instance of the `java.util.Set` interface containing a `javax.management.ObjectInstance` that was created, or a `java.lang.Throwable` for those that could not be created. There should be an entry in the `Set` for each `<MLET>` tag in the MLet text file.

The MLet text file used in the example in Listing 8-19 is shown in Listing 8-20.

**Listing 8-20: The MLet text file**

```
<MLET CODE="SimpleObject.class" ARCHIVE="mbeans.jar"
NAME="SimpleObject:name=simple"></MLET>
```

# Summary

In this chapter you have looked at one of the most important components of a JMX agent, the MBean Server. The MBean Server is the repository in which you store references to MBeans so that they can be accessed by management applications. MBeans are referred to by instances of the `ObjectName` class. The MBean Server maintains a list of registered MBeans by object name. When a management client wants to access an MBean, it must supply the object name of the MBean it wants to access. The management client then must use one of several methods such as `invoke()`, `getAttribute()`, or `setAttribute()` to manipulate the MBean.

In the next chapter you'll look at another feature of the MBean Server, the MBean Server's query facilities, which enable you to perform queries for MBeans in an MBean Server.

## Chapter 9

# Using MBean Server Query Facilities

In Chapter 8, you examined the MBean Server and learned how to get access to a particular MBean using its name. The name is represented as an implementation of the `javax.management.ObjectName` class. The `javax.management.ObjectInstance` class maintains the association between the `ObjectName` and the `MBean` class. Although it is fine to access a single MBean by name, it's not particularly efficient or flexible. In cases where you want to access beans for which you may not know the name, or have only partial information, you need to be able to query the MBean Server. This is why we have tools such as search engines on the Internet. If you knew where everything was, you probably wouldn't need a search engine.

The capability to query for managed resources becomes even more important when the size of the managed system is extremely large, with components numbering in the hundreds or thousands. Imagine if you were a systems administrator and your manager suddenly asked you to identify all the printers with an error status. The capability to query for managed resources also makes writing management agents simpler because they face the same challenges that users of management agents do. They need a flexible and efficient way to find management resources.

This chapter examines the query capabilities provided by the MBean Server. You will learn how to construct various queries, what valid queries are, and how to use queries. The MBean Server's query capabilities enable you to construct a variety of expressions using Boolean operators and pattern matching phrases to find one or more MBeans that satisfy the query. They also enable you to do substring-matching queries, which could, for instance, return all managed resources with name that begin with the letter "M."

The query capabilities enable you to find MBeans based on the values of attributes. This enables you to ask questions such as "Which MBeans that managed fixed-storage have available storage that is below five gigabytes," or, perhaps, to write canned queries that can be executed in the management console to provide you with highlights and summary information about managed devices. Going further, you can use the timer agent service and kick off a Java application that uses the query facilities to build a summary, which you can have e-mailed to you each morning.

> **NOTE:** The queries mentioned here do not imply some sort of natural language querying capabilities. The queries as worded above can be broken down into a series of pseudo-code or programming language statements that will result in the answers to those questions.

The JMX specification discusses queries in the scope of a single MBean Server, but also indicates that it expects a remote interface to an MBean Server to operate in a manner similar to an MBean Server running locally.

# Scope of a Query

Before looking at exactly how to perform a query, this section briefly discusses the scope in which a query operates. Initially, the scope for all queries exists inside a single MBean Server. However, within an MBean Server, the scope is refined even further, down to a single MBean. The necessity to refine the scope of a query can also have an impact on the time it takes for the query to execute. Imagine if the query were always run against every MBean and then possibly against every MBean in a distributed system. Refining the scope also ensures that the values specified by the query expression are only run against the smallest set of MBeans that might match the expression.

When a query is executed, the scope is first determined based on the name of the MBean or `ObjectName` passed into one of the query methods of the `MBeanServer` interface. The name is matched based on a pattern-matching scheme, which was briefly described in Chapter 8.

## Name pattern matching

When locating an MBean, you use the name of the MBean represented by an instance of the `javax.management.ObjectName` class. You construct an instance of this class using a string consisting of a domain and one or more key/value pairs. The line of code here illustrates a typical way you would construct an instance of the `ObjectName` class.

> **CROSS-REFERENCE:** You can refer to the section "Registering an MBean" in Chapter 8 for more information on the `ObjectName` class.

```
ObjectName mletName = new ObjectName("SimpleObject:name=simple");
```

The text that appears in the constructor of the `ObjectName` class is considered the value of the name of the MBean. The portion of text that appears to the left of the colon is the domain, and the portion that appears to the right of the colon is considered an arbitrary set of one or more key/value pairs.

In some cases, when retrieving an MBean from the MBean Server, an exact match is achieved. For instance, the `getObjectInstance()` method of the `javax.management` `.MBeanServer` interface looks at the exact value of the name to find the instance of an MBean. This is generally not considered a query in the strictest sense of the term, but it is perfectly reasonable to perform a query and supply an expression or value that returns an exact match. This type of comparison might be accomplished using a piece of Java code that looks like the following:

```
public boolean mbeanExists(String newName) {

    // retrieve mbean from local list //

    String name = "SimpleObject:name=simple";

    if (newName.equals(name))
        return true;
    else
        return false;
}
```

After the pattern matching has been applied as a primary filter, the remaining set of MBeans is matched against the query expression specified by the arguments to the query methods themselves.

You can use some special characters to specify an object name that could match more than one MBean. The JMX specification defines the question mark (?) and the asterisk (*) as characters that can be used to build patterns for object names. When these types of object names are used, you can apply your query to multiple MBeans. Without this feature, it would be difficult to perform queries because you would have to first retrieve each MBean and then see if the object name you created matches that, and then apply the remaining query parameters yourself. These special characters can be applied to virtually all parts of the object name, such as the domain or the key/value pair.

Some of the examples shown in this chapter use this ObjectName definition to select all MBeans in an MBean Server. This ObjectName uses the asterisk to indicate that any MBean in any domain and any key/value pair is allowed, as shown here:

```
ObjectName objName = new ObjectName("*:*");
```

The JMX specification formally defines the meaning of the asterisk and question mark when used in object names as follows:

♦ The asterisk matches any character sequence, including an empty one.

♦ The question mark matches any one single character.

So let's take a few examples of object names and see how using these two characters would affect the MBeans matched. Assume the following ObjectNames in Listing 9-1.

**Listing 9-1: Sample MBean object names**

```
PrinterObject:name=HP Deskjet,location=First Floor,domain=Metropolis
PrinterObject:name=HP Deskjet,location=Second Floor,domain=Metropolis
PrinterObject:name=HP Deskjet,location=First Floor,domain=Gotham
PrinterObject:Name=HP 600 Color,location=Third Floor,domain=Gotham
PrinterObject:Name=HP LaserJet,location=Third Floor,domain=Metropolis
```

You could construct valid object names for these MBean names using the following code. The first `ObjectName` would match each of the MBeans listed in Listing 9-1.

```
ObjectName name = new ObjectName("PrinterObject:*");
ObjectName name = new ObjectName("*:*,location=First Floor,*");
ObjectName name = new ObjectName("PrinterObject:*,location=Second
Floor");
```

The second `ObjectName` would match the first and third object names by matching any domain plus any `name` key, but the `location` key must be equal to the value of `First Floor`. The third `ObjectName` would match the second MBean, which has the `location` key with a value of `Second Floor`.

As mentioned, these patterns are matched against registered MBeans in an MBean Server instance, which then limits the number of MBeans against which the query will be executed.

## Building and executing queries

To execute the queries, use the `MBeanServer` interface and one of two methods for performing queries. The arguments to these methods, which are described shortly, operate basically the same way — the Java type of the result is what differentiates them. Table 9-1 describes the query methods of the `MBeanServer` interface.

### Table 9-1     MBeanServer Query Methods

| Method Name | Description |
|---|---|
| `queryMBeans(ObjectName name, QueryExp query);` | Returns a `java.util.Set` of `javax.management.ObjectInstance` instances representing MBeans matching the name and query |
| `queryNames(ObjectName name, QueryExp query)` | Returns a `java.util.Set` of `javax.management.ObjectName` instances representing MBeans matching the name and query |

### Query building blocks

The JMX API defines several classes and interfaces that comprise the necessary building blocks for constructing the various queries. These classes and interfaces represent an abstract query against an MBean, and enable you to specify constraints against values such as string values, attribute names, and MBean class names, to name just a few.

The primary class used when building a query is the `javax.management.Query` class. This class contains several fields representing Boolean operators, such as `and/or`, and other functions that enable you to perform comparisons and evaluate expressions given specific constraints. Table 9-2 describes the classes and interfaces used to build the expressions and constraints used in queries.

### Table 9-2     JMX Query Classes and Interfaces

| Classes and Interfaces | Description |
|---|---|
| Query | Class that is used for building QueryExp, ValueExp, AttributeValueExp, and StringValueExp |
| QueryEval | Class that enables a query to be performed in the context of a specific MBean Server |
| QueryExp | Interface representing a query expression that can be used with one of the MBeanServer interface query methods |
| ValueExp | Interface representing a value expression that can be used to build a query expression |
| AttributeValueExp | Class that represents an attribute value expression that can be used to build a query expression |
| StringValueExp | Class that represents a string value expression that can be used to build a query expression |

The Query class and related classes and interfaces, when used together, form the basis for constructing the arguments that are then passed to the query methods of the MBeanServer interface. You'll learn how to use each of these classes and interfaces shortly.

The process of building the necessary arguments is somewhat iterative in that to construct constraints you must use the various classes to build an appropriate expression object, which is then passed into another method to form a value expression. It is this value expression that is actually passed as the argument to the query method. None of the query methods or methods that build expression objects take simple strings. There is no equivalent Structured Query Language (SQL) for building expressions. Rather, the arguments and values are represented as the Java classes, which are listed in Table 9-2.

Basically, you build the query by executing one of the many static methods of the Query class in one long line of code. You can also call the methods in several lines of code, passing the result to the next line until the expression you desire has been constructed.

Two other relevant methods for applying queries exist in the QueryExp and ValueExp interfaces. These interfaces are implemented by the StringValueExp and AttributeValueExp classes that you'll see in the next section. The QueryExp and ValueExp define two methods:

- apply(javax.management.ObjectName mbean)
- setMBeanServer(MBeanServer server)

The apply() method is used to apply a query to the named MBean. You name the MBean using an instance of the ObjectName class. The setMBeanServer() method indicates the MBean Server in which the MBean used in the apply() method is located.

The apply() method is only one method of executing a query against an MBean. You have already seen the queryNames() and queryMBeans() methods in Table 9-1. The apply() method returns an instance of the ValueExp interface.

## Constructing AttributeValue and StringValue expressions

To perform any queries, you need to be able to construct Java objects that represent the values and arguments that will be used in the queries. The queries you execute with the MBeanServer use the values represented by these Java objects to build the queries.

The values are represented as either a javax.management.AttributeValueExp object or the javax.management.StringValueExp object, both of which implement the javax .management.ValueExp interface. The string value represented by the StringValueExp object represents a static literal string value. The AttributeValueExp object, on the other hand, represents the value of an MBean attribute, which could be a primitive, a string, or some other complex object.

You can construct both the StringValueExp object and the AttributeValueExp object using an empty constructor or by passing a value into its second constructor. For example, to construct a string expression, you could execute some code that looks like the following:

```
StringValueExp ex = new StringValueExp("JMX Programming");
```

This is very similar to constructing a string using the java.lang.String constructor, as follows:

```
String ex = new String("JMX Programming");
```

The AttributeValueExp object is not that much different, except instead of an arbitrary string, you pass in the name of an attribute you want the AttributeValueExp object to represent, as follows:

```
AttributeValueExp attr = new AttributeValueExp("name");
```

When you construct a StringValueExp or AttributeValueExp object in the manner just shown, these objects are then used as arguments to other Query class methods. These objects are most often constructed by using one of the Query class methods you will see shortly, (although it's also possible to use something like the code shown in Listing 9-4). First, consider the MBean in Listing 9-2.

**Listing 9-2: The SimpleQueryObjectMBean interface**

```
public interface SimpleQueryObjectMBean{

        public String getName();

        public void setName(String newName);

}
```

The `SimpleQueryObjectMBean` interface defines the accessor methods `getName()` and `setName()` that you can use to manipulate the `Name` attribute. The implementation of this interface is shown in Listing 9-3.

**Listing 9-3: Simple MBean to be queried against**

```java
public class SimpleQueryObject implements SimpleQueryObjectMBean{

    private String name = "simple";

    public SimpleQueryObject(){
    }

    public SimpleQueryObject(String iName){
        name = iName;
    }

    public String getName(){
        return name;
    }

    public void setName(String newName){
        name = newName;
    }

}
```

The `SimpleQueryObject` class has a single attribute (`name`) that is assigned an initial value of `simple`. It then includes accessor methods for getting and setting the value of this attribute. The class in Listing 9-4 loads an instance of this MBean and performs a query against the `name` attribute.

**Listing 9-4: Using the StringValueExp and AttributeValueExp manually**

```java
import javax.management.ObjectName;
import javax.management.MalformedObjectNameException;
import javax.management.MBeanServer;
import javax.management.MBeanServerFactory;
import javax.management.StringValueExp;
import javax.management.AttributeValueExp;
import javax.management.Query;
import javax.management.QueryExp;
import javax.management.ValueExp;
import java.util.Iterator;
import java.util.Set;

public class MBeanQuery {

    private static MBeanServer server = null;
```

```
    public MBeanQuery() {
        server = MBeanServerFactory.createMBeanServer();
    }

    public static void main(String[] args) {

        MBeanQuery agent = new MBeanQuery();
        ObjectName simpleObject = agent.loadBean("SimpleQueryObject",
                              "SimpleQueryObject:name=simple");

        StringValueExp arg1 = new StringValueExp("simple");

        AttributeValueExp arg2 = new AttributeValueExp("Name");

        QueryExp q1 = Query.match(arg2,arg1);

        Set results = server.queryNames(simpleObject,q1);

        Iterator iter = results.iterator();

        System.out.println("Query 1 >>>>>>>>>>>>>>>>>>>>>>>>>>>>>>");
        System.out.println("Results Found: " + results.size());
        while (iter.hasNext()) {
          ObjectName beanName = (ObjectName)iter.next();
          System.out.println(beanName + " was found as a matching
bean");
        }

        System.out.println("Query 2 >>>>>>>>>>>>>>>>>>>>>>>>>>>>>>");

        arg1 = new StringValueExp("complex");

        q1 = Query.match(arg2,arg1);

        results = server.queryNames(simpleObject,q1);

        System.out.println("Results Found: " + results.size());

        while (iter.hasNext()) {
          ObjectName beanName = (ObjectName)iter.next();
          System.out.println(beanName + " was found as a matching
bean");
        }

    }

    private ObjectName loadBean(String className,String objectName) {

        ObjectName mbeanObjectName = null;
```

```
        String mbeanName = className;
        try {
            mbeanObjectName = new ObjectName(objectName);
        } catch(MalformedObjectNameException e) {
          e.printStackTrace();
          System.exit(1);
        }
          // Create our simple object to manage //
          try {
            server.createMBean(mbeanName,mbeanObjectName);
          }catch(Exception ex){
                ex.printStackTrace();
                System.exit(1);
          }

          return mbeanObjectName;
      }
}
```

The MBeanQuery class executes two queries. The first is constructed by creating a StringValueExp object with the value of simple and an AttributeValueExp object using the name of the attribute you want to query against. Note that the case used in the value for the AttributeValueExp object is uppercase, just like the accessor get method.

The AttributeValueExp and StringValueExp objects are then used to construct a QueryExp object using the match() method. The QueryExp object is then used in the queryNames() method of the MBeanServer interface, which also uses the ObjectName created earlier in the same application.

The output from running the MBeanQuery Java application looks like the following:

```
Query 1 >>>>>>>>>>>>>>>>>>>>>>>>>>>>>>
Results Found: 1
SimpleQueryObject:name=simple was found as a matching bean
Query 2 >>>>>>>>>>>>>>>>>>>>>>>>>>>>>>
Results Found: 0
```

The query that generated the second result set is constructed like the first except that a new instance of the StringValueExp class is constructed. This was done to show the re-use of the Query class and also to show the results when a match is not found. Because the Query class uses static methods to create instances of the QueryExp interface, you can re-use the previous instance and just change it to use the new instance of StringValueExp. You then execute the query in the same manner as the first by using the queryNames() method of the MBeanServer interface method.

The methods of the query class are split between those that build value expressions and those that build query expressions. The query expressions are arguments to the query methods of the MBeanServer interface. Table 9-3 describes a subset of the methods of the Query class. A few overloadings of the value() method have been omitted.

## Table 9-3    Subset of Query Class Methods

| Method Name | Description |
|---|---|
| `and(QueryExp ex1, QueryExp ex1)` | Returns a query expression where both expressions must evaluate to true |
| `anySubString(AttributeValueExp ex1, StringValueExp sx1)` | Returns a query expression where the `StringValueExp` argument must exist in the `AttributeValueExp` |
| `attr(java.lang.String name)` | Returns an `AttributeValueExp` for the named attribute |
| `attr(java.lang.String classname, java.lang.String name)` | Returns an `AttributeValueExp` for the named attribute in the named class |
| `between(ValueExp ex1, ValueExp ex2, ValueExp ex3)` | Returns an expression where the first expression must be between the second two expressions |
| `classattr()` | Returns an `AttributeValueExp` that enables you to query against an MBean class name |
| `div(ValueExp ex1, ValueExp2)` | Returns a `ValueExp` that is the product of the first `ValueExp` divided by the second `ValueExp` |
| `eq(ValueExp ex1, ValueExp2)` | Returns a `QueryExp` where the first `ValueExp` must be equal to the second `ValueExp` |
| `finalSubString(AttributeValueExp ex1, StringValueExp sx1)` | Returns a `QueryExp` where the `StringValueExp` must exist as a suffix of the `AttributeValueExp` |
| `geq(ValueExp ex1, ValueExp ex2)` | Returns a `QueryExp` where the first `ValueExp` must be greater than or equal to the second `ValueExp` |
| `gt(ValueExp ex1, ValueExp ex2)` | Returns a `QueryExp` where the first `ValueExp` must be greater than the second `ValueExp` |
| `in(ValueExp ex1, ValueExp[] list)` | Returns a `QueryExp` where the first `ValueExp` must exist in the array of `ValueExp` objects |
| `initialSubString(AttributeValueExp ex1, StringValueExp sx1)` | Returns a `QueryExp` where the `StringValueExp` must exist as a prefix of the `AttributeValueExp` |
| `leq(ValueExp ex1, ValueExp ex2)` | Returns a `QueryExp` where the first `ValueExp` must be less than or equal to the second `ValueExp` |

| Method Name | Description |
|---|---|
| `lt(ValueExp ex1, ValueExp ex2)` | Returns a `QueryExp` where the first `ValueExp` must be less than the second `ValueExp` |
| `match(AttributeValueExp ex1, StringValueExp sx1)` | Returns a `QueryExp` that is the product of the pattern in the `StringValueExp` applied to the `AttributeValueExp` |
| `minus(ValueExp ex1, ValueExp ex2)` | Returns a `ValueExp` that is the product of the second `ValueExp` subtracted from the first `ValueExp` |
| `not(ValueExp ex1)` | Returns the negative result of the `ValueExp`. This is how you can indicate not equal to something. |
| `or(ValueExp ex1, ValueExp ex2)` | Returns a `QueryExp` where the first or the second `ValueExp` may be true |
| `plus(ValueExp ex1, ValueExp ex2)` | Returns a `ValueExp` that is the product of the first `ValueExp` added to the second `ValueExp` |
| `times(ValueExp ex1, ValueExp ex2)` | Returns a `ValueExp` that is the product of the first `ValueExp` multiplied by the second `ValueExp` |
| `value(boolean val)` | Returns a `ValueExp` that is the value of the boolean argument |
| `value(java.lang.String val)` | Returns a `ValueExp` that is the value of the string argument |

This lists only a couple of the `value()` methods that appear in the `Query` class. You can view the remaining overloadings of the `value()` method in the JavaDoc for the `Query` class. There are methods for `double`, `float`, `int`, `long`, and `Number` primitive types.

Some of the methods in Table 9-3 return values that are used in some of the other methods. Those methods are then used to build the query that is ultimately executed. These methods can be further divided into one of the following categories:

♦ Methods that build a boolean expression

♦ Methods that build a string expression

♦ Methods that build a numerical expression

♦ Methods that build a relational expression

The results returned by these methods are expression objects that are then used as arguments to query methods, or used as arguments to construct more complex queries. Before examining each of the methods listed in Table 9-3 consider the MBean interface code in Listing 9-5, which presents an MBean that is used in each of the subsequent sections.

**Listing 9-5: PrinterObject MBean interface**

```
public interface PrinterObjectMBean{

        public String getName();

        public void setName(String newName);

        public String getManufacturer();

        public void setManufacturer(String newManufacturer);

        public String getDomainName();

        public void setDomainName(String newDomainName);

        public String getDepartment();

        public void setDepartment(String newDepartment);

        public int getStatus();

        public void setStatus(int newStatus);

        public int getNumberOfSheets();

        public void setNumberOfSheets(int newNumberOfSheets);

        public int getNumberOfJobs();

        public void setNumberOfJobs(int newNumberOfJobs);

}
```

The `PrinterObjectMBean` interface represents a managed resource that exists in a theoretical network. This type of object could be used to represent any number of printers that exist. This managed resource is implemented as a standard MBean with a number of methods and attributes. Some of the attributes are read-only, such as `numberOfSheets`, `numberOfJobs`, and `status`. The corresponding MBean implementation for this interface is shown in Listing 9-6.

**Listing 9-6: MBean with multiple attributes**

```
public class PrinterObject implements PrinterObjectMBean{

        private String name = "printer";
        private String manufacturer = "";
        private String domainName = "";
        private String department = "";
        private int numberOfSheets = 0;
```

```java
private int numberOfJobs = 0;
private int status = 0;

public PrinterObject(){
}

public PrinterObject(String iName){
      name = iName;
}

public String getName(){
      return name;
}

public void setName(String newName){
      name = newName;
}

public String getManufacturer(){
      return manufacturer;
}

public void setManufacturer(String newManufacturer){
      manufacturer = newManufacturer;
}

public String getDomainName(){
      return domainName;
}

public void setDomainName(String newDomainName){
      domainName = newDomainName;
}

public String getDepartment(){
      return department;
}

public void setDepartment(String newDepartment){
      department = newDepartment;
}

public int getStatus(){
      return status;
}

public void setStatus(int newStatus){
      status = newStatus;
}
```

```
    public int getNumberOfSheets(){
        return numberOfSheets;
    }

    public void setNumberOfSheets(int newNumberOfSheets){
        numberOfSheets = newNumberOfSheets;
    }

    public int getNumberOfJobs(){
        return numberOfJobs;
    }

    public void setNumberOfJobs(int newNumberOfJobs){
        numberOfJobs = newNumberOfJobs;
    }

}
```

The first set of methods you'll look at perform queries that use Boolean operators to retrieve information such as "which printers have an error status code of 3."

## Boolean expression methods

Methods that return a boolean value are used to determine results such as whether a particular value exists in a list of values, whether or not a value is greater than another value, or whether a particular value is false. The methods that fall into this category are and(), or(), and not().

The Boolean result methods operate on QueryExp objects, unlike the string and numerical methods. The Boolean methods evaluate one or two QueryExp objects, depending on the method being used. The result returned from all three of the Boolean methods is a QueryExp object. Listing 9-7 show the source code for an application that demonstrates the use of the Boolean methods.

**Listing 9-7: Using the Boolean query constructors**

```
import javax.management.Attribute;
import javax.management.AttributeList;
import javax.management.ObjectName;
import javax.management.InstanceNotFoundException;
import javax.management.MalformedObjectNameException;
import javax.management.MBeanServer;
import javax.management.MBeanServerFactory;
import javax.management.ReflectionException;
import javax.management.StringValueExp;
import javax.management.AttributeValueExp;
import javax.management.Query;
import javax.management.QueryExp;
import javax.management.ValueExp;
```

```java
import java.util.Iterator;
import java.util.Set;

public class MBeanQueryBoolean {

    private static MBeanServer server = null;
    private static ObjectName printer1 = null;
    private static ObjectName printer2 = null;
    private static ObjectName printer3 = null;

    public MBeanQueryBoolean() {
        server = MBeanServerFactory.createMBeanServer();
    }

    public static void main(String[] args)
            throws InstanceNotFoundException,
                   MalformedObjectNameException,
                   ReflectionException {

        MBeanQueryBoolean agent = new MBeanQueryBoolean();
        printer1 = agent.loadBean("PrinterObject",
                                  "PrinterObject:name=HP Inkjet");
        printer2 = agent.loadBean("PrinterObject",
                                  "PrinterObject:name=HP Deskjet");
        printer3 = agent.loadBean("PrinterObject",
                                  "PrinterObject:name=HP 600 Color");

        // Fill MBeans with some data //
        AttributeList atts1 = new AttributeList();
        atts1.add(new Attribute("Manufacturer","Hewlett Packard"));
        atts1.add(new Attribute("Department","IT"));
        atts1.add(new Attribute("DomainName","Metropolis"));
        server.setAttributes(printer1,atts1);
        AttributeList atts2 = new AttributeList();
        atts2.add(new Attribute("Manufacturer","Hewlett Packard"));
        atts2.add(new Attribute("Department","Purchasing"));
        atts2.add(new Attribute("DomainName","Gotham"));
        server.setAttributes(printer2,atts2);
        AttributeList atts3 = new AttributeList();
        atts3.add(new Attribute("Manufacturer","Hewlett Packard"));
        atts3.add(new Attribute("Department","IT"));
        server.setAttributes(printer3,atts3);


        // Boolean query #1 //
        QueryExp ex = Query.eq(new AttributeValueExp("Manufacturer"),
                            new StringValueExp("Hewlett Packard"));

        QueryExp ex2 = Query.not(ex);
```

```
        Set results = server.queryNames(new ObjectName("*:*"),ex2);
        printBeans(results,ex2);

        // Boolean query #2 //
        ex = Query.eq(new AttributeValueExp("Department"),
                    new StringValueExp("IT"));
        results = server.queryNames(new ObjectName("*:*"),ex);
        printBeans(results,ex);

        // Boolean query #3 //
        ex = Query.and(Query.eq(new AttributeValueExp("Manufacturer"),
                            new StringValueExp("Hewlett Packard")),
                    Query.eq(new AttributeValueExp("Department"),
                            new StringValueExp("IT")));
        results = server.queryNames(new ObjectName("*:*"),ex);
        printBeans(results,ex);

        // Boolean query #4//
        ex = Query.or(Query.eq(new AttributeValueExp("Department"),
                            new StringValueExp("IT")),
                    Query.eq(new AttributeValueExp("Department"),
                            new StringValueExp("Purchasing")));
        results = server.queryNames(new ObjectName("*:*"),ex);
        printBeans(results,ex);


    }

    private static void printBeans(Set beans,QueryExp q) {
            System.out.println("Query used: " + q);
            System.out.println("Results: " + beans.size());
            Iterator iter = beans.iterator();
            while (iter.hasNext()) {
                    ObjectName beanName = (ObjectName)iter.next();
                    System.out.println(beanName + " was found");
            }
    }

    private ObjectName loadBean(String className,String objectName) {

    ObjectName mbeanObjectName = null;
    String domain = server.getDefaultDomain();
    String mbeanName = className;
    try {
            mbeanObjectName = new ObjectName(objectName);
    } catch(MalformedObjectNameException e) {
            e.printStackTrace();
            System.exit(1);
    }
```

```
                    // Create our simple object to manage //
                    try {
                        server.createMBean(mbeanName,mbeanObjectName);
                    }catch(Exception ex){
                            ex.printStackTrace();
                            System.exit(1);
                    }


                    return mbeanObjectName;
        }
}
```

The MBeanQueryBoolean application shown in Listing 9-7 begins by creating three hypothetical printer objects from the PrinterObject class shown in Listing 9-5. Each MBean that is created is assigned a unique ObjectName based on the name of the printer.

Next, each of the MBean printer objects is filled with some fictitious data about the department, domain name, and manufacturer of the printer. These attributes of the PrinterObject class correspond to the Department, DomainName, and Manufacturer attributes defined in the class. This gives you something to query on. The other attributes, which are read-only, such as status, numberOfSheets, and numberOfJobs, are set by the MBean implementation. In Chapter 13, you'll learn how to initialize an MBean against a real printer.

The output from running the MBeanQueryBoolean application looks like the following:

```
Query used: not ((Manufacturer) = ('Hewlett Packard'))
Results: 0
Query used: (Department) = ('IT')
Results: 2
PrinterObject:name=HP 600 Color was found
PrinterObject:name=HP Inkjet was found
Query used: ((Manufacturer) = ('Hewlett Packard')) and ((Department) =
('IT'))
Results: 2
PrinterObject:name=HP 600 Color was found
PrinterObject:name=HP Inkjet was found
Query used: ((Department) = ('IT')) or ((Department) = ('Purchasing'))
Results: 3
PrinterObject:name=HP 600 Color was found
PrinterObject:name=HP Deskjet was found
PrinterObject:name=HP Inkjet was found
```

The first query uses both the eq() and not() methods to find all printer objects whose manufacturer attribute is not equal to a value of Hewlett Packard. The first query object is built to create a query expression that will compare the manufacturer attribute to the value of Hewlett Packard. Next, to build the "not equal to" part of the expression, the not() method is used. (For some reason, the JMX specification doesn't include a ne() method for not equals.) The first query also demonstrates constructing two instances of the QueryExp interface separately, and then piecing them together to form the final expression.

The second query uses the eq() method to find all the printer objects whose department attribute is equal to IT.

The third query uses the eq() method to find all the printer objects whose department attribute is equal to IT and whose manufacturer attribute is equal to Hewlett Packard. This query demonstrates using the Query class directly in the boolean method calls. Recall from the "Query building blocks" section earlier in this chapter that many of the methods of the Query class return an instance of the QueryExp interface.

Finally, the fourth query uses the or() method to find all printer objects with a department attribute whose value is IT or Purchasing. This query uses the same style of using the Query class directly in the call to the or() method.

Each time a query is completed, you pass the java.util.Set that was returned, and the QueryExp object to the printBeans() method. This method prints each result found, the number of results found, and the query that was used.

## String expression methods

The methods that return a string value are used to determine results that contain an exact copy of a string and those that return a portion of a string. This portion could be from either the beginning or end of a string. The methods that fall into this category are anySubString(), initialSubString(), and finalSubString().

If you've been programming in Java, JavaScript, or virtually any other programming language, you've probably used similar functions before. String matching functions are needed to perform the queries against character-based attribute values. Listing 9-8 shows the source code for a Java application that performs different string-based queries.

**Listing 9-8: Using the string-based query constructors**

```
import javax.management.Attribute;
import javax.management.AttributeList;
import javax.management.ObjectName;
import javax.management.InstanceNotFoundException;
import javax.management.MalformedObjectNameException;
import javax.management.MBeanServer;
import javax.management.MBeanServerFactory;
import javax.management.ReflectionException;
import javax.management.StringValueExp;
import javax.management.AttributeValueExp;
import javax.management.Query;
import javax.management.QueryExp;
import javax.management.ValueExp;
import java.util.Iterator;
import java.util.Set;

public class MBeanQueryString {

    private static MBeanServer server = null;
    private static ObjectName printer1 = null;
```

```
private static ObjectName printer2 = null;
private static ObjectName printer3 = null;

public MBeanQueryString() {
    server = MBeanServerFactory.createMBeanServer();
}

public static void main(String[] args)
        throws InstanceNotFoundException,
                MalformedObjectNameException,
                ReflectionException {

    MBeanQueryString agent = new MBeanQueryString();
    printer1 = agent.loadBean("PrinterObject",
                            "PrinterObject:name=HP Inkjet");
    printer2 = agent.loadBean("PrinterObject",
                            "PrinterObject:name=HP Deskjet");
    printer3 = agent.loadBean("PrinterObject",
                            "PrinterObject:name=HP 600 Color");

    // Fill MBeans with some data //
    AttributeList atts1 = new AttributeList();
    atts1.add(new Attribute("Manufacturer","Hewlett Packard"));
    atts1.add(new Attribute("Department","IT"));
    atts1.add(new Attribute("DomainName","Metropolis"));
    server.setAttributes(printer1,atts1);
    AttributeList atts2 = new AttributeList();
    atts2.add(new Attribute("Manufacturer","Hewlett Packard"));
    atts2.add(new Attribute("Department","Purchasing"));
    atts2.add(new Attribute("DomainName","Gotham"));
    server.setAttributes(printer2,atts2);
    AttributeList atts3 = new AttributeList();
    atts3.add(new Attribute("Manufacturer","Hewlett Packard"));
    atts3.add(new Attribute("Department","IT"));
    server.setAttributes(printer3,atts3);


    // String query #1 //
    QueryExp ex =
        Query.anySubString(new AttributeValueExp("Manufacturer"),
                        new StringValueExp("Packard"));

    Set results = server.queryNames(new ObjectName("*:*"),ex);
    printBeans(results,ex);

    // String query #2 //
    ex = Query.match(new AttributeValueExp("Department"),
                    new StringValueExp("IT"));
    results = server.queryNames(new ObjectName("*:*"),ex);
```

```java
        printBeans(results,ex);

        // String query #3 //
        ex = Query.initialSubString(Query.attr("Manufacturer"),
                            new StringValueExp("HP"));
        results = server.queryNames(new ObjectName("*:*"),ex);
        printBeans(results,ex);

        // String query #4//
        ex = Query.finalSubString(Query.attr("Manufacturer"),
                            new StringValueExp("ard"));
        results = server.queryNames(new ObjectName("*:*"),ex);
        printBeans(results,ex);


    }

private static void printBeans(Set beans,QueryExp q) {
        System.out.println("Query used: " + q);
        System.out.println("Results: " + beans.size());
        Iterator iter = beans.iterator();
        while (iter.hasNext()) {
                ObjectName beanName = (ObjectName)iter.next();
                System.out.println(beanName + " was found");
        }
}

private ObjectName loadBean(String className,String objectName) {

 ObjectName mbeanObjectName = null;
 String domain = server.getDefaultDomain();
 String mbeanName = className;
 try {
        mbeanObjectName = new ObjectName(objectName);
 } catch(MalformedObjectNameException e) {
        e.printStackTrace();
        System.exit(1);
 }
        // Create our simple object to manage //
        try {
           server.createMBean(mbeanName,mbeanObjectName);
        }catch(Exception ex){
                ex.printStackTrace();
                System.exit(1);
        }

        return mbeanObjectName;
}
}
```

The MBeanQueryString application in Listing 9-8 begins in the same manner as the MBeanQueryBoolean application in Listing 9-7, by loading three PrinterObject MBeans and then initializing them with fictitious data.

The output from running the MBeanQueryString application looks like the following:

```
Query used: Manufacturer like '%Packard%'
Results: 3
PrinterObject:name=HP 600 Color was found
PrinterObject:name=HP Inkjet was found
PrinterObject:name=HP Deskjet was found
Query used: Department like 'IT'
Results: 2
PrinterObject:name=HP 600 Color was found
PrinterObject:name=HP Inkjet was found
Query used: Manufacturer like 'HP%'
Results: 0
Query used: Manufacturer like '%ard'
Results: 3
PrinterObject:name=HP 600 Color was found
PrinterObject:name=HP Deskjet was found
PrinterObject:name=HP Inkjet was found
```

The first query uses the anySubString() method to find any printer objects that have a manufacturer attribute containing the string Packard in it. Because all of the printer objects created in this example have a manufacturer attribute with a value of Hewlett Packard, all three printer objects created are returned.

The second query uses the match() method to find any printer objects that have a department attribute with a value of IT.

The third query uses the initialSubString() method to find any printer objects that have a manufacturer attribute whose value begins with the letters HP. Because none of the printer objects have a manufacturer that begins with HP, no results are returned.

The fourth and final query uses the finalSubString() method to find any printer objects that have a manufacturer attribute that ends with the letters ard. Because all three printer objects have a manufacturer attribute that was initialized with the value Hewlett Packard, all three printer objects are returned.

## Numerical expression methods

Numerical result methods are used to determine results that reflect the manipulation of two values: addition, subtraction, division, or multiplication. The methods that fall into this category are minus(), plus(), times(), and div().

The numerical result methods enable you to perform queries based on the results of calculations. Listing 9-9 shows the source code for an application that uses different numerical methods to build expressions.

**Listing 9-9: Using the numerical-based query constructors**

```
import javax.management.Attribute;
import javax.management.AttributeList;
import javax.management.ObjectName;
import javax.management.InstanceNotFoundException;
import javax.management.MalformedObjectNameException;
import javax.management.MBeanServer;
import javax.management.MBeanServerFactory;
import javax.management.ReflectionException;
import javax.management.StringValueExp;
import javax.management.AttributeValueExp;
import javax.management.Query;
import javax.management.QueryExp;
import javax.management.ValueExp;
import java.util.Iterator;
import java.util.Set;

public class MBeanQueryNumerical {

    private static MBeanServer server = null;
    private static ObjectName printer1 = null;
    private static ObjectName printer2 = null;
    private static ObjectName printer3 = null;

    public MBeanQueryNumerical() {
        server = MBeanServerFactory.createMBeanServer();
    }

    public static void main(String[] args)
            throws InstanceNotFoundException,
                    MalformedObjectNameException,
                    ReflectionException {

        MBeanQueryNumerical agent = new MBeanQueryNumerical();
        printer1 = agent.loadBean("PrinterObject",
                                "PrinterObject:name=HP Inkjet");
        printer2 = agent.loadBean("PrinterObject",
                                "PrinterObject:name=HP Deskjet");
        printer3 = agent.loadBean("PrinterObject",
                                "PrinterObject:name=HP 600 Color");

        // Fill MBeans with some data //
        AttributeList atts1 = new AttributeList();
        atts1.add(new Attribute("Manufacturer","Hewlett Packard"));
        atts1.add(new Attribute("Department","IT"));
        atts1.add(new Attribute("DomainName","Metropolis"));
        atts1.add(new Attribute("NumberOfSheets",new Integer(10)));
        atts1.add(new Attribute("NumberOfJobs",new Integer(5)));
```

```
        atts1.add(new Attribute("Status",new Integer(1)));
        server.setAttributes(printer1,atts1);
        AttributeList atts2 = new AttributeList();
        atts2.add(new Attribute("Manufacturer","Hewlett Packard"));
        atts2.add(new Attribute("Department","Purchasing"));
        atts2.add(new Attribute("DomainName","Gotham"));
        atts2.add(new Attribute("NumberOfSheets",new Integer(10)));
        atts2.add(new Attribute("NumberOfJobs",new Integer(15)));
        atts2.add(new Attribute("Status",new Integer(1)));
        server.setAttributes(printer2,atts2);
        AttributeList atts3 = new AttributeList();
        atts3.add(new Attribute("Manufacturer","Hewlett Packard"));
        atts3.add(new Attribute("Department","IT"));
        atts3.add(new Attribute("NumberOfSheets",new Integer(10)));
        atts3.add(new Attribute("NumberOfJobs",new Integer(50)));
        atts3.add(new Attribute("Status",new Integer(3)));
        server.setAttributes(printer3,atts3);


        // String query #1 //
        QueryExp ex = Query.gt(Query.value(20),
                    Query.div(Query.attr("NumberOfSheets"),
                    Query.attr("NumberOfJobs")));

        Set results =
            server.queryNames(new ObjectName("*:*"),ex);
        printBeans(results,ex);

        // String query #2 //
        ex = Query.lt(Query.value(20),
                    Query.times(Query.attr("NumberOfSheets"),
                    Query.attr("NumberOfJobs")));

        results = server.queryNames(new ObjectName("*:*"),ex);
        printBeans(results,ex);
}

private static void printBeans(Set beans,QueryExp q) {
        System.out.println("Query used: " + q);
        System.out.println("Results: " + beans.size());
        Iterator iter = beans.iterator();
        while (iter.hasNext()) {
                ObjectName beanName = (ObjectName)iter.next();
                System.out.println(beanName + " was found");
        }
}

private ObjectName loadBean(String className,String objectName) {
```

```
    ObjectName mbeanObjectName = null;
    String domain = server.getDefaultDomain();
    String mbeanName = className;
    try {
            mbeanObjectName = new ObjectName(objectName);
    } catch(MalformedObjectNameException e) {
            e.printStackTrace();
            System.exit(1);
    }

            // Create our simple object to manage //
            try {
                server.createMBean(mbeanName,mbeanObjectName);
            }catch(Exception ex){
                    ex.printStackTrace();
                    System.exit(1);
            }


            return mbeanObjectName;
    }
}
```

The MBeanQueryNumerical application shown in Listing 9-9 begins like the previous two examples, but instead creates three MBeans. However, to demonstrate the numeric query capabilities, I updated the PrinterObject class and PrinterObjectMBean interface to have set methods for setting the number of jobs, the number of sheets, and status attributes of the PrinterObject class.

The first query uses the gt() method in conjunction with the div() method to find all printer objects whose NumberOfSheets divided by the NumberOfJobs is less than a value of twenty. The second query is similar except that it uses the times() method to find all printer objects whose NumberOfSheets multiplied by the NumberOfJobs is less than the value of twenty. This type of numerical processing can be used to identify problems before they occur by indicating when the values are approaching numbers that suggest a problem.

Running the MBeanQueryNumerical application produces output that looks like the following:

```
Query used: (20) > (NumberOfSheets / NumberOfJobs)
Results: 3
PrinterObject:name=HP 600 Color was found
PrinterObject:name=HP Deskjet was found
PrinterObject:name=HP Inkjet was found
Query used: (20) < (NumberOfSheets * NumberOfJobs)
Results: 3
PrinterObject:name=HP 600 Color was found
PrinterObject:name=HP Deskjet was found
PrinterObject:name=HP Inkjet was found
```

### Relational expression methods

Relational expressions enable you to build queries that compare the values of two or more attributes of an MBean. The relational expressions enable you to perform comparisons such as equals, less than, greater than, or equal to. The methods that fall into this category are `eq()`, `gt()`, `geq()`, and `lt()`.

Listing 9-10 shows the source code for an application that uses several of the relational expression methods.

**Listing 9-10: Relational query constructors**

```
import javax.management.Attribute;
import javax.management.AttributeList;
import javax.management.ObjectName;
import javax.management.InstanceNotFoundException;
import javax.management.MalformedObjectNameException;
import javax.management.MBeanServer;
import javax.management.MBeanServerFactory;
import javax.management.ReflectionException;
import javax.management.StringValueExp;
import javax.management.AttributeValueExp;
import javax.management.Query;
import javax.management.QueryExp;
import javax.management.ValueExp;
import java.util.Iterator;
import java.util.Set;

public class MBeanQueryRelational {

    private static MBeanServer server = null;
    private static ObjectName printer1 = null;
    private static ObjectName printer2 = null;
    private static ObjectName printer3 = null;

    public MBeanQueryRelational() {
        server = MBeanServerFactory.createMBeanServer();
    }

    public static void main(String[] args)
            throws InstanceNotFoundException,
                MalformedObjectNameException,
                ReflectionException {

        MBeanQueryRelational agent = new MBeanQueryRelational();
        printer1 = agent.loadBean("PrinterObject",
                                "PrinterObject:name=HP Inkjet");
        printer2 = agent.loadBean("PrinterObject",
                                "PrinterObject:name=HP Deskjet");
        printer3 = agent.loadBean("PrinterObject",
```

```
                                     "PrinterObject:name=HP 600 Color");

      // Fill MBeans with some data //
      AttributeList atts1 = new AttributeList();
      atts1.add(new Attribute("Manufacturer","Hewlett Packard"));
      atts1.add(new Attribute("Department","IT"));
      atts1.add(new Attribute("DomainName","Metropolis"));
      atts1.add(new Attribute("NumberOfSheets",new Integer(10)));
      atts1.add(new Attribute("NumberOfJobs",new Integer(5)));
      atts1.add(new Attribute("Status",new Integer(1)));
      server.setAttributes(printer1,atts1);
      AttributeList atts2 = new AttributeList();
      atts2.add(new Attribute("Manufacturer","Hewlett Packard"));
      atts2.add(new Attribute("Department","Purchasing"));
      atts2.add(new Attribute("DomainName","Gotham"));
      atts2.add(new Attribute("NumberOfSheets",new Integer(10)));
      atts2.add(new Attribute("NumberOfJobs",new Integer(15)));
      atts2.add(new Attribute("Status",new Integer(1)));
      server.setAttributes(printer2,atts2);
      AttributeList atts3 = new AttributeList();
      atts3.add(new Attribute("Manufacturer","Hewlett Packard"));
      atts3.add(new Attribute("Department","IT"));
      atts3.add(new Attribute("NumberOfSheets",new Integer(10)));
      atts3.add(new Attribute("NumberOfJobs",new Integer(50)));
      atts3.add(new Attribute("Status",new Integer(3)));
      server.setAttributes(printer3,atts3);


      // String query #1 //
      QueryExp ex = Query.gt(Query.attr("NumberOfJobs"),
                             Query.value(5));

      Set results = server.queryNames(new ObjectName("*:*"),ex);
      printBeans(results,ex);

      // String query #2 //
      ex = Query.geq(Query.attr("NumberOfSheets"),
                     Query.value(10));

      results = server.queryNames(new ObjectName("*:*"),ex);
      printBeans(results,ex);

      // String query #3 //
      ex = Query.eq(Query.attr("Status"),
                    Query.value(3));
      results = server.queryNames(new ObjectName("*:*"),ex);
      printBeans(results,ex);
```

```
    }

    private static void printBeans(Set beans,QueryExp q) {
        System.out.println("Query used: " + q);
        System.out.println("Results: " + beans.size());
        Iterator iter = beans.iterator();
        while (iter.hasNext()) {
                ObjectName beanName = (ObjectName)iter.next();
                System.out.println(beanName + " was found");
        }
    }
}

    private ObjectName loadBean(String className,String objectName) {

    ObjectName mbeanObjectName = null;
    String domain = server.getDefaultDomain();
    String mbeanName = className;
    try {
            mbeanObjectName = new ObjectName(objectName);
    } catch(MalformedObjectNameException e) {
            e.printStackTrace();
            System.exit(1);
    }
            // Create our simple object to manage //
            try {
                server.createMBean(mbeanName,mbeanObjectName);
            }catch(Exception ex){
                    ex.printStackTrace();
                    System.exit(1);
            }

            return mbeanObjectName;
    }
}
```

The MBeanQueryRelational application in Listing 9-10 begins like the previous two examples, but instead creates three MBeans. However, to demonstrate the numeric query capabilities, I updated the PrinterObject class and PrinterObjectMBean interface to have set methods for setting the number of jobs, the number of sheets, and the status attributes of the PrinterObject class.

The first query uses the gt() method to find all printer objects with more than five print jobs. The second query uses the geq() method to find all printer objects with at least ten sheets of paper in the paper tray. In reality, this type of attribute would be very hard to discover, as people generally put a random number of sheets in the paper tray each time.

The third and final query uses the eq() method to find all the printer objects whose status code is a value of three. You could also use this type of query to find all printers in an error state. The status code of three used for this example would be defined as an error state.

Running the `MBeanQueryRelational` application produces output that looks like the following:

```
Query used: (NumberOfJobs) > (5)
Results: 2
PrinterObject:name=HP 600 Color was found
PrinterObject:name=HP Deskjet was found
Query used: (NumberOfSheets) >= (10)
Results: 3
PrinterObject:name=HP 600 Color was found
PrinterObject:name=HP Deskjet was found
PrinterObject:name=HP Inkjet was found
Query used: (Status) = (3)
Results: 1
PrinterObject:name=HP 600 Color was found
```

## Other expression methods

A few other methods enable you to do matching on a pattern like the object name, but define several other characters to build expressions. You can also use methods that enable you to find a value that falls between a specified range and check for inclusion in a list. The methods that fall into this last category are `between()`, `in()`, and `match()`.

Before continuing, however, you should understand the arguments to the `match()` method. The `match()` method enables you to perform a string comparison of an attribute to a single string value or a pattern. The JMX specification defines the following special characters that can be used in constructing an expression for the `match()` method:

◆ Wildcard characters of * and ?

◆ Character sets [Aa]

◆ Character set ranges [A–Z]

Listing 9-11 shows the source code for an application that uses the three aforementioned methods.

**Listing 9-11: Using the between, in, and match methods**

```
import javax.management.Attribute;
import javax.management.AttributeList;
import javax.management.ObjectName;
import javax.management.InstanceNotFoundException;
import javax.management.MalformedObjectNameException;
import javax.management.MBeanServer;
import javax.management.MBeanServerFactory;
import javax.management.ReflectionException;
import javax.management.StringValueExp;
import javax.management.AttributeValueExp;
import javax.management.Query;
import javax.management.QueryExp;
import javax.management.ValueExp;
```

```
import java.util.Iterator;
import java.util.Set;

public class MBeanQueryOther {

    private static MBeanServer server = null;
    private static ObjectName printer1 = null;
    private static ObjectName printer2 = null;
    private static ObjectName printer3 = null;

    public MBeanQueryOther() {
        server = MBeanServerFactory.createMBeanServer();
    }

    public static void main(String[] args)
            throws InstanceNotFoundException,
                    MalformedObjectNameException,
                    ReflectionException {

        MBeanQueryOther agent = new MBeanQueryOther();
        printer1 = agent.loadBean("PrinterObject",
                                    "PrinterObject:name=HP Inkjet");
        printer2 = agent.loadBean("PrinterObject",
                                    "PrinterObject:name=HP Deskjet");
        printer3 = agent.loadBean("PrinterObject",
                                    "PrinterObject:name=HP 600 Color");

        // Fill MBeans with some data //
        AttributeList atts1 = new AttributeList();
        atts1.add(new Attribute("Manufacturer","Hewlett Packard"));
        atts1.add(new Attribute("Department","IT"));
        atts1.add(new Attribute("DomainName","Metropolis"));
        atts1.add(new Attribute("NumberOfSheets",new Integer(10)));
        atts1.add(new Attribute("NumberOfJobs",new Integer(5)));
        atts1.add(new Attribute("Status",new Integer(1)));
        server.setAttributes(printer1,atts1);
        AttributeList atts2 = new AttributeList();
        atts2.add(new Attribute("Manufacturer","Hewlett Packard"));
        atts2.add(new Attribute("Department","Purchasing"));
        atts2.add(new Attribute("DomainName","Gotham"));
        atts2.add(new Attribute("NumberOfSheets",new Integer(10)));
        atts2.add(new Attribute("NumberOfJobs",new Integer(15)));
        atts2.add(new Attribute("Status",new Integer(1)));
        server.setAttributes(printer2,atts2);
        AttributeList atts3 = new AttributeList();
        atts3.add(new Attribute("Manufacturer","Hewlett Packard"));
        atts3.add(new Attribute("Department","IT"));
        atts3.add(new Attribute("NumberOfSheets",new Integer(10)));
        atts3.add(new Attribute("NumberOfJobs",new Integer(50)));
```

```
    atts3.add(new Attribute("Status",new Integer(3)));
    server.setAttributes(printer3,atts3);


    // String query #1 //

    QueryExp ex = Query.between(Query.attr("NumberOfJobs"),
                                Query.value(10),
                                Query.value(50));
    Set results = server.queryNames(new ObjectName("*:*"),ex);
    printBeans(results,ex);

    // String query #2 //

    ex = Query.in(Query.attr("DomainName"),
              new ValueExp[]{new StringValueExp("Gotham"),
              new StringValueExp("Metropolis")});

    results = server.queryNames(new ObjectName("*:*"),ex);
    printBeans(results,ex);

    // String query #3 //

    ex = Query.match(Query.attr("Department"),
                new StringValueExp("*T"));

    results = server.queryNames(new ObjectName("*:*"),ex);
    printBeans(results,ex);

}

private static void printBeans(Set beans,QueryExp q) {
    System.out.println("Query used: " + q);
    System.out.println("Results: " + beans.size());
    Iterator iter = beans.iterator();
    while (iter.hasNext()) {
            ObjectName beanName = (ObjectName)iter.next();
            System.out.println(beanName + " was found");
    }
}

private ObjectName loadBean(String className,String objectName) {

 ObjectName mbeanObjectName = null;
 String domain = server.getDefaultDomain();
 String mbeanName = className;
 try {
        mbeanObjectName = new ObjectName(objectName);
 } catch(MalformedObjectNameException e) {
```

```
            e.printStackTrace();
            System.exit(1);
      }

            // Create our simple object to manage //
            try {
               server.createMBean(mbeanName,mbeanObjectName);
            }catch(Exception ex){
                  ex.printStackTrace();
                  System.exit(1);
            }

            return mbeanObjectName;
      }
}
```

The `MBeanQueryOther` application shown in Listing 9-11 demonstrates the use of the `between()`, `in()`, and `match()` methods by first performing a query to find all printers that have a number of jobs between ten and fifty. The between is inclusive, meaning that values equal to or greater than ten and with a value less than or equal to fifty will be considered.

The second query finds all printers whose domain name is in a list containing the values `Gotham` and `Metropolis`. The third query uses the `match()` method to find all printers whose `DomainName` attribute begin with any character and the second character is a letter `T`.

The output from running the `MBeanQueryOther` application looks like the following:

```
Query used: (NumberOfJobs) between (10) and (50)
Results: 2
PrinterObject:name=HP 600 Color was found
PrinterObject:name=HP Deskjet was found
Query used: DomainName in ('Gotham', 'Metropolis')
Results: 2
PrinterObject:name=HP Inkjet was found
PrinterObject:name=HP Deskjet was found
Query used: Department like '%T'
Results: 2
PrinterObject:name=HP 600 Color was found
PrinterObject:name=HP Inkjet was found
```

# Summary

In this chapter you've looked at how to query for MBeans in an MBean Server using the two methods, `queryNames()` and `queryMBeans()`, in the `MBeanServer` interface. You learned how to construct a query and execute it. You also learned how to construct different types of queries based on numerical or string constraints. The arguments to queries are represented as one of four types of expressions: numerical, string, relational, and boolean.

The next chapter continues by taking you into more of the agent environment where you will look at the monitor and timer services. These services enable you to watch the values of managed resources and initiate some action at a specified interval.

# Chapter 10

# Using Monitoring and Timer Facilities

One of the key features of a management solution is the capability to watch the value of an entity over time. Computer operators and system administrators are two of the primary users of the type of data presented by monitoring facilities. Monitoring and notification form the basis of many management solutions and are critical for catching and reporting problems in a system.

In Chapter 1, I mentioned systems that have thousands of nodes, where a node represents a managed resource that can be a physical device such as a printer or computer terminal, an application program, or operating system software. Having an automated piece of software keeping an eye on everything ensures system integrity from a management standpoint. System problems can escalate quickly, so being able to watch critical system functions is essential to keep the system running efficiently.

The JMX specification defines two agent services: One is used for monitoring attributes of a managed resource and sending a notification should some condition be met. The JMX specification also defines a service for sending notifications at periodic intervals for a set number of iterations. The monitoring and timer services are mandatory services for a JMX-compliant agent.

In this chapter, you'll look at the monitoring and timer services. You will learn how to set up and monitor MBean attributes and respond to notifications of different events. You'll also learn how to use the monitor service to trigger different notifications.

> **CROSS-REFERENCE:** Although this chapter talks about notifications, it is only in the context of the monitoring and timer services. Chapter 11 provides a complete discussion of the notification facilities provided by the various JMX components.

## Using the Monitor Service

You've seen various references in this book to the types of information you could theoretically monitor, such as CPU percentage in use, amount of free storage on a fixed-storage device, or the error status of a printer, to name a few. Each of these types of information can be represented as a Java datatype. The JMX monitoring service monitors three basic types. Data that can be monitored can be categorized as `java.lang.String`, `java.lang.Integer`, or `java.lang.Float`. These types are often represented in a management console as a bar graph, a progress bar, a dial or gauge, or a counter. Specifically, the JMX specification defines the following names for the types of monitors that can be established:

♦ CounterMonitor

♦ GaugeMonitor

♦ StringMonitor

To enable the monitoring of a managed resource, you don't have to do anything special to the managed resource other than ensure that it has accessor methods for the attributes you want to monitor. Of course, the managed resource has to be present for a monitor to work, but a monitor can be active without its managed resource present. The JMX specification defines the behavior that the monitoring service takes when a managed resource is not present or suddenly disappears from view. In the section "The MonitorNotification class," later in this chapter, you'll be introduced to the error notifications that a monitor can send.

Given the various Java types and managed resources, which could represent any mixture of the three datatypes, it is necessary to ensure that you use the correct monitor for the correct type of data. This means that you cannot use the `StringMonitor` to monitor a `boolean` or `integer` value. When monitors are created, runtime type checking is performed against the attribute you requested to be monitored. If the Java type of the attribute is not compatible with the type of monitor being used, an exception is thrown.

## The anatomy of a monitor

Monitoring managed resources currently requires that the managed resource and monitor exist in the same Java Virtual Machine (JVM). The monitor MBeans can be instantiated in the same MBean Server in which the other MBeans have been loaded. When the Distributed Services phase of the of JMX specification is defined, perhaps it will include the capability to monitor attributes and MBeans that exist in other JVMs. However, although the JMX specification does not define the capability to monitor remote attributes, you could easily imagine a remote interface that would act as a proxy to a remotely managed resource using RMI. This type of remote interaction is where connectors can be utilized. If you recall, connectors are software components of the JMX agent layer that enable remote management clients to interact with managed resources.

You don't have to implement the remote monitoring in the `Monitor` class itself. You can also utilize the notification services to propagate notifications generated by an MBean running in a separate JVM to a central JVM. Again, the JMX specification does not define the capability to propagate notifications between JVMs, but in Chapter 12 you'll learn how to do this as well.

## Monitor base classes

The `javax.management.monitor.Monitor` class is the superclass of all monitor classes in JMX. The `Monitor` class provides the base methods that are common to all types of monitors. In addition, each subclass of the `Monitor` class defines a set of methods and attributes that are unique to the given type of monitor. The subclasses that extend the `Monitor` interface are the `javax.management.CounterMonitor`, `javax.management.GaugeMonitor`, and `javax.management.StringMonitor` classes. These subclasses are described in more detail later in this chapter.

The `Monitor` class extends the `javax.management.NotificationBroadcaster` class that can be used for MBeans that want to send notifications. It also implements the `MBeanRegistration` interface so that it can receive notifications of its own life cycle events as they occur in the MBean Server. The `Monitor` class itself is an abstract class, so it cannot be istantiated directly using the `new` operator. Figure 10-1 shows the relationship between the `Monitor` class and its direct subclasses.

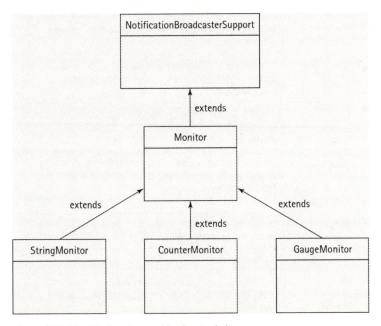

**Figure 10-1:** The Monitor class and its direct subclasses.

Table 10-1 describes each of the methods of the `Monitor` class.

## Table 10-1    Monitor Class Methods

| Method Name | Description |
|---|---|
| `getGranularityPeriod()` | Returns a Java `long` primitive representing the granularity period in milliseconds. If no granularity period has been set, the default value of ten is returned. |
| `getObservedAttribute()` | Returns a `java.lang.String` representing the name of the attribute being monitored by this monitor. If no attribute has been set, the value of `null` is returned. No default value is assigned to this attribute. |

| Method Name | Description |
|---|---|
| getObservedObject() | Returns a `javax.management.ObjectName` representing the MBean being observed. If no observed object has been set, a `null` value is returned. No default value is assigned to this attribute. |
| isActive() | Returns a Java `boolean` primitive indicating whether the monitor is active |
| postDeregister() | Called by the MBean Server after the MBean has been unregistered. See Chapter 8 for more information. |
| postRegister(java.lang.Boolean registrationDone) | Called by the MBean Server after the MBean has been registered. See Chapter 8 for more information. |
| preDeregister() | Called by the MBean Server before the MBean is about to be unregistered. See Chapter 8 for more information. |
| preRegister(javax.management. MBeanServer server,javax.management.Object Name bean) | Called by the MBean Server before the MBean is about to be registered. See Chapter 8 for more information. |
| setGranularityPeriod(long period) | Sets the granularity period to be used. The value must be greater than zero. |
| setObservedAttribute(java.lang .String attr) | Sets the attribute that will be monitored |
| setObservedObject(javax. management.ObjectName bean) | Sets the MBean that contains the attribute to be monitored |
| start() | Starts the monitor |
| stop() | Stops the monitor |

If you haven't caught on yet, the `Monitor` class is actually implemented as an MBean. In fact, all of the agent services, such as the monitoring and timer services described in this chapter, are implemented as MBeans. This enables a JMX agent to dynamically load and remove new services, and keeps the agent implementation itself that much easier.

This chapter does not cover the methods of the `MBeanRegistration` interface, such as `postRegister()` and `postDeregister()`. You can read about the `MBeanRegistration` interface in Chapter 8. The remaining methods in Table 10-1 are covered in the context of one of the subclasses that you'll look at shortly. Until then, the descriptions provided in Table 10-1 should be sufficient for an understanding of their purpose.

The term *monitor* implies an entity that watches and waits for some condition to occur. Usually, a predefined threshold or condition is defined, which, when met, results in some action occurring. With respect to JMX, monitors send notifications when a specified condition has been met. When monitors send the notification, they send it as an instance of the `javax.management.MonitorNotification` class, which is a subclass of the `javax.management.Notification` class. The `MonitorNotification` class defines a set of methods that are unique to monitored objects.

The `MonitorNotification` class is also used to describe error conditions that are sent as notifications. The `Monitor` class also inherits several methods from the `javax.management.NotificationBroadcaster` interface, which enables other components to register interest in the events this monitor may emit. In Chapter 11, you'll learn how to write a Java application that registers interest in receiving notifications. The examples you'll see in this chapter do not formally discuss notifications except in the context of the monitor that emits them.

## The MonitorNotification class

The `MonitorNotification` class is the class that describes an event or notification of some condition being met in a monitor. The `MonitorNotification` class is used to represent notifications for all the types of monitors that are currently defined in the JMX specification. When a `MonitorNotification` object is created, it is filled out with all the information about the particular event that has occurred. The types of conditions that can trigger a notification are when a threshold value has been reached for a counter, when a string value has changed, or when a value exceeds or drops below a threshold value. You can also use the `MonitorNotification` class to send an error notification when a managed resource suddenly disappears from the JVM due to an error condition. This might occur if someone unplugged a printer that was being monitored.

The `MonitorNotification` object includes methods that enable you to extract information about the notification and determine what happened and to whom. Table 10-2 describes the methods of the `MonitorNotification` class. (Not listed are the methods that the `MonitorNotification` class inherits from the `javax.management.Notification` class.) You can learn more about the `javax.management.Notification` class in Chapter 11. You can also view the JavaDoc for this class for more information.

## Table 10-2   MonitorNotification Class Methods

| Method Name | Description |
|---|---|
| `getDerivedGauge()` | Returns a `java.lang.Number` representing the derived gauge |
| `getObservedAttribute()` | Returns a `java.lang.String` representing the name of the attribute being monitored |
| `getObservedObject()` | Returns a `javax.management.ObjectName` representing the object name of the MBean being monitored |
| `getTrigger()` | Returns a `java.lang.Object` representing the value that triggered this notification |

All notifications include the same base set of information common to all monitors. Those pieces of information are accessible using the methods described in Table 10-1, and include the following: the observed object's name (the MBean), the observed attribute's name, the gauge value or the last value before the notification was sent, and the threshold value or string value that triggered the notification.

There are different types of notifications, some of which are common to all types of monitors, and some of which are specific to a monitor. The format of notification types is discussed in Chapter 11. The types of notifications that are common to all monitors are as follows:

- ◆ jmx.monitor.error.mbean — This notification is sent when the observed MBean is no longer registered in the MBean Server.

- ◆ jmx.monitor.error.attribute — This notification is sent when the observed attribute does not exist in the observed object.

- ◆ jmx.monitor.error.type — This notification is sent when the observed attribute is null or is not of the appropriate Java type.

- ◆ jmx.monitor.error.runtime — This notification is sent when an exception occurs while trying to retrieve the value of an observed attribute.

Each type of monitor has notification types that are unique to it. You will examine these notification types in the discussion of each monitor that follows in this chapter.

Monitors have some common characteristics, one of which is the granularity period of the notification.

## Specifying the granularity of a monitor

The granularity period that you can define using setGranularityPeriod() is the time between each query of the monitored attribute. Setting this value to a low number can result in too many queries of the attribute, whereas too high a number can result in delayed results. Setting the granularity period of monitors is usually represented in a user interface as a slider, dial, or spinner control that can easily increment or decrement a value.

The unit of measure for granularity is milliseconds, which gives you a wide range of options for determining how often you want to check the value of an observed attribute. Being able to specify the unit in milliseconds gives you the capability to observe an attribute in nearly real time. It also enables you to specify units such as seconds and minutes by doing the appropriate conversions. For example, five hundred milliseconds is approximately one second.

The next few sections describe how to use the different types of monitors. Each of the examples presented follows a simple pattern of defining a managed resource that represents a printer, and defining a class that implements the java.lang.Runnable interface, which is used to modify a specified attribute of the managed resource. Finally, the example defines an application that will load both the managed resource and the monitor being used.

In each section, I've omitted inherited methods because those can easily be looked up in the JavaDoc, and some are present in this chapter itself. For instance, the Monitor class is covered, so you can see the methods that all monitors inherit. The same goes for the

Notification class and the MonitorNotification class. I've tried to cover only the declared methods of each class.

The examples make use of a fictional managed object called PrinterObject, which, as its name implies, represents a printer. Listing 10-1 shows the source code for the PrinterObjectMBean interface.

**Listing 10-1: The PrinterObjectMBean interface**

```
public interface PrinterObjectMBean{

        public String getName();

        public void setName(String newName);

        public String getManufacturer();

        public void setManufacturer(String newManufacturer);

        public String getDomainName();

        public void setDomainName(String newDomainName);

        public String getDepartment();

        public void setDepartment(String newDepartment);

        public int getStatus();

        public void setStatus(int newStatus);

        public int getNumberOfSheets();

        public void setNumberOfSheets(int newNumberOfSheets);

        public int getNumberOfJobs();

        public void setNumberOfJobs(int newNumberOfJobs);

}
```

The implementation of the PrintObjectMBean interface is shown in the source code for the PrinterObject class in Listing 10-2.

**Listing 10-2: The PrinterObject class**

```
public class PrinterObject implements PrinterObjectMBean{

        private String name = "printer";
        private String manufacturer = "";
```

```java
    private String domainName = "";
    private String department = "";
    private int numberOfSheets = 0;
    private int numberOfJobs = 0;
    private int status = 0;

public PrinterObject(){
}

public PrinterObject(String iName){
    name = iName;
}

public String getName(){
    return name;
}

public void setName(String newName){
    name = newName;
}

public String getManufacturer(){
    return manufacturer;
}

public void setManufacturer(String newManufacturer){
    manufacturer = newManufacturer;
}

public String getDomainName(){
    return domainName;
}

public void setDomainName(String newDomainName){
    domainName = newDomainName;
}

public String getDepartment(){
    return department;
}

public void setDepartment(String newDepartment){
    department = newDepartment;
}

public int getStatus(){
    return status;
}
```

```
    public void setStatus(int newStatus){
         status = newStatus;
    }

    public int getNumberOfSheets(){
         return numberOfSheets;
    }

    public void setNumberOfSheets(int newNumberOfSheets){
         numberOfSheets = newNumberOfSheets;
    }

    public int getNumberOfJobs(){
         return numberOfJobs;
    }

    public void setNumberOfJobs(int newNumberOfJobs){
         numberOfJobs = newNumberOfJobs;
    }
}
```

You can compile the `PrinterObject` class and `PrinterObjectMBean` interface now or wait until you attempt the examples later in this book. You must explicitly compile these components, however, because the examples in this chapter refer to them dynamically, and will not cause them to be compiled along with the application they are used in.

## Monitoring string attributes

You can monitor changes in the value of a string attribute using the `javax.management` `.monitor.StringMonitor` class. This monitor can detect two different conditions with respect to an attribute of `java.lang.String` type. It can detect when an attribute value matches a string value, and when an attribute value is different from a string value.

This monitor does not automatically check for both of these conditions; rather, it provides accessor methods to toggle the checking of these two conditions on and off. It also enables you to set the string that will be compared against the attribute value. Table 10-3 describes the methods of the `StringMonitor` class. Not included are methods that are inherited from the `Monitor` class, except those that are overridden by the `StringMonitorMBean` interface.

### Table 10-3    StringMonitorMBean Interface Methods

| Method Name | Description |
|---|---|
| `getNotifyDiffer()` | Returns a boolean indicating whether notifications for string differences will be emitted |
| `getNotifyMatch()` | Returns a boolean indicating whether notifications for string matches will be emitted |

| Method Name | Description |
|---|---|
| getStringToCompare() | Returns the string that will be used to compare against the attribute value |
| setNotifyDiffer(boolean value) | Sets a flag indicating that the StringMonitor should emit notifications for differences in the strings it detects |
| setNotifyMatch(boolean value) | Sets a flag indicating that the StringMonitor should emit notifications for matches in the strings it detects |
| setStringToCompare(java.lang. String value | Sets the value against which the monitored attribute will be compared |

To test this example, I'm going to create a thread that can be launched from the management application. The thread's purpose is to repeatedly modify the value of an attribute until stopped. The thread will retrieve the value of a specified attribute, check its value, and change it if it's not equal to a predefined value. Listing 10-3 shows the source code for the BeanModifierThread class.

**Listing 10-3: A thread to modify the bean values**

```
import javax.management.MBeanServer;
import javax.management.ObjectName;
import javax.management.Attribute;

public class BeanModifierThread implements Runnable{

        private MBeanServer server = null;
        private ObjectName bean = null;

        public BeanModifierThread(MBeanServer theServer,
                                  ObjectName theBean){
                server = theServer;
                bean = theBean;
        }

        public void run(){

                while (true) {

                        try {

                        String attrVal =
                            (String)server.getAttribute(bean,"DomainName");

                        if (attrVal.equals("Metropolis"))
                            server.setAttribute(bean,
                                new Attribute("DomainName","Gotham"));
```

```
                    else
                server.setAttribute(bean,
                     new Attribute("DomainName","Metropolis"));

            Thread.sleep(500);

            } catch (Exception ex){
            }
        }
    }

}
```

The `BeanModifierThread` class uses a `while` loop to execute indefinitely. The value of the `DomainName` attribute is retrieved using the `getAttribute()` method of the `MBeanServer` interface. The value is checked against the string value `Metropolis`. This value is set by the application shown in Listing 10-2. If the current value of the attribute is equal to the string `Metropolis`, the `setAttribute()` method is called to change the value of the `DomainName` attribute to a value of `Gotham`. If the current value of the attribute is not equal to the string `Metropolis`, the value is set to `Metropolis`.

You now need a simple Java application that will load both the MBean you want to monitor and the MBean representing the monitor service. Listing 10-4 shows the source code for the `MBeanMonitorString` application.

**Listing 10-4: Monitoring a string value**

```
import javax.management.Attribute;
import javax.management.AttributeList;
import javax.management.ObjectName;
import javax.management.InstanceAlreadyExistsException;
import javax.management.InstanceNotFoundException;
import javax.management.MalformedObjectNameException;
import javax.management.MBeanException;
import javax.management.MBeanServer;
import javax.management.MBeanServerFactory;
import javax.management.NotCompliantMBeanException;
import javax.management.Notification;
import javax.management.NotificationFilter;
import javax.management.NotificationListener;
import javax.management.monitor.MonitorNotification;
import javax.management.ReflectionException;
import javax.management.monitor.StringMonitor;
import java.util.Iterator;
import java.util.Set;

public class MBeanMonitorString implements NotificationListener {

    private static MBeanServer server = null;
    private static ObjectName printer1 = null;
```

```java
private static ObjectName monitorBean = null;

public MBeanMonitorString() {
    server = MBeanServerFactory.createMBeanServer();
}

public static void main(String[] args)
        throws InstanceNotFoundException,
                MalformedObjectNameException,
                ReflectionException,
                MBeanException,
                InstanceAlreadyExistsException,
                NotCompliantMBeanException {

    MBeanMonitorString agent = new MBeanMonitorString();

        //JMXDebug debug = new JMXDebug(agent);

        printer1 = agent.loadBean("PrinterObject",
                        "PrinterObject:name=HP Inkjet");

        // Fill MBeans with some data //
        AttributeList atts1 = new AttributeList();
        atts1.add(new Attribute("Manufacturer",
                                "Hewlett Packard"));
        atts1.add(new Attribute("Department","IT"));
        atts1.add(new Attribute("DomainName","Metropolis"));
        atts1.add(new Attribute("NumberOfSheets",
                                new Integer(10)));
        atts1.add(new Attribute("NumberOfJobs",new Integer(5)));
        atts1.add(new Attribute("Status",new Integer(1)));
        server.setAttributes(printer1,atts1);

        // Setup monitor //
        monitorBean =
            new ObjectName("StringMonitor:type=printer");

        StringMonitor sMonitor = new StringMonitor();
        sMonitor.setObservedObject(printer1);
        sMonitor.setObservedAttribute("DomainName");
        sMonitor.setNotifyDiffer(true);
        sMonitor.setStringToCompare("Gotham");
        sMonitor.setGranularityPeriod(5);
        sMonitor.addNotificationListener(agent,null,null);
        server.registerMBean(sMonitor,monitorBean);

        // Start the monitor //
        sMonitor.start();
        // Setup modifier thread //
```

```
                    Thread p =
                        new Thread(new BeanModifierThread(server,printer1));
                    p.start();


    }

    public void handleNotification(Notification notif,Object who){
            MonitorNotification mNotif = (MonitorNotification)notif;
            System.out.println("Notification>>>>>>>>>>>>>>>>>>>> Value
is: " + (String)mNotif.getTrigger());
            System.out.println("Type: " + mNotif.getType());
    }

    private ObjectName loadBean(String className,String objectName) {

    ObjectName mbeanObjectName = null;
    String domain = server.getDefaultDomain();
    String mbeanName = className;
    try {
            mbeanObjectName = new ObjectName(objectName);
    } catch(MalformedObjectNameException e) {
            e.printStackTrace();
            System.exit(1);
    }
            // Create our simple object to manage //
            try {
                server.createMBean(mbeanName,mbeanObjectName);
            }catch(Exception ex){
                    ex.printStackTrace();
                    System.exit(1);
            }

            return mbeanObjectName;
    }
}
```

The application starts by loading a managed resource represented by the PrinterObject class. This MBean is then initialized with several pieces of information, including the domain name, the department, and the manufacturer. The domain name will serve as your attribute to be monitored.

Next, the application creates a new instance of the javax.management.StringMonitor class. Note that this does not create a new instance of the MBean in the MBean Server. You will register this instance in the MBean Server later in this application.

To set up the monitor, the setObservedObject() method is called, passing in the ObjectName of the PrinterObject MBean that was created earlier in the application. Next, you call the setObservedAttribute() method and supply a value of DomainName. The type of notification you want to receive is one that indicates when the value of the attribute is different than a supplied value. In the next line, you supply the string against which you want the monitor to compare the value of the attribute. This monitor will compare the value of the DomainName attribute to the string value of Gotham.

Set the granularity period to five milliseconds using the setGranularityPeriod() method. Setting it to this low of a value ensures that you get a chance to see a changed value. In the run() method of the BeanModifierThread() class, there is a call to the static java.lang .Thread method sleep(). If you set the value in the BeanModifierThread() to low, and set the value in the monitor too high, you may run into a condition where you can't seem to detect a change. In reality, the value of the DomainName would probably not change this frequently. Next, register the monitor in the MBean Server using the registerMBean() method of the MBeanServer interface, and finally call the start() method, which starts the monitor.

Calling the start() method does not result in any notifications being printed yet because you haven't changed the value of the attribute. Next, create an instance of the BeanModifierThread class by passing in the reference to the MBeanServer and PrinterObject MBean and calling the start() method of the Thread class. The BeanModifierThread class will then begin executing and changing the values of the DomainName attribute.

If all goes well, the monitor will begin detecting changes and periodically print messages indicating such. A few seconds after the MBeanMonitorString application starts, you should begin to see messages print that look like the following:

```
Notification>>>>>>>>>>>>>>>>>>>>>> Value is: Gotham
Type: jmx.monitor.string.differs
Notification>>>>>>>>>>>>>>>>>>>>>> Value is: Gotham
Type: jmx.monitor.string.differs
Notification>>>>>>>>>>>>>>>>>>>>>> Value is: Gotham
Type: jmx.monitor.string.differs
Notification>>>>>>>>>>>>>>>>>>>>>> Value is: Gotham
Type: jmx.monitor.string.differs
Notification>>>>>>>>>>>>>>>>>>>>>> Value is: Gotham
Type: jmx.monitor.string.differs
Notification>>>>>>>>>>>>>>>>>>>>>> Value is: Gotham
Type: jmx.monitor.string.differs
```

Each time a notification is generated, the handleNotification() method of the javax .management.NotificationListener interface is called. The value of Gotham is printed by calling the getTrigger() method of the MonitorNotification class. Because the handleNotification() method takes a Notification class as the first argument, you first cast it to the MonitorNotification type because the getTrigger() method does not exist in the Notification class. The value returned from the getTrigger() method is the value that caused the notification to be sent.

## Monitoring counter attributes

Sometimes, attributes represent numerical values that increase steadily over time. The `javax.management.monitor.Counter` class can be used to monitor numerical values, and can send a notification when the value reaches a certain threshold value. The counter can also be used to continuously monitor an increasing value by specifying a *modulus value,* after which the counter will start at its initial value again.

Counters often increase to a set value and then start over. Because the `CounterMonitor` class maintains its own internal counter to match against the attribute it is monitoring, it needs to be able to reset itself. You don't want to have to instantiate a new `CounterMonitor` each time, so the `CounterMonitor` can be given a modulus value so that it will reset itself each time the threshold is reached. Table 10-4 describes a subset of the methods of the `CounterMonitorMBean` interface.

### Table 10-4   CounterMonitorMBean Interface Methods

| Method Name | Description |
|---|---|
| getModulus() | Returns the modulus for this counter. The type returned is `java.lang.Number`, so you need to use an appropriate subclass, such as `java.lang.Integer`. |
| getNotify() | Returns a primitive Java `boolean` indicating whether notifications will be emitted |
| getOffset() | Returns the offset value for this counter |
| getThreshold() | Returns the threshold value for this counter |
| getDifferenceMode() | Returns a primitive Java `boolean` indicating whether difference mode is being used |
| setDifferenceMode(boolean value) | Sets a flag indicating that difference mode should be used |
| setModulus(java.lang.Number value) | Sets the modulus value for this counter |
| setOffset(java.lang.Number value) | Sets the offset value for this counter |
| setThreshold(java.lang.Number value) | Sets the threshold value for this counter |

The `CounterMonitor` has a couple of values that deserve a little more explanation. The threshold value is simple enough to understand: It basically sets a ceiling that when met, causes the monitor to emit a notification indicating that the threshold has been reached. The offset value is used to increment the threshold value by adding it to the threshold value as many times as necessary so that the threshold value exceeds the counter value.

The difference mode is used to provide a value that is equal to the difference between two successive threshold notifications.

To provide a constantly increasing value, I've written a thread class very similar to the `BeanModifierThread` class from Listing 10-3. The `BeanModifierCounterThread` class modifies the `NumberOfJobs` attribute in the `PrinterObject` MBean. Listing 10-5 shows the source code for the `BeanModifierCounterThread` class. When the counter in this class reaches a value greater than twenty, the counter is set to `zero`. This will cause the monitor to emit new notifications.

**Listing 10-5: Counter monitoring thread**

```
import javax.management.MBeanServer;
import javax.management.ObjectName;
import javax.management.Attribute;

public class BeanModifierCounterThread implements Runnable{

        private MBeanServer server = null;
        private ObjectName bean = null;

        public BeanModifierCounterThread(MBeanServer theServer,ObjectName
theBean) {
                server = theServer;
                bean = theBean;
        }

        public void run(){

                int counter = 0;

                while (true) {

                        try {

                                Integer attrVal =
(Integer)server.getAttribute(bean,"NumberOfJobs");

                                server.setAttribute(bean,
                                                new
Attribute("NumberOfJobs",new Integer(counter++)));

                                if (counter > 20)
                                        counter = 0;

                                Thread.sleep(500);

                        } catch (Exception ex){
                        }
```

```
        }
    }
}
```

Listing 10-6 shows the MBeanMonitorCounter class, which serves as your JMX agent and loads the CounterMonitor MBean and the PrinterObject MBean. The CounterMonitor MBean monitors the integer attribute representing the number of jobs currently in the printer's queue and emits a notification if the number of jobs reaches a threshold of twenty.

**Listing 10-6: Monitoring the counter of the number of jobs**

```
import javax.management.Attribute;
import javax.management.AttributeList;
import javax.management.ObjectName;
import javax.management.InstanceAlreadyExistsException;
import javax.management.InstanceNotFoundException;
import javax.management.MalformedObjectNameException;
import javax.management.MBeanException;
import javax.management.MBeanServer;
import javax.management.MBeanServerFactory;
import javax.management.NotCompliantMBeanException;
import javax.management.Notification;
import javax.management.NotificationFilter;
import javax.management.NotificationListener;
import javax.management.monitor.MonitorNotification;
import javax.management.ReflectionException;
import javax.management.monitor.CounterMonitor;
import java.util.Iterator;
import java.util.Set;

public class MBeanMonitorCounter implements NotificationListener {

    private static MBeanServer server = null;
    private static ObjectName printer1 = null;
    private static ObjectName monitorBean = null;

    public MBeanMonitorCounter() {
        server = MBeanServerFactory.createMBeanServer();
    }

    public static void main(String[] args)
            throws InstanceNotFoundException,
                MalformedObjectNameException,
                ReflectionException,
                MBeanException,
                InstanceAlreadyExistsException,
                NotCompliantMBeanException {

        MBeanMonitorCounter agent = new MBeanMonitorCounter();
```

```
        //JMXDebug debug = new JMXDebug(agent);

        printer1 = agent.loadBean("PrinterObject",
                             "PrinterObject:name=HP Inkjet");

        // Fill MBeans with some data //
        AttributeList atts1 = new AttributeList();
        atts1.add(new Attribute("Manufacturer","Hewlett Packard"));
        atts1.add(new Attribute("Department","IT"));
        atts1.add(new Attribute("DomainName","Metropolis"));
        atts1.add(new Attribute("NumberOfSheets",new Integer(10)));
        atts1.add(new Attribute("NumberOfJobs",new Integer(5)));
        atts1.add(new Attribute("Status",new Integer(1)));
        server.setAttributes(printer1,atts1);

        // Setup monitor //
        monitorBean = new ObjectName("CounterMonitor:type=printer");

        CounterMonitor sMonitor = new CounterMonitor();
        sMonitor.setObservedObject(printer1);
        sMonitor.setObservedAttribute("NumberOfJobs");
        sMonitor.setNotify(true);
        sMonitor.setThreshold(new Integer(20));
        sMonitor.setGranularityPeriod(5);
        sMonitor.addNotificationListener(agent,null,null);
        server.registerMBean(sMonitor,monitorBean);

        // Start the monitor //
        sMonitor.start();
        // Setup modifier thread //
        Thread p = new Thread(new
BeanModifierCounterThread(server,printer1));
        p.start();

    }

    public void handleNotification(Notification notif,Object who){
            MonitorNotification mNotif = (MonitorNotification)notif;
            System.out.println("Notification>>>>>>>>>>>>>>>>>>>>
Value is: " + mNotif.getTrigger());
            System.out.println("Type: " + mNotif.getType());

    }

    private ObjectName loadBean(String className,String objectName) {

    ObjectName mbeanObjectName = null;
    String domain = server.getDefaultDomain();
```

```
    String mbeanName = className;
    try {
         mbeanObjectName = new ObjectName(objectName);
    } catch(MalformedObjectNameException e) {
         e.printStackTrace();
         System.exit(1);
    }

         // Create our simple object to manage //
         try {
             server.createMBean(mbeanName,mbeanObjectName);
         }catch(Exception ex){
              ex.printStackTrace();
              System.exit(1);
         }

         return mbeanObjectName;
    }
}
```

The `CounterMonitor` MBean is instantiated using the `new` operator and registered using the `registerMBean()` method of the `MBeanServer` interface. The notifications are turned on for this monitor by calling the `setNotify()` method, and the monitored object and attribute are set using the `setObservedObject()` and `setObservedAttribute()` methods, respectively. The threshold value is set to twenty by calling the `setThreshold()` method. The `CounterMonitor` checks the value approximately every five milliseconds, as set by the `setGranularityPeriod()` method.

Once the `MBeanMonitorCounter` application starts, you will begin to see output that looks like the following:

```
Notification>>>>>>>>>>>>>>>>>>>>>>> Value is: 20
Type: jmx.monitor.counter.threshold
Notification>>>>>>>>>>>>>>>>>>>>>>> Value is: 20
Type: jmx.monitor.counter.threshold
Notification>>>>>>>>>>>>>>>>>>>>>>> Value is: 20
Type: jmx.monitor.counter.threshold
Notification>>>>>>>>>>>>>>>>>>>>>>> Value is: 20
Type: jmx.monitor.counter.threshold
```

## Monitoring fluctuating values

Attributes that change their values by an increasing or decreasing amount can be monitored using the `javax.management.monitor.GaugeMonitor` class. This class can monitor an attribute value to see if it dips below a low value or exceeds a high value. This type of monitor can be used to watch a managed resource with sensitive attributes that must stay within a predefined range. Table 10-5 shows the methods of the `GaugeMonitorMBean` interface and provides a description of each.

## Table 10-5 GaugeMonitorMBean Interface Methods

| Method Name | Description |
|---|---|
| getDifferenceMode() | Returns a primitive Java boolean indicating whether difference mode is being used |
| getHighThreshold() | Returns a java.lang.Number Java type representing the high threshold value |
| getLowThreshold() | Returns a java.lang.Number Java type representing the low threshold value |
| getNotificationInfo() | Returns an array of MBeanNotificationInfo objects containing information about the notifications emitted by the GaugeMonitor MBean |
| getNotifyHigh() | Returns a primitive Java boolean indicating whether notifications for high threshold values should be emitted |
| getNotifyLow() | Returns a primitive Java boolean indicating whether notifications for low threshold values should be emitted |
| setDifferenceMode(boolean value) | Sets a flag indicating whether to use difference mode |
| setNotifyHigh(boolean value) | Sets a flag indicating whether notifications for high threshold values should be emitted |
| setNotifyLow(boolean value) | Sets a flag indicating whether notifications for low threshold values should be emitted |
| setThresholds(java.lang.Number highValue, java.lang.Number lowValue) | Sets the high and low threshold values for the monitor |

When the GaugeMonitor is started, and the value is equal to or greater than the high threshold. A notification will be sent if you have called the setNotifyHigh() method with a value of true. Likewise, if the value is equal to or less than the low value, a notification will be sent if you have called the setNotifyLow() method with a value of true.

To demonstrate the GaugeMonitor class, you can use the following example that operates very similarly to the previous examples. The BeanModifierGaugeThread class in Listing 10-7 supplies the high and low values for the NumberOfJobs attribute in the PrinterObject MBean.

**Listing 10-7: The BeanModifierGaugeThread class**

```
import javax.management.MBeanServer;
import javax.management.ObjectName;
import javax.management.Attribute;
```

```
public class BeanModifierGaugeThread implements Runnable{

        private MBeanServer server = null;
        private ObjectName bean = null;

        public BeanModifierGaugeThread(MBeanServer theServer,ObjectName
theBean){
                server = theServer;
                bean = theBean;
        }

        public void run(){

                int counter = 0;
        boolean incr = true;

                while (true) {

                        try {

                        Integer attrVal =
(Integer)server.getAttribute(bean,"NumberOfJobs");

                                if (incr) {
                                    if (counter >= 20){
                                        counter = 20;
                                        incr = false;
                                    }else
                                        counter++;
                                } else {

                                if (counter >= 5)
                                        counter--;
                                    else
                                        incr = true;
                                }

                                server.setAttribute(bean,
                                                    new
Attribute("NumberOfJobs",new Integer(counter)));

                                Thread.sleep(500);

                        } catch (Exception ex){
                        }
                }
        }
}
```

The `BeanModiferGaugeThread` class operates by steadily increasing the `NumberofJobs` attribute up to a high threshold value of `twenty`. When the value of `twenty` is passed, the class begins decrementing the value to a low threshold value of `five`. When this low threshold value is reached, the process repeats. This example simulates a value that increases and decreases like a gauge.

The `MBeanMonitorGauge` class in Listing 10-8 shows the source code for the application that uses the `BeanModifierGaugeThread` class and loads the `GaugeMonitor` MBean and the `PrinterObject` MBean.

### Listing 10-8: The MBeanMonitorGauge application class

```
import javax.management.Attribute;
import javax.management.AttributeList;
import javax.management.ObjectName;
import javax.management.InstanceAlreadyExistsException;
import javax.management.InstanceNotFoundException;
import javax.management.MalformedObjectNameException;
import javax.management.MBeanException;
import javax.management.MBeanServer;
import javax.management.MBeanServerFactory;
import javax.management.NotCompliantMBeanException;
import javax.management.Notification;
import javax.management.NotificationFilter;
import javax.management.NotificationListener;
import javax.management.monitor.MonitorNotification;
import javax.management.ReflectionException;
import javax.management.monitor.GaugeMonitor;
import java.util.Iterator;
import java.util.Set;

public class MBeanMonitorGauge implements NotificationListener {

    private static MBeanServer server = null;
    private static ObjectName printer1 = null;
    private static ObjectName monitorBean = null;

    public MBeanMonitorGauge() {
        server = MBeanServerFactory.createMBeanServer();
    }

    public static void main(String[] args)
            throws InstanceNotFoundException,
                MalformedObjectNameException,
                ReflectionException,
                MBeanException,
                InstanceAlreadyExistsException,
                NotCompliantMBeanException {
```

```
        MBeanMonitorGauge agent = new MBeanMonitorGauge();

            //JMXDebug debug = new JMXDebug(agent);

        printer1 = agent.loadBean("PrinterObject","PrinterObject:name=HP
Inkjet");

            // Fill MBeans with some data //
            AttributeList atts1 = new AttributeList();
            atts1.add(new Attribute("Manufacturer","Hewlett
Packard"));
            atts1.add(new Attribute("Department","IT"));
            atts1.add(new Attribute("DomainName","Metropolis"));
            atts1.add(new Attribute("NumberOfSheets",new
Integer(10)));
            atts1.add(new Attribute("NumberOfJobs",new Integer(5)));
            atts1.add(new Attribute("Status",new Integer(1)));
            server.setAttributes(printer1,atts1);

            // Setup monitor //
            //monitorBean =
agent.loadBean("javax.management.monitor.StringMonitor","StringMonitor:t
ype=printer");
            monitorBean = new
ObjectName("CounterMonitor:type=printer");

            GaugeMonitor sMonitor = new GaugeMonitor();
            sMonitor.setObservedObject(printer1);
            sMonitor.setObservedAttribute("NumberOfJobs");
            sMonitor.setNotifyHigh(true);
            sMonitor.setNotifyLow(true);
            sMonitor.setThresholds(new Integer(20),new Integer(5));
            sMonitor.setGranularityPeriod(5);
            sMonitor.addNotificationListener(agent,null,null);
            server.registerMBean(sMonitor,monitorBean);

            // Start the monitor //
            sMonitor.start();
            // Setup modifier thread //
            Thread p = new Thread(new
BeanModifierGaugeThread(server,printer1));
            p.start();

    }

    public void handleNotification(Notification notif,Object who){
            MonitorNotification mNotif = (MonitorNotification)notif;
            System.out.println("Notification>>>>>>>>>>>>>>>>>>>>>>
Value is: " + mNotif.getTrigger());
```

```
            System.out.println("Type: " + mNotif.getType());
    }

    private ObjectName loadBean(String className,String objectName) {

    ObjectName mbeanObjectName = null;
    String domain = server.getDefaultDomain();
    String mbeanName = className;
    try {
            mbeanObjectName = new ObjectName(objectName);
    } catch(MalformedObjectNameException e) {
            e.printStackTrace();
            System.exit(1);
    }

            // Create our simple object to manage //
            try {
                server.createMBean(mbeanName,mbeanObjectName);
            }catch(Exception ex){
                    ex.printStackTrace();
                    System.exit(1);
            }

            return mbeanObjectName;
    }
}
```

The MBeanMonitorGauge application works almost identically to the StringMonitor example in Listing 10-4 and the CounterMonitor example in Listing 10-6. The real difference, of course, is that you're using the GaugeMonitor class, indicating that you want to receive notifications of high and low threshold values being reached by calling the setNotifyHigh() and setNotifyLow() methods, respectively. For the example in Listing 10-8, you set twenty as the high value and five as the low value. The MBeanMonitorGauge application sets the high and low threshold values using the setThresholds() method. Alternatively, you could have called the setHighThreshold() and setLowThreshold() methods to accomplish the same thing.

After starting the MBeanMonitorGauge application, you'll begin to see output that looks like the following:

```
Notification>>>>>>>>>>>>>>>>>>>>> Value is: 5
Type: jmx.monitor.gauge.low
Notification>>>>>>>>>>>>>>>>>>>>> Value is: 20
Type: jmx.monitor.gauge.high
Notification>>>>>>>>>>>>>>>>>>>>> Value is: 5
Type: jmx.monitor.gauge.low
Notification>>>>>>>>>>>>>>>>>>>>> Value is: 20
Type: jmx.monitor.gauge.high
Notification>>>>>>>>>>>>>>>>>>>>> Value is: 5
Type: jmx.monitor.gauge.low
```

# Using the Timer Service

In managed systems, it is sometimes desirable to start a process on a specified date — for instance, to start a batch process, to retrieve the value of a managed resource, or to create more instances of a managed resource. The timer service is like a utility feature in that it is required but not critical for implementing management systems. Nevertheless, the capability to send a notification at a specific time is a useful feature for the scheduling of tasks or for forwarding notifications from another MBean. The latter could be used to forward error notifications on behalf of another managed resource.

The timer service is another mandatory JMX component in a compliant JMX agent implementation. The timer service is an MBean that enables you to send dated notifications. The notifications covered in the last section on monitors send notifications when a particular condition has been met. Similarly, the condition that must be met in order for the timer MBean to send a notification is that a particular date has occurred.

The timer MBean can send notifications in two different ways. It can send them only once, or it can send them repeatedly, up to a specified number or until a specified amount of time has elapsed. In other words, you can send a notification a specified number of times, or send it as many times as possible for an hour.

The timer service maintains a list of notifications, each of which bears a date or a number of occurrences indicating either how long it should be sent or how many should be sent. The notifications are user-defined, unlike the notifications you have already seen in this chapter. The timer service does not maintain the list of notifications should the timer service be shut down, but it does have the capability to acknowledge notifications whose date has passed, and it can be configured to act appropriately on them.

The timer service is implemented as the `javax.management.timer.Timer` class, which implements the `TimerMBean` interface. Table 10-6 describes the methods of the `TimerMBean` interface.

### Table 10-6    TimerMBean Interface Methods

| Method Name | Description |
|---|---|
| `addNotification(java.lang.String type, java.lang.String message, java.lang.Object userData, java.util.Date date)` | Adds a new notification with the given type, message, user data, and date |
| `addNotification(java.lang.String type, java.lang.String message, java.lang.Object userData, java.util.Date date, long period)` | Adds a new notification with the given type, message, user data, date, and period |
| `addNotification(java.lang.String type, java.lang.String message, java.lang.Object userData, java.util.Date date, long period, long nbOccurences)` | Adds a new notification with the given type, message, user data, date, and period |

| Method Name | Description |
|---|---|
| getAllNotificationIDs() | Returns a `java.util.Vector` containing all the notification IDs, regardless of their type |
| getDate(java.lang.Integer id) | Returns a `java.util.Date` representing the date for a notification |
| getNbNotifications() | Returns a primitive Java `int` representing the number of notifications in the Timer |
| getNbOccurences(java.lang.Integer id) | Returns a `java.lang.Long` representing the number of occurrences remaining for a notification |
| getNotificationIDs(java.lang.String type) | Returns a `java.util.Vector` containing the notification IDs for a notification of a specific type |
| getNotificationMessage(java.lang.Integer id) | Returns a `java.util.String` representing the detailed message for a notification |
| getNotificationType(java.lang.Integer id) | Returns a `java.util.String` representing the notification type for the associated notification ID |
| getNotificationUserData(java.lang.Integer id) | Returns a `java.lang.Object` representing user data associated with a particular notification |
| getPeriod(java.lang.Integer id) | Returns a `java.lang.Long` representing the period in milliseconds for a notification |
| getSendPastNotifications() | Returns a primitive Java `boolean` indicating whether or not past notifications will be sent |
| isEmpty() | Returns a primitive Java `boolean` indicating whether or not the Timer contains any notifications |
| removeAllNotifications(java.lang.Integer id) | Removes all notifications from the Timer |
| removeNotification(java.lang.String type) | Removes a notification by type |
| setSendPastNotifications(boolean value) | Sets a flag indicating that notifications whose date has passed should be sent when loaded |

Because the `Timer` class extends the `NotificationBroadcaster` class, it inherits the methods necessary for adding new notifications. The `removeNotification()` method and related methods are part of the `TimerMBean` interface. The `isEmpty()` method enables you to quickly check if any notifications are in the timer. When the timer emits a notification and determines either that the period has elapsed or the number of occurrences has been met, the notification is removed from the list. However, it is possible for the timer MBean to be active with no notifications to send.

You can schedule notifications to be sent on a specified date and to be limited by a number of occurrences or by a period of time. These two parameters are specified when adding the notification to the timer using one of the addNotification() methods in Table 10-6. When notifications are loaded into the Timer class, it checks the dates to see if the notifications have passed the date allowed. If you have set the sendPastNotifications flag to true, notifications with past dates will be sent. The sendPastNotifications flag is set to false by default. You should keep this in mind if you have a large number of old notifications that will be loaded, because it could cause a rush of notifications to be sent.

When a notification is added using one of the addNotification() methods, an instance of java.lang.Integer is returned representing an ID for the notification. This ID is used as input to many of the other methods of the TimerMBean interface to retrieve information about a particular notification. Once a notification has been added, it is immutable, which means you cannot change any of the information the notification was originally created with. You must remove the old one and add a new one or wait for the current notification to expire.

When notifications arrive, they do so as an instance of the javax.management.timer .TimerNotification class, which is a subclass of the Notification class. The TimerNotification class declares one method, getNotificationID(), which retrieves the java.lang.Integer for the notification. It also inherits several methods from the Notification class. (You can review the methods of the Notification class in Chapter 11.)

The MBeanTimers application shown in Listing 10-9 demonstrates the use of the timer service. It illustrates the use of three different timers.

**Listing 10-9: Using the timer service**

```
import javax.management.Attribute;
import javax.management.AttributeList;
import javax.management.ObjectName;
import javax.management.InstanceAlreadyExistsException;
import javax.management.InstanceNotFoundException;
import javax.management.MalformedObjectNameException;
import javax.management.MBeanException;
import javax.management.MBeanServer;
import javax.management.MBeanServerFactory;
import javax.management.NotCompliantMBeanException;
import javax.management.Notification;
import javax.management.NotificationFilter;
import javax.management.NotificationListener;
import javax.management.timer.Timer;
import javax.management.timer.TimerNotification;
import javax.management.ReflectionException;
import javax.management.timer.Timer;
import java.util.Calendar;
import java.util.Date;

public class MBeanTimers implements NotificationListener {

    private static MBeanServer server = null;
```

```
    private static ObjectName printer1 = null;
    private static ObjectName timerBean = null;

    public MBeanTimers() {
        server = MBeanServerFactory.createMBeanServer();
    }

    public static void main(String[] args)
            throws InstanceNotFoundException,
                    MalformedObjectNameException,
                    ReflectionException,
                    MBeanException,
                    InstanceAlreadyExistsException,
                    NotCompliantMBeanException {

        MBeanTimers agent = new MBeanTimers();

        Timer sTimer = new Timer();
        timerBean = new ObjectName("Timer:parm=timer");

        Calendar cal = Calendar.getInstance();
        cal.add(Calendar.SECOND,5);
        Date date = cal.getTime();

        sTimer.addNotification("jmx.programming.type",
                            "Times Up!",null,date);

//sTimer.addNotification("jmx.programming.type.period","Times
Up!",null,date,Timer.ONE_SECOND);

        sTimer.addNotification("jmx.programming.type.period.expire",
                            "Times Up!",null,date,Timer.ONE_SECOND,10);
        sTimer.addNotification("jmx.programming.type.expire",
                            "Times Up!",null,date,0,10);

        sTimer.addNotificationListener(agent,null,null);

        server.registerMBean(sTimer,timerBean);

        // Start the monitor //
        sTimer.start();

    }

    public void handleNotification(Notification notif,Object who){
        TimerNotification mNotif = (TimerNotification)notif;
        System.out.println("Notification>>>>>>>>>>>>>>>>>>>> Value
is: " + mNotif.getType());
```

```
        System.out.println("Notification Message >>>>>>>>>>> Value
is: " + mNotif.getMessage());
        System.out.println("Notification Timestamp >>>>>>>>> Value
is: " + new Date(mNotif.getTimeStamp()));
    }

}
```

The timer service is instantiated using the `new` operator and is registered at the end of the `main()` method using the `registerMBean()` method of the `MBeanServer` interface. The first timer is created using the `addNotification()` method, which creates a date notification with a type of `jmx.programming.type`. The date used is calculated to be approximately five seconds after the application starts. This notification will execute exactly once and then be removed from the timer service.

The second notification is given the type `jmx.programming.type.period.expire`. This notification will start on the same date as the first and will be triggered every second after that up to a maximum of ten times, as indicated by the last argument to the `addNotification()` method.

The last notification is given the type `jmx.programming.type.expire`, and is set up almost exactly like the second notification except that the `period` argument is given a value of `zero`. The last argument is given a value of `ten`, which might lead you to believe it will execute up to ten times, but because the period argument is `zero`, the notification is triggered exactly once.

When the `MBeanTimers` application is run, you will see output that looks like the following. Please note that the system time where the timer service is executed may cause the dates to appear differently.

```
Notification>>>>>>>>>>>>>>>>>>>>> Value is: jmx.programming.type.expire
Notification Message >>>>>>>>>>> Value is: Times Up!
Notification Timestamp >>>>>>>>> Value is: Mon Feb 11 20:36:50 EST 2002
Notification>>>>>>>>>>>>>>>>>>>>> Value is:
jmx.programming.type.period.expire
Notification Message >>>>>>>>>>> Value is: Times Up!
Notification Timestamp >>>>>>>>> Value is: Mon Feb 11 20:36:50 EST 2002
Notification>>>>>>>>>>>>>>>>>>>>> Value is: jmx.programming.type
Notification Message >>>>>>>>>>> Value is: Times Up!
Notification Timestamp >>>>>>>>> Value is: Mon Feb 11 20:36:50 EST 2002
Notification>>>>>>>>>>>>>>>>>>>>> Value is:
jmx.programming.type.period.expire
Notification Message >>>>>>>>>>> Value is: Times Up!
Notification Timestamp >>>>>>>>> Value is: Mon Feb 11 20:36:51 EST 2002
Notification>>>>>>>>>>>>>>>>>>>>> Value is:
jmx.programming.type.period.expire
Notification Message >>>>>>>>>>> Value is: Times Up!
Notification Timestamp >>>>>>>>> Value is: Mon Feb 11 20:36:52 EST 2002
Notification>>>>>>>>>>>>>>>>>>>>> Value is:
jmx.programming.type.period.expire
```

```
Notification Message >>>>>>>>>> Value is: Times Up!
Notification Timestamp >>>>>>>>> Value is: Mon Feb 11 20:36:53 EST 2002
Notification>>>>>>>>>>>>>>>>>>> Value is:
jmx.programming.type.period.expire
Notification Message >>>>>>>>>> Value is: Times Up!
Notification Timestamp >>>>>>>>> Value is: Mon Feb 11 20:36:54 EST 2002
Notification>>>>>>>>>>>>>>>>>>> Value is:
jmx.programming.type.period.expire
Notification Message >>>>>>>>>> Value is: Times Up!
Notification Timestamp >>>>>>>>> Value is: Mon Feb 11 20:36:55 EST 2002
Notification>>>>>>>>>>>>>>>>>>> Value is:
jmx.programming.type.period.expire
Notification Message >>>>>>>>>> Value is: Times Up!
Notification Timestamp >>>>>>>>> Value is: Mon Feb 11 20:36:56 EST 2002
Notification>>>>>>>>>>>>>>>>>>> Value is:
jmx.programming.type.period.expire
Notification Message >>>>>>>>>> Value is: Times Up!
Notification Timestamp >>>>>>>>> Value is: Mon Feb 11 20:36:57 EST 2002
Notification>>>>>>>>>>>>>>>>>>> Value is:
jmx.programming.type.period.expire
Notification Message >>>>>>>>>> Value is: Times Up!
Notification Timestamp >>>>>>>>> Value is: Mon Feb 11 20:36:58 EST 2002
Notification>>>>>>>>>>>>>>>>>>> Value is:
jmx.programming.type.period.expire
Notification Message >>>>>>>>>> Value is: Times Up!
Notification Timestamp >>>>>>>>> Value is: Mon Feb 11 20:36:59 EST 2002
```

From the preceding output, you can see that the `jmx.programming.expire` notification and the `jmx.programming.type` notification were emitted exactly once, whereas the notification `jmx.programming.type.period.expire` was emitted ten times before ending. Listing 10-9 includes a commented-out timer that will execute once every second indefinitely.

There may be times when you want to send additional data along with the notification (other than what is normally included), keeping in mind that the `TimerNotification` class inherits the `getSource()` method from the `javax.management.Notification` source class. The `getSource()` method enables you to retrieve the object from which the notification was triggered.

## Summary

In this chapter you've looked at two agent services — the monitor and timer services. These services provide valuable supporting features that enable you to send notifications at a specified interval or based on the value of an attribute. The monitor service enables you to monitor the values of an attribute in one of three ways: as a changing string value, a fluctuating value, or a steadily increasing value. With the monitor service you can send a notification when the value of a specified attribute reaches a certain value. The timer service can send a notification once or several times and can be used as a crude scheduling service.

In the next chapter you'll look at the notification model that MBeans use. The notifications you've seen in this chapter are based on the notification model described in Chapter 11.

## Chapter 11

# Working with JMX Notifications

So far in this book, you've seen several references to notifications. You've learned that MBeans can emit notifications, and that the notification model is defined in the instrumentation level where managed resources reside. You've also learned that MBeans, as well as other pieces of code, can register their interest in notifications and act as listeners.

The JMX specification defines a model for sending and receiving notifications that behave like events. It defines a set of classes for sending notifications, as well as an interface for listening for notifications. It also provides the capability to filter the types of notifications that a listener may receive.

The capability to send notifications also forms the underlying foundation for some of the agent services described in this book. For example, the monitor service sends notifications when specific events have occurred regarding changes in attribute values. The timer service emits notifications based on date, period (in milliseconds) between timer notifications, and number of occurrences.

In a somewhat similar vein, if you've worked with Java Abstract Windowing Toolkit Classes (AWT) or Swing, you've undoubtedly run across listeners and events. By clicking on a user-interface component such as a button, an event is fired, which can be received by classes implementing the `ActionListener` interface.

Notifications provide an important component to management systems, just as monitoring services do. Like monitoring services, notifications enable management systems to notify other software components or personnel that something has gone wrong or some task has completed. Current hardware systems are becoming increasingly smart about reporting problems; they can, for example, notify technical personnel to perform fixes, and then send another notification to computer operators that a service call has been made.

The notification system must also be extensible, as notifications are often sent to different types of devices and along different transports. Some notifications may go directly to another software component via RMI, while some may go to a pager via HTTP. Notifications can be broadcast to a recipient or they can be collected and then picked up by some other process. In addition, notification systems must also enable senders to pack the notifications with as much useful information as needed. A message that provides only a simple one-line note and time stamp is not very helpful.

In this chapter, you'll take a closer look at the notification model in JMX, and the base classes for sending and receiving notifications. You'll also learn how you can send notifications to devices using other transports.

> **NOTE:** In the current phase of the JMX specification, notifications can only be sent to listeners that exist in the same JMX agent. In the "Remote Notifications" section of this chapter, you'll learn how to send notifications to a listener in a remote JMX agent.

# Notification Basics

Notifications can be broken down into three basic areas: sending, receiving, and filtering. The last two categories are optional, as there is no rule requiring a listener for a notification, and filtering is necessary only if there is a chance that a listener will receive a lot of notifications that it doesn't need. Of course, a listener may also use filtering to find specific events and act on those in a given manner.

Notifications are implemented using the `javax.management.Notification` class. This class forms the base for other notification implementations that exist in other parts of the JMX API, such as the monitoring and timer services. The `Notification` class enables you to build a notification or message that consists of the following pieces of information:

- A message
- A sequence number that can be used to order notifications
- The source of the notification
- A time stamp showing when the notification was created
- The type of notification
- An arbitrary object representing user data that you want to send along

You've seen the term *notification type* used quite a bit in previous chapters. This term does not imply any sort of real datatype; it is just the name of the notification. Notifications are named using a dot notation similar to the way Java packages are named. Some examples of notification types are as follows:

- jmx.programming
- jmx.programming.part.one
- jmx.programming.wiley

These types are used in several places in the notification API to find notifications, disable or enable notifications, or filter notifications. There are no defined syntax rules, other than that the type must be able to be represented as a valid `java.lang.String` type. The specification also states that the letters `jmx` are reserved for JMX reference implementation use only.

## Notification class

The `Notification` class contains fields and methods that enable you to provide all of the pieces of information described in the preceding section. The `Notification` class is the primary implementation of a notification in any JMX-compliant management solution. This class is used as the argument for sending notifications, constructing new notifications, and disabling notifications. Table 11-1 describes the methods of the `Notification` class.

### Table 11-1   Notification Class Methods

| Method Name | Description |
| --- | --- |
| getMessage() | Returns a `java.lang.String` representing the text of the message |
| getSequenceNumber() | Returns a primitive Java `long` representing a sequence number |
| getSource() | Returns a `java.lang.Object` representing the source of the notification |
| getTimeStamp() | Returns a primitive Java `long` representing the time the notification was generated |
| getType() | Returns a `java.lang.String` representing the type of the notification |
| getUserData() | Returns a `java.lang.Object` representing arbitrary user data that was packaged with the notification |
| setSequenceNumber(long sequenceNumber) | Sets the sequence number of a notification. This has no real effect, as the notification broadcaster does not guarantee order. |
| setSource(java.lang.Object source) | Sets the source of the notification |
| setTimeStamp(long timeStamp) | Sets the time stamp of the notification |
| setUserData(java.lang.Object userData) | Sets arbitrary user data that the broadcaster wants to send with the notification |

The message of a notification can be as short or as long as needed, but generally, it is succinct. It's primarily intended to be a description of the notification, but it should not be so short that the meaning could not be discerned from reading it. The message is what might be displayed in some management consoles that list all notifications of a managed system. Examples of such messages include the following:

- ◆ "Warning: disk space on volume three is running low."
- ◆ "CPU utilization of processor three is 40%."
- ◆ "The printer is out of paper."

## Notification sequencing

Sequencing is not done automatically by the sender or receiver of a notification; however, a sequence number can be assigned to a notification that is sent, and a listener can sequence them so that they are received in the proper order. If you have a recipient of notifications that relies on an order of messages, then the sequence number is important. You could, for instance, have a management console that monitors the shutdown of a large computer system, and the order in which things occur can influence the actions of a computer operator monitoring the system.

The sender of messages may or may not care about sending the messages in a certain sequence. Additionally, the actual sequence of messages can be influenced by factors such as when the message was created and what path it takes before being sent out as a notification. Once the notification leaves the sender, the route it takes can influence when it arrives (or whether it arrives at all). The time stamp of the message can be used to support the sequencing of messages, but it is more commonly used for determining when something occurred.

Of course, depending on the underlying transport for the notifications, you may have the sequencing of messages done for you automatically. If you are using Java Message Service (JMS) to send distributed notifications, for instance, you could use the JMS sequencing feature to sequence notifications.

## Notifications travel one-way

Notifications are considered one-way traffic in that no response is required, and no receipt is provided indicating that the notification was received intact. In some cases, like distributed notifications, you will not know whether your notifications have been received by the listeners. It's sort of like shouting off the top of a building. Some people might hear you and respond, others may hear and give no notice, and still others may not hear you at all. When a notification is emitted, the broadcaster of the notification examines its list of listeners and sends the notification to each by calling a method of the listener. Other than returning without an exception being thrown, the listener does not indicate any successful sort of receipt.

The notification system is not to be interpreted as anything other than an event listener model. There are no underlying mechanisms for persistence or delayed delivery of a notification. Therefore, if receipt of your messages is important for your implementation, you have to implement that portion yourself. This is where complementary technologies such as JMS can be of use. They come with message forwarding and persistence built in.

You can construct notifications using one of four overloaded constructors for the `Notification` class, two of which are shown in the following list. You can view the others in the JMX API documentation. No checking of arguments is performed during construction of a notification, so you can put pretty much anything that is type-compatible in as an argument.

- **Notification**(java.lang.String type, java.lang.Object source, long sequenceNumber)

- **Notification**(java.lang.String type, java.lang.Object source, long sequenceNumber, long timeStamp)

Once you have a notification constructed, you need a vehicle for sending it. Because the underlying JMX infrastructure handles the actual implementation of sending a notification from point A to point B, you merely need to understand how to make a managed component enable itself for sending notifications.

## Sending and receiving notifications

The JMX specification defines the `javax.management.NotificationBroadcaster` interface for classes that want to send notifications. Note that this is just an interface, which leaves some implementation details to those of you who want to implement your own notification sending. To facilitate the sending of notifications, you can use the `javax.management.NotificationBroadcasterSupport` class, an implementation of the `NotificationBroadcaster` interface. You can extend this class and have the notification handling done for you.

### Sending notifications with the NotificationBroadcasterSupport class

Without the `NotificationBroadcasterSupport` class, you would have to implement a way to store notifications before they were sent, broadcasting the actual notification to listeners and removing notifications from internal lists. The `NotificationBroadcaster` interface enables implementations of notification handling to appear the same to any components acting as listeners, regardless of the underlying implementation. The various agent services, such as the monitor and timer, use the `NotificationBroadcasterSupport` class to facilitate the delivery of monitor and timer notifications, respectively. Table 11-2 describes the methods of the `NotificationBroadcasterSupport` class.

#### Table 11-2    NotificationBroadcasterSupport class

| Method Name | Description |
|---|---|
| `addNotificationListener(javax .management.NotificationListener, javax.management.NotificationFilter, java.lang.Object handback)` | Adds a notification listener. Takes an argument representing the notification listener, an argument representing a notification filter, and a handback object used to associate a notification with the broadcaster. |
| `getNotificationInfo()` | Returns an array of `javax.management.MBean NotificationInfo` objects representing the notifications that can be sent |
| `removeNotificationListener(javax .management.NotificationListener)` | Removes a notification listener. If a listener has been registered several times with the broadcaster, all instances are removed. |

| Method Name | Description |
|---|---|
| sendNotification(javax.management<br>.Notification) | Sends a notification to registered listeners |

Listing 11-1 shows how you can use the `NotificationBroadcasterSupport` class to send a notification.

**Listing 11-1: Java application that sends a JMX notification**

```
import javax.management.Notification;
import javax.management.NotificationBroadcasterSupport;


public class MBeanNotifier extends NotificationBroadcasterSupport {

        public static void main(String args[]){

                MBeanNotifier notifier = new MBeanNotifier();
                notifier.sendNotification(new Notification("hmi.jmx.message",
                                          notifier,
                                          0,
                                          "MBean Notifier Message"));
        }

}
```

The `MBeanNotifier` acts as the sender and receiver of its own notifications in this example. I'll cover the `NotificationListener` interface shortly. As you can see, it's quite simple to send a notification. By extending the `NotificationBroadcasterSupport` class, you have the `sendNotification()` method available, and you can create a simple notification with `hmi.jmx.message` as the type. I've provided the notification with the following: a reference to the `MBeanNotifier` class as the source object, `zero` as the sequence number, and the string `MBean Notifier Message` as the text of the message. This will send the message to any registered listeners (in this case, there are none).

Enabling receipt of a notification is almost as easy and involves implementing a single interface.

### Receiving notifications with the NotificationListener interface

The `javax.management.NotificationListener` interface is used by classes that want to be able to receive notifications. This is not the only requirement for receiving notifications, as you must still use the `addNotificationListener()` method of the `NotificationBroadcaster` interface to add the listener to the list of registered listeners. However, the `NotificationListener` interface defines the method `handleNotification()`, which is called by the underlying JMX infrastructure when a notification arrives for this listener. (The underlying JMX infrastructure refers here to the code implemented in the `NotificationBroadcaster` class.)

> **NOTE:** You can create a notification listener using a simple, non-MBean class, or an MBean. The `NotificationBroadcaster` class you have seen only has methods for adding a listener using a class that implements the `NotificationListener` interface. You can add a listener to a class using an instance of the `ObjectName` class, using the `addNotificationListener()` method of the `MBeanServer` interface that takes an `ObjectName` argument.

The `handleNotification()` method has two arguments: an instance of the `Notification` class and an instance of `java.lang.Object` that was passed by the notification broadcaster. This object is used by the notification system to associate a notification with the emitter of the notification. You can see how easy it is to receive a notification by looking at the code in Listing 11-2, which is an updated version of the `MBeanNotifier` application in Listing 11-1.

**Listing 11-2: Updating MBeanNotifier to receive notifications**

```
import javax.management.Notification;
import javax.management.NotificationBroadcasterSupport;
import javax.management.NotificationListener;


public class MBeanNotifier extends NotificationBroadcasterSupport
                        implements NotificationListener{


    public static void main(String args[]){

        MBeanNotifier notifier = new MBeanNotifier();
        notifier.addNotificationListener(notifier,null,null);
        notifier.sendNotification(new Notification("hmi.jmx.message",
                            notifier,
                            0,
                            "MBean Notifier Message"));
    }
    public void handleNotification(Notification notif,
                            Object handback) {

        System.out.println("Notification Type: " +
                        notif.getType());
        System.out.println("Notification Seq: " +
                        notif.getSequenceNumber());
        System.out.println("Notification Msg: " +
                        notif.getMessage());

    }
}
```

The preceding example implements the `NotificationListener` interface and the required `handleNotification()` method. In the `handleNotification()` method, you print the type, sequence number , and message of the notification. Running the `MBeanNotifier` application produces the following output:

```
Notification Type: hmi.jmx.message
Notification Seq: 0
Notification Msg: MBean Notifier Message
```

The delivery and printing of the message happen almost instantly and the application ends.

> **NOTE:** When you receive a notification, respond and return from the `handleNotification()` method as quickly as possible, because the notification broadcaster is calling a method on your listener and is waiting for the method to return. The notification broadcaster is the `MBeanNotifier` class. A delay in returning from the `handleNotification()` method could delay delivery of other notifications. The cause of the delay could be a number of things, such as doing lengthy I/O operations to the file system or a database.

The notification broadcaster does not usually care who gets its message. Generally, when a component is set up to send notifications, it is expected that only listeners that are interested in the notifications will register as listeners. In some cases, however, a managed resource may emit a number of notifications that are meant for a number of different recipients. In cases like this, you can supply a filter that only allows messages you are interested in to be accepted.

## Filtering notifications

To filter the types of notifications that are received by a recipient, the JMX notification model defines the `javax.management.NotificationFilter` interface. This interface defines a single method that is used to check whether a particular notification is enabled. It has a complementary class called the `javax.management.NotificationFilterSupport` class that exposes a set of methods for enabling and disabling notifications by type. The notification broadcaster can use the `NotificationFilter` implementation class to determine whether it should send a particular notification to a registered listener. Table 11-3 describes each of the `NotificationFilterSupport` class methods.

### Table 11-3    NotificationFilterSupport Class Methods

| Method Name | Description |
|---|---|
| `disableAllTypes()` | Disables all notifications regardless of the type |
| `disableType(java.lang.String prefix)` | Disables all notifications with the specified prefix |
| `enableType(java.lang.String prefix)` | Enables all notifications with the specified prefix |
| `getEnabledTypes()` | Returns a `java.util.Vector` of `java.lang.String` containing all the enabled types |
| `isNotificationEnabled(javax.management .Notification notification)` | Returns a primitive Java `boolean` indicating whether a notification is enabled |

The types do not have to exist as actual registered notifications. Thus, you can disable notifications of certain types before they are even created. The filters can also be set against prefixes of types. This enables you to specify parts of a notification type instead of the entire type name. For example, if you had fifty notification types that all began with the prefix `wiley.jmx`, you could disable all fifty notification types using the `disableType()` method of the `NotificationFilterSupport` class. This could be done using code that looks like the following:

```
NotificationFilterSupport filter = new NotificationFilter();
filter.disableType("wiley.jmx");
```

There is no wildcard or pattern matching facility for naming the types that you want to enable or disable. Rather, you use the different parts of the notification type to indicate the prefix of the notification type you want to disable. When you specify a prefix, the prefix is not assumed to actually exist, so if you give the `NotificationFilterSupport` class the wrong information, the API will not complain with an exception.

When using notification filters, you need to enable the types that you want to send. Although the JMX specification does not state this explicitly, if you add a notification filter and don't enable any types, you won't see any notifications come to a listener. If you pass a null value as the second argument to the `addNotificationListener()` method, in effect indicating that there is no notification filter, it is assumed that no filtering is to be done, and all notification types will be sent to registered listeners.

Listing 11-3 shows the source code for an application that registers itself as a notification listener and broadcaster, and then enables all but one type of notification.

**Listing 11-3: Filtering notifications**

```
import javax.management.Notification;
import javax.management.NotificationBroadcasterSupport;
import javax.management.NotificationListener;
import javax.management.NotificationFilterSupport;


public class MBeanNotifierFilter extends NotificationBroadcasterSupport
                        implements NotificationListener{


        public static void main(String args[]){

                MBeanNotifierFilter notifier = new MBeanNotifierFilter();

                NotificationFilterSupport filter =
                        new NotificationFilterSupport();

                filter.disableType("hmi.jmx");
                filter.enableType("wiley");

                notifier.addNotificationListener(notifier,filter,null);
```

```
                    notifier.sendNotification(new Notification("hmi.jmx.message",
                                      notifier,
                                      0,
                                      "MBean Notifier Message"));
            notifier.sendNotification(new
Notification("hmi.jmx.message.system",
                                 notifier,
                                 1,
                                 "MBean Notifier Message System"));

            notifier.sendNotification(new
Notification("hmi.jmx.message.broadcast",
                                 notifier,
                                 2,
                                 "MBean Notifier Message Broadcast"));
            notifier.sendNotification(new
Notification("wiley.jmx.message",
                                 notifier,
                                 3,
                                 "Wiley JMX Message"));

    }
    public void handleNotification(Notification notif,
                                Object handback) {

        System.out.println("Notification Type: " +
                           notif.getType());
        System.out.println("Notification Seq: " +
                           notif.getSequenceNumber());
        System.out.println("Notification Msg: " +
                           notif.getMessage());
    }

}
```

The output from running the `MBeanNotifierFilter` application should look like the following:

```
Notification Type: wiley.jmx.message
Notification Seq: 3
Notification Msg: Wiley JMX Message
```

You can enable and disable types at runtime, which means you can interactively control notification flow in a managed system. For example, if you notice that a particular managed resource is emitting a high number of error notifications, you can disable that particular type until the problem is resolved and then enable it again later.

## Attribute change notifications

In Chapter 10, you looked at the monitoring facilities that enable you to receive notifications based on different conditions. One of these conditions occurs when an attribute changes in some way. The JMX notification model defines a type of notification that can be sent when an attribute change has occurred. Managed resources are not required to indicate changes in attribute values, but there are two classes they can use to do so.

The `AttributeChangeNotification` class is a subclass of the `Notification` class and is tailored toward relating information about a change in attribute value. The `AttributeChangeNotificationFilter` class operates similarly to the `NotificationFilter` class, enabling you to filter which attribute changes you receive notifications about. The notification type for all attribute change notifications is `jmx.attribute.change`.

To send attribute notifications, you follow the same steps that you would for sending normal notifications, but you create `AttributeChangeNotification` classes instead of `Notification` classes. The `AttributeChangeNotification` class has a single constructor that takes the following arguments:

- The source of the object emitting the attribute change notification
- A sequence number
- A time stamp indicating when the notification was generated
- A message describing the notification
- The name of the attribute
- A string indicating the Java type of the attribute
- An object representing the old value of the attribute
- An object representing the new value of the attribute

The following code fragment illustrates how you might construct an attribute change notification in an MBean:

```
public String setName(String newName) {


    AttributeChangeNotification att =
        new AttributeChangeNotification(this,
                                        0,
                                        0,
                                        "Name changed",
                                        "Name",
                                        "java.lang.String",
                                        name,
                                        newName);

    name = newName;
```

```
sendNotification(att);

}
```

This example assumes that the MBean implements the necessary interfaces and classes. It constructs an `AttributeChangeNotification` class indicating that the `name` attribute has changed. The time stamp and sequence are set to zero because these parameters are not relevant to this example. Note also that this example highlights why a notification listener should process notifications as soon as possible, because the call to the `setName()` method will not exit until the `sendNotification()` method returns.

You should also carefully consider whether it's absolutely necessary to send notifications for every attribute change, as this could quickly become a problem if you have managed resources with many attributes and are sending notifications each time an attribute changes. However, you could also use the `AttributeChangeNotificationFilter` class to ensure that only necessary attribute change notifications are sent.

When an attribute change notification arrives at the listener, you can retrieve information about it using the methods of the `AttributeChangeNotification` class. Table 11-4 describes the declared methods of this class (but not the inherited methods).

### Table 11-4   AttributeChangeNotification Class Declared Methods

| Method Name | Description |
|---|---|
| getAttributeName() | Returns a `java.lang.String` representing the name of the attribute |
| getAttributeType() | Returns a `java.lang.String` representing the Java type of the attribute |
| getOldValue() | Returns a `java.lang.Object` representing the old value of the attribute |
| getNewValue() | Returns a `java.lang.Object` representing the new value of the attribute |

When creating `AttributeChangeNotification` class instances, it is up to the MBean to properly fill out the arguments. You must enter the correct old and new values, and the correct type and attribute name. When implementing support for attribute change notifications, it might be a good idea to implement this type of support in a superclass, which will ensure that all attribute change notifications are done the same way.

Filtering attribute change notifications is performed in a manner similar to normal notifications. The `AttributeChangeNotificationFilter` class defines a set of methods for filtering which attributes will generate change notifications. Table 11-5 describes the declared methods of the `AttributeChangeNotificationFilter` class.

## Table 11-5    AttributeChangeNotificationFilter Class Methods

| Method Name | Description |
|---|---|
| disableAllAttributes() | Disables notifications of all attributes |
| disableAttribute(String name) | Disables notifications of a single attribute. Takes a single java.lang.String representing the name of the attribute. |
| enableAttribute(String name) | Enables notifications of a single attribute. Takes a single java.lang.String representing the name of the attribute. |
| getEnabledAttributes() | Returns a java.util.Vector of all enabled attributes |
| isNotificationEnabled(javax. management.Notification) | Returns a primitive Java boolean indicating whether a particular attribute change notification is enabled |

To illustrate the attribute change notification, you can create a simple MBean that signals an attribute change notification when its Name attribute is changed. Listing 11-4 shows the source code for the SimpleObjectNotifierMBean interface.

**Listing 11-4: SimpleObjectNotifierMBean interface**

```
public interface SimpleObjectNotifierMBean{

    public String getName();

    public void setName(String newName);

}
```

The implementation of this interface is shown in the SimpleObjectNotifier class in Listing 11-5.

**Listing 11-5: SimpleObjectNotifier class**

```
import javax.management.AttributeChangeNotification;
import javax.management.NotificationBroadcasterSupport;

public class SimpleObjectNotifier extends NotificationBroadcasterSupport
                            implements SimpleObjectNotifierMBean{

    private String name = "";

    public SimpleObjectNotifier(){
    }

    public SimpleObjectNotifier(String iName){
```

```
                    name = iName;
        }


        public String getName(){
                return name;
        }


        public void setName(String newName){


                AttributeChangeNotification att =
                 new AttributeChangeNotification(this,
                                                0,0,
                                                "Name Attribute Changed",
                                                "Name",
                                                "java.lang.String",
                                                name,
                                                newName);


                sendNotification(att);
                name = newName;
        }


}
```

The `SimpleObjectNotifier` class extends the `NotificationBroadcasterSupport` class so that it can use the `sendNotification()` method to send the notifications. The `setName()` method includes the construction of an `AttributeChangeNotification()` object containing the information about the attribute change, including the new and previous values of the attribute. This `AttributeChangeNotification` object is then sent using the `sendNotification()` method, which is inherited from the `NotificationBroadcasterSupport` class.

To exercise this MBean, I've created a simple Java application that will act as the listener for the attribute change notification events, as well as provide the changes to the attribute of the MBean. Listing 11-6 shows the source code for the `MBeanNotifierAttr` application.

**Listing 11-6: MBeanNotifierAttr application**

```
import javax.management.AttributeChangeNotification;
import javax.management.MBeanServer;
import javax.management.MBeanServerFactory;
import javax.management.Notification;
import javax.management.NotificationBroadcasterSupport;
import javax.management.NotificationListener;
import javax.management.ObjectName;


public class MBeanNotifierAttr extends NotificationBroadcasterSupport
                        implements NotificationListener{
```

```
public static void main(String args[]){

        MBeanServer server =
            MBeanServerFactory.createMBeanServer();

        MBeanNotifierAttr notifier = new MBeanNotifierAttr();

        SimpleObjectNotifier simpleObj =
            new SimpleObjectNotifier();

        simpleObj.addNotificationListener(notifier,null,null);

        try {

                ObjectName simpleObjName =
                    new ObjectName("SimpleObjectNotifier:name=attr");

                server.registerMBean(simpleObj,simpleObjName);


                // Invoke several name change method //
                server.invoke(simpleObjName,
                              "setName",
                              new Object[]{"Simple Object"},
                              new String[]{"java.lang.String"});

                server.invoke(simpleObjName,
                              "setName",
                              new Object[]{"Simpler Object"},
                              new String[]{"java.lang.String"});

        } catch (Exception ex){
                System.out.println(ex);
        }

}
public void handleNotification(Notification notif,
                               Object handback) {

        AttributeChangeNotification attNotif =
                (AttributeChangeNotification)notif;

        System.out.println("Notification Type: " +
                           attNotif.getType());
        System.out.println("Attribute Name: " +
                           attNotif.getAttributeName());
        System.out.println("Attribute Type: " +
                           attNotif.getAttributeType());
```

```
                    System.out.println("Previous Value: " +
                                    attNotif.getOldValue());
                    System.out.println("New Value: " +
                                    attNotif.getNewValue());
        }

}
```

The `MBeanNotifierAttr` application registers the `SimpleObjectNotifier` MBean using the `registerMBean()` method of the `MBeanServer` interface, and then proceeds to invoke the `setName()` method twice. Each time the method is invoked, this triggers a notification to be sent to the `MBeanNotifierAttr` application. The `MBeanNotifierAttr` application registered itself as a listener, and each time a notification comes in, the `handleNotification()` method is called.

In the `handleNotification()` method, you print the notification type, the attribute name, the attribute type, and the new and old values of the attribute. The output from running the `MBeanNotifierAttr` application looks like the following:

```
Notification Type: jmx.attribute.change
Attribute Name: Name
Attribute Type: java.lang.String
Previous Value:
New Value: Simple Object
Notification Type: jmx.attribute.change
Attribute Name: Name
Attribute Type: java.lang.String
Previous Value: Simple Object
New Value: Simpler Object
```

The first notification that comes in indicates that the previous value is blank. This occurs because when the `SimpleObjectNotifier` MBean is created, the `Name` attribute is initialized to a blank string value.

The discussion up to this point has covered notifications that are sent from a broadcaster to one or more listeners in the same JMX agent. In the following section, you will examine notifications that are sent from a broadcaster to one or more listeners in a different JMX agent.

# Remote Notifications

When you want to send a notification to a listener, you use the `sendNotification()` method of the `NotificationBroadcasterSupport` class. When you want to add a listener to a broadcaster, you use the `addNotificationListener()` method of the `NotificationBroadcaster` interface. You can also use the `addNotificationListener()` method of the `MBeanServer` interface. These methods take either a Java reference to a class implementing the `NotificationListener` interface or an instance of the `ObjectName` class. Sometimes the notification broadcaster is in the same JMX agent, but in some cases it is not. This section examines such remote notifications, and explains how you listen for notifications from a broadcaster in a different JMX agent and hence, a different JVM.

In Chapter 2, you were presented with an overview of the JMX architecture and its key components. Two of those key components were protocol adapters and connectors. You use these components to enable management applications to connect and manage your JMX-based applications. In the same chapter, you also learned that you can use connectors to enable remote notifications.

The current JMX specification does not define any details for remote notifications; nor does the Sun JMX reference implementation attempt to define any support for remote notifications. However, a number of other JMX reference implementations provide support for remote notifications. One such implementation is the Java Dynamic Management Kit (JDMK). The JDMK provides an implementation based on the JMX specification, in addition to other features, such as remote notifications.

> **NOTE:** Because you have been introduced to many JMX concepts in this book, this section discusses the JDMK implementation only as it relates to remote notifications. It also covers basic usage of the components, and not architectural details about them. If you peruse the JDMK documentation, you will see remote notifications also referred to as *notification forwarding*.

You can download the JDMK from `www.sun.com/products-n-solutions /nep/software/java-dynamic`.

## Implementing remote notifications with JDMK

Using the JDMK to implement remote notifications is quite simple, and you only have to be familiar with a couple of components. At the beginning of this section, I stated that you can use the connector component of the JMX architecture to enable remote notifications. In the JDMK, you will find two components that are used to enable remote notifications:

♦ `com.sun.jdmk.comm.RmiConnectorServer`

♦ `com.sun.jdmk.comm.RmiConnectorClient`

To listen for notifications in a remote JMX agent, you must be able to connect to that agent and register a notification listener. To do this, you use both the `RmiConnectorServer` and `RmiConnectorClient`. You use the `RmiConnectorClient` in the JMX agent where the notification listener resides to connect to the JMX agent where the notification broadcaster resides. To be able to use the `RmiConnectorClient`, you need to have an instance of the `RmiConnectorServer` running in the JMX agent where the notification broadcaster resides.

> **NOTE:** The remote notifications feature of the JDMK uses a notification cache to buffer notifications before they are sent. You can also receive these notifications in either a push or pull mode.

The relationship between the `RmiConnectorServer` and `RmiConnectorClient` is similar to that of many remote objects and their clients that use RMI. You register a remote object on a host, and a client connects to that host and manipulates the remote object as if it were running locally. The `RmiConnectorServer` is modeled as an MBean for ease of use and administration. Figure 11-1 shows the relationship between the RmiConnectorServer and RmiConnectorClient components.

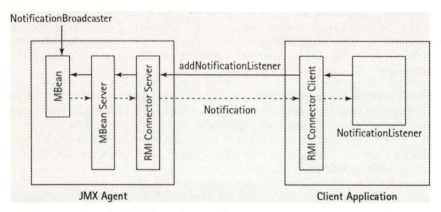

**Figure 11-1:** Using remote notifications with the JDMK.

In Figure 11-1, I have omitted some architectural details in the interest of simplicity. The lines that travel between the notification listener and RmiConnectorClient pass through a proxy object created on behalf of the notification listener. There is also an internal listener that is created in the JMX agent when you register a listener. The internal listener is used as a proxy in the JMX agent to listen for notifications and then forward them back to the notification listener through the RmiConnectorServer and RmiConnectorClient.

The RmiConnectorServer MBean enables remote clients to connect to a JMX agent and manipulate MBeans, including adding notification listeners to them. The RmiConnector class enables you to establish the connection with the remote host and add the notification listener to an MBean. It has a set of methods that are very similar to those of the MBeanServer interface described in Chapter 8. These methods enable you to access remote MBeans in a way that is nearly identical to accessing local MBeans.

To illustrate the use of remote notifications, you are going to examine a simple example that uses a JMX agent and client application to listen for remote notifications. You will use the JMX agent to run the RmiConnectorServer and SimpleObjectNotifier MBean from this chapter. You will have the JMX agent modify the Name attribute of the SimpleObjectNotifier MBean, which will trigger a notification.

## Writing the JMX agent

You will use the client application to run the RmiConnectorClient, and add the client application as a notification listener on the SimpleObjectNotifier MBean. As the notifications are broadcast, they will appear in the client application that is running in a different JVM.

The source code for the JMX agent that you will run is shown in Listing 11-7.

**Listing 11-7: The JMXAgentRemote application**

```
import javax.management.Attribute;
import javax.management.InstanceNotFoundException;
import javax.management.IntrospectionException;
import javax.management.MalformedObjectNameException;
import javax.management.ReflectionException;
import javax.management.ObjectName;
import javax.management.MBeanServer;
import javax.management.MBeanServerFactory;

import com.sun.jdmk.comm.CommunicatorServer;
import com.sun.jdmk.comm.RmiConnectorAddress;
import com.sun.jdmk.comm.RmiConnectorServer;

public class JMXAgentRemote {

    private static MBeanServer server = null;
    private static int MAX = 50;

    public JMXAgentRemote() {
        server = MBeanServerFactory.createMBeanServer();
    }

    public static void main(String[] args) {

        JMXAgentRemote agent = new JMXAgentRemote();
            CommunicatorServer rmiConnector = new
RmiConnectorServer(8888);
            SimpleObjectNotifier simpleObj = new
SimpleObjectNotifier();
            int i = 0;

            try {

                server.registerMBean(rmiConnector,null);
                rmiConnector.start();

                ObjectName simpleObjName = new
ObjectName("SimpleObjectNotifier:name=simple");
                server.registerMBean(simpleObj,simpleObjName);

                // Invoke an attribute change, pause between each
iteration
                while (i++ < MAX) {
                    server.setAttribute(simpleObjName,new
Attribute("Name","New Value"+i));
                    Thread.sleep(500);
                    System.out.println("Attribute change made....");
```

```
                        }


            }catch(Exception ex){
                System.out.println(ex);
            }

    }


}
```

The `JMXAgentRemote` application in Listing 11-7 begins by creating an instance of the `RmiConnectorServer` MBean. You pass a value of `8888` to its constructor, indicating that port `8888` will be used to listen for remote requests. You can also pass no value, which means that the default port specified in the `com.sun.jdmk.ServiceName.RMI_CONNECTOR_PORT` will be used. You can review the JDMK API documentation for a complete list of the constructors available for the `RmiConnectorServer` class.

Next, you create an instance of the `SimpleObjectNotifier` MBean that will serve as your notification broadcaster. You then register the `RmiConnectorServer` MBean using the `registerMBean()` method of the `MBeanServer` interface. You pass in the reference to the `RmiConnectorServer` class you just created, and a value of `null` for the object name you want to use. A value of `null` causes the default names specified by these two static fields in the `com.sun.jdmk.ServiceName` class to be used:

- ♦ `ServiceName.DOMAIN`
- ♦ `ServiceName.RMI_CONNECTOR_SERVER`

At this point, the `RmiConnectorServer` is configured but not running. You can start the `RmiConnectorServer` using its `start()` method. This method is inherited from the `CommunicatorServer` class from which the `RmiConnectorServer` class extends. Now you need to register the `SimpleObjectNotifier` MBean. To do this, you again use the `registerMBean()` method of the `MBeanServer` interface.

Once the `SimpleObjectNotifier` MBean is running, you go into a `while` loop, changing the value of the `Name` attribute using the `setAttribute()` method of the `MBeanServer` interface. Each time the attribute is changed, an `AttributeChangeNotification` will be sent to any registered listeners. The loop will execute up to the value defined in the `MAX` field specified at the top of the class. The next step is to create the client application that will register a notification listener.

## Writing the remote listener

You use the `RmiConnectorClient` class in the client application to connect to the JMX agent represented by the `JMXAgentRemote` application and to register a notification listener. The client application implements the `NotificationListener` interface to receive the notifications from the `SimpleObjectNotifier` MBean running in the `JMXAgentRemote` application. Listing 11-8 shows the source code for the `JMXAgentClient` application.

**Listing 11-8: The JMXAgentClient application**

```
import com.sun.jdmk.*;
import com.sun.jdmk.comm.*;
import javax.management.*;


public class JMXRemoteClient implements NotificationListener {

    public static void main(String args[]){

        JMXRemoteClient client = new JMXRemoteClient();

        RmiConnectorClient rmiClient = new RmiConnectorClient();
        RmiConnectorAddress rmiAddress =
            new
RmiConnectorAddress("localhost",8888,ServiceName.RMI_CONNECTOR_SERVER);

        try {

            rmiClient.connect(rmiAddress);
            ObjectName name = new
ObjectName("SimpleObjectNotifier:name=simple");

rmiClient.addNotificationListener(name,client,null,null);

        } catch (Exception ex){
          System.out.println(ex);
        }

    }

    public void handleNotification(Notification notif,Object
handback){
        System.out.println("Notification Received!!!!!!!!");
    }
}
```

The JMXRemoteClient application in Listing 11-8 begins by creating an instance of the RmiConnectorClient class. You pass in a single argument representing an instance of the RmiConnectorAddress class, which you construct with three arguments. Those arguments are the host name of the JMX agent where the RmiConnectorServer is running, the port number on which the RmiConnectorServer is listening, and the service name that the RmiConnectorServer used to register itself in the RMI registry.

Next, you construct an instance of the ObjectName class that represents the object name of the MBean to which you want to add a listener. To add the JMXRemoteClient application as a notification listener, you first use the connect() method of the RmiConnectorClient class to connect to the host where the RmiConnectorServer MBean is running. You then call the addNotificationListener() method of the RmiConnectorClient class and

pass in four arguments. The first argument is the object name of the
SimpleObjectNotifier MBean; the second is a reference to the notification listener (the
JMXRemoteClient application); and the third and fourth are the notification filter and hand
back object, which can be null for this example.

## Running the application

To run this application, you first need to compile both classes. Because this example is based
on the JDMK, you need to ensure that the JDMK jar located in
%JDMK_INSTALL%/lib/jdmkrt.jar is in your CLASSPATH before the Sun or other JMX
reference implementations, or conflicts may arise in versions of classes.

Once you have compiled both applications, you start the JMXAgentRemote application first,
because the client application needs a server to connect to. When you start the
JMXAgentRemote application, you will see output that looks like the following:

```
F:\files\JMX-Wiley>java JMXAgentRemote
Attribute change made....
Attribute change made....
Attribute change made....
Attribute change made....
```

Next, you can start the JMXRemoteClient application, which yields output that looks like
this:

```
F:\files\JMX-Wiley>java JMXRemoteClient
Notification Received!!!!!!!!
Notification Received!!!!!!!!
Notification Received!!!!!!!!
Notification Received!!!!!!!!
Notification Received!!!!!!!!
Notification Received!!!!!!!!
Notification Received!!!!!!!!
```

The messages from the JMXAgentRemote and JMXRemoteClient applications will continue
until the JMXAgentRemote application ends its loop.

# Summary

This chapter described a key component of the instrumentation layer of JMX — notifications.
The notification model defined in the instrumentation layer enables managed resources to emit
notifications, messages that indicate either a change in the value of an attribute or some user-
defined event. You construct notifications using the Notification class or one of its
subclasses. To send the notification, you use the sendNotification() method of the
NotificationBroadcasterSupport class. This class is provided as a convenience class
that managed resources can extend to enable notification support.

In the next chapter, you'll look at an important component of the agent layer — protocol
adapters and connectors. These components enable management clients to access managed
resources remotely using protocols such as HTTP and SNMP. They also enable management
agents to exchange information, such as notifications.

# Chapter 12

# Protocol Adapters and Connectors

The JMX specification defines two components, the *protocol adapter* and the *connector*, that are used by management clients to interact with managed resources. Protocol adapters enable application clients and managers to connect to a JMX agent. For example, a JMX agent provides an HTTP protocol adapter that Web browsers can connect to and use to manage the system. The JMX agent could also have a protocol adapter that uses the Wireless Access Protocol (WAP) to enable handheld devices to manage applications.

A connector is similar to a protocol adapter, except it primarily utilizes protocols that are used by applications and other management applications. You can implement a connector using RMI or CORBA, which enables applications written in other languages to manage your applications.

Although the JMX specification identifies protocol adapters and connectors, it does not define them other than to say that they can be implemented as MBeans. Other than the `MBeanServer` interface, there is no defined interface to an MBean Server that a protocol adapter can use. Implementing protocol adapters and connectors as MBeans enables you to take advantage of the JMX architecture. It also reduces development time, as the decision about how these components fit into a managed system architecture has already been made. They can be managed just like other resources, and you can provide new protocols on the fly. Depending on what you are developing, you may be able to take advantage of an existing infrastructure — such as an HTTP server — that comes with many servlet engines to act as a protocol adapter.

In this chapter, you'll learn how management clients connect remotely to JMX agents and managed MBeans. You will build a Hypertext Transfer Protocol (HTTP) protocol adapter and a Remote Method Invocation (RMI) connector that enable Web browsers and standalone applications to connect to JMX agents as well. Connectors enable heavier client applications and other JMX agents to connect to one another and perform management functions.

The chapter includes a primer on HTTP so that you'll gain the knowledge necessary to build the protocol adapter. It also includes an RMI primer to prepare you to build the connector.

# Protocol Adapters

A protocol adapter is responsible for translating requests from a client into commands, executing those commands, and then sending the results back to the client. The types of clients that can interact with a managed system are determined by the protocol adapters in the system. The JMX agent is responsible for making sure that at least one protocol adapter or connector is available at all times. Without a protocol adapter available, a system cannot be managed.

A protocol adapter speaks a specific network transport protocol. Protocols exist at different levels of communication; and each level defines protocols that perform specific tasks. A protocol adapter receives requests, examines each request, extracts the data from the request, and builds a structure that represents the request. It then must translate the request into a command or request for a resource, execute the request, and formulate a success or failure response.

Fortunately for developers, many of these levels are handled automatically. The Java networking libraries handle interaction with the lower-level TCP/IP calls, and include classes for working with, retrieving, and sending resources using HTTP.

The Java libraries, however, do not include any classes or interfaces for packaging and unpackaging HTTP messages. The HTTP classes that exist enable only the most basic access to HTTP messages. For standalone applications, you need something along the lines of the `HttpRequest` and `HttpResponse` classes. You may have worked with these classes if you've written Java servlets or worked with server-side scripting languages such as JavaServer Pages (JSP). Ideally, you want to implement an adapter as an MBean.

> **NOTE:** If you are already familiar with HTTP, or are not interested in a brief tour of the protocol, you may want to skip ahead to the section titled "Building a request with HTTP," which describes how to build a Java class that represents an HTTP request.

## An HTTP primer

HyperText Transfer Protocol (HTTP) is all about requests and responses. At a high level, an HTTP request comes in and identifies the resource being requested using a Uniform Resource Locator (URL) that contains a Uniform Resource Identifier (URI). In other words, the request comes in with a string that identifies the resource being requested, which could be a static HTML page, a GIF image file, or a request to execute a software program. Once the request has been executed, a response is built that contains the result of the request. The response will either contain the requested resource, or the results of executing a program, or an error. HTTP provides a standard way of implementing this type of request/response conversation.

Understanding HTTP is quite easy, and is essential if you want to implement a standalone protocol adapter that speaks HTTP.

> **CROSS-REFERENCE:** In Chapters 14 and 15, you'll learn how to use the existing infrastructure of an application server to act as a protocol adapter. You can also utilize an existing third-party library that performs the functions of the classes you'll create in this chapter.

HTTP requests and responses contain headers that provide meta-information about the request or response. They also consist of headers that apply to both request and response as well as the payload of the request or response. HTTP headers can be categorized as follows:

- ♦ General headers
- ♦ Request headers
- ♦ Response headers
- ♦ Entity headers

At a lower level, HTTP requests and responses can be described as messages that consist of a conceptual envelope describing the request, the type of client making the request, and any parameters the request might require. An HTTP response also includes a conceptual envelope that describes the response, the type of recipient sending the response, and the result of the response in the payload section of the response.

If you've ever used a Web browser, then you've used HTTP. Web browsers use HTTP to send requests to Web servers to display Web pages or image files, or to execute software programs. In the context of JMX, a Web browser might send a request to view the attributes of an MBean. The protocol adapter translates that into a request to the MBean Server to get the attribute values. The protocol adapter then builds the response and sends it back to the Web browser. A typical HTTP request might look like the following:

```
GET /index.html HTTP/1.1
User-Agent: Mozilla/4.0 (compatible; MSIE 4.01; Windows NT)
Host: localhost:8888
Connection: Keep-Alive
```

This request is for the resource named `index.html`, which exists at the root directory of the Web server. The client is identifying itself as Internet Explorer 4.01 with the `User-Agent` header. This header simply identifies the client; in reality, the Web server does not know if it's a Web browser. The `Host` header identifies the address and port of the Web server, and the `Connection` header indicates that the client would like to keep the connection open.

The response to this request might look like the following:

```
HTTP 200 OK
Content-Type: text/html
Content-Length: 36

<HTML>
<BODY>
A Web Page
</BODY>
</HTML>
```

By returning a status code of `200` and a reason phrase of `OK`, the response indicates that the request was received successfully. The content of the response is described in the `Content-Type` header as MIME type `text/html` and is expected to be 36 bytes in length. Two carriage return line-feed pairs follow the headers, followed by the content of the response, which is the HTML, contained in the index.html page.

### Status codes

The response to an HTTP request can indicate varying degrees of success. The *status code* is part of the first line of the response (along with another component, the reason phrase, which I'll cover in a moment). I'm sure that you have used a Web browser to access a Web page and received the following result:

```
404 Not Found
```

The number 404 is the status code of the response. The HTTP protocol defines a set of status codes and ranges within each set. Table 12-1 describes the commonly used sets of HTTP status codes and their categories.

### Table 12-1   Common HTTP Status Codes

| Status Code | Category | Description |
|---|---|---|
| 1xx | Informational | Request received, continue processing |
| 2xx | Success | The request was received and accepted |
| 3xx | Redirection | The resource was not at the location that was specified and further information is required to continue |
| 4xx | Client Error | The request was received but has incorrect syntax or the client is not authorized |
| 5xx | Server Error | A severe error has occurred while processing your request. This can occur when some type of memory exception occurs and the address space of the server is compromised. |

An HTTP request can succeed (or fail) at two distinct junctures: the receipt or the execution. A request to execute an application program, for instance, might be received and accepted (code 200), but the application program you executed might have returned a failure that is contained in the body of the response.

Listing the entire range of status codes is beyond the scope of the book, but you can find the complete list in the HTTP specification at www.w3c.org. Remembering all the status codes can be quite a challenge, so the HTTP specification includes an additional component called the *reason phrase*.

### Reason phrase

The reason phrase provides additional information about a specific HTTP status code. Along with the status code number, it provides a description containing more detailed information than the status code itself. Common reason phrases (prefaced by the HTTP status code) include 200 OK, indicating a successful request, and 500 Server Error, indicating that a severe problem occurred.

Now that you've examined the components of an HTTP request and HTTP response, you can begin building some classes that represent these components.

## Building a request with HTTP

When a request comes in, it must be parsed into different parts that represent the various components of the request. To parse the request, the parser needs to determine several things, such as whether the request method is GET or POST. The request method determines whether the data within the request contains its parameters and data in the payload of the request or in the request URI.

The request URI is the resource that is being requested. For example, when you type http://www.web.com/page.html, the resource being requested is page.html. The next major components are the headers, followed by the payload of the message (if a payload exists). Without going into all the details just yet, take a look at the HTTPRequest class. Listing 12-1 shows the source code for a class named HTTPRequest that represents the HTTP request.

**Listing 12-1: The HTTPRequest class**

```
package com.hmi.http;

/***
 *
 *  Notes:
 *  - www-x-application-form-encoded processing
 *  - Escaped QueryString processing
 *
 ***/

import java.util.Hashtable;
import java.util.StringTokenizer;
import java.util.Enumeration;
import java.io.ByteArrayOutputStream;
import java.io.IOException;
import java.util.StringTokenizer;
import java.net.MalformedURLException;

public class HTTPRequest{

    private Hashtable headers = new Hashtable();
    private Hashtable parameters = new Hashtable();
    private ByteArrayOutputStream out = new ByteArrayOutputStream();
    private byte[] content = null;
    private String requestURI = "";
    private String method = "";

    private static int AMPERSAND = 0x26;
```

```java
private static int EQUALS = 0x3D;

public HTTPRequest(byte[] headers){
parseHeaders(headers);
}

private void parseHeaders(byte[] rawHeaders){

     // Find end of Headers //
int eoh = findEOH(rawHeaders);
String heads = new String(rawHeaders,0,eoh);

//Setup StringTokenizer
StringTokenizer st = new StringTokenizer(heads,"\r\n");

// Process Method and URI
StringTokenizer st_firstLine = new StringTokenizer(st.nextToken(),"
");
method = st_firstLine.nextToken().trim();
     // Need to truncate the querystring from the request URI
requestURI = st_firstLine.nextToken().trim();

// Process the rest of the headers//
while (st.hasMoreTokens()){
     String requestLine = st.nextToken();
     int separator = requestLine.indexOf(": ");
     String header = requestLine.substring(0,separator);
     String value =
requestLine.substring(separator+1,requestLine.length());
     headers.put(header.trim(),value.trim());
}

// If "POST" Method, get message body and put in array //
if (getMethod().equals("POST")){
    content = new byte[Integer.parseInt(getHeader("Content-
Length"))];
    System.arraycopy(rawHeaders,eoh+1,content,0,content.length);
}

// if "GET" Method, build request parameters //
if (getMethod().equals("GET"))
    processQueryString(getRequestURI());

}

public static int findEOH(byte[] headers){
     int l = 0;
     for (int i=0;i<headers.length;i++){
```

```
                    if (i+2 < headers.length && headers[i] == 0x0D &&
headers[i+1] == 0x0A){
                        if (headers[i+2] == 0x0D && headers[i+3] == 0x0A){
                            l=i+3;
                            break;
                        }
                    }
                }
            return l;
    }


    /**
     *
     * Parse a query string from an HTTP get into a hashtable
     *
     **/
    private void processQueryString(String requestURI){
            System.out.println("REQUEST URI: " + requestURI);
            //requestURI = requestURI.substring(1,requestURI.length());
            int qIdx = requestURI.indexOf('?');
            // Change to malformed url exception later //
            if (qIdx == -1)
                throw new IllegalArgumentException("Could not determine
start of query string");
            else{
                requestURI =
requestURI.substring(qIdx,requestURI.length());
                byte data[] = requestURI.getBytes();
                int pos = 1;    // skip first character ? //
                int lastpos = 0;
                String parm = null;
                String value = null;
                boolean parmStarted = false;
                boolean valueStarted = false;
                while (pos<data.length) {
                        if (data[pos]==HTTPRequest.AMPERSAND){
                            parmStarted = true;
                            valueStarted = false;
                            value = new String(data,lastpos+1,pos-
(lastpos+1));

                            lastpos=pos;
                            // Store parameter and value //
                            parameters.put(parm,value);
                        }
                        if (data[pos]==HTTPRequest.EQUALS && !valueStarted){
                            valueStarted = true;
                            parm = new String(data,lastpos+1,(pos-1)-
lastpos);

                            lastpos=pos;
```

```
                              parmStarted=false;
                      }
                  if(pos+1==data.length) {
                      if (parmStarted)
                          parm = new String(data,lastpos+1,(pos-1)-
lastpos);
                      if (valueStarted)
                          value = new String(data,lastpos+1,pos-
(lastpos));

                  }

                  pos++;
          }
          if (parm != null)
              parameters.put(parm,value);
      }

  }
  public String getRequestURI(){
  return requestURI;
  }
  public String getMethod(){
      return method;
  }
  public String getParameter(String name){
      return (String)parameters.get(name);
  }
  public Enumeration getParameters(){
      return parameters.keys();
  }
  public String getHeader(String name){
      return (String)headers.get(name);
  }
  public Enumeration getHeaders(){
      return headers.keys();
  }
  public String getContentType(){
      return getHeader("Content-Type");
  }
  public byte[] getContent(){
      return content;
  }
  // This method allows setting the body of an HTTP Request //
  public void setContent(byte[] newContent){
      content = newContent;
  }

}
```

The `HTTPRequest` class has a single constructor that takes a byte array representing the request, including headers. The `parseHeaders()` method begins by finding the end of the HTTP headers using a private method named `findEOH()`. This method scans through the data from the beginning until it finds the two carriage-return line-feed pairs that signal the end of the headers. As each header is found, it is placed into a `java.util.Hashtable` along with the value of the header. (The nice thing about headers is that duplicates are not allowed, so using a hashtable won't run the risk of overwriting an existing header.)

Once the headers have been processed, the `HTTPRequest` class continues by checking whether the method being used is POST. If this is the case, then the body of the HTTP message is copied into a buffer representing the content of the message.

If the request is using the GET method, the request URI is processed for query string parameters. Requests that use the GET method send all parameters in one long line, as opposed to the POST method, where everything is sent in the body of the HTTP message. The request parameters start with a single question mark followed by a name/value pair. This is a string followed by an equal sign, followed by another string. Subsequent name/value pairs are separated using the ampersand character (&).

## Building a response with HTTP

Building a response to a client request is a lot easier than building the request because you don't do any parsing to figure anything out. You need to construct a response that contains the necessary headers, and place any response data in the body of the HTTP message. Listing 12-2 shows the source code for the `HTTPResponse` class.

**Listing 12-2: The HTTPResponse class**

```
package com.hmi.http;

import java.io.DataOutputStream;
import java.net.Socket;
import java.io.IOException;
import java.util.Date;

public class HTTPResponse{

        private byte[] content = null;
        private String contentType = "text/html";
        private DataOutputStream client = null;
        private Socket clientSock = null;
        private int httpCode = 200;
        private int contentLength = 0;
        private String CRLF = "\r\n";


        public HTTPResponse(int responseCode,Socket sock){
                clientSock = sock;
                httpCode = responseCode;
```

```java
        }

        public void setContentType(String type){
                contentType = type;
        }

        public String getContentType(){
                return contentType;
        }

        public void write(byte[] writeMe) throws IOException{
                client =
                   new DataOutputStream(clientSock.getOutputStream());
                client.write(buildResponseHeaders(writeMe).getBytes());
                /* Write out data of resource */
                client.write(writeMe);
                client.flush();
                client.close();
                clientSock.close();
        }

        private String buildResponseHeaders(byte[] content){
                StringBuffer headers = new StringBuffer();
                int content_length = content.length;
                String content_type = getContentType();
                Date toDay = new Date();
                String expire_date = toDay.toString();

                headers.append("HTTP "+httpCode+" OK"+CRLF);
                headers.append("Server: Personal Web Server - Java
Edition"+CRLF);
                headers.append("Content-Type: " + content_type + CRLF);
                headers.append("Content-Length: "+content_length+CRLF);
                headers.append("Connection: close"+CRLF);
                headers.append("Expires: "+expire_date);
                headers.append(CRLF+CRLF);

                return headers.toString();
        }

}
```

The HTTPResponse class has a single constructor that takes an integer representing the status code, and a java.net.Socket instance, which is the socket where the client who made the request can be contacted. This socket is what you'll use to write back your response.

When using the HTTPResponse class, you need to set the content type to ensure that the client understands the response. The content type you'll be using in this example is text/html, which you'll see set later. The other method of primary interest is the `write()` method, which is what you'll call when you want to write back data to the client.

The `write()` method first builds the necessary response headers, which identify the response as an HTTP response, and the status code and reason phrase of the request. The current date and the date on which the content should expire are also set, as well as the `Content-Type` and `Content-Length` headers. Finally, the double carriage return and line-feed pair is appended to the end of the headers, and the buffer of headers is then returned.

The headers are written to the client socket, followed by the data of the response itself, using the `write()` method of the `java.io.DataOutputStream` class. The `write()` method can throw an `IOException` while writing, so the `write()` method of the `HTTPResponse` class also declares the `IOException`. An `IOException` can occur, for example, because of a dropped network connection or because the client has been disconnected from the server.

## Creating a handler

Ideally, when dealing with HTTP, the less you have to work with the actual bits, the better. Java developers who have worked with JSP and servlets are used to working only with the `HTTPRequest` and `HTTPResponse` classes when dealing with HTTP clients, and not the data that makes up the whole request.

You can provide a construct, similar in nature to a servlet, that provides a single access method. You can implement the method to receive requests in the form of an `HTTPRequest` object, and then provide an `HTTPResponse` object to write the response back. Listing 12-3 shows the source code for a simple interface that you can use to write a handler for your HTTP requests.

**Listing 12-3: The IMServlet interface**

```
package com.hmi.http;

import java.io.IOException;

public interface IMServlet{
        void onRequest(HTTPRequest req,HTTPResponse res) throws
IOException;
}
```

The `IMServlet` interface defines a single method that implementers must use to receive requests. Whenever a request comes in, you can access the request parameters and data, as well as write the response back to the recipient. A simple implementation of this interface looks like the code shown in Listing 12-4.

**Listing 12-4: Example implementation of IMServlet interface**

```
package com.hmi.http;

import java.io.IOException;
import java.util.Enumeration;
```

```java
import javax.management.MBeanServer;

public class IMServerServlet implements IMServlet{

    private MBeanServer localServerRef = null;

    public void setLocalServerRef(MBeanServer server){
        localServerRef = server;
    }


    public void onRequest(HTTPRequest request,HTTPResponse response)
      throws IOException
    {
        String responseText =
"<HTML><BODY><I>IMServerServlet</I><BR/>";
        Enumeration headers = request.getHeaders();
        while (headers.hasMoreElements()){
            String headerName = (String)headers.nextElement();
            String headerValue = request.getHeader(headerName);
            responseText+=headerName+": "+headerValue+"<BR/>";
        }
        responseText+=">>>>>>>>>>>>>>>>>>>>>>>>>>>>>>>><BR/>";
        Enumeration parameters = request.getParameters();
        while (parameters.hasMoreElements()){
            String parmName = (String)parameters.nextElement();
            String parmValue = request.getParameter(parmName);
            responseText+=parmName+" = "+parmValue+"<BR/>";
        }
        responseText+="</BODY></HTML>";
    response.setContentType("text/plain");
    response.write(responseText.getBytes());
    }

}
```

This implementation gathers and prints out all the HTTP headers that were sent in the request by using the getHeaders() method. It then prints out all the request parameters by getting a list using the getParameters() method.

## Putting the bits together

Along with the nicer interface you built for working with the HTTPRequest and HTTPResponse classes, you need a way to populate the structures and implement support for client requests. You need a component that provides simple listening capabilities on a single network port and then processes each request by constructing an HTTPRequest object. Ideally, you need to do this in a thread for each client request that comes in, so that multiple requests can be handled almost simultaneously. To do this, you'll need to define two more classes. The first class will act as the thread for the client request, and the second will act as the listener for requests.

The first class of interest is the `IMClient` class itself. This class is responsible for taking the bits from the socket and creating instances of the `HTTPRequest` class and `HTTPResponse` class. Listing 12-5 shows the source code for the `IMClient` class.

**Listing 12-5: The IMClient class**

```
package com.hmi.http;

import java.io.*;
import java.net.*;
import java.util.*;

public class IMClient extends Thread{

    Socket socket;
    ByteArrayOutputStream bos = new ByteArrayOutputStream();
    DataOutputStream out = null;
    IMServlet servlet = null;

    public IMClient(Socket socket,IMServlet handler){
        this.socket = socket;
        this.servlet = handler;
        setPriority( NORM_PRIORITY-1 );
        start();
    }

    public void run(){

        try{

    BufferedReader requestReader = new BufferedReader(new
InputStreamReader(socket.getInputStream()));
    ByteArrayOutputStream requestBA = new ByteArrayOutputStream();
    int rch = socket.getInputStream().available();
    while (rch-- > 0){
    requestBA.write(requestReader.read());
            }

        HTTPRequest request = new
HTTPRequest(requestBA.toByteArray());
        HTTPResponse response = new HTTPResponse(200,socket);

        servlet.onRequest(request,response);

        }catch(IOException ioe){
    System.out.println(ioe);
        }
```

```
        }

}
```

The IMClient class extends the java.lang.Thread class and defines a run() method, which is where all the work takes place. The constructor takes the client socket instance and the IMServlet instance and stores these for later use in the run() method. The run() method uses a java.io.BufferedReader to read all the data from the socket, and writes it into a temporary java.io.ByteArrayOutputStream. A byte array is then extracted from the ByteArrayOutputStream and passed to the constructor of the HTTPRequest class. The HTTPResponse class is created by passing the client socket instance and a response code of 200 to its constructor.

In a full implementation, you would want to try to catch any exception from the onRequest() method and set the response code accordingly, but for this example, the 200 value works fine. With the HTTPRequest and HTTPResponse class constructed, you then pass them to the onRequest() method of the IMServlet instance that was passed to the constructor of the IMClient class.

Listing 12-6 shows the source of the IMListener class.

**Listing 12-6: The IMListener class**

```
package com.hmi.http;

import java.io.*;
import java.net.*;
import java.util.*;

public class IMListener implements Runnable{

        private ServerSocket serversocket = null;
        private int port = 0;
        private IMServlet servlet = null;

        public IMListener(int thePort){
                port = thePort;
        }

        public void setHandler(IMServlet handler){
                servlet = handler;
        }

        public void begin(){
                /* Start Server */
                Thread server_thread = new Thread(this);
                server_thread.start();
        }

        public void run(){
                try{
```

```
            serversocket = new ServerSocket(port);

        }catch(IOException e){
        System.out.println("Error: " + e);
        }

        while(true){

            try{

                new IMClient(serversocket.accept(),servlet);

            }catch(Exception e){
                System.out.println("Error: " + e);
            }
        }
    }
}
```

The `IMListener` class implements the `Runnable` interface so that it can be passed as an argument to the constructor of a thread and scheduled to run. This class includes a `setHandler()` method, which sets the instance of the handler that will handle the request. The `run()` method is implemented as required by the `Runnable` interface, and it uses a try/catch to spawn new `IMClient` class instances, which are defined as a subclass of the `java.lang.Thread` class. This `try/catch` block is enclosed in a `while` loop that executes until the thread is interrupted outside this class. The `while` loop will wait due to the use of the `accept()` method, which blocks execution until a new request is sent over the socket.

Now that you have a nice separation from the details of parsing and constructing an `HTTPRequest` object, you can examine how the `IMServerServlet` class from Listing 12-4 will interact with the MBean Server.

## Creating the HttpAdapterMBean

To interact with the MBean Server, you need to define an MBean for the HTTP and IM classes you've defined so far. This MBean will serve as your HTTP adapter, sending requests for the MBean Server to an instance of the `IMServerServlet` class. You've seen many examples so far of how to write MBeans of the standard, dynamic, or model variety; this example uses a standard MBean. Listing 12-7 shows the source code for the MBean interface for your HTTP adapter.

**Listing 12-7: HttpAdapterMBean interface**

```
package com.hmi.http.adapter;

public interface HttpAdapterMBean{

        void setPort(int port);
        int getPort();
}
```

This simple interface enables the changing of the port on which the HttpAdapter listens. In this example, however, you won't be using the accessor methods for the interface. The implementation of this interface is also quite simple. Listing 12-8 shows the source code for the HttpAdapterMBean interface implementation.

**Listing 12-8: HttpAdapterMBean interface implementation**

```
package com.hmi.http.adapter;

import com.hmi.http.IMListener;
import com.hmi.http.IMServerServlet;
import javax.management.MBeanServer;
import javax.management.MBeanRegistration;
import javax.management.ObjectName;

public class HttpAdapter implements HttpAdapterMBean,MBeanRegistration{

        private IMListener listener = null;
        private IMServerServlet servlet = new IMServerServlet();
        private int port = 8888;

        public HttpAdapter(int port){
               listener = new IMListener(port);
               listener.setHandler(servlet);
               listener.begin();
        }

        public int getPort(){
               return port;
        }

        public void setPort(int newPort){
               port = newPort;
        }

        // MBeanRegistration interface methods
        public void postDeregister(){};
        public void postRegister(Boolean done){};
        public void preDeregister(){};
        public ObjectName preRegister(MBeanServer beanServer,
                                      ObjectName name){
               servlet.setLocalServerRef(beanServer);
               return name;
        }
}
```

This MBean takes a single integer representing the port to listen on and then defines a new IMListener class on that port. It then sets the handler, so for this example, it creates a new instance of the `IMServerServlet` class each time. This means that every request that comes in will have its own instance of the servlet. Finally, the `begin()` method is called, which starts the thread of the `IMListener` class, and requests can now be taken.

The next thing you need to do is write a JMX agent that will load the `HttpAdapterMBean`, as well as a set of MBeans upon which it can operate.

# Managing a Simple Object with HTTP

Now that you have a protocol adapter that can speak HTTP, you can write a simple example to utilize it. In this example, you use the HTTP protocol adapter to access an arbitrary MBean and view its attributes. You also enable the capability to set the values of attributes using the protocol adapter. Listing 12-9 shows the source code for the MBean interface of the object you'll manage in this example.

**Listing 12-9: The ProtocolMBean interface**

```java
public interface ProtocolMBean {

    public String getName();

    public void setName(String newName);

    public String doNothing();
}
```

The `ProtocolMBean` interface contains a single attribute, `Name`, as identified by its `getName()` and `setName()` methods. Listing 12-10 shows the source of the `Protocol` class, which implements the `ProtocolMBean` interface.

**Listing 12-10: The Protocol class**

```java
public class Protocol implements ProtocolMBean {

    private String name = "Protocol MBean";

    public void setName(String newName){
        name = newName;
    }

    public String getName(){
        return name;
    }

    public String doNothing(){
        return "Nothing";
    }
}
```

The user interface for interaction with the MBeans is presented as HTML, and setting the values of attributes is done using HTML forms. The first thing you do is write a simple JMX agent that loads the HttpAdapterMBean and a couple of simple MBeans that you can experiment with. Listing 12-11 shows the source code for the JMX agent.

**Listing 12-11: The JMXAgent class**

```java
import javax.management.InstanceNotFoundException;
import javax.management.IntrospectionException;
import javax.management.MalformedObjectNameException;
import javax.management.ReflectionException;
import javax.management.ObjectName;
import javax.management.MBeanServer;
import javax.management.MBeanServerFactory;

import com.hmi.http.adapter.HttpAdapter;

public class JMXAgent {

    private static MBeanServer server = null;

    public JMXAgent() {
        server = MBeanServerFactory.createMBeanServer();
    }

    public static void main(String[] args) {

        JMXAgent agent = new JMXAgent();
        ObjectName simpleObject =
                agent.loadBean("Protocol",
                               "Protocol:name=simple");

        ObjectName httpObjName = null;
        HttpAdapter httpAdapter = new HttpAdapter(8888);

        try {

            httpObjName =
                new ObjectName("HttpAdapter:port=8888");
            server.registerMBean(httpAdapter,httpObjName);

        }catch(Exception ex){
            System.out.println(ex);
        }
    }

    private ObjectName loadBean(String className,String objectName) {
```

```
        ObjectName mbeanObjectName = null;
        String domain = server.getDefaultDomain();
        String mbeanName = className;
        try {
             mbeanObjectName = new ObjectName(objectName);
        } catch(MalformedObjectNameException e) {
          e.printStackTrace();
          System.exit(1);
        }
           // Create our simple object to manage //
           try {
               server.createMBean(mbeanName,mbeanObjectName);
           }catch(Exception ex){
                ex.printStackTrace();
                System.exit(1);
           }

           return mbeanObjectName;
     }
}
```

If you read Chapters 4 and 8 of this book, on standard MBeans and the MBean Server, then this example code is probably old hat to you. The `JMXAgent` class loads the `HttpAdapter` MBean using the `registerMBean()` method of the `MBeanServer` interface. Another MBean, `Protocol`, is also loaded, but it uses dynamic registration through the use of the `createMBean()` method of the `MBeanServer` interface. Creating a new instance of the `HttpAdapter` class will start the listening thread, and you are now ready to proceed with making the updates to the `IMServerServlet` class to process requests.

## Defining a common parent

Protocol adapters, like connectors, need to be able to interact with the MBean Server. It's useful to define a common parent class that enables this access by providing an instance of an MBean Server. This keeps the adapter class a bit cleaner, as it doesn't need the code to find the MBean Server. (Alternatively, the `HttpAdapter` MBean could implement the `MBeanRegistration` interface and receive a notification. It could then store a reference to the MBean Server into which it has been loaded.)

You need to define a parent class that stores the reference to its MBean Server. Having a parent class enables you to separate some of the JMX specifics from your MBean. Listing 12-12 shows the source code for the parent class.

**Listing 12-12: Parent MBean class**

```
package com.hmi;

import javax.management.MBeanRegistration;
import javax.management.MBeanServer;
import javax.management.MBeanServerFactory;
```

```
import javax.management.ObjectName;

public class ProtocolAdapter implements MBeanRegistration {

    private MBeanServer server = null;

    public ProtocolAdapter(){
    }

    public MBeanServer getMBeanServer(){
        return server;
    }

    // MBeanRegistration interface methods
    public void postDeregister(){};
    public void postRegister(Boolean done){};
    public void preDeregister(){};
    public ObjectName preRegister(MBeanServer beanServer,
                                  ObjectName name){
        server = beanServer;
        return name;
    }

}
```

The `ProtocolAdapter` class implements the `MBeanRegistration` interface and uses the `preRegister()` method to store a reference to the MBean Server it is about to be registered in. (Recall that the `preRegister()` method is called before the MBean has been registered in the MBean Server.) That is all the `ProtocolAdapter` class does, but if you ever want to change how the MBean Server is located, you can make the change in the `ProtocolAdapter` class without having to change the individual MBeans.

## Updating the IMServerServlet class

The `IMServlet` class is the application class that will act as the intermediary between the protocol adapter and the MBean Server. You've already seen the basic implementation of the `IMServlet` interface as the `IMServerServlet` class in Listing 12-4. The first implementation just listed some information about the HTTP request. You now need to update it so that it returns real information from the MBean Server. I've removed from the original implementation the code that displayed information about the request.

Listing 12-13 shows the source code for the `IMServerServlet` class that has been updated to interact with the MBean Server.

**Listing 12-13: Updated IMServerServlet class**

```
package com.hmi.http;

import java.io.IOException;
import java.util.Enumeration;
```

```java
import java.util.Iterator;
import java.util.Set;
import javax.management.Attribute;
import javax.management.ObjectName;
import javax.management.MBeanInfo;
import javax.management.MBeanServer;
import javax.management.MBeanAttributeInfo;

import java.net.URLDecoder;


public class IMServerServlet implements IMServlet {

        private MBeanServer localServerRef = null;

        public void setLocalServerRef(MBeanServer server){
                localServerRef = server;
        }

        public void onRequest(HTTPRequest request,HTTPResponse response)
          throws IOException
        {

                String responseText
="<HTML><BODY><I>IMServerServlet</I><BR/>";

                if
(request.getParameter("op").equalsIgnoreCase("listBeans"))
                        responseText+=listBeans(request,response);

                if
(request.getParameter("op").equalsIgnoreCase("showBean")){
                        responseText+=showBean(request,response);
                        responseText+="<a href='/?op=listBeans'>Show
Beans</a>";
                }

                if
(request.getParameter("op").equalsIgnoreCase("updateAtts")){
                        String ret = updateAtts(request,response);
                        if (!ret.equals(""))
                            responseText+=ret;
                        responseText+=showBean(request,response);
                        responseText+="<a href='/?op=listBeans'>Show
Beans</a>";
                }


                responseText+="</BODY></HTML>";
```

```
        response.setContentType("text/html");
        response.write(responseText.getBytes());


    }

     public String listBeans(HTTPRequest request, HTTPResponse
response){
            String temp = "";
            Set beans = localServerRef.queryNames(null,null);
            Iterator beanIter = beans.iterator();
            while (beanIter.hasNext()){
                 ObjectName bean = (ObjectName)beanIter.next();
                 temp+="<a
href='/?op=showBean&bean="+bean.getCanonicalName()+"'>"+
                                 bean.getCanonicalName()+"</a><BR/>";
             }
             return temp;
     }


     public String showBean(HTTPRequest request, HTTPResponse
response){
            String temp = "";
            String bean =
URLDecoder.decode(request.getParameter("bean"));
            temp+="Information about " + bean +"<BR/>";
            try {
               temp+="<FORM NAME='MBEANATTS' METHOD='GET'
ACTION='/'>";
                 temp+="<TABLE BORDER='1' CELLPADDING='4'
CELLSPACING='2'>";

temp+="<TR><TD>Name</TD><TD>Type</TD><TD>R/W</TD><TD>Value</TD></TR>";
                 ObjectName beanObj = new ObjectName(bean);
                 MBeanInfo beanInfo =
localServerRef.getMBeanInfo(beanObj);
                 MBeanAttributeInfo attInfo[] =
beanInfo.getAttributes();
                 for (int i=0;i<attInfo.length;i++){
                    temp+="<TR><TD>"+attInfo[i].getName()+"</TD>";
                    temp+="<TD>"+attInfo[i].getType()+"</TD>";

temp+="<TD>"+attInfo[i].isReadable()+"/"+attInfo[i].isWritable()+"</TD>"
;
                    Object value =
(String)localServerRef.getAttribute(beanObj,attInfo[i].getName());
                    if (attInfo[i].isWritable() &&
attInfo[i].getType().equals("java.lang.String"))
                         temp+="<TD><INPUT TYPE=TEXT
NAME="+attInfo[i].getName()+" VALUE="+value+"></TD></TR>";
```

```
                              else
                                  temp+="<TD>"+value+"</TD></TR>";
                          }
                          temp+="<TR><TD><INPUT TYPE=SUBMIT
VALUE='Submit'/></TD></TR>";
                          temp+="</TABLE>";
                          temp+="<INPUT TYPE=HIDDEN NAME='op'
VALUE='updateAtts'/>";
                          temp+="<INPUT TYPE=HIDDEN NAME='bean'
VALUE='"+bean+"'/>";
                          temp+="</FORM>";
                      }catch(Exception ex){
                          temp+="An error occurred getting attributes for " +
bean + "<BR/>";
                          temp+=ex;
                      }
                      return temp;
            }


        public String updateAtts(HTTPRequest request, HTTPResponse
response){
                String temp = "";
                String bean =
URLDecoder.decode(request.getParameter("bean"));
                try {
                    ObjectName objName = new ObjectName(bean);
                    Enumeration parms = request.getParameters();
                    while (parms.hasMoreElements()){
                      String parm =
URLDecoder.decode((String)parms.nextElement());
                        if (!parm.equals("op") && !parm.equals("bean")){
                            String parmValue = request.getParameter(parm);
                            System.out.println("PARM: " + parm + ",VALUE: "
+ parmValue);

                            // Update the attribute
                            Attribute newAttr = new
Attribute(parm,parmValue);
                            localServerRef.setAttribute(objName,newAttr);
                        }
                    }
                }catch(Exception ex){
                    temp+="An error occurred setting attributes for " +
bean + "<BR/>";
                    temp+=ex;
                }
                return temp;
        }

}
```

The IMServerServlet class has been updated to respond to three types of requests. The first type is a request for all the MBeans that a JMX agent knows about. The second type requests a list of information about a particular MBean. The third type of request is for updating the attributes of an MBean. The IMServerServlet figures out which of the three requests has been made by examining the parameters that were passed in the HTTP request. I have defined the use of a parameter named op that you must pass in order to utilize the HttpAdapter.

If the op parameter equals a value of listBeans, then the IMServerServlet accesses the MBean Server using the localServerRef instance variable. It calls the queryNames() method of the MBeanServer interface and passes a value of null for both arguments. This has the effect of saying "Give me all beans regardless of their name." You then wrap the results that are returned in hyperlinks and separate each hyperlink with a break tag <BR/>.

If the op parameter equals a value of showBean, then the IMServerServlet retrieves the MBeanInfo object associated with the MBean. The name of the MBean is passed as a string in the parameter bean. This string must be a valid object name; and it should be, as it was generated from a list of MBeans using the listBeans operation.

If the op parameter equals a value of updateAtts, the IMServerServlet retrieves the new values you passed in from the HTML form. These are provided using the name of the attribute that is specified in the NAME attribute of the INPUT element of the HTML form, and its new value you typed in the text field. You then create an javax.management.Attribute object from these two values and pass it to the setAttribute() method of the MBeanServer interface. After you update the attribute, the attributes for the MBean are redisplayed so you can see your changes.

> **NOTE:** I haven't taken the trouble to separate the building of the presentation in this example. The IMServerServlet class builds the HTML tags and the display, which is then written back to the client. You could use a number of techniques to accomplish this, but I think one of the best solutions would be to use XML and an XSL stylesheet.

The last few lines of code set the content type of the response. For this example, the content type is text/html. The very last line of code writes the entire HTML page to the client.

The updates to the IMServerServlet class complete the coding steps for this example. You can now launch the agent and point a Web browser at it to manage some MBeans.

## Launching the agent and using the adapter

You are going to use the JMXAgent application that was defined in Listing 12-11. This agent loads two MBeans: the Protocol MBean and the HttpAdapter MBean. There is no output from the JMXAgent application, but once it starts, you can start your favorite Web browser at this address:

```
http://localhost:8888/?op=listBeans
```

I used Internet Explorer to find the URL. Figure 12-1 displays the result.

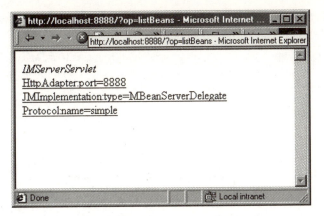

**Figure 12-1:** Using the HttpAdapter with Internet Explorer.

From Figure 12-1, you can see that the `HttpAdapter` MBean and the `Protocol` MBean are present, as well as an MBean called `JMImplementation`. You may recall from Chapter 8 that the `MBeanServerDelegate` MBean is used internally by the MBean Server. Each MBean is listed by the object name it was created with and links to another URL that enables you to display information about the MBean. Figure 12-2 shows the display information shown for the `Protocol` MBean.

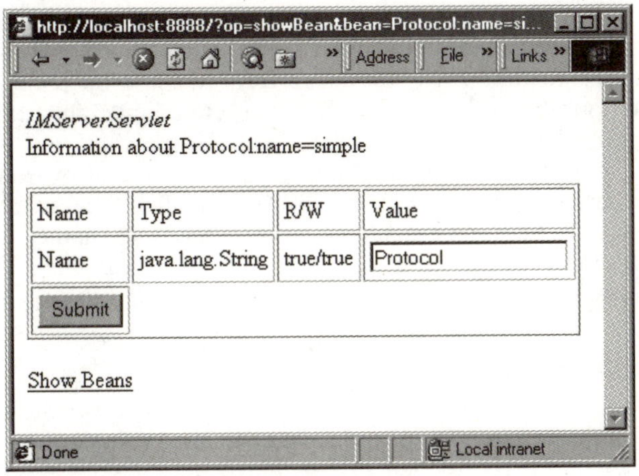

**Figure 12-2:** The attributes of the Protocol MBean displayed.

The attributes are displayed in a table with the name, type, whether it's read/write, and its current value. If an attribute is writable, a text field is displayed with the value so you can change it and press the Submit button. If an attribute is read-only, the value of the attribute is displayed as text. In order to keep this example simplified, you are only allowed to update attributes of type `java.lang.String`. You will see other attributes displayed, but if they are not `java.lang.String` type, their value is displayed as text. You can navigate back to the list of MBeans using the hyperlink labeled `Show Beans`.

The `HttpAdapter` example enables you to use a Web browser to send requests to a JMX agent to manage resources. You can extend it to perform other management-related operations, such as invoking operations or handling attributes of other datatypes like `java.lang.Integer`. Now it's time to get acquainted with the second type of component used for remote interaction: the connector.

# Connectors

A connector is conceptually similar to a protocol adapter. It takes a request using a specified protocol, translates the request into a command or request for a resource, executes the command, and then formulates a response. The primary difference is that heavyweight clients or other management agents typically use connectors, and protocol adapters are used by lightweight clients such as Web browsers or handheld devices. However this difference is not set in stone, and you may see a protocol adapter used like a connector. Like a protocol adapter, a connector is usually comprised of different components, each providing a specific piece of functionality such as mapping a request to an action, or interpreting protocol headers.

A connector is not restricted to a specific protocol, and you could just as easily implement a connector using the HTTP protocol. In this example, however, you are going to implement a connector using Java's Remote Method Invocation (RMI). For those not familiar with RMI, I provide a brief overview of how it works.

Using RMI has both advantages and disadvantages. Using RMI for this application means that you (the developer) will not be responsible for many of the details regarding how the protocol works or how threads are managed. This does not mean that the details aren't important; it just means that your job will be easier. One drawback to RMI is that it's a Java-specific technology, so it's not as accessible as the `HTTPAdapter` you worked with earlier. However, as you are no doubt aware by now, JMX does not limit the number or type of protocol adapters or connectors that you can use, so you can mix and match them to suit your needs. In the preceding section, you used a class named `JMXAgent` to load the `HttpAdapter`. In this section, the `JMXAgent` class will load both the `HttpAdapter` and the RMI connector.

## RMI primer

RMI is a Java-specific technology that facilitates distributed applications by enabling objects to be remotely accessed. An application running on one host can execute the methods of an object that physically exists on another host. To the client making the request, it looks as if the object is running in the same Java Virtual Machine (JVM). In reality, however, sets of classes called *stubs* are handling the packaging and unpackaging of arguments to the methods, and are used by the RMI runtime. There is a set of client stubs on each end of an RMI conversation: one on the client end and one on the server end.

Objects that want to be remotely accessed register themselves in the RMI registry or via the Java Naming Directory Interface (JNDI). When a client application wants to access the remote object, it connects to the registry running on the host on which the object is located and asks for the object. You don't get an actual instance of the object back, but an instance of a remote interface representing the object.

The registry can be started in one of two ways: either programmatically, using the `java.rmi.server.LocateRegistry` class, or by using the `registry.exe` executable that comes with the Java Development Kit (JDK). For developing the RMI connector, you will use the `LocateRegistry` class.

When the registry is started, it uses a default port of `1099`. You can easily change this by specifying a new port when the registry is created using the Java API. It cannot be changed when the `registry.exe` application that is part of the JDK is used. If you used the `registry.exe` application, you would need a way to launch it, which could be a part of normal system operations, and the RMI connector MBean would need to be passed the port so that it could bind remote objects to it.

## Remote exceptions

You'll find that methods that exist in remote interfaces must be defined to throw `java.rmi.RemoteException`. The `java.rmi.RemoteException` class is used to wrap local exceptions or those exceptions that happen in the RMI runtime. This means that if you execute a remote method on a remote object, and an exception is thrown, such as a `NullPointerException`, a `RemoteException` will be sent back to the client with the `NullPointerException` included in the detail. The following code snippet shows what a `RemoteException` might look like:

```
Msg: Nothing
Exception in thread "main" java.util.NoSuchElementException
        at
sun.rmi.transport.StreamRemoteCall.exceptionReceivedFromServer(Unknow
n Source)
        at sun.rmi.transport.StreamRemoteCall.executeCall(Unknown
Source)
        at sun.rmi.server.UnicastRef.invoke(Unknown Source)
        at com.hmi.rmi.RemoteMBeanServerImpl_Stub.getAttribute(Unknown
Source)
        at com.hmi.rmi.TestRMIAdapter.main(TestRMIAdapter.java:26)
```

You can see from the stack trace that the exception originates from the stub class for the `RemoteMBeanServerImpl` class, indicating an attempt to access an element of a collection that does not exist. Any exceptions that you might catch in the `RMIAdapter` should be re-thrown as a `RemoteException` so that the RMI runtime can properly deal with them.

You might then want to design a proxy class that handles dealing with the `RemoteException` and re-throwing the exception in your client as some other exception. This relieves client applications of the burden of dealing with the details of RMI exceptions.

## The RMI compiler

After you've created the implementation of the remote interface, you must create the stub and skeleton code that the RMI runtime will use. To do this, you use a utility included with the Java Development Kit called `rmic`. The `rmic` utility is a compiler that takes the implementation of a remote interface and generates a skeleton and stub. For example, if you have an interface called RemoteMBeanServer and a class named RemoteMBeanServerImpl, you would execute a command like the following:

```
rmic RemoteMBeanServerImpl
```

After you run the rmic against that class, you have two additional classes named RemoteMBeanServerImpl_Stub.class and RemoteMBeanServerImpl_Skel.class. The rmic utility includes a host of options, which are similar to those of the javac compiler, such as being able to specify a classpath, as well as a directory for the output files. If you run rmic with no options and just a class name, the stub and skel files are placed in the same directory as the class.

The idea behind the RMI connector is to expose an object that looks and behaves like an MBean Server running locally. Because there is no specification for what this remote interface should look like or how it should behave, it's really up to you to come up with this interface. In the interest of simplicity, it is easiest to make the interface look nearly identical to the MBeanServer interface. The implementation of that remote RMI interface can then be delegated to a local copy of an MBean Server. Table 12-2 shows the classes used for the RMI example.

### Table 12-2   RMI Connector Classes

| Class Name | Description |
| --- | --- |
| RMIAdapter | Implementation of the RMI connector |
| RMIAdapterMBean | Management interface for the RMI connector |
| RMIListener | Starts the RMI registry to listen for requests |
| RemoteMBeanServer | Implemenation of a remote MBean Server |
| RemoteMBeanServerImpl | Remote interface for an MBean Server |

In RMI, you need to define the remote interface and then the implementation of that interface, just as you do with an MBean. Methods that are not defined in the remote interface but are defined in the implementation are not considered part of the remote interface. Each of the classes in Table 12-2 serves a purpose similar to those in the HTTPAdapter you saw earlier. Table 12-3 shows this comparison.

### Table 12-3   RMI vs. HTTP

| RMI | HTTP Equivalent | Function |
| --- | --- | --- |
| RMIAdapter | HttpAdapter | MBean management interface |
| RMIAdapterMBean | HttpAdapterMBean | Implementation of MBean interface |

| RMI | HTTP Equivalent | Function |
|-----|-----------------|----------|
| RMIListener | HttpListener | Listens for requests from clients |
| RemoteMBeanServer | IMServlet | Remote interface for working with the MBean Server |
| RemoteMBeanServerImpl | IMServerServlet | Implementation of remote interface for working with the MBean Server |

Let's take a look at each of these components, starting with the RMIListener. This component is critical to the RMI connector because it is what listens for remote requests; it also binds the remote interface of the MBeanServer to the registry.

## The RMI listener

The RMIListener class acts as the class that starts the RMI registry and binds the remote MBean Server instance into the registry. The binding process enables remote clients to obtain an instance of the RemoteMBeanServer interface, which in turn gives them an instance of the RemoteMBeanServerImpl class.

This remote MBean Server instance holds a reference to a locally defined MBean Server instance. The RMIListener class is intended to be used inside an MBean like the HTTPAdapter you worked with earlier. This enables the RMI connector to be dynamically loaded and unloaded. You could even potentially expose the capability to change the port on which the RMI listener listens for requests, although this example does not expose such a capability.

Listing 12-14 shows the source code for the RMIListener class.

**Listing 12-14: The RMIListener class**

```
package com.hmi.rmi.adapter;

import java.net.MalformedURLException;
import java.rmi.Naming;
import java.rmi.Remote;
import java.rmi.RemoteException;
import java.rmi.registry.Registry;
import java.rmi.registry.LocateRegistry;
import java.rmi.server.UnicastRemoteObject;

public class RMIListener {

        private Registry rmiRegistry = null;
        private Remote serverRef = null;
        private int port = 12000;

        public RMIListener(int newPort){
                port = newPort;
```

```
        }

        public void setRemoteInterface(Remote objRef) throws
RemoteException{
                serverRef = objRef;
        }

        public void begin() throws RemoteException{
                //rmiRegistry = LocateRegistry.getRegistry(port);
                //if (rmiRegistry == null) {
                    rmiRegistry = LocateRegistry.createRegistry(port);
                try {

Naming.rebind("//localhost:"+port+"/RemoteMBeanServer",serverRef);
                }catch(MalformedURLException ex){
                    throw new RemoteException("Unable to bind remote MBean
Server",ex);
                }
        }

}
```

The `RMIListener` is structured very similarly to the `HttpListener` in that the port is passed in the constructor and the class includes a `begin()` method. The `begin()` method is what starts the actual threads that listen for requests. Unlike the `HttpListener`, though, you must rely on the RMI registry to handle the threading and opening of network ports. As a result, you have little control over the threading of the RMI registry, unlike with the `HttpListener`, which includes the `IMClient` thread class, of which you were responsible for creating instances.

When the `begin()` method is called, an `RMIRegistry` instance is created, and then an attempt is made to bind the remote MBean Server to it. The `rebind()` method of the `java.rmi.Naming` class is used to do the binding and takes two arguments. The first argument is a URL that includes the host, the port, and the name of the object. The second argument is the instance of the remote MBean Server or an instance of the `RemoteMBeanServer` interface. I used the `rebind()` method so that if an existing reference existed, this new one would replace it.

The `createRegistry()` method of the `java.rmi.server.LocateRegistry` class is used to create an instance of the RMI registry. When you call this method to create the registry, the network port is opened. Again, you have no real control over exactly when the port is opened, although it is usually immediate.

With a listener capable of starting an RMI registry and binding your remote MBean Server out of the way, you can proceed to define the remote interface of the MBean Server.

# Defining the remote interface and implementation

The purpose of the connector is to make an object that looks and behaves like an MBean Server accessible to remote clients. When you want to make a class accessible via RMI, you must define an interface that extends the `java.rmi.Remote` interface and then define an implementation of that interface. This idea is conceptually similar to the way that MBeans must define a management interface and an implementation of that interface, but that's where the similarity ends.

For your RMI connector, you define a remote interface named `RemoteMBeanServer` that has a set of methods that look almost identical to the interfaces of the `MBeanServer` interface in the JMX API. Listing 12-15 shows the source of the `RemoteMBeanServer` interface.

**Listing 12-15: The RemoteMBeanServer interface**

```
package com.hmi.rmi;

import javax.management.Attribute;
import javax.management.ObjectName;
import java.rmi.Remote;
import java.rmi.RemoteException;

public interface RemoteMBeanServer extends Remote{

        Object invoke(ObjectName name,String operation,Object
parms[],String types[]) throws RemoteException;
        Object getAttribute(ObjectName objName,String attrName) throws
RemoteException;
        void setAttribute(ObjectName objName, Attribute attr) throws
RemoteException;

}
```

The `RemoteMBeanServer` interface works similarly to the `MBeanServer` interface by defining the common methods for working with MBeans. The `invoke()` method is for invoking the operations of an MBean, and the `getAttribute()` method retrieves the value of an attribute. One difference between these methods and the `MBeanServer` interface methods is that each of the remote methods is defined to throw the `java.rmi` `.RemoteException` exception. When a JMX-specific exception occurs in the local MBean Server, it is propagated back to the calling client as an instance of the `RemoteException` class. The original exception can be extracted from the exception to find out what went wrong.

Listing 12-16 shows the source code of the `RemoteMBeanServerImpl` class that implements the `RemoteMBeanServer` interface.

**Listing 12-16: The RemoteMBeanServerImpl class**

```
package com.hmi.rmi;

import java.rmi.MarshalledObject;
import java.rmi.RemoteException;
```

```java
import java.rmi.Remote;
import javax.management.Attribute;
// Temporary
import javax.management.AttributeChangeNotification;
import javax.management.InstanceNotFoundException;
import javax.management.MalformedObjectNameException;
import javax.management.MBeanException;
import javax.management.MBeanServer;
import javax.management.NotificationListener;
import javax.management.NotificationFilter;
import javax.management.Notification;
import javax.management.ObjectName;
import javax.management.ObjectInstance;
import java.util.Set;
import java.rmi.server.UnicastRemoteObject;


public class RemoteMBeanServerImpl extends UnicastRemoteObject
implements RemoteMBeanServer{

        private MBeanServer localServerRef = null;

        public RemoteMBeanServerImpl() throws RemoteException{};

        public Object invoke(ObjectName objectName,
                             String actionName,
                             Object parms[],
                             String types[]) throws RemoteException{

            Object returnValue = null;
            try {
              returnValue =
localServerRef.invoke(objectName,actionName,parms,types);
            }catch(Exception ex){
                throw new RemoteException("General Exception",ex);
            }

            return returnValue;
        }

        public void setAttribute(ObjectName objName,Attribute attr)
            throws RemoteException{

            try {
                localServerRef.setAttribute(objName,attr);
            } catch(Exception ex){
                throw new RemoteException("Could not set attribute",ex);
            }
        }
```

```
        public Object getAttribute(ObjectName objName,String attrName)
throws RemoteException{

            Object attr = null;
            try {
                attr = localServerRef.getAttribute(objName,attrName);
            }catch(Exception ex){
                throw new RemoteException("Could not retrieve
attribute",ex);
            }
            return attr;
        }

        // Sets the reference to the local MBeanServer
        public void setLocalServerRef(MBeanServer local){
            localServerRef = local;
        }

}
```

The `RemoteMBeanServerImpl` class implements the `RemoteMBeanServer` interface and extends the `java.rmi.server.UnicastRemoteObject` class. You must extend this class or the `RemoteObject` class in order for an object to be remotely accessible using RMI.

The two implemented methods `invoke()` and `getAttribute()` delegate the calls to the real methods of the `MBeanServer` interface of the same name. Before delegating the call to the MBean Server, the `getMBean()` method is used to find the actual MBean instance. The `invoke()` and `getAttribute()` methods of your `RemoteMBeanServer` interface define `java.lang.String` as the type of the first argument. This must be translated into a real `ObjectName` instance and then returned. This `ObjectName` instance is then passed to the real methods of the `MBeanServer` interface.

## Interacting with the MBean Server

Because the whole point of this exercise is to access MBeans remotely, you need, of course, to interact with an MBean Server. Like the `HTTPAdapter`, the RMI connector needs to enable interaction with an MBean Server and the MBeans it has registered.

To load the RMI connector, you define an MBean that acts as the container for the RMI connector so that it can be loaded and unloaded like any other MBean. This MBean doesn't need any other methods right now, so the management interface will be empty. Listing 12-17 shows the source of the `RMIAdapterMBean` interface.

**Listing 12-17: The RMIAdapterMBean interface**

```
package com.hmi.rmi.adapter;

public interface RMIAdapterMBean {
```

```
}
```

Currently, the RMIAdapterMBean interface does not define any methods, which is perfectly acceptable. The implementation of this interface is shown in Listing 12-18, the RMIAdapter class.

**Listing 12-18: The RMIAdapterMBean implementation**

```
package com.hmi.rmi.adapter;

import javax.management.MBeanServer;
import javax.management.ObjectName;
import javax.management.MBeanException;
import javax.management.MBeanRegistration;
import java.rmi.RemoteException;

import com.hmi.rmi.RemoteMBeanServerImpl;

public class RMIAdapter implements RMIAdapterMBean,MBeanRegistration{

        private RMIListener rmiListener = null;
        private RemoteMBeanServerImpl mbeanImpl = null;

        public RMIAdapter(int port) throws MBeanException{
                rmiListener = new RMIListener(port);
                try {
                    mbeanImpl = new RemoteMBeanServerImpl();
                    rmiListener.setRemoteInterface(mbeanImpl);
                    rmiListener.begin();
                } catch (RemoteException ex) {
                    ex.printStackTrace();
                    throw new MBeanException(ex,"Could not start
RMIAdapter");
                }
        }
        // MBeanRegistration interface methods
        public void postDeregister(){};
        public void postRegister(Boolean done){};
        public void preDeregister(){};
        public ObjectName preRegister(MBeanServer beanServer,
                                      ObjectName name){
                mbeanImpl.setLocalServerRef(beanServer);
                return name;
        }
}
```

The RMIAdapter class implements its required management interface as well as the MBeanRegistration interface. The MBeanRegistration interface enables you to obtain a reference to the MBean Server that has loaded it without having to resort to finding the MBean Server. This may be desirable if you want to use a string identifier to find a particular MBean

Server to use. The intent here, however, is to use the `MBeanServer` reference as the local copy, meaning the remote MBean Server will delegate all calls to this local copy.

The constructor takes a single argument specifying the port on which the `RMIListener` should listen for requests, and a new `RMIListener` object is created using this port. At this point, the RMI registry has been created, but the remote MBean Server has not been bound in it, nor is the registry accepting requests.

A new `RemoteMBeanServerImpl` object is created and the `setRemoteInterface()` method of the `RMIListener` class is called and passed the `RemoteMBeanServerImpl` instance just created. This is done so that the `RemoteMBeanServerImpl` object can be bound in the registry and accessed via remote method calls. Once this is done, the `begin()` method of the `RMIListener` class is called, which actually causes the registry to be created and the remote MBean Server reference to be bound.

Another point of interest is the `preRegister()` method, which is implemented as required by the `MBeanRegistration` interface. This method calls the `setLocalServerRef()` method of the `RemoteMBeanServerImpl` class to store a copy of the MBean Server into which the `RMIAdapter` MBean was loaded.

## Updating the JMXAgent

Before trying to use the RMI connector, you need to update the `JMXAgent` application used in the `HttpAdapter` example shown earlier in this chapter. These minor updates cause the `JMXAgent` to load the `RMIAdapter` MBean. Listing 12-19 shows the `JMXAgent` source code updated to load the `RMIAdapter`.

**Listing 12-19: JMXAgent updated for the RMI connector**

```
import javax.management.InstanceNotFoundException;
import javax.management.IntrospectionException;
import javax.management.MalformedObjectNameException;
import javax.management.ReflectionException;
import javax.management.ObjectName;
import javax.management.MBeanServer;
import javax.management.MBeanServerFactory;

import com.hmi.http.adapter.HttpAdapter;
import com.hmi.rmi.adapter.RMIAdapter;

public class JMXAgent {

    private static MBeanServer server = null;

    public JMXAgent() {
        server = MBeanServerFactory.createMBeanServer();
    }

    public static void main(String[] args) {
```

```
        JMXAgent agent = new JMXAgent();
        ObjectName simpleObject =
                agent.loadBean("Protocol",
                               "Protocol:name=simple");

            ObjectName httpObjName = null;
            HttpAdapter httpAdapter = new HttpAdapter(8888);
            ObjectName rmiObjName = null;

            try {

                httpObjName =
                    new ObjectName("HttpAdapter:port=8888");
                server.registerMBean(httpAdapter,httpObjName);
                RMIAdapter rmiAdapter =
                    new RMIAdapter(12000);
                rmiObjName =
                    new ObjectName("RMIAdapter:port=12000");
                server.registerMBean(rmiAdapter,rmiObjName);

            }catch(Exception ex){
                System.out.println(ex);
            }
    }

    private ObjectName loadBean(String className,String objectName) {

    ObjectName mbeanObjectName = null;
    String domain = server.getDefaultDomain();
    String mbeanName = className;
    try {
            mbeanObjectName = new ObjectName(objectName);
    } catch(MalformedObjectNameException e) {
            e.printStackTrace();
            System.exit(1);
    }

        // Create our simple object to manage //
        try {
        server.createMBean(mbeanName,mbeanObjectName);
        }catch(Exception ex){
                ex.printStackTrace();
                System.exit(1);
        }

        return mbeanObjectName;

    }
}
```

The `main()` method has been updated to create a new instance of the `RMIAdapter` MBean, which is then passed to the `registerMBean()` method of the `MBeanServer` interface. A value of 12000 is passed as the port number that the RMI registry will use.

> **NOTE:** Management clients that want to use the RMI connector need to know this port number if they want to use the connector.

The next example shows how to connect to the RMI connector. The `HttpAdapter` example was a little more straightforward in that it involved using Internet Explorer and typing in a URL, but the RMI example is not that much more difficult. The Web browser also needs to use the URL, so the client applications are actually similar in this respect.

## Managing a Simple Object with RMI

To test the RMI connector, you can write a simple application that gains access to the remote MBean Server and then invokes methods to access MBeans running remotely. The MBean you will manage is the `ProtocolMBean` you created in the "Managing a simple object with HTTP" section earlier in this chapter.

The `TestRMIAdapter` class is shown in Listing 12-20. Before running the `TestRMIAdapter` application, make sure that the `JMXAgent` application that loads the MBeans and RMI connector is running.

**Listing 12-20: The TestRMIAdapter class**

```
package com.hmi.rmi;

import javax.management.Attribute;
import javax.management.MalformedObjectNameException;
import javax.management.ObjectName;
import java.rmi.Naming;
import java.net.MalformedURLException;
import java.rmi.NotBoundException;
import java.rmi.RemoteException;


import com.hmi.rmi.RemoteMBeanServer;

public class TestRMIAdapter {

    public static void main(String args[]){

        try {

            ObjectName simpleObj = new
ObjectName("Protocol:name=simple");

            RemoteMBeanServer beanServer =
```

```
(RemoteMBeanServer)Naming.lookup("//localhost:12000/RemoteMBeanServer");

        String msg = (String)beanServer.invoke(simpleObj,
                                               "doNothing",
                                               new Object[]{},
                                               new String[]{});
        System.out.println("Msg: " + msg);

        // Get an attribute
        String attr = (String)beanServer.getAttribute(simpleObj,
                                                      "Name");

        System.out.println("Name attr = " + attr);

        // Set an attribute

        beanServer.setAttribute(simpleObj,new
Attribute("Name","Wiley"));

        // Get the attribute
        attr = (String)beanServer.getAttribute(simpleObj,"Name");
        System.out.println("Name attr = " + attr);

    }catch(MalformedURLException ex){
    }catch(MalformedObjectNameException ex){
    }catch(NotBoundException ex){
    }catch(RemoteException ex){
        ex.printStackTrace();
        System.out.println("Exception: " + ex);
    }


    }

}
```

The first thing the `TestRMIAdapter` application does is obtain a reference to the remote MBean Server using the `lookup()` method of the `java.rmi.Naming` class. This method takes a string representing the URL of the MBean Server; and in this case, the `MBeanServer` can be contacted at `localhost` on port `12000`, and has been bound with a name of `RemoteMBeanServer`.

The output from the `TestRMIAdapter` application looks like the following:

```
Msg: Nothing
Name attr = Protocol MBean
Name attr = Wiley
```

You could extend this simple model of an RMI connector to allow distributed notifications, which currently are not defined in the JMX specification. The `RMIAdapter` could be run on every JMX agent that you wanted to be able to send a notification to, and could use the `RemoteMBeanServerImpl` class to locate an MBean to send a notification to.

You've seen how to utilize an HTTP adapter and RMI connector to enable access to MBeans by management clients. Now you'll look at how to use SNMP to accomplish the same task.

# Managing Objects with SNMP

In Chapter 1, you learned that SNMP is the prevalent network management protocol used today. No network management software solution would be complete without support for SNMP, and JMX is no exception. You can utilize SNMP to monitor and manage MBeans in a JMX agent similar to the way in which the HTTP adapter and RMI connector in this chapter accomplish this task.

> **CROSS-REFERENCE:** Appendix A includes a list of network-monitoring products that use SNMP.

Although SNMP is relatively simple at a high level, completely describing it is beyond the scope of this book. This section addresses some of the key concepts, followed by the example. The example for this chapter shows you how to use one of the leading JMX/SNMP toolkits on the market today, the AdventNet ManageEngine, which enables you to build a JMX agent that contains an SNMP agent you can use for managing MBeans registered in an MBean Server.

> **NOTE:** I used the beta 2 version of the AdventNet ManageEngine product to generate the code for this example. You can download a evaluation version of this product from `www.adventnet.com`.

There is also a tool named `mibgen` that comes with the Java Dynamic Management Kit (JDMK). The JDMK can be downloaded from `www.sun.com/products-n-solutions /nep/software/java-dynamic`. This tool enables you to generate the necessary MBeans from a MIB. You must then implement a JMX agent and use an SNMP adapter to enable management of the MBeans. However, from this example, you will see how easy it is to implement management via SNMP using the AdventNet ManageEngine product.

The code you generate with the ManageEngine product can be customized manually using a text editor or the ManageEngine editor. The ManageEngine also enables you to generate the SNMP MIB that is needed by the SNMP agent and the SNMP manager. The MIB defines what objects and attributes can be managed.

Because of the complexity behind implementing a fully functional SNMP adapter, this example shows you how to use the ManageEngine product to generate the necessary JMX agent, SNMP agent, and MBean for this example.

## Getting started

In previous examples throughout this book, you've seen the logical sequence of steps used to create the examples. You first define your managed object's interface. Next, you define the implementation of that interface, which becomes the managed object itself. Finally, you create a JMX agent, which is a Java application that hosts the MBean Server and protocol adapters or connectors used to enable access by management clients. The JMX agent also loads any requisite MBeans and registers them in the MBean Server. The example shown next is not that different, except you use the ManageEngine product to generate the code.

When you install the ManageEngine product, an entry is created on your Start menu (and, optionally, an icon on the desktop). After you launch the product, you are presented with an application window that looks like the one shown in Figure 12-3.

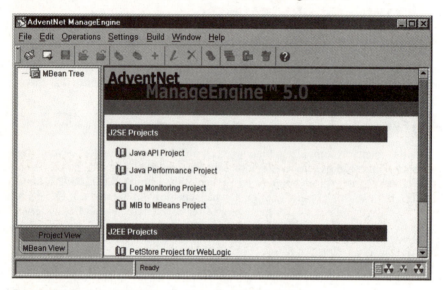

**Figure 12-3:** The AdventNet ManageEngine main application window.

Like many IDEs, the files you work with in the ManageEngine editor are organized into projects. The projects contain not only the source files you create and edit, but also the directories and libraries that are created after you compile your code. These directories include one that stores logs that are created when running your JMX agent, a bin directory that contains a script to start your agent, and a lib directory that contains the JAR archive containing the compiled class files representing your JMX agent, MBeans, and associated files, just to name a few.

## Creating the manageable class

Before you proceed with the ManageEngine portion of this example, you need to create a class that will be managed. For this example you need to create a simple class with two accessor methods for a single attribute. You do not need to create an MBean interface for this class because, as you will see in the next section, this class will be used with a model MBean. If you recall from Chapter 6, model MBeans use a handle to the object they are managing. The code you'll generate in the next section will use a handle to the manageable class whose source is shown in Listing 12-21

**Listing 12-21: The Sample class**

```
public class Sample {


    private String name = "SampleMBean";

    public String getName(){
        return name;
    }

    public void setName(String newName){
        name = newName;
    }

}
```

You need to save this class in a file named `Sample.java` and then compile it. You'll need the compiled class file for the next section.

## Creating the project

You start the next step of this example by creating a project. From there, you add an MBean, compile the project files, and execute the agent. You then test it using the ManageEngine MIB browser, which acts like an SNMP manager and enables you to communicate with the SNMP adapter in your JMX agent. Use the following steps to create the project files for this example:

1. Launch the AdventNet ManageEngine
2. Select File ➪ New Project from the menu bar. This presents the New Project dialog box.
3. In the New Project dialog box, enter the project name **SNMPJMX** in the Project Name text field. You also need to select the type of application. Select J2SE for this example, using the Application Type radio button. This indicates that this is for a non-J2EE JMX application. Click the Next button to continue.
4. On this second page of the dialog box, deselect the check box next to the HTML adaptor in the Adaptors section. This tells the ManageEngine that you want to have an SNMP adaptor added to your JMX agent for this project. Click the Finish button.

At this point, you have an empty project with no files. You now need to add the class that will be managed.

## Creating the MBean and JMX agent

In the ManageEngine editor, a tree view at the left offers a project view and an MBean view. The project view shows the files you have in your project, and the MBean view shows the MBeans in your project, as well as any attributes, operations, and notifications of the MBeans. The root node of the tree is labeled *MBean Tree*.

To add a class to this project, follow these steps:

1. Select File ➪ Load ➪ Java API from the menu bar. This launches the Application Class Loader dialog box.

2. Select the button labeled Browse that launched the Load Java API dialog. Navigate to the directory where you compiled the `Sample.class` class file that you created in the "Create the manageable class" section. After you select this, the class will appear in the Application Classes panel at the left. Select the class and click on the button labeled Add, which adds the selected class to the Application Classes for Management panel on the right. Click OK to finish this part. You will have a single MBean named `SampleMBean` in the MBean view of the ManageEngine application window.

3. Select Build ⇨ Generate Agent from the menu bar. This launches the Code Generation Settings Dialog box. You can leave all the options but one set at the default. Select the radio button labeled Ignore and Generate and click the OK button. This causes the JMX agent and supporting files to be generated.

This creates the Java code that represents the agent. It also generates some XML documents that are used by the JMX agent to configure your MBean. You can safely ignore those XML documents for this example. The three source files that are of interest are the following:

♦ `ReferenceProvider.java` — This class is used by the `SampleMBean` class to return a reference to the managed class.

♦ `SampleMBean.java` — This class is used by the model MBean to access the `Sample.class` class.

♦ `MyProjectStartup.java` — This is the JMX agent class that loads the model MBean and `SampleMBean`.

Before continuing, you need to modify the `ReferenceProvider.java` and `SampleMBean.java` code generated by the ManageEngine tool. You need to update the `ReferenceProvider.java` file so that it returns a reference to your `Sample.class` class. Listing 12-22 shows the source of the `ReferenceProvider.java` class with the lines in bold representing the updates you need to make. You can edit this class by selecting the `ReferenceProvider.java` class from the Project View pane.

**Listing 12-22: The source code for the ReferenceProvider class**

```java
// Code generated from AdventNet ManageEngine 5.0
// Any changes made will be lost if regenerated
// Please use User tags to add custom code

package com.agent;

import Sample;

public class ReferenceProvider {

 private static Sample sample = new Sample();

 public static Sample getSample() {
  return sample;
 }

}
```

Once you have finished making these changes, save the file by selecting File ⇨ Save File. Now you need to make a minor change to the SampleMBean class. Listing 12-23 shows the source of the SampleMBean class, with boldface marking those lines you need to change. You can make these changes in the ManageEngine editor, just like the SampleMBean change you made in the last step.

**Listing 12-23: The source code for the SampleMBean**

```
// Code generated from AdventNet ManageEngine 5.0
// Any changes made will be lost if regenerated
// Please use User tags to add custom code

package com.agent;

import com.adventnet.agent.utilities.common.AgentException;
import com.adventnet.agent.utilities.common.CommonUtils;

import Sample;

public class SampleMBean {

 protected java.lang.String name = null;

 public SampleMBean() {
 }

 ///////////////////// Attributes /////////////////////

 public java.lang.String getName() throws Exception {
  Sample sample = ReferenceProvider.getSample();
  if(sample == null)
   throw new AgentException("null reference got", CommonUtils.GENERR);
  return sample.getName();

 }

 public void setName(java.lang.String value) throws Exception {
  Sample sample = ReferenceProvider.getSample();
  if(sample == null)
   throw new AgentException("null reference got", CommonUtils.GENERR);
  sample.setName(value);

 }

 ///////////////////// Operations /////////////////////

}
```

Now you are ready to build the agent and compiled the project. Select Build ⇨ Build Agent, which instructs the ManageEngine to generate the JMX agent code for this example.

That's it for the code portion of this example. You are now ready to test your agent and MBean.

## Testing the agent and MBean

To test the agent, you need to execute the `run.bat` script that is generated by the ManageEngine editor. To execute this script, change to the directory in which the project is stored. For this example, you used the default project location, which should put the script in `%ADVENTNET_INSTALL%/ManageEngine/projects/SNMPJMX/bin`. You can execute the script by simply typing the following:

```
run.bat
```

When you execute this script, the following output should be displayed on the console (the exact pathnames shown in this output will vary depending on your installation location):

```
F:\Program Files\AdventNet\ManageEngine\projects\SNMPJMX\bin>run

F:\Program Files\AdventNet\ManageEngine\projects\SNMPJMX\bin>cd ..

F:\Program Files\AdventNet\ManageEngine\projects\SNMPJMX>set
JAVA_HOME=F:\jdk1.3
.1\jre

F:\Program Files\AdventNet\ManageEngine\projects\SNMPJMX>set
CLASSPATH=classes;F
:\Program
Files\AdventNet\ManageEngine\jars\AdventNetAppServerStats.jar;lib\SNMP
JMX_Agent.jar;F:\jdk1.3.1\jre\lib\classes.zip;F:\Program
Files\AdventNet\ManageE
ngine\jars\AdventNetJmx.jar;F:\Program
Files\AdventNet\ManageEngine\jars\AdventN
etJmxAgent.jar;F:\Program
Files\AdventNet\ManageEngine\jars\AdventNetAgentRuntim
eUtilities.jar;F:\Program
Files\AdventNet\ManageEngine\jars\AdventNetManageEngin
eRuntime.jar;F:\Program
Files\AdventNet\ManageEngine\jars\AdventNetLogging.jar;F
:\Program Files\AdventNet\ManageEngine\jars\jaxp.jar;F:\Program
Files\AdventNet\
ManageEngine\jars\crimson.jar;F:\Program
Files\AdventNet\ManageEngine\jars\xalan
.jar;F:\Program
Files\AdventNet\ManageEngine\jars\AdventNetSnmp.jar;F:\Program F
iles\AdventNet\ManageEngine\jars\AdventNetSnmpAgent.jar;;F:\files\JMX-
Hungrymind
s\snmp-1;
```

```
F:\Program Files\AdventNet\ManageEngine\projects\SNMPJMX>set
JAVA_COMPILER=NONE


F:\Program
Files\AdventNet\ManageEngine\projects\SNMPJMX>F:\jdk1.3.1\jre\bin\jav
a com.agent.MyProjectStartup
SnmpAgent is started... at port 8001
RuleEngineServer started at 4050
```

The key line in this output is the second from the last: *SnmpAgent is started... at port 8001*. This line of output indicates that the SNMP agent is started on port 8001. You need this information when you use the MIB browser to access the JMX agent. Now launch the MIB browser by selecting Start ⇨ Programs ⇨ AdventNet ManageEngine 5.0 Beta 2 ⇨ MIB Browser. After starting the MIB browser, you need to load the MIB generated in the previous section of this chapter. The MIB is stored in the root directory of your project and is named after the project. It is named `SNMPJMXMib.mib` for this example. You can load the MIB by selecting File ⇨ Load MIB from the menu bar.

After loading the MIB, you should have a screen that looks like the one shown in Figure 12-4.

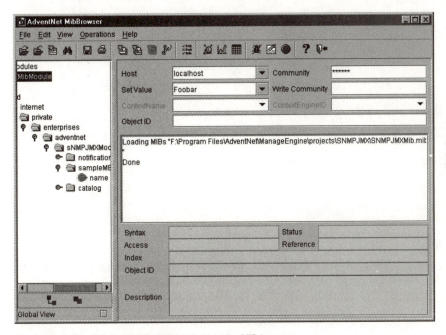

**Figure 12-4:** The SNMPJMXMib MIB loaded into the MIB browser.

When you first load the MIB, the tree view at the left is collapsed; you need to drill down into the `SampleMBean` node shown in Figure 12-4. Underneath this node is a node for the `name` attribute. When you select this attribute, you will see the MIB information appear in the panel at the right.

You can set the value of the `name` attribute by entering a value in the Set Value drop-down list and selecting Operations ⇨ Set from the menu. This results in a request being sent to the JMX agent and subsequently the `SampleMBean` to change the value of the `name` attribute. Figure 12-5 shows the results of setting the `name` attribute to a value of `Foobar`, and then getting the value using the Operations ⇨ Get menu option.

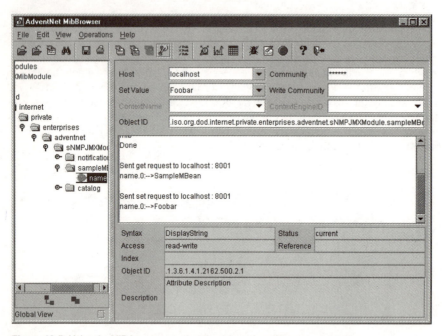

**Figure 12-5:** Using the MIB browser to set and get the value of the name attribute.

From the output shown in Figure 12-5, you can see that the value of the `name` attribute was successfully set and retrieved.

## Summary

In this chapter, you learned how to provide two key components of the JMX specification that have not been defined in detail yet: protocol adapters and connectors. You learned how to implement a simple HTTP protocol adapter and an RMI connector. The protocol adapter enabled a Web browser to connect and manage a simple MBean, and the RMI connector was used by a Java application for the same purpose.

In the next chapter, you'll start putting your knowledge of JMX to work. Chapter 13 presents a use case of building a JMX-based print monitor that can observe attributes such as the number of printers attached to a system, and how many print jobs are queued.

# Part IV

# Programming JMX

**Chapter 13: Monitoring Hardware with JMX**

**Chapter 14: Managing Servers Remotely**

**Chapter 15: Managing J2EE Components**

# Monitoring Hardware with JMX

Modern hardware devices have SNMP agents or other management agents built into them. When you attach one of these hardware devices to a network, it becomes manageable using standard tools and technologies. A management application can query the status of a device to determine the health of the device or receive notifications from the device if a problem occurs.

In this chapter, you'll look at examples that implement management of a locally connected printer, and learn how to monitor its attributes. Previous chapters used a fictional MBean called `PrinterObjectMBean` to illustrate various JMX concepts. In this chapter, you'll build a functioning version of the `PrinterObjectMBean` that is associated with a real printer. The printer used in the examples is an HP DeskJet 610C, but you can substitute any locally connected printer.

You will use the Java Native Interface (JNI) and C programming language to build this example.

> **NOTE:** You do not need to be intimately familiar with JNI or C. The compiled versions of the Dynamic Link Library (DLL) that you'll create are also available from the companion Web site for this book at `www.wiley.com/extras`. You can choose to simply download the library and use it.

## Managing a Printer

At a high level, you'll be talking to a Windows library called `WINSPOOL.DRV` that enables you to obtain information about the printers and printing subsystems in Windows. The jmxprinter.dll you'll create will use Windows APIs to access `WINSPOOL.DRV` and extract the information that will then be passed on to your MBeans. Figure 13-1 illustrates the architecture of this example.

Unfortunately, there is no easy way to embed the example application into a hardware device. Perhaps in the near future there will be a way to program common household devices and personal computer peripherals directly.

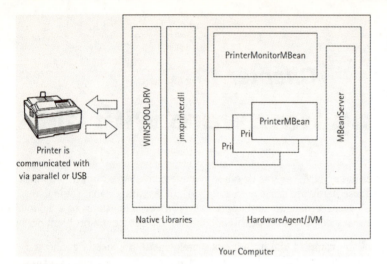

**Figure 13-1:** Accessing printer hardware using JMX.

The example application will enable you to monitor the following attributes of printers attached to a computer:

♦ Number of printers
♦ Name of each printer
♦ General information about each printer
♦ Status of each printer (paper jammed, out of paper, idle/ready, printing)
♦ Number of jobs queued

You won't be able to create, delete, or update the attributes of the printer directly but you will be able to monitor the changes in them.

The DLL you'll build will make use of common Windows API functions for accessing locally installed printers. You'll also be able to monitor and control various attributes of the printer through the management interface you'll create for the printer. The management interface, of course, will be built using the Java programming language and implemented as an MBean. You'll then build a Java Swing application client that makes use of the MBeans to monitor the printer.

The files that you'll create for this example are listed in Table 13-1.

## Table 13-1    Files for Print Monitor Example

| File Name | Description |
|-----------|-------------|
| `PrinterMonitor.java` | MBean that serves as logical grouping of printers. It is responsible for building the list of printer MBeans. |
| `PrinterMonitorMBean.java` | Management interface for `PrinterMonitor` MBean |

| File Name | Description |
|-----------|-------------|
| `Printer.java` | MBean that serves as a logical representation of a printer |
| `PrinterMBean.java` | Management interface for `Printer` MBean |
| `HardwareAgent.java` | JMX agent that will host MBean Server and the Printer MBeans for this example |
| `ManagementConsole.java` | A Swing-based application you will use to monitor the printer |
| `com_hmi_hardware_PrinterMonito r.h` | Header file containing function prototypes for native functions |
| `jmxprinter.c` | C source file for dynamic link library |
| `jmxprinter.dll` | Windows Dynamic Link Library for accessing information about printers |

Before you dive into the dynamic link library portion of this example, you need to build each of the Java classes. A portion of the dynamic link library section depends on the Java classes being available.

## Building the MBeans

The MBeans for the printer include one MBean that represents the actual printer. This `PrinterMBean` has attributes that represent data such as the name of the printer, its model, its location, and how many documents the printer currently has queued to print.

Rather than having the JMX agent build these bean instances directly, I've decided to employ the use of a second MBean named the `PrinterMonitorMBean`. The purpose of this MBean is to create instances of the `Printer` MBeans and register them with the MBean Server. It is also responsible for loading the dynamic link library and all interactions with the operating system. When the MBeans are loaded for the first time, the `PrinterMonitorMBean` queries the operating system for printers that it has defined, and creates instances of the `PrinterMBean` class, populated with information directly from the printer definitions. Listing 13-1 shows the source code for the `PrinterMBean` interface.

**Listing 13-1: The PrinterMBean interface**

```
package com.hmi.hardware;


/**
 *
 * This is the interface for a managed printer
 *
 **/

public interface PrinterMBean {
```

```
        String getPrinterName();
        void setPrinterName(String name);
        String getManufacturer();
        void setManufacturer(String mf);
        String getLocation();
        void setLocation(String loc);
        String getPort();
        void setPort(String nPort);
        String getDriver();
        void setDriver(String drv);
        String getStatus();
        void setStatus(String state);
        int getNumberQueuedJobs();
        void setNumberQueuedJobs(int jobs);
        String getComment();
        void setComment(String comment);

}
```

The interface for the `PrinterMBean` defines read-write methods for the attributes. The ability to display these attributes is exposed via the user interface through a common user-interface control — a table. The interface also defines the write methods so that you can change the values of the attributes.

The `PrinterMBean` acts as a container for runtime information about a printer. The example application does not allow the creation or deletion of printers, and no information is persisted between runs of the application. Listing 13-2 shows the source code for the implementation of this interface.

**Listing 13-2: The PrinterMBean interface implementation**

```
package com.hmi.hardware;

/**
 *
 * Represents a physical printer locally attached
 * to a computer
 *
 **/

import java.io.Serializable;

public class Printer implements PrinterMBean,Serializable {

        private String printerName = "Unnamed";
        private String manufacturer = "Unknown";
        private boolean isdefault = false;
        private String port = "";
        private String status = "";
        private int numberQueuedJobs = 0;
```

```java
private String location = "";
private String driver = "";
private String comment = "";

public String getPrinterName(){
      return printerName;
}

public void setPrinterName(String name){
      printerName = name;
}

public String getManufacturer(){
      return manufacturer;
}

public void setManufacturer(String mf){
      manufacturer = mf;
}

public String getLocation(){
      return location;
}

public void setLocation(String loc){
      location = loc;
}

public String getDriver(){
      return driver;
}

public void setDriver(String drv){
      driver = drv;
}

public String getStatus(){
      return status;
}

public void setStatus(String state){
      status = state;
}

public int getNumberQueuedJobs(){
      return numberQueuedJobs;
}

public void setNumberQueuedJobs(int jobs){
```

```
            numberQueuedJobs = jobs;
    }

    public String getPort(){
            return port;
    }

    public void setPort(String nPort){
            port = nPort;
    }

    public String getComment(){
            return comment;
    }

    public void setComment(String newComment){
            comment = newComment;
    }

    public String toString(){
            return "Name: " + getPrinterName() + "\n" +
                    "Port: " + getPort() + "\n" +
                    "Location: " + getLocation() + "\n" +
                    "Status: " + getStatus() + "\n" +
                    "Jobs: " + getNumberQueuedJobs() + "\n";
    }
}
```

The `PrinterMBean` class is instantiated by the `PrinterMonitor` class, and its accessor methods are populated with runtime information about the printer. Some of the information about a printer is stored in the Windows registry and can be queried even when the printer is offline. When instances of this object are initially created, they contain only information that can be obtained while the printer is not connected. In fact, you can add new printers using the NT control panel and view them with this sample application.

Listing 13-3 shows the source code for the management interface of the `PrinterMonitor` MBean.

**Listing 13-3: The PrinterMonitorMBean interface**

```
package com.hmi.hardware;

import java.util.List;

public interface PrinterMonitorMBean {

        List getPrinters();
        void refresh();
        void init();

}
```

The getPrinters() method is self-explanatory, but the init() method deserves a little explanation. The init() method must be called after the PrinterMonitorMBean is loaded to initialize the list of Printer MBeans. The next section shows you the implementation of this method.

The PrinterMonitor class implements this interface and provides the necessary details and code for establishing a list of printers, or retrieving information about a specific printer. The PrinterMonitorMBean will be loaded initially by the JMX agent. Listing 13-4 shows the source code for the implementation of the PrinterMonitorMBean interface.

**Listing 13-4: The PrinterMonitorMBean interface implementation**

```
package com.hmi.hardware;

/****
 *
 *
 * Periodically update array of printer structures and
 * all registered PrinterMBeans then send notifications
 * So that the agent can update its data model and the UI
 *
 * Each PrinterMBean can have a monitor associated with it
 * to watch (status, jobs, etc.)
 *
 * It can also have a notification associated with it to
 * watch specific attributes
 *
 * setPrinter() WIN32/API can change stat of printer (pause,resume,etc)
 *
 ****/

import javax.management.MBeanServer;
import javax.management.MBeanRegistration;
import javax.management.NotificationBroadcasterSupport;
import javax.management.ObjectName;
import java.util.Arrays;
import java.util.List;
import java.util.LinkedList;


public class PrinterMonitor extends NotificationBroadcasterSupport
                            implements PrinterMonitorMBean,
                                       MBeanRegistration{

    /* Native methods */
    private native Printer[] getNativePrinterInfo();

    private MBeanServer beanServer = null;
    private ObjectName objName = null;
```

```
    static {
System.loadLibrary("jmxprinter");
    }

    private List printers = new LinkedList();

    public List getPrinters(){
            return printers;
    }


    /**
     *
     * Called during agent startup to initialize
     * list of printers
     *
     **/
    public void init(){
            // Call printerInfo
            Printer[] ntvPrinters = getNativePrinterInfo();
            for (int j=0;j<ntvPrinters.length;j++){
                // internal list
                printers.add(ntvPrinters[j]);
                // register in MBeanServer
                try {
                    ObjectName pName = new
ObjectName("Printers:type=printer,name="+

ntvPrinters[j].getPrinterName());
                    beanServer.registerMBean(ntvPrinters[j],pName);
                }catch(Exception ex){
                    // Print error and continue
                    ex.printStackTrace();
                    System.out.println("Could not register printer: "
+ ex);
                }
            }

            // Start refresh thread
            RefreshThread rfThread = new RefreshThread(this);
            rfThread.start();
    }

    /**
     *
     * Called to refresh list of printers
     *
     **/
```

```
        public void refresh(){

                // Refresh all registered MBeans
                printers.clear();
                Printer[] ntvPrinters = getNativePrinterInfo();
                for (int j=0;j<ntvPrinters.length;j++)
                        printers.add(ntvPrinters[j]);

                // Send notification that all is refreshed
                HardwareNotification hwNote =
                 new
HardwareNotification("com.hmi.hardware.printers.refresh",
                                        this,
                                        0);
                sendNotification(hwNote);
        }


        // MBeanRegistration interface methods
        public void postDeregister(){};
        public void preDeregister(){};
        public void postRegister(Boolean r){};
        public ObjectName preRegister(MBeanServer server,
                                ObjectName name){
                beanServer = server;
                objName = name;
                return name;
        }


        // Observation thread that causes monitor to
        // refresh its cache of information about printers
        class RefreshThread extends Thread {
                private PrinterMonitorMBean parent = null;
                public RefreshThread(PrinterMonitorMBean bean){
                        parent = bean;
                }

                public void run(){
                        while (true){
                            try {
                                Thread.sleep(1000);
                                parent.refresh();
                            }catch(InterruptedException ex){
                                System.out.println(ex);
                            }
                        }
                }
        }
}
```

In this code, you see the implementation of the `init()` method, which calls the native method `getNativePrinterInfo()` from the `jmxprinter.dll` library. This usage is no different from a normal method invocation, except that it is not defined within the `PrinterMonitor` class or a superclass. The `getNativePrinters()` method returns an array of `java.lang.String` objects. Each element of the array represents the name of a printer, such as HP Deskjet 610C.

When an update occurs to the internal list of MBeans, a notification of type `com.hmi.hardware.printers.refreshed` is emitted to listeners. Listeners who receive this message should take the necessary steps to update their view of the printers. I've created a subclass of the `javax.management.Notification` class called `HardwareNotification` to represent hardware-specific notifications. Listing 13-5 shows the source code for the `HardwareNotification` class.

**Listing 13-5: The HardwareNotification class**

```
package com.hmi.hardware;

import javax.management.Notification;

public class HardwareNotification extends Notification{

        public HardwareNotification(String type,Object src,long sn){
                super(type,src,sn);
        }
}
```

The rationale for using a subclass, rather than a regular notification class, with the notification type is that it enables you to extend it in the future. You could add a method that specifically deals with hardware-related attributes. For example, you could have a `getDevice()` method, which returns the device that generated the notification.

A loop is used to process all elements of the array, and with each iteration of the array, a `Printer` object is created and added to the `java.util.List`. This list is returned from the `getPrinters()` method. The Printer class instances in the array were created by the jmxprinter.dll library in the `getNativePrinterInfo()` function. Once all the Printer class instances have been processed, you send a notification using the `sendNotification()` method that you inherited from `NotificationBroadcasterSupport`. You construct the notification with the `HardwareNotification` class. This notification tells listeners that the list of printers has been refreshed and they can query the `PrinterMonitorMBean` again for the list.

The `PrinterMonitorMBean` acts as the organizer and creates instances of the `PrinterMBean` classes. It  also handles calling the native library (as you'll see shortly). The `PrinterMBean` acts as the container for all the information about a printer. When changes occur in a printer, the `PrinterMonitor` MBean will update the attributes of that managed printer.

Now that you have the managed objects and their interfaces defined, you can proceed with building a key component, the dynamic link library. This library will be coded with the C programming language. Don't worry if you've never used C before; I've commented the source where needed to indicate the function of each particular section of code.

# Building the DLL

This section examines the source files needed to build the dynamic link library that will enable you to obtain printer information from the operating system. You'll need utilities for building C source as well as a Java utility named javah. The javah utility is covered in depth in the Tools section of the JDK documentation, but its basic usage is covered here for the purposes of the example. The javah utility is used to generate the header files with the appropriate JNI-style function prototypes. You can then include these header files into your applications as is.

If you've worked with C before, or worked with Visual Studio, then building this example will be old hat to you. If you haven't, don't worry; I attempt to present the steps in as easy a way as possible. You'll learn how to build the header file first because it drives the creation of the source for this example.

## Generating the header file for the PrinterMonitor class

To generate the header file that contains the appropriate JNI-style function prototypes for an application, you use the javah utility. A header file contains a set of commonly used code that can be shared among source files and included in your compiled application.

The javah utility is run against a compiled Java class that contains *native method declarations*. Native method declarations are those that define methods that exist in an external library. When you define a native method you use the native keyword, and do not define the body or implementation of the method because it exists in the native library.

To build the header that you need for the example, run the javah utility against the PrinterMonitor class you created earlier. You need to make sure that you have compiled the PrinterMonitor class since the javah utility runs against a class file, not a source file.

If you run the javah utility with no arguments except for the class, it generates the header file in the same directory in which the utility was run. For this example, it generates a file named com_hmi_hardware_PrinterMonitor.h. Listing 13-6 shows the source code for the header file.

**Listing 13-6: The header file for the PrinterMonitor class**

```
/* DO NOT EDIT THIS FILE - it is machine generated */
#include <jni.h>
/* Header for class com_hmi_hardware_PrinterMonitor */

#ifndef _Included_com_hmi_hardware_PrinterMonitor
#define _Included_com_hmi_hardware_PrinterMonitor
#ifdef __cplusplus
extern "C" {
#endif
/*
 * Class:     com_hmi_hardware_PrinterMonitor
 * Method:    getNativePrinterInfo
```

```
 * Signature: ()[Lcom/hmi/hardware/Printer;
 */
JNIEXPORT jobjectArray JNICALL
Java_com_hmi_hardware_PrinterMonitor_getNativePrinterInfo
  (JNIEnv *, jobject);

#ifdef __cplusplus
}
#endif
#endif
```

You can safely ignore most of this file and focus your attention on the function prototype that begins with the line JNIEXPORT. The return type of the method is defined here and the fully qualified class name becomes part of the function name. When the javah utility is run against the Java class, it takes the package name and replaces the dot separators with an underscore that turns com.hmi.hardware into com_hmi_hardware.

The header file contains the necessary function prototypes for each of the native functions you defined in the PrinterMonitor class. You can create this file for the example by either typing it in as it appears above or by running the javah utility against your own PrinterMonitor class. If you decide to type it in, you can safely leave out the comments. If you change this file manually and then use the javah utility to create a header file in the same directory, your manually typed copy will be overwritten. The javah utility automatically creates the header file in the same directory from which you execute it, but it also has a –d argument to indicate the output directory.

The main source code file that implements the methods in the header file is shown in Listing 13-7. This source file contains the DllMain() method, which is the entry point for a dynamic link library. It's like the main() method of a Java application, and is passed three arguments (which can be ignored for this example). You also see a function prototype for a function named mapStatusToStr(), which is used to map an integer value representing the status of a printer to a string representation.

**Listing 13-7: The source file for the DLL**

```
/***
 *
 * Native library for interfacing with printers
 *
 ***/

#include <jni.h>
#include <jni_md.h>
#include <windows.h>
#include <winspool.h>

#include "com_hmi_hardware_PrinterMonitor.h"

// local method prototype
```

```
LPSTR mapStatusToStr(DWORD state);


BOOL APIENTRY DllMain( HANDLE hModule,
                       DWORD  ul_reason_for_call,
                       LPVOID lpReserved
      )
{
    return TRUE;
}



/**
 *
 * Returns full structure about printer
 *
 **/

JNIEXPORT jobjectArray JNICALL
Java_com_hmi_hardware_PrinterMonitor_getNativePrinterInfo
(JNIEnv *env, jobject obj){

 DWORD dwBytesNeeded;
 DWORD dwBytesRead;
 LPPRINTER_INFO_2 prntInfo2 = NULL;

  // First call to figure out how much
  EnumPrinters(PRINTER_ENUM_LOCAL,
            NULL,
      2, /* use 4 for printer/server name only */
      NULL,
      0,
      &dwBytesNeeded,
      &dwBytesRead);

  // Second call to get actual prt data
  // Allocate structure
  prntInfo2= (LPPRINTER_INFO_2)LocalAlloc(LPTR,dwBytesNeeded);

  EnumPrinters(PRINTER_ENUM_LOCAL,
            NULL,
      2,
      /*(LPBYTE)prntInfo2,*/
      (PBYTE)prntInfo2,
      dwBytesNeeded,
      &dwBytesNeeded,
      &dwBytesRead);
```

```c
// Allocate new String array object to contain the printer names
const char *str = "com/hmi/hardware/Printer";
const char *init = "<init>";
const char *returnType = "()V";
jclass prtCls = env->FindClass(str);
// MethodID for GetMethodID
jmethodID prtObjectID = env->GetMethodID(prtCls,init,returnType);
jobjectArray sArray = NULL;
if (prtCls != NULL) {
   sArray = env->NewObjectArray((int)dwBytesRead,
                                prtCls,
                                (jobject)NULL);

} else {
   printf("Array is null");
   }


// Populate array with printer information
for (int i=0;i< (int)dwBytesRead;i++){
   jobject value = env->NewObject(prtCls,prtObjectID);
   jclass cls = env->GetObjectClass(value);
   // Call all get/set methods here
      env->CallVoidMethod(value,env-
>GetMethodID(prtCls,"setPrinterName","(Ljava/lang/String;)V"),env-
>NewStringUTF(prntInfo2[i].pPrinterName));
   env->CallVoidMethod(value,env-
>GetMethodID(cls,"setManufacturer","(Ljava/lang/String;)V"),env-
>NewStringUTF(" "));
    env->CallVoidMethod(value,env-
>GetMethodID(cls,"setLocation","(Ljava/lang/String;)V"),env-
>NewStringUTF(prntInfo2[i].pLocation));
    env->CallVoidMethod(value,env-
>GetMethodID(cls,"setPort","(Ljava/lang/String;)V"),env-
>NewStringUTF(prntInfo2[i].pPortName));
    env->CallVoidMethod(value,env-
>GetMethodID(cls,"setDriver","(Ljava/lang/String;)V"),env-
>NewStringUTF(prntInfo2[i].pDriverName));
    env->CallVoidMethod(value,env-
>GetMethodID(cls,"setStatus","(Ljava/lang/String;)V"),env-
>NewStringUTF(mapStatusToStr(prntInfo2[i].Status)));
    env->CallVoidMethod(value,env-
>GetMethodID(cls,"setNumberQueuedJobs","(I)V"),(jint)prntInfo2[i].cJobs)
;
    env->CallVoidMethod(value,env-
>GetMethodID(cls,"setComment","(Ljava/lang/String;)V"),env-
>NewStringUTF(prntInfo2[i].pComment));
   // Set array of element with Printer object
   env->SetObjectArrayElement(sArray,i,value);

}
```

```c
  // Free local memory after constructing new Java object
  LocalFree(prntInfo2);

 return sArray;
}



// Maps printer status to a printable string
LPSTR mapStatusToStr(DWORD state){

 switch((int)state){
 case PRINTER_STATUS_BUSY:
     return "Busy";
  break;
 case PRINTER_STATUS_DOOR_OPEN:
  return "Door Open";
  break;
 case PRINTER_STATUS_ERROR:
  return "Error";
  break;
 case PRINTER_STATUS_INITIALIZING:
  return "Initializing";
  break;
 case PRINTER_STATUS_WAITING:
  return "Waiting";
  break;
 case PRINTER_STATUS_PAUSED:
  return "Paused";
  break;
 case PRINTER_STATUS_PROCESSING:
  return "Processing";
  break;
 case PRINTER_STATUS_PRINTING:
  return "Printing";
  break;


    case PRINTER_STATUS_OFFLINE | PRINTER_STATUS_IO_ACTIVE:
  return "Wierd";
  break;
 default:
  return "Ready";
  break;

 }
}
```

The `jmxprinter` DLL contains the one native function you declared in the `PrinterMonitor` class. The `getNativePrinterInfo()` function uses the `PRINTER _INFO_2` structure, which returns detailed information about a printer. This function also creates an array to return, but the array is of `Printer` class objects. Each `Printer` class object that is created is filled out with information returned in the `PRINTER_INFO_2` structure by calling the set accessor methods of the `Printer` class. To call the accessor methods, use the `CallVoidMethod()` function (used to call a Java method which returns void). The JNI specification has a `CallXXXMethod()` definition for different Java types. The `CallVoidMethod()` function, like others, takes the following as arguments:

- A reference to the object represented as an object
- A method ID of the method to call. This method is retrieved using the `GetMethodID()` function
- A set of values representing the arguments to the method

After the newly created `Printer` object has been created, it is placed into an element of the array. When all the `Printer` objects have been processed, the array is returned.

The function `mapStatusToStr()` method is not exposed as a native method that the `PrinterMonitor` class can call. It is used just to return a friendly string version of the status. Normally, the status is stored as a `DWORD` value, which wouldn't make much sense to a user of the application.

Save this source code in a file named `jmxprinter.c`. This code and the header shown previously will be included in the Visual Studio project you'll create in the next section.

## Compiling the DLL

Now that you have the necessary header and source file, you can build a project and compile the source into a binary object represented by the `jmxprinter.dll`. Setting up a project in Visual Studio for this example is quite straightforward. I used Visual C++ 5.0 for this example. You can follow these steps to build the DLL for this example:

1. Launch Visual Studio and select File ⇒New. A dialog box for selecting a project type pops up.

2. Select `Win32 Dynamic Link Library` from the list of project types. In the Project Name field at the top-right, type in **jmxprinter**.

3. Click OK when you are are finished. The workspace for your project is created. At this point, no files have been added to the project.

4. Make sure you are in File view by selecting the File View tab in the workspace window. This window is the one with the tree view of all the files in a project, at the middle-left of the application.

5. Right-click on the project name in the navigation tree and select Add Files To Project.

6. Select the `com_hmi_hardware_PrinterMonitor.h` file and click OK. Follow the same procedure for the `jmxprinter.c` file. Once this step is complete, you are almost ready to compile the project.

7. Before compiling, you need to add the dependent headers for JNI. These headers are distributed with the JDK and can be found in the `%JAVA_HOME%\include` and `%JAVA_HOME%\include\win32` directories. You need to add these directories to the paths the compiler searches when looking for included header files. Recall that the header and source for your files contain includes for `jni.h` and `jni_md.h`.

8. To add the dependent headers to the project, you must update the settings for the project by selecting the Project ⇨ Settings menu selection from the menu bar.

9. When the dialog box appears, select the tab labeled `C++` from the set of tabs at the right.

10. When the tab appears, select PreProcessor from the Category drop-down list.

11. The dialog box will change after you make your selection and a set of fields will appear. One of these fields is labeled Additional include directories. Type in the values specified from Step 7, separating each value with a comma. Figure 13-2 shows the dialog box with the required entries.

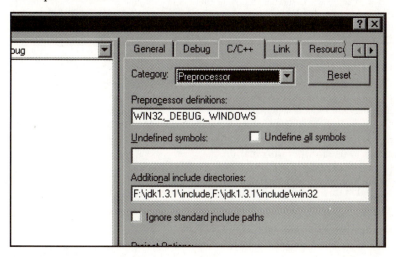

**Figure 13-2:** Settings for the jmxprinter project.

12. Once you have typed in the appropriate entries, click OK. At this point, you are ready to compile. (You will need to change the directories and/or drive letter to match those of your own system.)

13. You can build the project by pressing the F7 key or by selecting Build ⇨ Build jmxprinter.dll from the menu bar. If all goes well, you should have a new directory under the directory in which you created your project, named Debug and containing the DLL. When you create a new project in Visual Studio, VS chooses Debug as the target. When you deploy the DLL, you need to switch to Release as the target. Using Release results in a smaller DLL that contains no debugging symbols.

With the native portion of the example built, you can move on to the next Java portion. Here is where you create the agent for using the `PrinterMonitorMBean`. The JMX agent you'll write will load the `PrinterMonitorMBean` that in turn loads the native library you just created.

> **NOTE:** If you do not have MS Visual Studio, you can find a compiled version of the DLL on the companion Web site for the book. Along with the DLL, you will find instructions for using the GNU compiler and linker.

# Building the agent

The next component you need to build is the JMX agent that will host the MBeans and provide remote connectivity to the agent. The agent performs the typical agent tasks of loading the `PrinterMonitor` MBeans, but it also enables you to connect remotely to the JMX agent using the RMI connector from the Java Dynamic Management Kit (JDMK).

> **NOTE:** The RMI connector is part of the Java Dynamic Management Kit. It is discussed in Chapter 11 in the "Remote Notifications" section. The jdmkrt.jar that is shipped with the JDMK needs to be in your CLASSPATH when you compile and run the HardwareAgent, and later, in the "Building the management console" section of this chapter, the Management Console. Place it in your CLASSPATH before other JMX reference implementations.

The user interface will be implemented using a Swing `JFrame` and `JTable`. Each row of a `JTable` presents a small set of details about a specific printer, such as the name, the documents queued, the status, the location, a comment, and the model of the printer. The data that appears in the `JTable` is constructed from a table model that is an inner class to the agent. The `PrinterTableModel` class extends from the `AbstractTableModel` class to provide the necessary functionality for manipulating the data model for the table. The table model also understands the `Printer` class and how to extract information about its attributes, as well as the proper headings to use for that information.

The agent uses the monitor service to watch the status of each printer, issuing a dialog box to indicate an abnormal status. Listing 13-8 shows the source code for the JMX agent class, `HardwareAgent`.

**Listing 13-8: The HardwareAgent JMX agent**

```
package com.hmi.hardware;

/**
 *
 * This application serves as a JMX Agent
 * with a user interface to allow monitoring
 * of printers defined locally to a computer
 *
 **/

import javax.management.InstanceNotFoundException;
import javax.management.IntrospectionException;
import javax.management.MalformedObjectNameException;
import javax.management.Notification;
import javax.management.NotificationListener;
import javax.management.NotificationBroadcasterSupport;
```

```java
import javax.management.ReflectionException;
import javax.management.ObjectName;
import javax.management.MBeanServer;
import javax.management.MBeanServerFactory;
import java.util.Iterator;
import java.util.List;
import java.util.LinkedList;
import java.util.Set;

import com.sun.jdmk.comm.RmiConnectorAddress;
import com.sun.jdmk.comm.RmiConnectorServer;

public class HardwareAgent extends NotificationBroadcasterSupport{

    private static MBeanServer server = null;
    private static ObjectName prntObject = null;

    public HardwareAgent() {
        server = MBeanServerFactory.createMBeanServer();
    }

    public static void main(String args[]) {

            HardwareAgent agent = new HardwareAgent();

            try {

                RmiConnectorServer rmiConnector = new
RmiConnectorServer(8888);
                server.registerMBean(rmiConnector,null);

                rmiConnector.start();

        prntObject = new ObjectName("PrinterMonitor:name=printer");

                PrinterMonitor prntMon = new PrinterMonitor();
                server.registerMBean(prntMon,prntObject);
                prntMon.init();

                // Get list of printers
                List prnts =
(List)server.getAttribute(prntObject,"Printers");

                // Print list of printers
                Iterator iter = prnts.iterator();
                while (iter.hasNext()){
                    Printer printer = (Printer)iter.next();
```

```
                      // Send Notifications
                      HardwareNotification hwNotify =
                        new
HardwareNotification("com.hmi.hardware.printers.added",agent,0);
                      hwNotify.setUserData(printer);
                      agent.sendNotification(hwNotify);
                }

            }catch(Exception ex){
                  System.out.println(ex);
            }


      }

}
```

What looks like a lot of code in the HardwareAgent class can best be understood by reviewing its various functions. The HardwareAgent class follows these basic steps:

1. Creates an instance of MBeanServer in the constructor.

2. Creates the RmiConnectorServer MBean, registers it, and starts it using the start() method of the RmiConnectorServer class.

3. Creates PrinterMonitorMBean and registers it.

4. Initializes the list of printers in PrinterMonitorMBean by calling the init() method.

5. Retrieves the list of printers and sends a HardwareNotification to any registered listeners.

6. Waits for the program to exit.

With the JMX agent built, you now need to provide a way to monitor the printer MBeans that are registered within it. To do this, you'll need to build a management console that can connect to the JMX agent and access the information about the printer MBeans.

## Building the management console

In this section you'll build a Swing-based management console that you can use to monitor the printer via JMX. The management console will utilize an RMI connector to access the MBeans in the agent and monitor them. You will also establish monitors to and see notifications emitted from the MBeans.

The management console presents the set of printers in a JTable and also has a scrollable area at the bottom to display notifications being emitted from MBeans in the agent. When the management console starts, it establishes a connection to the JMX agent using the RMI connector and establishes itself as a notification listener. It also uses the RMI connector to discover the printer MBeans that have been registered in the MBean Server in the agent. Listing 13-9 shows the source code for the management console.

**Listing 13-9: The JMX management console**

```java
package com.hmi.hardware;


import javax.management.NotificationListener;
import javax.management.Notification;
import javax.management.ObjectName;

import java.awt.BorderLayout;
import javax.swing.*;
import javax.swing.table.AbstractTableModel;
import javax.swing.event.TableModelEvent;
import javax.swing.event.MouseInputAdapter;
import java.awt.event.*;
import java.util.Iterator;
import java.util.List;
import java.util.LinkedList;

import com.sun.jdmk.comm.RmiConnectorClient;
import com.sun.jdmk.comm.RmiConnectorAddress;
import com.sun.jdmk.ServiceName;

public class ManagementConsole extends JFrame implements
NotificationListener{

    private static JFrame frame_ = null;
    private static JTable table_ = null;
    private static PrinterTableModel model_ = null;
    private static RmiConnectorClient rmiClient_ = null;

    public static void main(String args[]) {

            frame_ = new JFrame("JMX Print Monitor");
            frame_.setSize(600,200);
            frame_.addWindowListener(new WindowAdapter(){
                public void windowClosing(WindowEvent evn){
                    // Initiate clean shutdown before exit
                    System.exit(0);
                }
            });

            model_ = new PrinterTableModel();
            table_ = new JTable(model_);
            model_.addTableModelListener(table_);

            JScrollPane scrollPane = new JScrollPane(table_);

frame_.getContentPane().add(BorderLayout.CENTER,scrollPane);
```

```
                    frame_.setVisible(true);

            ManagementConsole agent = new ManagementConsole();

                try {

                    rmiClient_ = new RmiConnectorClient();
                    RmiConnectorAddress rmiAddress =
                      new
RmiConnectorAddress("localhost",8888,ServiceName.RMI_CONNECTOR_SERVER);

                    rmiClient_.connect(rmiAddress);

                    ObjectName name = new
ObjectName("PrinterMonitor:name=printer");

rmiClient_.addNotificationListener(name,agent,null,null);


                    // Get list of printers upon initial start
                    List prnts =
(List)rmiClient_.getAttribute(name,"Printers");

                    // Print list of printers
                    Iterator iter = prnts.iterator();
                    while (iter.hasNext()){
                        Printer printer = (Printer)iter.next();
                        model_.addRow(printer);

                    }
                    // Update table rows

model_.fireTableRowsInserted(model_.getRowCount(),model_.getColumnCount(
));

                }catch(Exception ex){
                    System.out.println(ex);
                }

        }

    // TODO: Should check for specific notifications ?
    public void handleNotification(Notification notif,Object handback){

                    // Assume only printer notification for this example
                    try {

                        ObjectName name = new
ObjectName("PrinterMonitor:name=printer");
```

```
                    // Get list of printers
                    List prnts =
(List)rmiClient_.getAttribute(name,"Printers");

                    model_.removeAllRows();

                    // Print list of printers
                    Iterator iter = prnts.iterator();
                    while (iter.hasNext()){
                        Printer printer = (Printer)iter.next();
                        model_.addRow(printer);
                    }
                    // Update table rows
                    model_.fireTableRowsUpdated(0,model_.getRowCount());

                }catch (Exception ex){
                        System.out.println("Could not update Printers: "
+ ex);
                }
```

[AdventNet-Rev2] This function code is duplicated except
model.removeAllRows(), it can be easily made as one method and will be
called. If example size is small, user may feel comfortable.

```
        }

    // Table model for printer table
    private static class PrinterTableModel extends AbstractTableModel {

            private String columns[] = new
String[]{"Name","Documents","Status","Location","Comment","Model"};
            private List rows = new LinkedList();

            public void removeAllRows(){rows.clear();};
            public String getColumnName(int column){return
columns[column];};
            public int getColumnCount(){return columns.length; };
            public int getRowCount(){return rows.size();};
            public Object getValueAt(int row, int column){
                Object retValue = "";
                Printer prt = (Printer)rows.get(row);
                switch (column) {
                    case 0:
                        retValue = prt.getPrinterName();
                        break;
                    case 1:
                        retValue = new
Integer(prt.getNumberQueuedJobs());
                        break;
```

```
                case 2:
                    retValue = prt.getStatus();
                    break;
                case 3:
                    retValue = prt.getLocation();
                    break;
                case 4:
                    retValue = prt.getComment();
                    break;
                case 5:
                    retValue = prt.getDriver();
                    break;
            }
            return retValue;
        };
        public void addRow(Printer printer){
            rows.add(printer);
        };
    }

}
```

The ManagementConsole Java application starts by setting up the user interface components consisting of a JFrame that is the main window of the application. You then set up a JTable that will hold the information about each printer. The management console initializes its display of printers for the first time by retrieving the value of the getAttribute() method of the RmiConnectorClient class.

When a notification arrives, the agent retrieves a list of printers using the getAttribute() method of the RmiConnectorClient class. This causes the list of printers in the PrinterMonitor MBean's printers attribute to be retrieved. Next, the table model for the JTable is cleared and then refilled with data. Rather than updating individual rows in this example, it's better to just remove all rows and then add them again because you'll have only a few rows at most.

After the rows have been removed and re-added, use the fireTableRowsUpdated() method to tell the JTable to redraw itself. The agent automatically assumes that the notification is for new printers being added because that is the only notification that is to be sent. The PrinterMonitorMBean only emits a notification when printer information has successfully been retrieved and updated internally to it.

To tie the description of what the agent does more closely to the code, the main() method covers steps 1 through 7 from the previous section. The handleNotification() method waits for new hardware notifications to arrive. Currently, there should only be new notifications for new printers that are added. You could also create a NotificationFilter object to control which notifications you want to receive.

The inner class `PrinterTableModel` serves as the programmatic representation of the data behind the rows and columns you see in the `JTable`. It contains all of the information about the rows and columns and the data behind them, as well as accessor methods for retrieving the rows, updating the rows, retrieving column header information, and removing the rows from the model.

Now that you've built the management console you are ready to try it out. You'll also need to make sure you've built the JMX agent presented in the "Building the agent" section of this chapter.

## Running the example

To run the example, you first need to make sure that the directory containing the jmxprinter.dll library can be found in your PATH environment variable. The easiest thing to do is copy the DLL from the directory in which you compiled it to the same directory in which you will execute the `HardwareAgent` application. When the Java runtime attempts to load the library, it will look in the current directory. You need to make sure you compile the `HardwareAgent`, `Printer` and `PrinterMonitor`, and `ManagementConsole` classes as well.

You also need to make sure that the jdmkrt.jar from the JDMK is in your CLASSPATH. You used this JAR in the "Building the agent" section earlier in this chapter. You need to make sure it appears in your CLASSPATH before any other JMX reference implementation.

Once you have copied the DLL compiled the application, you can launch it using the following command:

```
java com.hmi.hardware.HardwareAgent
```

If you execute this example and receive the following Java exception, this is an indication that the DLL cannot be found in the path:

```
Exception in thread "main" java.lang.UnsatisfiedLinkError: no jmxprinter
in java
.library.path
        at java.lang.ClassLoader.loadLibrary(Unknown Source)
        at java.lang.Runtime.loadLibrary0(Unknown Source)
        at java.lang.System.loadLibrary(Unknown Source)
        at
com.hmi.hardware.PrinterMonitor.<clinit>(PrinterMonitor.java:43)
        at com.hmi.hardware.HardwareAgent.main(HardwareAgent.java:86)
```

This could occur because you failed to copy the DLL into the same directory from which you executed the `HardwareAgent`, or because the DLL is not in a directory that Windows will search. You can resolve this problem by making sure that the DLL exists in the same directory as the `HardwareAgent` application.

When the application starts the view, what you see may vary from what is presented here, depending on the number and types of printers that you have installed. The system on which I ran this example has an HP Deskjet 610C installed, and a fax printer was installed along with the operating system. The information you see is taken directly from the output of the PrinterMonitorMBean, which in turn uses the jmxprinter.dll native methods to retrieve the information from the operating system. Depending on the current printer activity, the values for status and number of documents might be different as well.

## Running the management console

Once the agent is running you can run the management console by executing the following command:

```
java com.hmi.hardware.ManagementConsole
```

Figure 13-3 shows what the management console looks like running on my system.

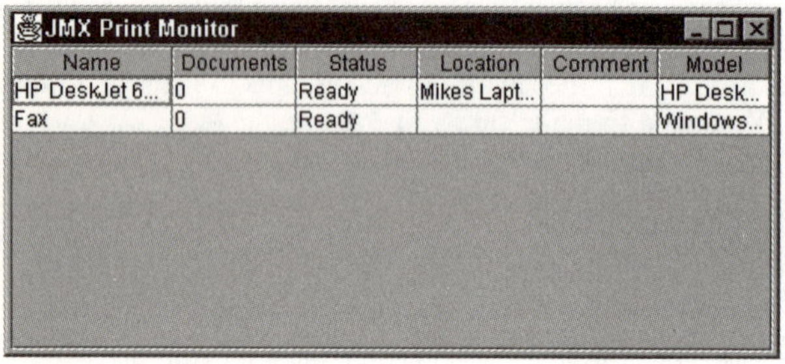

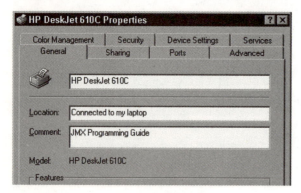

**Figure 13-3:** JMX Print Monitor running on Windows 2000.

To further illustrate the function of this application, you can open the options panel for this printer and change some values. Change the location attribute of the printer configuration and send a couple of documents to print. The display should automatically be updated to reflect these changes.

The options pane to configure the printer on Windows 2000 can be accessed by selecting Start ⇨ Settings ⇨ Printers. When the list of printers is displayed, right-click on it and select Properties from the menu. You should see a dialog box like the one shown in Figure 13-4.

**Figure 13-4:** Printer dialog box in Windows 2000.

The values displayed in Figure 13-5 reflect the updates, which I then made permanent by clicking the Apply button at the bottom-right of the dialog box (not visible in Figure 13-4). After clicking Apply, you should see the values reflected in the JMX print monitor display. I also sent two test pages to the printer, reflected in the values shown in the JMX print monitor.

| Name | Documents | Status | Location | Comment | Model |
|------|-----------|--------|----------|---------|-------|
| HP DeskJet ... | 2 | Ready | Connected t... | JMX Progra... | HP DeskJet ... |
| Fax | 0 | Ready | | | Windows N... |

**Figure 13-5:** JMX print monitor values update dynamically.

As you can see from the display, the values have dynamically changed to reflect the current state. Each time this dynamic update occurs, the `PrinterMonitorMBean`'s internal list of printers is updated, as are the MBeans represented by the `PrinterMBean` class. With these updates occurring automatically, you have a near real-time view of the printers, and obtain some state information about them.

## Summary

In this chapter, you learned how to expose the management of a hardware device using JMX. You created a `PrinterMonitorMBean` that represents a print monitor whose job is to keep a list of MBeans representing printer status updates. The print monitor uses the dynamic link library to communicate with Windows and gather information about the status of each installed printer. The print monitor uses a thread to periodically call the `refresh()` method, rebuilding its list of printers each time the thread's `run()` method executes the `getNativePrinterInfo()` method from the `jmxprinter.dll` library.

# Chapter 14

# Managing Servers Remotely

System management encompasses components such as applications and hardware devices, and it can extend to more abstract processes. You can monitor traffic on a network and look at packets of information zipping back and forth from device to device. Similarly, a network administrator can use system management tools to watch traffic coming into and going out of a network. He might also use these same tools to monitor the state of file servers, print servers, and application servers.

In addition to the different functions of these servers, each server could be from a different vendor. Moreover, various tools may be needed to connect each of these different servers, which might require additional administration. In the most complicated scenario, each of these could have a different administrative interface; one might have an MS Windows application, another might have a simple command-line interface, and a third might have a Web interface. Having different interfaces makes a system administrator's job extremely difficult, if not impossible. Not only would you need a machine capable of running all of these tools simultaneously, you would need to be able to do this remotely.

Imagine if an NT or Linux server required that you launch a system administration tool locally, or on the server itself, in order to administer it. This situation could be further compounded by the proximity of servers to one another. They could be in the same room, in different rooms on the same floor, in different buildings, or even scattered around the world, such as those connected to Wide Area Networks (WANs).

The importance of a single management interface and the capability to use this interface remotely is important. It not only makes a system administrator's job easier (and, frankly, possible) it also reduces the costs associated with administering and maintaining systems. Without remote administration, you would need several system administrators present, one for each location.

Many, if not all, of the examples that have been demonstrated thus far in the book have dealt more with single applications and components than with collections of components. You launched a JMX agent that loads a couple of simple MBeans and then prints some information about them or manipulates some of their attributes. Much of the information contained in these MBeans was present only at runtime.

In this chapter, you'll learn how to use JMX to monitor the runtime state of a server, both locally and remotely, including logging and administration. In particular, you'll explore some of the system management components of the BEA WebLogic Application Server version 7.0, hereafter referred to as *WLS*.

> **NOTE:** Before beginning this chapter you should have a general understanding of how WLS works and how to start a WLS server instance. Please consult the WLS documentation at `e-docs.bea.com` if you have any questions.

# Using WebLogic Server MBeans

This chapter examines some of the JMX facilities in the WebLogic Application Server 7.0. First you'll learn about accessing WebLogic MBeans that enable you to work with the WLS server configuration and set up and monitor server values. The number and types of MBeans in the WebLogic management library is extensive, and this chapter does not attempt to cover every available MBean. Consult the WebLogic JavaDoc and the WebLogic JMX overview guide for a more complete look at the JMX facilities present in the WebLogic product. You can find the WebLogic documentation at `e-docs.bea.com`.

WLS includes a host of components that enable you to track the state of various runtime and configuration components of a server or a cluster of servers. The MBeans used in the WebLogic server are categorized as follows:

♦ Administration

♦ Configuration

♦ Runtime

Each category includes a set of MBeans that exposes the management functionality of that variety. For example, there are MBeans that deal with the configuration of a WebLogic server; MBeans that deal with the runtime state of a WebLogic server; and MBeans that deal with administering a WebLogic server. WebLogic organizes administration using an administration server, which may be responsible for one or more managed servers. The administration server synchronizes configuration data between managed servers, among other functions.

The MBean names also follow a specific naming convention that indicates the function of the MBean. MBeans that have no suffix are considered administration MBeans. MBeans that have just the suffix `MBean` indicate a configuration MBean, and an MBean with a `Runtime` suffix indicates an MBean representing the runtime state of a WLS component. For example

♦ `ServerMBean` represents the configuration interface for a WLS server

♦ `ServerRuntimeMBean` represents the runtime state interface for a WLS server

Not all MBeans in WLS will have each of the three types (configuration, administration, and runtime) of interface. Figure 14-1 illustrates a hypothetical domain configuration. In this diagram, the largest outer circle with a box labeled `TheShire` is the WebLogic domain. The four circles labeled `Aragorn`, `Frodo`, `WLS1`, and `WLS2` are WebLogic servers. Additionally, the server labeled `Aragorn` is the WebLogic administration server for this domain.

Each server in a WebLogic domain is represented from a management perspective by a series of MBeans that perform specific functions. You already know that with JMX, when you want to manage an MBean, you first need to talk to the MBean Server of the agent with which the MBean is registered. In the WebLogic management system, the MBean Server of a host is represented by an instance of the `WebLogic.management.MBeanHome` interface.

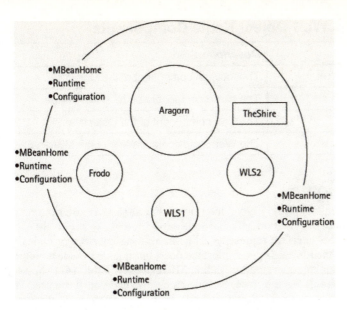

**Figure 14-1:** A WebLogic domain with four WebLogic servers.

# WebLogic JMX fundamentals

When you begin to work with WLS JMX, understanding a few basic concepts will make your life easier. When you write JMX applications, you work with a number of core components, such as the MBeanServer interface, the ObjectName class, and the DynamicMBean interface. If you are working with standard MBeans, then you need to understand the management interface of these beans. To use WLS JMX, you need to understand how WLS implements these core components.

The ObjectName class is used to build a string that uniquely identifies an MBean, as you have already learned. The WebLogic JMX support subclasses the ObjectName class from the JMX API to provide a specific set of constructors and accessors for building WebLogic-specific object names. The WebLogic.management.WebLogicObjectName class is used to build object names for use with WLS MBeans. The WebLogicObjectName enables you to build object names that follow WLS-specific rules.

The string values used to build object names have a few rules that govern their syntax. As you learned earlier in this book, the object name consists of an optional domain part, followed by a colon, followed by a set of one or more key/value pairs. If the domain part of the object name is omitted, a default domain defined by JMX is used.

In WLS, the string used to build object names needs to consist of four components that are also represented by static fields in the WebLogicObjectName class. Table 14-1 describes the four components of a WLS object name.

## Table 14-1 WLS Object Name Components

| Field | Description |
|---|---|
| WebLogicObjectName.LOCATION | The location component of the ObjectName |
| WebLogicObjectName.NAME | The name component of the ObjectName |
| WebLogicObjectName.TYPE | The type component of the ObjectName |
| WebLogicObjectName.WEBLOGIC | The WebLogic domain name of the MBean |

## Finding an MBeanHome

The MBeanHome interface presents a strongly typed interface to the MBeanServer running on the agent. It also provides an accessor method named getMBeanServer() to access the instance of the MBeanServer this interface represents. The MBeanHome interface provides many of the same methods that the MBeanServer interface does, but it also provide a plethora of other methods that make obtaining, querying, or finding MBeans easy. Table 14-2 shows a subset of the methods of the MBeanHome interface. Included are those that you'll see used later in this chapter and those that are most useful. Some methods, such as getMBean(), support multiple overloading. Consult the WebLogic JavaDoc for a complete list.

## Table 14-2 Subset of MBeanHome Interface Methods

| Method | Description |
|---|---|
| getActiveDomain() | Returns a DomainMBean representing the active domain of this server |
| getAdminMBean(String name,String type) | Returns a ConfigurationMBean for the specified admininstration server |
| getAllMBeans() | Returns a java.util.Set containing a list of the MBeans registered in this server |
| getMBean(ObjectName bean) | Returns a WebLogicMBean instance representing the object name supplied |
| getMBean(String name,String type) | Returns a WebLogicMBean instance with the name and type supplied |
| getMBeansByType(String type) | Returns a java.util.Set with the type specified |
| getMBeanServer() | Returns the MBean Server that this MBeanHome interface wraps. The returned object is an instance of the RemoteMBeanServer interface. |

Of course, you can also use the methods of the MBeanServer that underlies the MBeanHome interface instance that you retrieve. You first need to use the getMBeanServer() method, and then you call the normal methods such as getAttribute(), setAttribute(), or invoke(). As you will see later, however, WLS MBeans divide each component into a runtime view of a managed resource, and then back it with a configuration MBean for that component. The configuration MBean exposes the attributes and operations necessary for configuring that component.

To use the MBeanHome interface, you must retrieve an instance of it from the server you want to work with. You can retrieve an instance of the MBeanHome interface using a JNDI lookup. You can specify three qualifiers when determining which MBeanHome interface you want:

♦ MBeanHome.JNDI_NAME

♦ MBeanHome.ADMIN_JNDI_NAME

♦ MBeanHome.LOCAL_JNDI_NAME

Under most circumstances, the MBeanHome.JNDI_NAME is the qualifier you want to use. This enables you to access a remote MBean Server, and you can also use it to access an MBean Server running locally. The MBeanHome.ADMIN_JNDI_NAME qualifier is somewhat different from the other two qualifiers because it accesses a domainwide MBeanHome that represents the administration management view of a domain, whereas the MBeanHome.LOCAL_JNDI_NAME enables you to access the MBeanHome of the local server. When you use the MBeanHome.JNDI_NAME qualifier, you add the name of the server to the end to get the complete address. For example, to access a server named Aragorn, you would use the following syntax:

```
MBeanHome home = (MBeanHome)ctx.lookup(MBeanHome.JNDI_Name+".Aragorn");
```

The other two qualifiers are used as they are with no modification. Listing 14-1 shows the source of an application that retrieves the MBeanHome for a server named Aragorn running on the same host as the application. Before running this application, you need to ensure that you have a WLS server running. You also need to change the values of the username and password variables to match those of your WLS server.

**Listing 14-1: Retrieving the MBeanHome**

```
package com.hmi.wls;


/**
 *
 *
 * Client application that access WLS MBeanHome
 *
 *
 **/

import javax.naming.Context;
import javax.naming.InitialContext;
```

```
import javax.naming.AuthenticationException;
import javax.naming.CommunicationException;
import javax.naming.NamingException;
import weblogic.jndi.Environment;
import weblogic.management.MBeanHome;

public class WLSMBeanHome{

    public static void main(String args[]){

        MBeanHome home = null;

        String url = "t3://localhost:7001";
        String username = "YOURUSERNAME";
        String password = "YOURPASSWORD";
        String SERVER_NAME = "Aragorn";

        try {
            //Obtaining an MBeanHome Using JNDI
            Environment env = new Environment();
            env.setProviderUrl(url);
            env.setSecurityPrincipal(username);
            env.setSecurityCredentials(password);
            Context ctx = env.getInitialContext();
            home = (MBeanHome)ctx.lookup(MBeanHome.JNDI_NAME +
                            "." + SERVER_NAME);
            System.out.println(SERVER_NAME +
                            " MBeanHome was located");

            ctx.close();

        } catch (Exception ex) {
            System.out.println("Exception: " + ex);
        }

    }

}
```

The WLSMBeanHome application attempts to look up the MBeanHome of the WLS server
running on the localhost at port 7001. To look up the MBeanHome, you need to provide
some security information so that the request can be authenticated. The security information is
provided via the WebLogic.jndi.Environment class, which is a WLS-specific class that
serves to contain the environment information associated with a JNDI context. In this
example, we purposely omit the username and password used to access the WLS server. You
must replace these with the username and password of the WLS server you run this
application against.

If you want to construct your own set of environment properties, rather than use the WebLogic `Environment` class, you can use a `java.util.Hashtable`, which can be passed to the constructor of the `javax.naming.InitialContext` class. The `t3` protocol specifier in the URL is a WLS-specific protocol that is used heavily when dealing with WLS. When writing WLS JNDI applications, you can optionally use the `Environment` class.

For those familiar with JNDI and constructing an `InitialContext` object, the code for creating the `InitialContext` in this example could be rewritten as follows:

```
Hashtable env = new Hashtable();
env.put(CONTEXT.INITIAL_CONTEXT_FACTORY,"
weblogic.jndi.WLInitialContextFactory");
env.put(CONTEXT.PROVIDER_URL,url);
env.put(CONTEXT.SECURITY_PRINCIPAL,username);
env.put(CONTEXT.SECURITY_CREDENTIALS,password);
Context ctx = new InitialContext(env);
```

The WLS API provides some defaults if you use the `Environment` class and don't specify the username, password, URL, or initial context factory properties. These defaults are provided by the `Environment` class as follows:

♦ If you don't set the `INITIAL_CONTEXT_FACTORY` property, it is set to `WLInitialContextFactory`

♦ If you don't set the username or password, they are set to `guest` and `guest`, respectively

♦ If you don't set the URL of the server, it is set to the value of `t3://localhost:7001`

Once you've created an initial context and retrieved an instance of the `MBeanHome` interface, you can start accessing beans. The number of different MBean types in the WLS management API is mind-boggling; it seems they have thought of everything. Browsing through the JavaDoc for the `weblogic.management.configuration` package will show you all of the MBeans available to management applications. You'll examine those with relevance to server functions and server runtime monitoring in this chapter.

> **NOTE:** If you are creating an initial context from within a WLS server, you don't need to specify any properties. The WLS server sets the properties when constructing an initial context there. Setting the initial context from within a WLS server occurs when using a servlet or JavaServer Page. Additionally, the WLS API provides its own version of the `javax.naming.Context` interface, and defines a set of additional properties. You can view those additional properties in the JavaDoc for the `weblogic.jndi.WLContext` interface.

## Using the Helper class

In addition to constructing an initial context to find an `MBeanHome` interface, the WebLogic management API provides an additional class called `Helper`. This class is in the same package as the `MBeanHome` interface, and it is used to obtain the `MBeanHome` but without having to explicitly create an `InitialContext` object.

There are two methods in the Helper class. The first is getAdminMBeanHome(), which is used to obtain the MBeanHome of the administration server for a domain. The second is getMBeanHome(), which is used to obtain the MBeanHome interface of a WLS server. Listing 14-2 shows the use of the Helper class to obtain an MBeanHome.

> **NOTE:** Before you run this example, make sure to change the username, password, and SERVER_NAME variables to match those of the server you want to access.

**Listing 14-2: Using the Helper class to obtain the MBeanHome interface**

```
package com.hmi.wls;


/**
 *
 *
 * Client application that access WLS MBeans
 *
 *
 **/

import weblogic.management.Helper;
import weblogic.management.MBeanHome;

public class WLSMBeanHomeHelper{

        public static void main(String args[]){

                MBeanHome home = null;

                String url = "t3://localhost:7001";
                String username = "YOURUSERNAME";
                String password = "YOURPASSWORD";
                String SERVER_NAME = "Aragorn";

                try {
                        home = (MBeanHome)Helper.getMBeanHome(username,
                                                        password,
                                                        url,
                                                        SERVER_NAME);
                        System.out.println(SERVER_NAME +
                                        " MBeanHome was located");


                } catch (Exception ex) {
                        System.out.println("Exception: " + ex);
                }
```

```
        }

}
```

All MBean interfaces in WLS extend a super interface named WebLogicMBean, either directly or indirectly. This interface contains a standard set of methods that are inherited by all WLS MBeans. The WebLogicMBean interface extends from the standard JMX interfaces DynamicMBean, MbeanRegistration, and NotificationBroadcaster, which are discussed in Chapters 5, 8, and 11, respectively.

The WebLogicMBean provides the standard methods for obtaining the MBeanInfo object for an MBean, acting as a notification broadcaster and receiving notifications of MBean registration events. These standard methods, of course, are inherited from the interfaces that the WebLogicMBean interface extends from. Table 14-3 describes the declared methods of the WebLogicMBean interface.

### Table 14-3    WebLogicMBean interface methods

| Method | Description |
|---|---|
| getMBeanInfo() | Returns an instance of the javax.management.MBeanInfo interface representing the management interface for this MBean |
| getName() | Returns a java.lang.String representing the name of the MBean |
| getObjectName() | Returns a WebLogic.management.WebLogicObjectName class representing the JMX object name for this MBean |
| getParent() | Returns a WebLogic.management.WebLogicMBean interface instance representing the parent of this MBean. This attribute is not configurable. |
| getType() | Returns a java.lang.String representing the type of this MBean |
| isCachingDisabled() | Returns a primitive Java boolean indicating whether caching in proxies is disabled |
| isRegistered() | Returns a primitive Java boolean indicating whether this MBean is still registered in an MBean Server |
| setName() | Sets the name of the MBean |

Subclasses of the WebLogicMBean interface often declare methods that are specific to functionality required by an MBean implementing that interface.

You have now had an overview of the WLS architecture and how JMX fits into that architecture. You have also learned some of the fundamentals of using JMX in WLS, such as the core classes and interfaces used to access the MBeanServer and create an object name, and the syntax for constructing object names. This information should provide you with enough foundation to write a simple application that prints information about MBeans in WLS. The goal of this application is simply to explore the MBeans present in WLS. Later in this chapter, you'll build a Web-based version of this application that contains more features.

You're going to re-use some code from Chapter 4 of this book to display a Swing JTree containing the management information about MBeans running in a WebLogic server. The application will connect to a WLS and retrieve the MBeanHome interface for that server. Finally, it will retrieve all the MBeans using the getAllMBeans() method of that interface, and then populate the JTree with the information of each MBean returned.

The code you're going to re-use is the MBeanUtils class that was first introduced in Chapter 4. This class contains the buildBeanInfoTree() method, which takes a DefaultMutableNode instance and an MBeanInfo instance. This method modifies the JTree in place, and when the method exits, the JTree is populated with your management information. Listing 14-3 shows the source of the WLSMBeanClient application.

**Listing 14-3: Displaying WebLogic MBeans**

```
package com.hmi.wls;


/**
 *
 *
 * Client application that access WLS MBeans
 *
 *
 **/

import javax.management.ObjectName;
import javax.management.MBeanInfo;
import javax.management.MBeanAttributeInfo;
import javax.naming.Context;
import javax.naming.InitialContext;
import javax.naming.AuthenticationException;
import javax.naming.CommunicationException;
import javax.naming.NamingException;
import java.util.Iterator;
import java.util.Set;
import weblogic.jndi.Environment;
import weblogic.management.MBeanHome;
import weblogic.management.RemoteMBeanServer;
import weblogic.management.WebLogicMBean;
import weblogic.management.WebLogicObjectName;

import javax.swing.*;
import javax.swing.tree.*;
import java.awt.BorderLayout;
import java.awt.event.*;
import java.awt.Event.*;
```

```java
import com.hmi.mbean.utils.MBeanUtils;


public class WLSMBeanClient {

    public static void main(String args[]){

        JFrame frame = new JFrame("MBean Explorer");
        frame.setSize(400,400);

        frame.addWindowListener(new WindowAdapter(){
            public void windowClosing(WindowEvent ev){
                System.exit(0);
            }
        });

        new WLSMBeanClient(frame);

    }

    public WLSMBeanClient(JFrame frame){

        MBeanHome home = null;

        String url = "t3://localhost:7001";
        String username = "YOURSYSTEM";
        String password = "YOURPASSWORD";
        String SERVER_NAME = "Aragorn";

        try {
            //Obtaining an MBeanHome Using JNDI
            Environment env = new Environment();
            env.setProviderUrl(url);
            env.setSecurityPrincipal(username);
            env.setSecurityCredentials(password);
            Context ctx = env.getInitialContext();
            home = (MBeanHome)ctx.lookup(MBeanHome.JNDI_NAME + "."

                                          SERVER_NAME);
            System.out.println(SERVER_NAME +
                            " MBeanHome found externally");

            frame.getContentPane().setLayout(new BorderLayout());
            DefaultMutableTreeNode top =
                new DefaultMutableTreeNode("MBean");

            // New instance of MBean Utils //
            MBeanUtils beanUtils = new MBeanUtils();
```

```
            // Get all WLS MBeans registered in this server
            Set allBeans = home.getAllMBeans();
            Iterator beanIter = allBeans.iterator();
            while (beanIter.hasNext()){
                 WebLogicMBean wlBean =
                    (WebLogicMBean)beanIter.next();
                 MBeanInfo info = wlBean.getMBeanInfo();
                 beanUtils.buildBeanInfoTree(top,
                                             info,
                                       wlBean.getObjectName());
            }
            JTree tree = new JTree(top);
            JScrollPane scrollPane = new JScrollPane(tree);

            frame.getContentPane().add("Center",scrollPane);

            frame.setVisible(true);

            ctx.close();
        } catch (AuthenticationException ex) {
            System.out.println("Authentication Exception: " +
                                ex);
        } catch (CommunicationException ex) {
            System.out.println("Communication Exception: " +
                                ex);
        } catch (NamingException ex) {
            System.out.println("Naming Exception: " + ex);
        } catch (Exception ex) {
            System.out.println("Exception: " + ex);
        }

    }

}
```

The output from running the WLSMBeanClient application is shown in Figure 14-2. The application may take a minute to start because of the large number of MBeans present in a particular WLS server. Later, you'll add the capability to filter the MBeans shown and select a particular server for viewing.

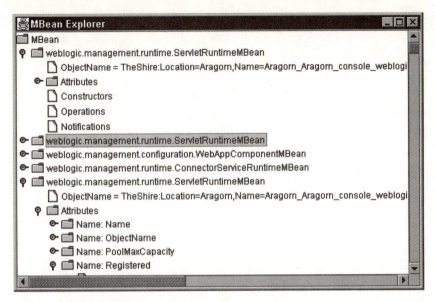

**Figure 14-2:** Viewing WebLogic MBean information.

From Figure 14-2, you can see a lot of interesting information about the MBeans running in a particular WebLogic server. The top level of the tree is a node labeled MBean. Each node under the top-level node represents a single MBean instance and is labeled with the class name of the MBean found. Under the MBean-specific node is the information about the management interface. This information includes the object name, and the attributes, constructors, operations, and notifications found in the `MBeanInfo` class retrieved from each MBean.

In my particular WLS server, I had over 500 MBeans registered. From Figure 14-2, you can see an MBean with a class name of `ServletRuntimeMBean`. I expanded this node in the tree to display some of the attributes of the MBean. If I expanded a particular node under the attributes node, I would see more detailed information about a particular attribute, such as whether it was `read-write`, or whether it has an `is` accessor method. The majority of MBeans and associated management attributes and operations have descriptions, to give you an idea of each attribute's or operation's purpose. Figure 14-3 shows the `ServletRuntimeMBean` expanded to show several attributes.

In this figure, you can see several of the attributes that exist for the `ServletRuntimeMBean`. This view can also give you an idea of the types of metrics that you could capture for a particular type of managed resource. For the `ServletRuntimeMBean`, you could see how many times the servlet was reloaded, how many times it was executed, as well as some average execution times. You can also find some normal MBean-specific information, such as the ObjectName of the MBean.

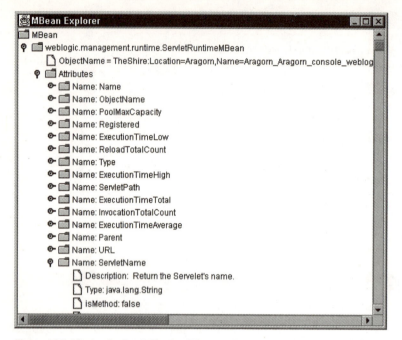

**Figure 14-3:** Viewing the ServletRuntimeMBean attributes with MBean Explorer.

## Specific WLS MBean types

The MBeans shown in the previous examples give you a big picture of what WLS enables you to manage. This section describes some key MBeans that you might have seen in the MBean Explorer. Table 14-4 lists some of these key WLS MBeans and provides a brief description of each. The MBeans listed deal with both runtime and configuration aspects of a WebLogic server and WebLogic domain.

### Table 14-4   Key WebLogic MBeans

| MBean | Description |
|---|---|
| ServerRuntime | Represents the runtime view of a WebLogic server |
| Server | Represents the configuration of a WebLogic server |
| DomainRuntime | Represents the runtime view of a WebLogic domain. WebLogic servers belong to domains. |
| Domain | Represents the configuration of a domain |

| MBean | Description |
|---|---|
| `WebServerRuntime` | Represents the runtime view of a Web server running in a WebLogic server. Each WebLogic server has at most one Web server. |
| `WebServer` | Represents the configuration for a Web server |
| `ServerLifeCycleRuntimeMBean` | Represents the life cycle of a server MBean. You use this MBean to start and stop a server. |

The `WLSMBeanClient` application has given you a picture of the JMX MBeans in a WebLogic server. The types of MBeans present should give you an idea of what things you can manage and monitor using these management beans. You could write your own servlet-specific monitoring console for a particular application or for all servlets running in a WebLogic server. You could also view the types of notifications for a particular MBean and then establish notification listeners using this information.

The rest of this chapter focuses on building a Web-based management application that enables you to monitor servlets running in a WebLogic server. The example utilizes JavaServer Pages (JSP) to build the application and present the user interface for the application.

## Monitoring WebLogic Servers with JMX

As you have seen in previous examples, WLS includes MBeans for many of the components that represent a WebLogic domain, including server, Web server, and cluster, just to name a few. We created a simple Java Swing application to browse the MBeans of a particular WLS server. In this example, you're going to build a Web-based version of the preceding example, but only to display information specific to servers.

You'll be making use of the MBeans representing a WLS domain, and the MBeans representing a WLS server. From these two sets of MBeans, you'll enable users to navigate and see information about a server, and alter the state of a server. You'll write a few JavaServer Pages that provide the user interface for the application. For this example, you'll also build two views of the management information.

The first view is geared toward viewing the raw attributes and operations of an MBean. Essentially, it will display the contents of the `MBeanInfo` class for a particular MBean. The second view is geared more toward a friendlier user interface, and will present management information and operations from a more task-oriented angle. For example, if you are looking at a Web server component of a WLS and it has a `stop()` operation, this is presented as something like "Stop this Web server."

This application is hosted inside a WebLogic server and utilizes one other WLS server to demonstrate the capability to manage multiple servers. These WLS servers will all be running on the same host for this example. The example also assumes that you have WLS installed.

Before continuing, you should familiarize yourself with an entity called the *NodeManager*. The WLS NodeManager is a daemon process that enables you to remotely start and stop WebLogic servers. You can run this process as an NT service; you can start it manually from the command line; or, on Unix, you can run it as a daemon process. You must have a NodeManager on each host from which you want to access a WebLogic server remotely.

The following section covers some basics used to set up this particular example, but the WebLogic Administration Guide includes many more details on working with NodeManagers. You can view the Administration Guide online at e-docs.bea.com.

## Setting up a NodeManager

Setting up and running a NodeManager is actually quite simple and can be done in a few simple steps. You can launch a NodeManager in a few ways. One way is to install and run it as an NT service. Running the NodeManager as an NT service has the added benefit that the NodeManager is automatically started and stopped when the system is rebooted. On Unix machines, the NodeManager can be set up to run as part of a startup shell script.

The second way involves manually typing the command to start the NodeManager Java application. This command is typed in at a command prompt and is relatively straightforward, but it requires that you have the appropriate environment variable CLASSPATH set. The last way involves using a script provided with WLS that has the appropriate environment variables set and issues the correct commands to start a NodeManager. I recommend the last method if you want to get up and running quickly or want to experiment with the NodeManager. You should, however, review the WebLogic documentation for the NodeManager, as a number of default values are provided for some key attributes — such as security — which should be changed before running a NodeManager in a production environment.

In the %BEA_HOME%\weblogic700\server\bin folder are two scripts: startNodeManager.cmd for Windows NT and startNodeManager.sh for Unix systems. You can use these to start a NodeManager. Before you use the NodeManager, however, you must configure a WebLogic server to identify which NodeManager can be used to start it remotely.

Setting up a NodeManager requires two basic steps:

1. Creating and configuring a Machine instance using the WLS administration console.
2. Configuring a WLS server to use that Machine instance.

The following section explains these steps in detail.

### Configuring a WebLogic server for a NodeManager

To configure a WebLogic server to be started remotely, you must configure at least one machine in the WebLogic domain where the NodeManager will run. To configure the machine, use the WebLogic administration console to indicate which machine to use. To access the WLS administration console, point your Web browser at http://localhost:7001. (The port and host name may be different depending on your installation.) By default, no machine is selected. In the WLS administration console, select the General tab for the server. On the field named Machine you will find a drop-down list of NodeManagers.

To add a NodeManager to this drop-down list, you can use the navigation tree at the left of the console. Alternatively, from the main start page of the administration console of WLS, select the hyperlink labeled `Machine`. To use the navigation tree, find a node in the tree labeled Machine. Using either method sends you to the same page for configuring the NodeManager. When you arrive at the page, you will see a list of currently configured machines, as well as options for creating a NodeManager for a Unix or Windows machine. For this example, you should select the Create a New Machine option, which will present a form for creating a Windows-based NodeManager.

In this case, all you need to do is change the name; if you have no preference, you can leave the default machine name in the field. You do need to change the name and click the Apply button before you can change other attributes of the configuration. You don't need to change anything else, however, so the defaults will be acceptable. The NodeManager will be listening on port `5555` for administrative requests to start and stop WebLogic servers.

The Servers tab of the NodeManager configuration page lists the available servers that you want to be able to start remotely. If you already have WebLogic servers created when you create the NodeManager, they will automatically be selected for use with the new NodeManager.

### Configuring the WLS server

After you create the NodeManager, you need to return to the WLS server configuration General tab. Change the value of the drop-down to be the name of the NodeManager. Now there is one final step. You need to indicate some necessary configuration parameters that will be passed to the NodeManager when starting a new WLS server instance. Once you have indicated that a WLS server can be started remotely, a new Remote tab appears at the far right of the configuration page for a WebLogic server. On this page, you can specify the following parameters:

- BEA Home
- Root Directory
- CLASSPATH
- Arguments
- Security Policy File
- UserName
- Password

If you do not specify values for these fields, the NodeManager uses the values that were used to start it. Optionally, the NodeManager can be passed a number of system properties that control these values as well. For this example, I provided the following values for my installation:

- BEA Home — F:\bea
- Root Directory — F:\bea
- CLASSPATH — F:\bea\weblogic700\server\lib\weblogic.jar

♦ UserName — The username for the administrator

♦ Password — The password for the administrator

After you set the values, click Apply to save them. At this point, you are ready for business and can start the NodeManager. To start the NodeManager, open a command prompt, navigate to the `%BEA_INSTALL%\weblogic700\server\bin` directory, and execute the startup script previously mentioned. You'll see output that looks like the following:

```
F:\bea\weblogic700\server\bin>startNodeManager

F:\bea\weblogic700\server\bin>set
CLASSPATH=.;F:\bea\jdk131_02\lib\tools.jar;F:\
bea\weblogic700\server\lib\weblogic_sp.jar;F:\bea\weblogic700\server\lib
\weblogi
c.jar;.;f:\jdk1.3.1\jre\lib\rt.jar;f:\files\cloudscape364\lib\cloudscape
.jar;f:\
files\cloudscape364\lib\tools.jar;f:\files\cloudscape364\demo\programs\t
ours;F:\
files\xalan\xalan\xalan.jar;f:\j2sdkee1.3.1\lib\j2ee.jar;f:\j2sdkee1.3.1
\lib\loc
ale;f:\files\tomcat\lib\ant.jar;f:\files\JMX-Hungryminds;f:\files\jmx-
1_1-ri\jmx
_1.1_ri_bin\lib\jmxri.jar;f:\files\jmx-1_1-
ri\jmx_1.1_ri_bin\lib\jmxtools.jar;f:
\files\jmx-1_1-
ri\jmx_1.1_ri_bin\lib\jmxgrinder.jar;F:\bea\wlserver6.1\lib\weblo
gic.jar;f:\files\goodstuff\TreeControl;f:\files\c\xlndnd

F:\bea\weblogic700\server\bin>set
PATH=F:\bea\weblogic700\server\bin;F:\bea\jdk1
31_02\bin;F:\Perl\bin\;E:\WINNT\system32;E:\WINNT;E:\WINNT\System32\Wbem
;f:\jdk1
.3.1\bin;F:\Program
Files\excelon\XIS\bin;F:\Emacs20.3.1\bin;F:\files\tomcat\bin
;F:\bpm3.0.1.mikej\os\bpm\buildtools;f:\j2sdkee1.3.1\bin;f:\files\jxul\j
xul-src2
1july2001\bin;f:\program files\devstudio\sharedide\bin\ide;f:\program
files\devs
tudio\sharedide\bin;f:\program
files\devstudio\vc\bin;f:\cygnus\cygwin~1\h-i586~
1\bin;f:\handspring\prc-tools\bin;e:\program files\microsoft visual
studio\commo
n\tools\winnt;e:\program files\microsoft visual
studio\common\msdev98\bin;e:\pro
gram files\microsoft visual studio\common\tools;e:\program
files\microsoft visua
l
studio\vc98\bin;C:\WINDOWS;C:\WINDOWS\COMMAND;C:\JDK1.3\BIN;C:\files\jav
a\work
```

```
flow;c:\j2sdkee1.3\bin

F:\bea\weblogic700\server\bin>cd F:\bea\weblogic700\common\nodemanager

F:\bea\weblogic700\common\nodemanager>"F:\bea\jdk131_02\bin\java.exe" -
hotspot -
Xms32m -Xmx200m  -classpath
".;F:\bea\jdk131_02\lib\tools.jar;F:\bea\weblogic700
\server\lib\weblogic_sp.jar;F:\bea\weblogic700\server\lib\weblogic.jar;.
;f:\jdk1
.3.1\jre\lib\rt.jar;f:\files\cloudscape364\lib\cloudscape.jar;f:\files\c
loudscap
e364\lib\tools.jar;f:\files\cloudscape364\demo\programs\tours;F:\files\x
alan\xal
an\xalan.jar;f:\j2sdkee1.3.1\lib\j2ee.jar;f:\j2sdkee1.3.1\lib\locale;f:\
files\to
mcat\lib\ant.jar;f:\files\JMX-Hungryminds;f:\files\jmx-1_1-
ri\jmx_1.1_ri_bin\lib
\jmxri.jar;f:\files\jmx-1_1-
ri\jmx_1.1_ri_bin\lib\jmxtools.jar;f:\files\jmx-1_1-
ri\jmx_1.1_ri_bin\lib\jmxgrinder.jar;F:\bea\wlserver6.1\lib\weblogic.jar
;f:\file
s\goodstuff\TreeControl;f:\files\c\xlndnd" "-Dbea.home=F:\bea" "-
Dweblogic.secur
ity.SSL.trustedCAKeyStore=F:\bea\weblogic700\server\lib\cacerts" "-
Djava.securit
y.policy=F:\bea\weblogic700\server\lib\weblogic.policy" "-
Dweblogic.nodemanager.
javaHome=F:\bea\jdk131_02" weblogic.nodemanager.NodeManager
<Jun 16, 2002 10:22:35 AM EDT> <Info> <NodeManager> <NodeManager: for
informatio
n on command line options,  try "java weblogic.nodemanager.NodeManager
help">
<Jun 16, 2002 10:22:35 AM EDT> <Info> <NodeManager> <Starting
NodeManager >
<Jun 16, 2002 10:22:40 AM EDT> <Info> <NodeManager@localhost:5555> <Node
Manager
 listening on localhost:5555..>
<Jun 16, 2002 10:22:40 AM EDT> <Info> <NodeManager@localhost:5555>
<NodeManager
started, log messages being written into file
F:\bea\weblogic700\common\nodemana
ger\NodeManagerLogs\NodeManagerInternal\NodeManagerInternal_102423735524
9>
```

You can now remotely start and stop a WebLogic server. From the last line of the output, you can see that the port 5555 is being used to listen for requests. Now that the NodeManager has been configured and can be used, let's begin looking at the code for the example.

# Getting started with the example

To start this example, you must identify exactly what types of information you want to monitor, and then you need to determine the types of MBeans that contain that information. This section describes how you would implement this example using JavaServer Pages. The good news is that writing this application will not be that different from any other of the examples you've seen so far. This reflects the true value of the JMX API, which enables you to write management applications using a small set of well-defined components in a standard way. There is no perceptible difference between writing a management application using Java and Swing, and writing the same application using JSP and servlets.

I've already alluded to the type of information you want to center this example on: information about WebLogic servers. With information about a WebLogic server, you can extract additional details about it, find out metrics about it, as well as start and stop control instances of the server by starting and stopping it. The types of information about a WebLogic server include the following:

♦ The name of the server

♦ The domain of the server

♦ What applications are deployed on that server

♦ How many Web servers are associated with the WebLogic server

♦ General information about the security of the server

♦ The log that the server is using

♦ The root directory of the configuration for the server

This is not an exhaustive list, but it serves as a good foundation for this example. In addition to the types of information presented above, you also want to be able to control instances of the servers. You might want to create new instances or stop and start instances. For this example, I limit the interaction with respect to instances to just starting and stopping instances. This is partly because of some of the manual intervention required to establish the NodeManager described above on a target machine. This example assumes the existence of at least one NodeManager on the same host as the administration server, although this is not generally the way it is configured. I have configured it this way to make it possible to easily execute this example without having to worry about multiple machines.

The flow of the management application begins with a view of the WebLogic domains you have defined. A domain in WLS serves as a logical grouping of WebLogic resources such as WebLogic servers. In previous examples, you've seen the string TheShire, which is the name of the domain I've assigned to my WLS installation. In this domain is one WebLogic server, which also happens to be the administration server for my domain. From this domain view, you can drill down into zero or more managed WebLogic servers. You can also view various bits of information about that particular domain.

The domain view will be built and presented by a JSP, as will the other pieces of this application. You're not going to build a deployment JAR for this application; rather, simply place the JSPs into the default Web application directory and execute them from a Web browser. In my particular installation, the default Web application directory is

F:\bea\theshire\TheShire\applications\DefaultWebApp. Obviously, the directory and drive that exist on your machine are different than mine, and your domain has a different name. For this example, the hierarchy of this application, and where the JSPs will be stored, will look like the following (although substituting your own drive and domain name). The filenames in bold-faced type are those you'll develop in this example.

```
F:\bea
    \theshire
        \TheShire
            \applications
                \DefaultWebApp
                    wlsdomainmonitor.jsp
                    wlsviewserver.jsp
                    wlsviewdomain.jsp
                    wlsoperation.jsp
```

Now that you have a few of the specifics and setup out of the way, you can begin with the first JSP. This JSP serves to show the display of domains defined in a WLS installation. (The colors in the HTML generated from the JSPs appear in black and white in the figures here.) You can tailor the values in the CSS stylesheets to your preferences. Each JSP will be developed independently and then tested before moving on to the next. There is no final demonstration of the application in this example; instead, you will exercise it as you build each JSP.

Over the course of the example, the JSP's you'll develop will flow downward from the initial domain-level page. This first page displays some primary details about the domains defined in a WLS installation. The next page shows more detail about a particular domain, including the number of WebLogic servers and a link to each. The next JSP you'll develop enables you to display detailed information about a particular WebLogic server, and the last JSP enables you to start and stop a WebLogic server, invoked from the JSP just preceding it.

### Displaying the domains

Displaying domains and information about domains involves finding the correct MBean that contains this information. Earlier in this chapter, you were introduced to several key WLS MBeans that represent core WLS server components, such as the DomainMBean. The JSP you need to build here must find the appropriate MBean and then display a set of information about it that you might find useful. The user interface should also provide a link from the domain to a set of WLS servers.

Finding a particular MBean with the WLS JMX management API is somewhat easier than using the standard MBeanServer interface query methods. In Chapter 9, you used the queryNames() and queryMBeans() methods to find MBeans of a particular type. The WLS management API provides several different methods for getting an MBean, each taking a different set of arguments. You can also rely on the naming standards WLS MBeans follow to find an MBean of a particular type. Throughout this example, I'll make use of the queryNames() method, which takes an object name pattern and an instance of the QueryExp interface. For a domain MBean, this will result in values of TheShire and Domain for the name and type, respectively.

Listing 14-4 shows the source of the JSP for displaying the domains.

**Listing 14-4: Displaying domains in WLS**

```
<%@ page import="weblogic.management.*;" %>
<%@ page import="weblogic.management.runtime.*;" %>
<%@ page import="weblogic.management.configuration.*;" %>
<%@ page import="javax.management.*;" %>
<%@ page import="java.util.*;" %>
<%@ page import="java.net.*;" %>
<HTML>
<STYLE TYPE="text/css">
TH {
   font-family:Arial Black;
   font-size:12pt;
   color: rgb(192,192,192);
   background-color: rgb(188,151,46);
   text-align: left;
}
BODY {
   background-color: rgb(178,190,107);
}
.TITLE {
   font-family:Arial Black;
   font-size:12pt;
   color: rgb(188,151,46);
}
.OFFSET {
   background-color: rgb(205,212,168);
}
.REGULAR{
   background-color: rgb(178,190,107);
}
</STYLE>
<TITLE>WebLogic Server JMX Monitor</TITLE>
<BODY>

<%

MBeanHome home = null;
Set mbeans = null;
MBeanServer beanSvr = null;
try {

    home = (MBeanHome)Helper.getAdminMBeanHome("system",
                                                "guyverx2",
                                                "t3://localhost:7001");

    beanSvr = home.getMBeanServer();
```

```
        mbeans = beanSvr.queryNames(new
ObjectName("*:*,Type=Domain,*"),null);


 }catch(Exception ex){
 }

%>
<SPAN CLASS=TITLE>WebLogic Domains</SPAN>
<TABLE BORDER="0" CELLPADDING="4" CELLSPACING="0">
<TR><TH>Type</TH><TH>Name</TH><TH>Directory</TH><TH>Domain</TH><TH>Class
Name</TH></TR>
<%
   int cntr = 1;
   String offsetClass = "OFFSET";
   Iterator iter = mbeans.iterator();
   while (iter.hasNext()){
      ObjectName bean = (ObjectName)iter.next();
      MBeanInfo info = beanSvr.getMBeanInfo(bean);
      String type = (String)beanSvr.getAttribute(bean,"Type");
      %>
      <TR>
        <%
         if (cntr/2==0)
             offsetClass = "REGULAR";
         else
             offsetClass = "OFFSET";
        %>
        <TD CLASS=<%=offsetClass%>><a
href="/wlsviewdomain.jsp?bean=<%=URLEncoder.encode(bean.toString())%>&ty
pe=<%=type%>&domain=<%=bean.getDomain()%>"><%=type%></a></TD>
        <TD
CLASS=<%=offsetClass%>><%=beanSvr.getAttribute(bean,"Name")%></TD>
        <TD
CLASS=<%=offsetClass%>><%=beanSvr.getAttribute(bean,"RootDirectory")%></
TD>
        <TD CLASS=<%=offsetClass%>><%=bean.getDomain()%></TD>
        <TD CLASS=<%=offsetClass%>><%=info.getClassName()%></TD>
      </TR>
      <%
      cntr++;
   }
%>
</TABLE>
</BODY>
</HTML>
```

You should save this JSP in a file named `wlsdomainmonitor.jsp` before continuing. This file retrieves the `MBeanHome` interface for the administration server using the `Helper` class and then gets all domain MBeans using the `queryNames()` method. The type of MBean you are looking for is *Domain*. The `queryNames()` method returns a `java.util.Set` of all the MBeans found. The MBean you are referencing is the configuration MBean for the domain. If you wanted to retrieve the runtime MBean for the domain, you could have used a value of `DomainRuntime` instead of just `Domain`.

After you have a collection of the MBeans, begin iterating through them in a `while` loop. Each time through the loop, retrieve an instance of the MBean and cast it to the `ObjectName` class. You could also have explicitly used the `DomainMBean` class, but it wasn't absolutely necessary for this page. The information you need for this page consists of the basic information about the MBean and nothing specific to a Domain MBean. The information you retrieve to display on this page is as follows:

♦ The type of the MBean
♦ The domain the MBean is in
♦ The name of the MBean
♦ The root directory for the configuration of this domain
♦ The class name of this MBean

Figure 14-4 shows the output from running this JSP. You do not present too much detail on this initial page; the second page has more detail about the domain. This JSP needs to be located in the `DefaultWebApp` directory specified in the "Getting started with the example" section of this chapter.

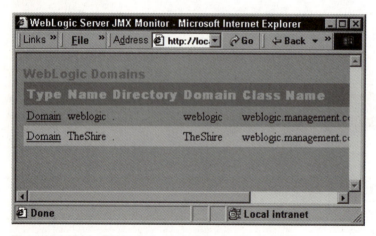

**Figure 14-4:** Viewing WebLogic domains using a JavaServer Page.

The hyperlinks that appear for the MBean type will lead you to the detail page that you'll be building next, so don't click on them just yet! The browser window that appears in Figure 14-4 has been resized; when running the example on your machine the browser window will appear at its normal size based on your settings.

## Domain details

When you click on one of the domains listed, you are taken to a detail page that presents more information about that particular domain. This detailed information includes which WebLogic servers are present in the domain, and provides links to more details about particular WebLogic servers. Because the primary goal of this example is to write a management application to work with WebLogic servers, there won't be much in the way of updates to the domain presented in the user interface. Nor will there be any capability to create or destroy domains, but feel free to extend the example. Listing 14-5 shows the source code of a JSP that displays some details about a WebLogic domain MBean.

**Listing 14-5: Showing the management interface of a domain bean**

```
<%@ page import="weblogic.management.*;" %>
<%@ page import="weblogic.management.runtime.*;" %>
<%@ page import="weblogic.management.configuration.*;" %>
<%@ page import="javax.management.*;" %>
<%@ page import="java.util.*;" %>
<%@ page import="java.net.*;" %>
<HTML>
<STYLE TYPE="text/css">
TD {
   font-family: Arial;
   font-size: 10pt;
}
TH {
   font-family:Arial Black;
   font-size:12pt;
   color: rgb(192,192,192);
   background-color: rgb(188,151,46);
   text-align: left;
}
BODY {
   background-color: rgb(178,190,107);
}
.TITLE {
   font-family:Arial Black;
   font-size:12pt;
   color: rgb(188,151,46);
}
.OFFSET {
   background-color: rgb(205,212,168);
}
.REGULAR{
   background-color: rgb(178,190,107);
}
</STYLE>
<TITLE>WebLogic Server JMX Monitor</TITLE>
<BODY>
```

```
<%

 MBeanHome home = null;
 Set mbeans = null;
 MBeanServer beanSvr = null;
 String type = "";
 String name = "";
 String domain = "";

 ObjectName objName = null;
 MBeanInfo info = null;

 try {

     home = (MBeanHome)Helper.getAdminMBeanHome("system",
                                                "guyverx2",
                                                "t3://localhost:7001");

     type = request.getParameter("type");
     name = request.getParameter("bean");
     domain = request.getParameter("domain");

     beanSvr = home.getMBeanServer();
     mbeans = beanSvr.queryNames(new ObjectName(name),null);
     Iterator iter = mbeans.iterator();
     objName = (ObjectName)iter.next();
     info = beanSvr.getMBeanInfo(objName);

 }catch(Exception ex){
 }

%>
<SPAN CLASS=TITLE><a href="/wlsdomainmonitor.jsp">WebLogic Domains</a> >
<%= new ObjectName(name).getDomain() %></SPAN>
<TABLE BORDER="0" CELLPADDING="4" CELLSPACING="0" WIDTH="100%">
<TR><TH COLSPAN="2"> </TH></TR>
<TR><TD WIDTH="5%">Type:</TD><TD><%= type %></TD></TR>
<TR><TD CLASS="OFFSET">Name:</TD><TD CLASS="OFFSET"><%= new
ObjectName(name).getDomain() %></TD></TR>
<TR><TD>Domain:</TD><TD><%= new ObjectName(name).getDomain()
%></TD></TR>
<TR><TD CLASS="OFFSET">ObjectName:</TD><TD CLASS="OFFSET"><%= objName
%></TD></TR>
<TR><TD>Root
Directory:</TD><TD><%=beanSvr.getAttribute(objName,"RootDirectory")%></T
D></TR>
<%
```

```
   ObjectName logObjName =
(ObjectName)beanSvr.getAttribute(objName,"Log");

%>
<TR><TD CLASS="OFFSET">Log File:</TD><TD
CLASS="OFFSET"><%=beanSvr.getAttribute(logObjName,"FileName")%></TD></TR
>
<%
   ObjectName svrObjName[] =
(ObjectName[])beanSvr.getAttribute(objName,"Servers");
%>
<TR><TD>Servers:</TD><TD><a
href="/wlsviewserver.jsp?server=<%=URLEncoder.encode(svrObjName[0].toStr
ing())%>&domain=<%=domain%>&domainname=<%=name%>"><%=
beanSvr.getAttribute(svrObjName[0],"Name") %></a></TD></TR>
<%
   //Process remaining servers
   for (int i=1;i<svrObjName.length;i++){
       out.println("<TR><TD> </TD>");
       out.println("<TD><a href=\"/wlsviewserver.jsp?server=" +
URLEncoder.encode(svrObjName[i].toString()) +
"&domain="+name+"&domainname="+name+"\">");
       out.println(beanSvr.getAttribute(svrObjName[i],"Name") +
"</a></TD></TR>");
   }
%>
</TABLE>
</BODY>
</HTML>
```

The wlsviewdomain.jsp JSP presents a small set of details about a particular domain. The name of the domain, and its type and object name are shown in the display. Three other pieces of information are included: the root directory where the configuration for this domain is found, the log file for this domain, and a list of the WebLogic servers that are configured in this domain. Each server that is listed is a hyperlink to the next detail page you'll be developing. In my domain, I have two WLS servers, only one of which was actually running at the time this example was created.

Unlike the domain list page in Listing 14-4, I am not using a loop to build the display because I know that I will only be working with a single MBean. I retrieve the relevant MBean using the following excerpt of code from Listing 14-4:

```
mbeans = beanSvr.queryNames(new ObjectName(name),null);
Iterator iter = mbeans.iterator();
objName = (ObjectName)iter.next();
```

The name, type, and domain variables were passed in the request from the domain view page. The hyperlink for each domain in that page contained a set of parameters that correspond to the name, type, and domain of the domain I wanted to view the details for.

Again, for this detail page, I've excluded many bits of information, as I wanted to focus on the initial set of information established at the beginning of this example. You could extend this example by allowing a way to establish new domains or remove domains.

Figure 14-5 shows the output of the domain detail page running on my installation.

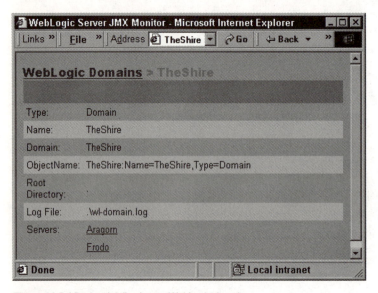

**Figure 14-5:** Viewing details about a WebLogic domain.

The detail page shows information similar to the summary page, such as the type, domain, and name of the MBean, but it continues with more specific information. Also included in the details for this domain are the following: the object name, the root directory where the configuration for this domain is found, the log file for this domain, and a list of WebLogic servers. A link at the top of the page shows the current domain detail being viewed, and provides a link back to the list of domains. You can click on the hyperlink for any WebLogic server to view the detail about that particular WebLogic server. This detail page for the WebLogic server will be constructed in the next part of this example.

### WebLogic server detail

The last detail screen you'll develop for this example is the one that shows detailed information about a particular WebLogic server. From this page, you'll also add access to operations to start and stop a particular server instance. This page uses information from the `ServerMBean` and `ServerStartMBean` to retrieve configuration information about a particular WLS. The `ServerStartMBean` represents the arguments you configured earlier for the remote aspects of a WebLogic server.

Listing 14-6 shows the source code for the JSP that will display detailed information about a particular WebLogic server.

**Listing 14-6: Viewing WLS server detail**

```
<%@ page import="weblogic.management.*;" %>
<%@ page import="weblogic.jndi.*;" %>
<%@ page import="weblogic.management.runtime.*;" %>
<%@ page import="weblogic.management.configuration.*;" %>
<%@ page import="javax.management.*;" %>
<%@ page import="javax.naming.*;" %>
<%@ page import="java.util.*;" %>
<%@ page import="java.net.*;" %>
<HTML>
<STYLE TYPE="text/css">
TD {
   font-family: Arial;
   font-size: 10pt;
}
TH {
   font-family:Arial Black;
   font-size:12pt;
   color: rgb(192,192,192);
   background-color: rgb(188,151,46);
   text-align: left;
}
BODY {
   background-color: rgb(178,190,107);
}
.TITLE {
   font-family:Arial Black;
   font-size:12pt;
   color: rgb(188,151,46);
}
.OFFSET {
   background-color: rgb(205,212,168);
}
.REGULAR{
   background-color: rgb(178,190,107);
}
</STYLE>
<TITLE>WebLogic Server JMX Monitor</TITLE>
<BODY>

<%

 MBeanHome home = null;
 Set mbeans = null;
 MBeanServer beanSvr = null;
 String type = "";
 String name = "";
 String domain = "";
```

```
String domainname = "";
MBeanInfo info = null;
String SERVER_NAME = "Aragorn";
ObjectName objName = null;

String theName = "";

try {


    //Obtaining an MBeanHome Using JNDI
    Environment env = new Environment();
    env.setProviderUrl("t3://localhost:7001");
    env.setSecurityPrincipal("system");
    env.setSecurityCredentials("guyverx2");
    Context ctx = env.getInitialContext();
    home = (MBeanHome)ctx.lookup(MBeanHome.JNDI_NAME + "." +
                                SERVER_NAME);


    type = "Server";
    name = request.getParameter("server");
    domain = request.getParameter("domain");
    domainname = request.getParameter("domainname");

    beanSvr = home.getMBeanServer();
    mbeans = beanSvr.queryNames(new ObjectName(name),null);
    Iterator iter = mbeans.iterator();
    objName = (ObjectName)iter.next();
    info = beanSvr.getMBeanInfo(objName);

    theName = (String)beanSvr.getAttribute(objName,"Name");

}catch(Exception ex){
}

%>
<SPAN CLASS=TITLE><a href="/wlsdomainmonitor.jsp">WebLogic Domains</a> >
<a
href="/wlsviewdomain.jsp?bean=<%=domainname%>&type=Domain&domain=<%=doma
in%>"><%= new ObjectName(domainname).getDomain() %></a> > <%= theName
%></SPAN>
<TABLE BORDER="0" CELLPADDING="4" CELLSPACING="0" WIDTH="100%">
<%
    String status = "Unknown";
    ObjectName sObjName = new ObjectName(name);
    ObjectName srvObjName =
(ObjectName)beanSvr.queryNames(sObjName,null).iterator().next();
```

```
    ServerLifeCycleRuntimeMBean srMBean =
(ServerLifeCycleRuntimeMBean)beanSvr.invoke(srvObjName,

"lookupServerLifeCycleRuntime",

                                                new Object[]{},
                                                new String[]{});

   if (srMBean == null)
       status = "Unknown";
   else
       status = srMBean.getState();

%>
<TR><TH>General</TH><TH ALIGN="RIGHT">Status: <%=status%></TH></TR>
<TR><TD WIDTH="15%">Name:</TD><TD><%=theName%></TD></TR>
<TR><TD CLASS="OFFSET">Port:</TD><TD
CLASS="OFFSET"><%=beanSvr.getAttribute(srvObjName,"ListenPort")%></TD></
TR>
<TR><TD>Address:</TD><TD><%=beanSvr.getAttribute(srvObjName,"ListenAddre
ss")%></TD></TR>
<TR><TD CLASS="OFFSET">Root Directory:</TD><TD
CLASS="OFFSET"><%=beanSvr.getAttribute(srvObjName,"RootDirectory")%></TD
></TR>
<%
   ObjectName ssObjName =
(ObjectName)beanSvr.getAttribute(srvObjName,"ServerStart");
%>
<TR><TH COLSPAN="2">Remote Start</TH></TR>
<TR><TD>Arguments:</TD><TD><%=beanSvr.getAttribute(ssObjName,"Arguments"
)%></TD></TR>
<TR><TD CLASS="OFFSET">Bea Home:</TD><TD
CLASS="OFFSET"><%=beanSvr.getAttribute(ssObjName,"BeaHome")%></TD></TR>
<TR><TD>Classpath:</TD><TD><%=beanSvr.getAttribute(ssObjName,"ClassPath"
)%></TD></TR>
<TR><TD CLASS="OFFSET">Root Directory:</TD><TD
CLASS="OFFSET"><%=beanSvr.getAttribute(ssObjName,"RootDirectory")%></TD>
</TR>
<TR><TD>Security Policy
File:</TD><TD><%=beanSvr.getAttribute(ssObjName,"SecurityPolicyFile")%><
/TD></TR>
</TABLE>
<HR/>
Commands:
<%

 String sName = sObjName.toString();

 if (status.equals("Not Running") || status.equals("SHUTDOWN")){
   out.println("<a
href=\"/wlsoperation.jsp?operation=start&name="+sName);
```

```
out.println("&domain="+domain+"&type=Server&server="+sName+"&domainname=
"+domain+"\">Start Server</a>");
}else
 out.println("Start Server");
%>
 | 
<%
  if (status.equals("RUNNING")){
     out.println("<a
href=\"/wlsoperation.jsp?operation=stop&name="+sName);

out.println("&domain="+domain+"&type=Server&server="+sName+"&domainname=
"+domain+"\">Stop Server</a>");
 }else
    out.println("Stop Server");
%>

</BODY>
</HTML>
```

The action of shutting down and starting a server instance is performed by the
wlsoperation.jsp JSP. This JSP receives an HTTP GET request that contains the
parameters necessary to identify a particular server instance, as well as whether you want to
start or stop the instance. The operation parameter is used to indicate whether or not to start or
stop a server, and the JSP wlsviewserver.jsp will set this parameter to the appropriate
value based on the state of the server at the time the JSP is requested. This means that you
should never send a start request to a started or starting WLS server instance, and never send a
stop request to an executing stopped or stopping request.

This servlet is requested from the wlsviewserver.jsp JSP page from either the Start Server
or Stop Server hyperlinks at the bottom of the page. Listing 14-7 shows the source code of the
wlsoperation.jsp JSP.

**Listing 14-7: The wlsoperation.jsp JSP**

```
<%@ page import="weblogic.management.*;" %>
<%@ page import="weblogic.jndi.*;" %>
<%@ page import="weblogic.management.runtime.*;" %>
<%@ page import="weblogic.management.configuration.*;" %>
<%@ page import="javax.management.*;" %>
<%@ page import="javax.naming.*;" %>
<%@ page import="java.util.*;" %>
<%@ page import="java.net.*;" %>

<%


                MBeanHome home = null;
                MBeanServer beanSvr = null;
```

```
            String SERVER_NAME = "Aragorn";

        try{

            //Obtaining an MBeanHome Using JNDI
            Environment env = new Environment();
            env.setProviderUrl("t3://localhost:7001");
            env.setSecurityPrincipal("system");
            env.setSecurityCredentials("guyverx2");
            Context ctx = env.getInitialContext();
            home = (MBeanHome)ctx.lookup(MBeanHome.JNDI_NAME +
"." +
                                        SERVER_NAME);

            beanSvr = home.getMBeanServer();

            String name = request.getParameter("name");
            String domain = request.getParameter("domain");

            ObjectName srvObjName =
(ObjectName)beanSvr.queryNames(new
ObjectName(name),null).iterator().next();

            ServerLifeCycleRuntimeMBean srMBean =
(ServerLifeCycleRuntimeMBean)beanSvr.invoke(srvObjName,

"lookupServerLifeCycleRuntime",
                                                              new
Object[]{},
                                                              new
String[]{});

            String op = request.getParameter("operation");
            if (op.equals("stop"))
               srMBean.shutdown();

            else
               srMBean.start();

            RequestDispatcher dispatcher =
request.getRequestDispatcher("/wlsviewserver.jsp");

            dispatcher.forward(request,response);

        }catch(Exception ex){
            ex.printStackTrace();
            System.out.println("Exception: " + ex);
        }
```

```
%>
```

The JSP retrieves the name and domain parameters from the request and uses these to retrieve the `ServerMBean` associated with a particular WLS server. The value used to retrieve the object name for the server uses the `queryNames()` method of the `MBeanServer` interface. After the appropriate `ObjectName` has been retrieved using the `queryNames()` method of the `MBeanHome` interface, the `ServerLifeCycleRuntimeMBean` for that server is retrieved using the `lookupServerLifeCycleRuntime()` method of that MBean. You can then stop or start the WLS server instance using the `ServerRuntimeMBean` `shutdown()` or `start()` methods. As mentioned earlier, only the method appropriate for the current state of the server will be invoked.

Shutting down a WLS server instance is not an immediate action. After the request has been received by the NodeManager, it takes a few moments to actually shut down the server instance. Numerous components and connections need to be cleanly shut down. Before the shutdown is complete, the user will be redirected back to the `wlsviewserver.jsp` page using the `forward()` method of the `RequestDispatcher` interface.

When the user sees the server status page again, the status of the server may be in an intermediate state, such as `Shut Down in Progess`. You need to refresh the page until the state is reflected at `Not Running`. Figure 14-6 shows an intermediate state of a WebLogic server displayed using our management console.

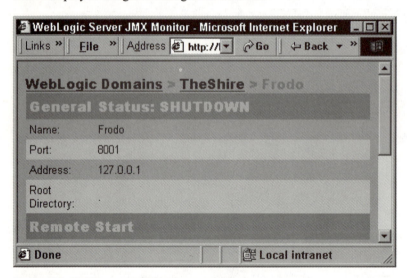

**Figure 14-6:** Shutting down a WebLogic server instance.

You can see the state of `Shutdown` displayed in the status column. The different states that a WLS server can be in are defined as constants in the `ServerRuntimeMBean` class:

♦ RUNNING

- SHUTDOWN IN PROGRESS
- SHUTDOWN PENDING
- SUSPENDED
- UNKNOWN
- STANDBY

Curiously, there does not seem to be a STARTING or STARTUP IN PROGRESS state for a WebLogic server. After you click the Start or Stop link and return to the server detail page, the state should have changed. You need to refresh the page by either using the Refresh button on the Web browser toolbar or clicking on the links at the top of the page.

## Summary

This chapter examined the remote aspects of JMX by writing a Web-based management console for managing a J2EE application server. You utilized the JMX components in the BEA WebLogic Application Server 7.0 to monitor various runtime aspects of domains and WebLogic server instances, and enabled the capability to start and stop instances of a WLS using MBean operations. By implementing a management console for a commercial product, you can see how the concepts in the rest of the book are implemented and used in a real product. I hope this will also enable you to see how different types of components would behave in a production server. Software vendors may approach exposing various runtime and configurable aspects of their products differently.

In the next chapter, you'll learn how to use JMX with J2EE components such as servlets and Message-Driven Beans. You'll also look at how BEA WebLogic 7.0 exposes these same components using JMX.

# Chapter 15

# Managing J2EE Components

In Chapter 14, you were introduced to some of the JMX capabilities of BEA WebLogic Server 6.1. You learned how to implement support for managing various runtime components of a WebLogic server, such as those representing a configuration and those representing a domain. The WebLogic Server management API includes many components, some of which are geared toward server configuration and some of which are geared toward managing applications and components running in a WebLogic server. With these MBeans, you can monitor the state of deployed components, gathering specific information about them that is exposed via their management interface. Like the runtime and server MBeans the J2EE component MBeans are implemented as standard MBeans.

Recall that the granularity of a managed resource can be a single component, several components, or an entire application. The WebLogic Server management API includes a set of MBeans representing components that have been deployed in a WebLogic server. When assembled, these components represent a Web application, and are commonly comprised of components such as Enterprise Java Beans, servlets, and JavaServer Pages.

In this chapter, you'll examine how to use the various J2EE component MBeans to manage these J2EE components. In order for application servers to be accepted into large data center environments, the capability to provide a standard management interface is critical. Also key is the capability to create custom-tailored management applications, as well as the capability to integrate the management of an application into an existing management infrastructure.

You'll learn how you can build management capabilities into your own applications and servlets to monitor them. Finally, you'll create a `JMXServlet` class that other servlets can extend from to make them manageable via JMX.

## Identifying Manageable Resources

A J2EE application can be composed of a number of available components. These components range in type from EJBs, servlets, Java Message Service (JMS) Message Queues, JMS Message Listeners, JavaServer Pages, to your own custom classes, to name just a few.

You can approach the management of J2EE components from three perspectives: monitoring the state of components, altering the state of components, or a combination of the two. When monitoring the state of a component, you might be interested in information such as the following:

- ◆ Number of instances of a particular servlet
- ◆ Number of instances of an Enterprise JavaBean
- ◆ Number of transactions being executed
- ◆ Number of transactions that have been rolled back
- ◆ Active number of connections to external data sources
- ◆ Whether any component is in an error state

When altering the state of a component, you might want to perform actions that relate to load balancing, or perhaps you want to change the security parameters required to execute a method of an EJB. The types of actions that could fall under these categories include the following:

- ◆ Controlling the number of instances or the pool of EJBs
- ◆ Controlling the number of instances of a servlet
- ◆ Controlling where a servlet or EJB can run
- ◆ Controlling the pool of connections to a data source
- ◆ Changing the security parameters of a Web component

These scenarios cover common components that appear in an application, but do not cover components that you may write yourself, or other customer or third-party components.

An administrator monitoring a J2EE system may be interested in different types of information. For example, a system administrator might be interested in how many servlets of a specific type are running in a servlet container. This information might be needed for performing load-balancing functions.

From an application perspective, an administrator might be interested in what components are in an application. For example, one might ask questions such as "How many Bank Account Withdrawal servlets have been created?" or "How much money has been withdrawn?" These types of questions could be answered in monitored systems. The latter question is more application-specific, while the former question regarding instances of servlets is more in line with common monitoring scenarios.

Implementing your own J2EE components can be challenging because they are managed by other application components called *containers*. These containers are responsible for managing instances by creating new instances, removing instances, and calling common entry points such as doPost() or doGet() for servlets. They are also responsible for calling methods such as ejbCreate() and ejbRemove() for EJBs. Basically, containers manage the lifecycle for these types of components. This is the source of the challenge, because you cannot simply hook into most servlet or EJB containers unless they explicitly provide hooks for you.

You might be able to get your hands on the source for Tomcat and implement some hooks yourself, but ideally, you should find a container that already provides hooks. The software developers who write a container know better than anyone else how and where to provide access without compromising the integrity of the container. You could conceivably write a servlet that implements a management interface that in turn finds an MBean Server when it is instantiated and records its existence. You could then record how many instances of a particular servlet were loaded, but you could not control how many instances occurred.

## Servlet lifecycle

When implementing components that are controlled by a container, it is helpful to understand the lifecycle of the component. The lifecycle of a component is a sequence of events that occurs from the time a new instance of the component is created to when it is destroyed. During the lifecycle, zero or more events can occur — events that determine when a component is available, when it is unavailable, and whether it goes into some abnormal state. Components with defined lifecycles often have special hooks or methods that you can override to be notified of the various states that the component passes through.

Servlets have a lifecycle that is specified by the servlet specification. It describes the sequence of events and states that a servlet can be in during its lifecycle. To implement a servlet, it is helpful to understand its lifecycle so you can make informed decisions, such as when to create the management interface or MBean for it, and when to make the MBean unavailable. For example, if you created an MBean before an instance of a servlet was available and then tried to use the MBean, you would not be able to find out any information about the servlet. The same is true when a servlet is destroyed, as you must ensure that the management interface is not present when the managed resource is not present. (This last concern may not be valid in every scenario if an MBean is also responsible for creating instances of a managed resource. For example, you might have an MBean that represents a servlet container.)

A servlet's lifecycle can be monitored at a high level using the `init()` and `destroy()` methods. These two methods define when the servlet is created and destroyed. When a request comes to a execute a servlet, the following steps occur:

1. If an instance of the servlet is not loaded, the following events occur:
   - The servlet class is loaded
   - A new object/instance is created
   - The servlet is initialized by calling the `init()` method
2. If an instance is already loaded, the `service()` method is called. If the servlet is an `HttpServlet`, the request is then passed to the `doGet()` or `doPost()` method.

With this knowledge of the servlet lifecycle, you can better anticipate when the MBean for a servlet would be available. You can also make better decisions about how you might implement the servlet. You can monitor the more fine-grained lifecycle events of a servlet by using listeners.

During the startup of a server, the MBean Server needs to be initialized before any MBeans are loaded. This could be done via a servlet that runs first during startup of the application server. It could also be done via a superclass that checks for the existence of an MBean Server and initializes one if it does not already exist. In either case, you want a single MBean Server instance per JVM that tracks the servlet instance. You would not be able to track the same granularity of information that would exist at the container level. Look at a simple example of monitoring a servlet in the J2EE server that comes with the J2EE reference implementation from Sun Microsystems.

## Building the example servlet

In this example, you implement a servlet using the standard MBean interface. You create a management interface that enables you to retrieve the following bits of information:

♦ The number of instances of this servlet

♦ The name of the servlet

You also use another servlet to initialize the MBean Server, and you extend your servlet from this one. To monitor the servlet, you create a single JavaServer Page that will display these pieces of information. Let's look at what you need for the servlet superclass first. Table 15-1 provides a summary of the components for this example. Also included is some J2EE deployment information that will make referencing the components easier.

### Table 15-1   Components for the Servlet Example

| Component | Alias | Description |
|---|---|---|
| JMXServlet | | Superclass that creates an MBean Server instance and registers the subclass as an MBean |
| JMXServletMBean | | Management interface for servlet MBeans |
| MBeanServlet | bean | Extends the JMXServlet class |
| monitorservlet.jsp | monitor | JSP to display MBean information about servlet MBeans that are registered in the MBean Server |
| viewinterface.jsp | viewinterface | JSP to display the management interface, such as attributes and operations |

The aliases in the table will be defined when you package the components for deployment into the J2EE server used in this example. In the "Packaging and deploying the servlet example" section of this chapter, I discuss the steps for deploying this example. One thing that is not covered in the deployment phase is a security setting that enables the JMX MBean Server to read system properties. The J2EE reference implementation server uses a Java security policy file that restricts what permissions are allowed in a JVM running the J2EE server and supporting services. During development, you add a temporary permission that grants read/write access for working with property files.

The file `server.policy` is in the `%J2EE_INSTALL%/lib/security` directory and contains the permissions that you need to update. The following code snippet needs to be added before you try to use the examples that follow:

```
// "standard" properties that can be read by anyone
grant {
 permission java.util.PropertyPermission "*", "read,write";
 permission javax.management.MBeanServerPermission "*";
};
```

You should add this code to the top of the file and save it. It would be a good idea to restart the J2EE server if you have it running, so that the new permissions can be discovered.

> **NOTE:** The `javax.management.MBeanServerPermission` is required for JMX agents that use a security manager and are using the JMX 1.1 maintenance release. Chapter 8 discusses the `javax.management.MBeanPermission` class.

Another step not covered in the deployment section is setting up automatic loading of the `MBeanServlet` servlet. This step is actually optional, as I describe the steps necessary to initialize the `MBeanServlet` later in the chapter. If you want to perform this step, however, you need to add the following code snippet to the `%J2EE_INSTALL%/conf/web.xml` file:

```
<servlet>
    <servlet-name>MBean Servlet</servlet-name>
    <display-name>MBean Servlet</display-name>
    <servlet-class>com.hmi.servlet.MBeanServlet</servlet-class>
    <load-on-startup>1</load-on-startup>
 </servlet>
```

One last environmental check you need to make is to ensure that the JMX runtime libraries are in the CLASSPATH of the J2EE server. The J2EE reference implementation comes with several scripts that are responsible for setting up various environmental attributes before the J2EE server is started. One such script is the `userconfig.bat` script, which enables you to add libraries to the CLASSPATH used by the J2EE server. This `userconfig.bat` script is located in the `%J2EE_INSTALL%/bin` directory. The following code snippet shows the area of the script and the relevant updates that you need to make (the changes are highlighted in boldfaced type):

```
rem Each directory is delimited by a semicolon.
rem
rem set J2EE_CLASSPATH=
set JMX=f:/files/jmx-1_1-ri/jmx_1.1_ri_bin/lib
set J2EE_CLASSPATH=%JMX%/jmxri.jar;%JMX%/jmxtools.jar
rem
rem JAVA_HOME refers to the directory where the Java(tm) 2 SDK
rem Standard Edition software is installed.
```

The agent for your example is the J2EE reference implementation server. The servlets are loaded manually, which causes the MBean Server to be instantiated and stored for later use. The protocol adapter functionality is performed using the built-in HTTP services of the application server. Technically, this is not the best way to implement the protocol adapter support, but for the purposes of this example, it makes it much easier and you can focus on implementing a servlet as an MBean. For a real implementation, you can review Chapter 12, which explains how to create a protocol adapter and connector.

Ideally, if you were to deploy these servlets in a production application, you would want to specify that the MBeanServlet should be loaded during the startup sequence. This would ensure that the JMX environment was initialized and that the MBean Server was available. To ensure that the JMX subsystem is initialized, the JMXServlet that you will see throws an exception if the MBean Server is not initialized.

Listing 15-1 shows the source of the management interface for the MBeans you want to use. Rather than define an interface that each servlet must implement directly, I've chosen to define an interface that will be implemented by a superclass, which other servlets must extend. Recall from Chapter 4 that the management interface can be inherited from a parent class.

**Listing 15-1: The JMXServletMBean interface**

```
package com.hmi.servlet;

/**
 *
 * This is the management interface for the Servlet
 *
 **/

public interface JMXServletMBean {

       public String getServletName();
       public void setServletName(String name);
       public int getServletInstances();

}
```

Listing 15-2 illustrates a simple interface that enables you to discover the name of a servlet, change the name of a servlet, and find out how many instances of this servlet are running.

**Listing 15-2: The JMXServlet implementation of JMXServletMBean**

```
package com.hmi.servlet;

import javax.servlet.*;
import javax.servlet.http.*;
import javax.management.MBeanServer;
import javax.management.MBeanServerFactory;
import javax.management.ObjectName;

public class JMXServlet extends HttpServlet
                        implements JMXServletMBean {
```

```
private String servletName = "Default Servlet Name";
private int servletInstances_ = 0;
private static MBeanServer server_ = null;
private static ObjectName servletObjectName_ = null;

public void init() throws ServletException{
    if (server_ == null)
        server_ = MBeanServerFactory.createMBeanServer();

    // Register this MBean
    try {
        servletObjectName_ =
            new ObjectName("Servlet MBean:type=servlet");

        server_.registerMBean((Object)this,servletObjectName_);

    }catch(Exception ex){
        // rethrown as ServletException so servlet isn't
initialized
        throw new ServletException(ex);
    }
}

public static MBeanServer getMBeanServer(){
    return server_;
}

public void doGet(HttpServletRequest req,
                  HttpServletResponse res)
    throws javax.servlet.ServletException,
        java.io.IOException {
    doPost(req,res);
}
public void doPost(HttpServletRequest req,
                   HttpServletResponse res)
    throws javax.servlet.ServletException,
        java.io.IOException {

}

public String getServletName(){
    return servletName;
}

public void setServletName(String name){
    servletName = name;
}

public int getServletInstances(){
```

```
                    return servletInstances_;
        }

}
```

The `JMXServlet` class is intended to act as the superclass for servlets that you want to expose through JMX. It is responsible for registering an instance of the servlet by creating an object name and passing it along with the class being registered to the `registerMBean()` method of the `MBeanServer` interface. Because this is a superclass, you don't have to explicitly create an instance of it or specify anything special during deployment of this servlet into a J2EE server.

Creating a new instance of a subclass of the `JMXServlet` class causes an instance of the `JMXServlet` class to be used, which in turn causes the appropriate MBean to be registered in the MBean Server. Subclasses of the `JMXServlet` should not override the `init()` method of the servlet interface. If they do, they should call `super.init()` as the first line of their implementation to ensure that the MBean Server is correctly set up.

The `JMXServlet` class also implements all the methods of the `JMXServletMBean` interface as required. The methods defined in that interface will enable you to access runtime information about the servlet. Although you've only defined one subclass so far, you could define other subclasses that look like `MBeanServlet` and they would automatically become manageable via JMX.

There are two ways in which the `JMXServlet` instance can be instantiated: if the J2EE server automatically loads the subclass servlet, or if an explicit request is made to execute a subclass servlet. I recommend employing the former method, as this will ensure that the MBean Server is always available. If a problem occurs during initialization, it will be caught much earlier and can be acted upon, rather than waiting for the first request to find out that a critical component might be missing. You could also return an error message indicating something like the following:

```
JMX Sub-system is not initialized... Please contact your administrator
```

The `JMXServlet` class also defines a static method named `getMBeanServer()` that returns an instance of the `MBeanServer` for the JMX agent. You can write subclasses of the `JMXServlet` class and find other servlet MBeans using the `getMBeanServer()` method. Management applications can also use the `getMBeanServer()` method of the `JMXServlet` class to find servlet MBeans. This method also ensures that a single instance of an MBean Server is available. This does not preclude someone from using the `findMBeanServer()` method of the `MBeanServerFactory` class; but the static method, `getMBeanServer()`, will make it more convenient to find the correct MBean Server.

The servlet that we want to manage is the `MBeanServlet`. This servlet MBean inherits its management interface from the `JMXServletMBean` interface in the `JMXServlet` class. Listing 15-3 shows the source code for the `MBeanServlet` class.

**Listing 15-3: MBeanServlet implementation of the JMXServletMBean interface**

```
package com.hmi.servlet;
```

```
/**
 *
 * This is the client servlet that needs to be instrumented
 * as an MBean
 *
 **/

import javax.servlet.*;
import javax.servlet.http.*;
import java.io.*;

public class MBeanServlet extends JMXServlet {


    public void doPost(HttpServletRequest req,
                        HttpServletResponse res)
        throws javax.servlet.ServletException,
                java.io.IOException {

        PrintWriter out = res.getWriter();

        res.setContentType("text/html");

        out.println("HelloWorld from MBeanServlet");

    }
}
```

The MBeanServlet class source shown here is intended to simply return a message to a caller, nothing else. Its purpose in this example is to serve as your managed resource, and to ensure that the JMX MBean Server is created and available for management applications to use. The management application or client used for this example is a JavaServer Page that can be accessed using a Web browser.

You learned in previous chapters that management clients interact with managed resources using an adapter or connector. For this example, you use the HTTP services in the J2EE reference implementation server to act as an HTTP adaptor.

Listing 15-4 shows the source code of the `monitorservlet.jsp` JSP.

**Listing 15-4: The JSP for monitoring the servlet MBeans**

```
<%@ page import="com.hmi.servlet.*" %>
<%@ page import="javax.management.*" %>
<%@ page import="java.util.*" %>
<%@ page import="java.net.*" %>
<HTML>
<STYLE type="text/css">
```

```
.HEADING {font-family:Arial;font-size:10pt;background-
color:rgb(98,161,162);}
.CELL {font-family:Arial;font-size:8pt;background-
color:rgb(173,200,217);}
</STYLE>
<BODY>

<H1>Servlet Monitoring Console</H1>

<%

 Set beans = null;

 MBeanServer beanServer = JMXServlet.getMBeanServer();

 if (beanServer != null)
     beans = beanServer.queryMBeans(new
ObjectName("*:type=servlet"),null);
 else
     beans = new HashSet();

%>

There are : <%= beans.size() %> servlet mbeans registered <BR/>

<TABLE BORDER="0" CELLSPACING="0" CELLPADDING="4">
<TR><TD CLASS="HEADING">Bean Canonical Name</TD><TD
CLASS="HEADING">Servlet Name</TD><TD CLASS="HEADING">Servlet
Class</TD></TR>
<%
  Iterator iter = beans.iterator();
  while (iter.hasNext()) {
      ObjectInstance bean = (ObjectInstance)iter.next();
      ObjectName beanObj = bean.getObjectName();
      out.println("<TR><TD
CLASS=\"CELL\">"+beanObj.getCanonicalName()+"</TD>");

      String servletName = "";
      // Print Servlet Name
      try {
       if (beanObj.getCanonicalName().indexOf("Servlet") != -1)
          servletName =
(String)beanServer.getAttribute(beanObj,"ServletName");
       else
          servletName = "Could not retrieve servlet name";
      } catch (Exception ex) {
          servletName = "Could not retrieve servlet name for " +
beanObj.getCanonicalName();
      }
```

```
       out.println("<TD CLASS=\"CELL\">"+servletName+"</TD>");
       String className = bean.getClassName();
       out.println("<TD CLASS=\"CELL\"><a
href=\"/jmx/viewinterface?bean="+URLEncoder.encode(beanObj.getCanonicalN
ame())+"\">"+className+"</a></TD></TR>");
       //out.println("<TD CLASS=\"CELL\"><a
href=\"/jmx/viewinterface\">"+className+"</a></TD></TR>");

   }
%>
</TABLE>

</BODY>
</HTML>
```

This JSP retrieves an instance of the MBeanServer using the getMBeanServer() method of the JMXServlet class, as described earlier. The JSP assumes that the JMXServlet class has at least been loaded and initialized by the servlet container. The purpose of this JSP page is to list all the registered servlet MBeans that you might want to manage. To retrieve a list of the MBeans registered, use the queryMBeans() method of the MBeanServer interface.

Previous examples used values of null for both arguments, which resulted in all MBeans being returned. This meant that the delegate MBean that the MBean Server manages is returned in the results. For this example, what you really want is just the servlet MBeans. When a servlet MBean is registered, part of its object name includes the name/value pair type=servlet. Using this information, you can construct an object name that will filter the MBeans and return only those that match the pattern. The full ObjectName *:type=servlet indicates that you want all MBeans with type=servlet regardless of the domain they are in.

The result from the queryMBeans() method is a java.util.Set of ObjectInstance objects, each representing a servlet MBean. You then use an iterator to move through the list and extract information about the MBean. This information includes the canonical name, the value of the ServletName attribute, and the class name to which the MBean belongs. In a later section, "Running the example," you will see the output of this JSP in Internet Explorer. Listing 15-5 shows the source code of the viewinterface.jsp JSP.

**Listing 15-5: Viewing the management interface for a servlet MBean**

```
<%@ page import="com.hmi.servlet.*" %>
<%@ page import="javax.management.*" %>
<%@ page import="java.util.*" %>
<HTML>
<STYLE type="text/css">
.HEADING {font-family:Arial;font-size:10pt;background-
color:rgb(98,161,162);}
.CELL {font-family:Arial;font-size:8pt;background-
color:rgb(173,200,217);}
</STYLE>
<BODY>
```

```
<H1>View Servlet MBean Interface</H1>

<%

 Set beans = null;

 MBeanServer beanServer = JMXServlet.getMBeanServer();

 if (beanServer != null)
    //beans = beanServer.queryMBeans(new
ObjectName(request.getParameter("bean")),null);
    beans = beanServer.queryMBeans(new
ObjectName("*:type=servlet"),null);
 else
    beans = new HashSet();

%>

Bean name: <%= request.getParameter("bean") %><BR/>

<TABLE BORDER="0" CELLSPACING="0" CELLPADDING="4">
<%
  Iterator iter = beans.iterator();
  while (iter.hasNext()) {
      ObjectInstance bean = (ObjectInstance)iter.next();
      ObjectName beanObj = bean.getObjectName();
      MBeanInfo beanInfo = beanServer.getMBeanInfo(beanObj);
      MBeanAttributeInfo attInfo[] = beanInfo.getAttributes();
      %>
 <TR><TD CLASS="HEADING">Attribute Name</TD><TD
CLASS="HEADING">Type</TD><TD CLASS="HEADING">Read</TD><TD
CLASS="HEADING">Write</TD></TR>
<%
      for (int i=0;i<attInfo.length;i++){
          out.println("<TR><TD
CLASS=\"CELL\">"+attInfo[i].getName()+"</TD>");
          out.println("<TD
CLASS=\"CELL\">"+attInfo[i].getType()+"</TD><TD CLASS=\"CELL\">"+
                      attInfo[i].isReadable()+"</TD>");
          out.println("<TD
CLASS=\"CELL\">"+attInfo[i].isWritable()+"</TD></TR>");
      }
%>
 <TR><TD CLASS="HEADING">Operation Name</TD><TD CLASS="HEADING">Return
Type</TD><TD CLASS="HEADING" COLSPAN="2"> </TD></TR>
<%

      MBeanOperationInfo opInfo[] = beanInfo.getOperations();
```

```
        for (int j=0;j<opInfo.length;j++){
            out.println("<TR><TD
CLASS=\"CELL\">"+opInfo[j].getName()+"</TD><TD CLASS=\"CELL\">"+
opInfo[j].getReturnType() + "</TD><TD CLASS=\"CELL\"
COLSPAN=\"2\"> </TD></TR>");
        }


    }
%>
</TABLE>

</BODY>
</HTML>
```

This JSP should be saved in a file named `viewinterface.jsp`. It will be deployed along with the servlet and MBean interfaces described earlier. This JSP is responsible for displaying more detail about the management interfaces, the Java types of the attributes, and information about the operations. The servlet MBean in this example does not define any operations, so when you run this example, only the headings will be printed.

The JSP obtains a handle to the `MBeanServer` running in the agent, using the static `getMBeanServer()` method of the `JMXServlet` interface. Then, like the `monitorservlet.jsp` JSP, it begins iterating over the set of MBeans returned from the `queryMBeans()` method. In this example, you have only one MBean; but if, for instance, servlet pooling were turned on, you may get several rows of information about each servlet MBean.

## Packaging and deploying the servlet example

To run this example, you need to create a Web Application Archive (WAR), and an Enterprise Application Archive (EAR) in which to deploy the example code. You can create these archives by hand, but the deployment tool that comes with the Sun J2EE SDK provides a nice user interface, and it can easily create these files for you in very few steps.

Recall the list of files and aliases for a couple of the files from Table 15-1. You'll need this information again when building your EAR and WAR to deploy. You can use the following steps to build the EAR and WAR using the deployment tool. Note that the WAR is created automatically when you add a new Web component to an enterprise application in the `deploytool`. If you are not familiar with using the `deploytool` or building and deploying J2EE applications, I have attempted to provide clear steps, but you can also view the J2EE Tutorial at `http://java.sun.com/j2ee/tutorial`, which provides a great deal of additional information about the packaging and deployment process.

The deployment tool itself is found in the `%J2EE_INSTALL%/bin` directory of your J2EE installation. To launch the tool, you need to have the bin directory in your PATH on Windows, or be in the bin directory itself. I recommend the former option, as it enables you to execute the tool from any location.

Once you have launched the `deploytool`, you must follow these steps to package and deploy the servlet example.

1. Click the File ⇨ New ⇨ Application menu option. Alternatively, you can click the New Application icon on the toolbar.

2. The New Application dialog box will appear, in which you must supply the name of the file that will function as the EAR file. The display name will be set based on the file name, but you can change it to something else if you want. For this example, I used the file name `JMX-Programming`. Click the OK button when finished.

3. Select the application from the navigation tree in the left pane if it is not already selected.

4. Click the File ⇨ New ⇨ Web Component menu option. Alternatively, you can click the New Web Component icon on the toolbar. This will launch the New Web Component Wizard, which will guide you step by step through the process of adding a Web component — in this case, servlets and a JSP — to your application.

5. In the dialog box, make sure the Create a New WAR file in Application radio button is selected, and that the application named JMX-Programming is selected in the drop-down list below the radio button.

6. In the WAR Display Name text field, enter the name that will be used to display the WAR to management and deployment tools. I used the same name as the application name: JMX-Programming. Next, you need to specify the files that will be used in Step 8 of the process.

7. In the Contents pane at the bottom of the dialog box, you will find a tree with the top-level node labeled WEB-INF. This is the main directory in which the components will reside when they are deployed. The J2EE specification defines a directory structure to which Web applications must adhere.

8. Click the Edit button to the right of the Contents pane. This launches a dialog box that enables you to specify the actual class names of the Web components. The top pane is a directory tree view of your local file system. The bottom pane is the directory view of the Web application. From the top pane labeled Available Files, navigate to the `com.hmi.servlet` directory. From the list of files, select the `MBeanServlet.class`, the `JMXServlet.class`, and the `JMXServletMBean.class`. After selecting each file, click the Add button in the middle-right of the dialog box. When you have added all three classes, click the OK button at the bottom-right to continue.

9. Click the Next button, which opens the Choose Component Type dialog box. Here, you indicate the primary component type that you are deploying. For this example, make sure that the Servlet radio button is selected, and click the Next button. This takes you to the Component Properties dialog box.

10. From the servlet drop-down class, select the `com.hmi.servlet.MBeanServlet`. In the Web Component Name text field, type in the name of the servlet. I used `MBean Servlet` for this example. When you are done, click the Finish button, which completes this part of the packaging.

11. Click on the tree node labeled MBeanServet, select the Aliases tab in the right pane, and click the Add button. This will add to the list of aliases a row in which you can type in a value of **bean** and enter Return. Now you are ready to add the JSP to the application.

12. Select the File ⇨ New ⇨ Web Component menu option, which again displays the New Web Component Wizard dialog box. This time, you are going to add a Web component to the WAR that you created in the previous steps. Rather than selecting the Create a New WAR file in Application radio button, you need to select the Add to existing WAR in Application radio button.

13. Follow Steps 7 and 8 to select the `monitorservlet.jsp` JSP file and then click the Next button to continue. This will display the Choose Component Type dialog box, where you need to select the JSP radio button. Click the Next button to continue to the Component General Properties dialog box.

14. Select the `monitorservlet.jsp` file from the JSP drop-down list and type in a name for the JSP in the Web Component text field. For this example, I used the value `Monitor JSP`.

15. Repeat Steps 13 and 14, but this time select `viewinterface.jsp` from the JSP drop-down list. I used `viewinterface` for the JSP name. Click the Finish button when you are done.

16. Repeat Step 11, but this time select the Monitor JSP node from the tree and type in a value of **monitor** for the alias of this JSP. Repeat this step, but this time select viewinterface for the JSP name and use a value of **viewinterface** for the alias of this JSP. After this step, you are ready to deploy the application.

17. Make sure that the J2EE reference implementation server is running before attempting to deploy.

18. Select the File ⇨ Add Server menu option. The Add Server dialog box appears with a default value of `localhost`; click the OK button to accept this value. You will see a new addition to the tree in the deployment tool.

19. Select the application labeled JMX-Programming from the tree and then select the Tool ⇨ Deploy menu option. This will launch the Deploy Introduction dialog box. Make sure that in the Object to Deploy drop-down list, the application name JMX-Programming is selected, and that the Target Server drop-down list contains the server named localhost. Click the Next button to continue to the WAR Context Root dialog box.

20. In the Context Root field of the row, type in a value of **/jmx**. This is the root of the Web components that you will use to access the application. Click the Finish button to initiate the deployment. A dialog box will appear indicating the progress of the deployment and any errors that occur during deployment. If all goes well, you should see a dialog box similar to the one shown in Figure 15-1.

The output from the dialog box indicates that your Web components were successfully deployed to the server. At this point, you are ready to go. You can open a Web browser and begin with the next set of instructions. When deploying the example application, you don't need to restart the J2EE server in order for it to be available.

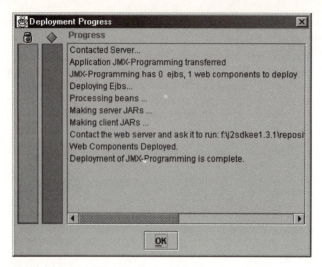

**Figure 15-1:** Successful deployment of the JMX-Programming J2EE Web application.

## Running the example

After you have deployed the example, you are ready to try it out. First, make sure that the `JMXServlet` and `MBeanServlet` have been initialized. You can initialize both of these using the alias bean that you defined during deployment by navigating your Web browser to `http://localhost:8000/jmx/bean`.

You should then see a message printed to your browser window that says `HelloWorld from MBeanServlet`. Once this is done, you are ready to launch the monitor and see what servlet MBeans have been loaded. You can launch the monitor JSP using another alias that was defined during deployment: monitor. Navigate your Web browser to `http://localhost:8000/jmx/monitor`. You should see a display similar to the one shown in Figure 15-2.

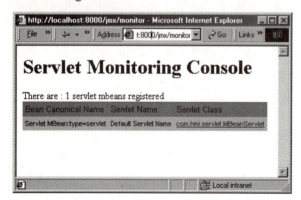

**Figure 15-2:** Monitoring your servlet using JMX.

You can see from Figure 15-2 that the MBean representing the `com.hmi.servlet` `.MBeanServlet` class has been loaded. You don't see the `JMMBeanDelegate` MBean that appeared in other examples in this book because of the pattern-matching used in the call to `queryMBeans()`, which filtered out only the MBeans with a key/value pair of `type=servlet`.

Clicking on the name of the servlet class takes you to the detail screen for that servlet. Here, you find detailed information about the attributes and operations of the servlet MBean. This information is about the management interface, rather than runtime information about the servlet MBean. Figure 15-3 shows the detail screen.

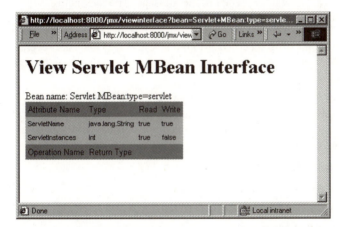

**Figure 15-3:** Viewing the management interface for a servlet MBean.

Servlets are only one type of component you might find in an enterprise application. Enterprise applications written in Java may make use of software components called EJBs. These beans can represent remote client functionality and persistent data that your application can access. Some developers argue that the inefficiency of EJBs has affected their acceptance into enterprise development with Java. Therefore, the capability to monitor and record metrics about their processing becomes even more important.

It is also interesting — from an administrator's perspective — to monitor enterprise components like EJBs to retrieve various statistics, such as how many EJBs of a particular type are pooled, how many requests have been made, and who the caller is.

Before the EJB 2.0 specification, there were only two types of EJBs: Session and Entity beans. With the EJB 2.0 specification, a new bean type was added: the Message-Driven Bean (MDB). This EJB enables you to asynchronously process requests, unlike Session beans, which process requests synchronously. The capability to process requests asynchronously is imperative because it decreases the load on applications.

The next example follows in the spirit of the preceding servlet example. For this one, you will implement a Message-Driven Bean. You'll then write some JavaServer Pages to monitor the bean.

# Monitoring Message-Driven Beans

A Message-Driven Bean (MDB), as its name implies, processes messages in a manner similar to a JMS message consumer. The basic concept of messaging works like this: A client sends messages to a queue, messages that are later taken off the queue by the JMS provider and delivered to a recipient (or, the recipient retrieves the messages off the queue). Message-Driven Beans act as receivers of messages, and messages are delivered to them in the same way that they are sent to a JMS message listener.

This is how asynchronous processing is accomplished: The sender of the message does not have to wait for the recipient to acknowledge receipt of the message. The messaging infrastructure in an application server will take the message off the queue and deliver it to the MDB later. A single message can be delivered to multiple MDBs because more than a single listener can register to receive events off a specified JMS queue. Messages can take several forms, from simple text to binary, and you can subclass the JMS API class `Message` to create your own variants.

The asynchronous nature of MDBs, the pooling of them, and the varying types of messages lend themselves to being candidates for monitoring. This example focuses on first implementing an MDB, and then providing attributes and operations of the MBean, which enable you to ask the following questions:

- How many instances of an MDB exist?
- How many messages has an MDB received?
- How many total bytes in size were the messages received?
- What types of messages have been received?

This example follows the same implementation procedure outlined for the servlet example. You will first review how to set up the example and create the JMS queue to which you'll send messages. Then, to demonstrate the use of the management interface, you'll also write a client application simulator that will send various types of messages to the queue that are then delivered to the MDB. You'll then use a JSP to monitor the MDB and view simple statistics about the messages.

Some good news about this example is that MDBs are quite a bit easier to implement than their Session and Entity counterparts. This is partly because of the way that applications interact with MDBs. With Session beans, for example, you need to access a remote interface before you can use the bean. This remote interface needs to be defined along with the implementation by you, the developer.

Because MDBs work with messages, rather than having methods called directly by applications, you are only responsible for developing the MDB implementation class. The remainder of the work, locating and executing the `onMessage()` method of the MDB, is handled by the EJB container. A client's interaction with an MDB is completely transparent because it sends requests and data to a JMS queue; there are no interface names to identify. The only thing that client applications using MDBs need to know is the name of the queue to which messages should be sent. Queues are located using the Java Naming and Directory Interface (JNDI). The J2EE SDK provides utilities with which you can create queues, as well as a JMS provider that the applications you write can use. You can find out more about JNDI from the Java Tutorial at `java.sun.com/tutorial`.

## MDB lifecycle

Like servlets, MDBs have a lifecycle that is controlled by the EJB container. MDBs have methods similar to those of servlets that you can use to track the lifecycle of the MDB. Understanding the lifecycle of an MDB enables you to properly implement the management interface, just as it was implemented in the servlet example. The lifecycle of an MDB, although similar to that of a servlet, is slightly different in that it has two states: it does not exist, and it's ready. When an MDB moves from the "does not exist" state to the "ready" state, the EJB container calls a set of methods defined in the `MessageDrivenBean` interface. These methods notify you of the state of the MDB.

The lifecycle of an MDB follows a series of lifecycle events similar to that of a servlet. An MDB instance is created if one does not exist, and the EJB container calls the `ejbCreate()` method and `ejbRemove()` method for creation and deletion of the MDB, respectively. When a message is delivered, the `onMessage()` method is called. Figure 15-4 illustrates the lifecycle of an MDB and the states that it passes through.

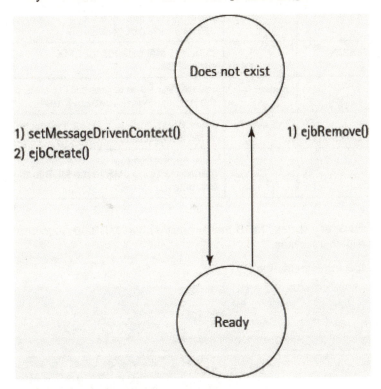

**Figure 15-4:** Lifecycle of a Message-Driven Bean.

What do Message-Driven Beans look like? They are quite simple, and implement only two interfaces: one that provides the necessary methods for receiving messages, and one that provides notification of two EJB lifecycle events. The first lifecycle event that MDBs and other EJBs receive is when an instance of the EJB has been created and instantiated into the container.

The second lifecycle event is when it is about to be removed from the container. Actually, these are not the only two events that an EJB can receive, but they are the only two that an MDB is required to implement methods for. Like the servlet example, these lifecycle event notifications enable you to make sure that a managed resource is actually available when the MBean exists in the MBean Server. The components for this example are summarized in Table 15-2.

### Table 15-2    Components for the MDB Example

| Component | Alias | Description |
| --- | --- | --- |
| JMXMessageDrivenBean | | Superclass for setting up the JMX MBean Server |
| JMXMessageDrivenBeanMBean | | Management interface for JMXMessageDrivenBean |
| ManagedMessageDrivenBean | | Subclass that extends the JMX superclass |
| monitormdb.jsp | /mdb | JavaServer Page to monitor the state of the ManagedMessageDrivenBean |
| viewmdbdetail.jsp | /viewmdb | JavaServer Page to monitor the values of MDB attributes |
| MDBClientSimulator | | Java application that sends a variety of messages using JMS to the MDB in this example |

Listing 15-6 shows the source of a skeletal MDB implementation. The MDB you implement for this example begins with this skeleton.

**Listing 15-6: Skeletal MDB implementation**

```
package com.hmi.mdb;

import javax.ejb.*;
import javax.jms.*;

public abstract class JMXMessageDrivenBean implements MessageDrivenBean,
                                                      MessageListener{

        public void ejbCreate(){};
```

```
        public void ejbRemove(){};

        public void onMessage(Message msg){
        }

        public void setMessageDrivenContext(MessageDrivenContext ctx){
        }

        public void onMessageInternal(Message msg){};

}
```

The class in this example is defined as abstract, which forces you to extend it. This is good for your example because you want the JMXMessageDrivenBean class to act as the owner of all JMX-specific tasks, such as registering and unregistering the MBean from the MBean Server and maintaining the values of attributes. Because you are going to subclass this class, you want to be able to intercept the messages and pass them on to your subclass. By intercepting the messages, you can record the information that you want to implement in the superclass.

However, you need a way to pass the message on to the subclass. If you subclass this class and override the onMessage() method, you will not be able to automatically access the message before passing it along. To accommodate this design, you specify a method called onMessageInternal(), which the subclass must implement to get its message. Because the JMXMessageDriveBean class is declared as abstract, a subclass must implement this message, even if it does not want to do anything with the message passed to it.

You now need to define a management interface that enables you to access the attributes representing the statistics you are compiling. This management interface, which enables you to ask the questions listed in the preceding section, looks like the source code in Listing 15-7.

**Listing 15-7: The JMXMessageDrivenBeanMBean interface**

```
package com.hmi.mdb;

import java.util.List;

public interface JMXMessageDrivenBeanMBean {

        public int getNumberInstances();
        public int getNumberMessagesProcessed();
        public int getTotalBytesProcessed();
        public List getMessageTypesProcessed();
}
```

Because this example illustrates monitoring various bits of information about an MDB, the methods listed in the interface result in a read-only view of an MBD. These methods will turn into accessor methods, not operations on the MDB, so you will use the getAttribute() method of the MBeanServer interface to retrieve the values of these fields.

The implementation of this interface is shown in Listing 15-8. This MDB implements the necessary management interface.

**Listing15-8: Implementation of the JMXMessageDrivenBeanMBean interface**

```
package com.hmi.mdb;

/**
 *
 * This MDB is responsible for implementing the parent
 * management interface. It manages interaction with the
 * MBeanServer and adding and removing itself from the
 * MBeanServer. It also handles the various metrics for
 * a sub-class of this bean.
 *
 **/

import javax.ejb.EJBException;
import javax.ejb.MessageDrivenBean;
import javax.ejb.MessageDrivenContext;
import javax.jms.Message;
import javax.jms.MessageListener;
import javax.jms.TextMessage;
import java.util.List;
import java.util.LinkedList;
import javax.management.ObjectName;
import javax.management.MBeanServer;
import javax.management.MBeanServerFactory;


public abstract class JMXMessageDrivenBean implements MessageDrivenBean,
                                          MessageListener,
                                          JMXMessageDrivenBeanMBean{

        private int numberInstances = 0;
        private int numberMessagesProcessed = 0;
        private int totalBytesProcessed = 0;
        private List messageTypesProcessed = new LinkedList();
        private static MBeanServer server_ = null;
        private static ObjectName mdbObjectName_ = null;

        public void ejbCreate(){

                if (server_ == null)
                    server_ = MBeanServerFactory.createMBeanServer();

                // Register this MBean
                try {
```

```
                    mdbObjectName_ = new
ObjectName("MessageDrivenMBean:type=mdb");

              server_.registerMBean((Object)this,mdbObjectName_);

         }catch(Exception ex){
             // rethrown as EJBException so MDB isn't initialized
             throw new EJBException(ex);
         }
    };
    public void ejbRemove(){
         System.out.println("ejbRemove called !!!!!!!!!!!!!!!!!");
    };

    public static MBeanServer getMBeanServer(){
         return server_;
    }

    public void onMessage(Message msg){

         // Increment counter
         numberMessagesProcessed++;

         // Calculate Bytes
         totalBytesProcessed+=calculateBytes(msg);

         // Pass message onto sub-class
         onMessageInternal(msg);
    }

    // Determines how to tabulate bytes based on
    // Message type
    private int calculateBytes(Message msg){
         int workingBytes = 0;
         try {
           if (msg instanceof TextMessage)

workingBytes+=((TextMessage)msg).getText().getBytes().length;
         }catch(Exception ex){};

         return workingBytes;
    }

    public void setMessageDrivenContext(MessageDrivenContext ctx){
    }

    // Management interface methods

    public int getNumberInstances(){
```

```
            return numberInstances;
        }

        public int getNumberMessagesProcessed(){
            return numberMessagesProcessed;
        }

        public int getTotalBytesProcessed(){
            return totalBytesProcessed;
        }

        public List getMessageTypesProcessed(){
            return messageTypesProcessed;
        }

        public void onMessageInternal(Message msg){};

}
```

The lifecycle of this MDB will enable you to perform the necessary initialization of required resources such as the MBean Server. The `ejbCreate()` method is called before the MDB is ready for work, and it is here where you create an instance of an MBean Server and store it in an instance variable for later use. This instance can later be accessed using the static method `getMBeanServer()` of this class.

You register an MBean using the object name `MessageDrivenMBean:type=mdb`. In the servlet example, you used a similar technique of registering the MBean for this MDB. If any exceptions are thrown during this initialization process, an `EJBException` is thrown and wraps the real exception, which could be a JMX-specific exception such as `InstanceAlreadyExistsException` or `MalformedObjectNameException`. By throwing an exception during this phase, you can prevent the MDB from being initialized.

## Compiling statistics

After the MBean has been registered and the MDB is available to receive messages, it is ready for work. Each time a message is delivered, the `onMessageInternal()` method will be called and you will perform the necessary calculations, storing the results in the instance variables. What happens if an exception is thrown while passing the information to a subclass? The `onMessage()` method does not define any checked exceptions, so it is possible that a runtime exception could occur while the subclass is processing the message.

For simplicity, I have chosen not to try to catch any exceptions that may be thrown during processing. If an exception were thrown, it could conceivably affect the statistics, because you could argue that the message was not really processed. Conversely, you could also argue that the definition of processing a message implies that the `onMessage()` method has been called and that the message be delivered regardless of what the MDB does with the message after delivery. I have taken the latter view for this example.

The `JMXMessageDrivenBean` is not meant to be used directly, so I have defined a subclass named `ManagedMessageDrivenBean`. This class will serve as the real working MDB for this example, although it is not going to do anything with the messages. Listing 15-9 shows the source of the `JMXMessageDrivenBeanMBean` class.

**Listing 15-9: Subclass of the JMXMessageDrivenBeanMBean MDB**

```
package com.hmi.mdb;

import javax.jms.Message;

public class ManagedMessageDrivenBean extends JMXMessageDrivenBean{

        public void onMessageInternal(Message msg){
                System.out.println("Message retrieved!!!!!!!!!");
        }

}
```

There's not a lot to say about the `ManagedMessageDrivenBean` class because this example doesn't do much with it. The real point of interest here is the `JMXMessageDriveBean` class that this class extends from. With this in mind, you simply print a message indicating that a message was received. Listing 15-10 shows the source of the `monitormdb.jsp` JSP.

**Listing 15-10: JavaServer Page to view management information**

```
<%@ page import="com.hmi.mdb.*" %>
<%@ page import="javax.management.*" %>
<%@ page import="java.util.*" %>
<%@ page import="java.net.*" %>
<HTML>
<STYLE type="text/css">
.HEADING {font-family:Arial;font-size:10pt;background-
color:rgb(98,161,162);}
.CELL {font-family:Arial;font-size:8pt;background-
color:rgb(173,200,217);}
</STYLE>
<BODY>

<H1>Message Driven Bean Monitoring Console</H1>

<%

 Set beans = null;

 MBeanServer beanServer = JMXMessageDrivenBean.getMBeanServer();

 if (beanServer != null)
    beans = beanServer.queryMBeans(new ObjectName("*:type=mdb"),null);
 else
```

```
    beans = new HashSet();

%>

There are : <%= beans.size() %> MDB mbeans registered <BR/>

<TABLE BORDER="0" CELLSPACING="0" CELLPADDING="4">
<TR><TD CLASS="HEADING">Bean Canonical Name</TD><TD CLASS="HEADING">MDB
Name</TD><TD CLASS="HEADING">MDB Class</TD><TD CLASS="HEADING">Messages
Processed</TD><TD CLASS="HEADING">Bytes Processed</TD></TR>
<%
  Iterator iter = beans.iterator();
  while (iter.hasNext()) {
      ObjectInstance bean = (ObjectInstance)iter.next();
      ObjectName beanObj = bean.getObjectName();
      out.println("<TR><TD
CLASS=\"CELL\">"+beanObj.getCanonicalName()+"</TD>");

      String mdbName = "Message Driven Bean";

      Integer msgsProcessed =
(Integer)beanServer.getAttribute(beanObj,"NumberMessagesProcessed");
      Integer bytesProcessed =
(Integer)beanServer.getAttribute(beanObj,"TotalBytesProcessed");
      out.println("<TD CLASS=\"CELL\">"+mdbName+"</TD>");
      String className = bean.getClassName();
      out.println("<TD CLASS=\"CELL\"><a
href=\"/jmx/viewmdb?bean="+URLEncoder.encode(beanObj.getCanonicalName())
+"\">"+className+"</a></TD>");
      out.println("<TD
CLASS=\"CELL\">"+msgsProcessed.intValue()+"</TD>");
      out.println("<TD
CLASS=\"CELL\">"+bytesProcessed.intValue()+"</TD></TR>");
      //out.println("<TD CLASS=\"CELL\"><a
href=\"/jmx/viewinterface\">"+className+"</a></TD></TR>");

  }
%>
</TABLE>

</BODY>
</HTML>
```

This JSP prints some high-level information about the MDB MBean. It should be saved into a file named monitormdb.jsp. In addition to the canonical name, the MDB name, and the class name, the JSP prints two statistics that the parent JMX MBean class compiles: the number of messages processed and the size in bytes of those messages. These values are retrieved using the getAttribute() method of the MBeanServer interface. The attributes retrieved are TotalBytesProcessed and NumberMessagesProcessed, and are integers.

You also need to build a detail page — just as you did for the servlet example — that will show you the attributes and operations. This detail page will go a little further and display the current values of the attributes. Listing 15-11 shows the source of the `viewmdbdetail.jsp` JSP.

**Listing 15-11: Detail page for the MDB example**

```
<%@ page import="com.hmi.mdb.*" %>
<%@ page import="javax.management.*" %>
<%@ page import="java.util.*" %>

<HTML>
<STYLE type="text/css">
.HEADING {font-family:Arial;font-size:10pt;background-
color:rgb(98,161,162);}
.CELL {font-family:Arial;font-size:8pt;background-
color:rgb(173,200,217);}
</STYLE>
<BODY>

<H1>View MDB MBean Interface</H1>

<%

 Set beans = null;

 MBeanServer beanServer = JMXMessageDrivenBean.getMBeanServer();

 if (beanServer != null)
    beans = beanServer.queryMBeans(new ObjectName("*:type=mdb"),null);
 else
    beans = new HashSet();

%>

Bean name: <%= request.getParameter("bean") %><BR/>

<TABLE BORDER="0" CELLSPACING="0" CELLPADDING="4">
<%
  Iterator iter = beans.iterator();
  while (iter.hasNext()) {
      ObjectInstance bean = (ObjectInstance)iter.next();
      ObjectName beanObj = bean.getObjectName();
      MBeanInfo beanInfo = beanServer.getMBeanInfo(beanObj);
      MBeanAttributeInfo attInfo[] = beanInfo.getAttributes();
      %>
 <TR><TD CLASS="HEADING">Attribute Name</TD><TD
CLASS="HEADING">Type</TD><TD CLASS="HEADING">Read</TD><TD
CLASS="HEADING">Write</TD><TD CLASS="HEADING">Current Value</TD></TR>
```

```
<%
        for (int i=0;i<attInfo.length;i++){
            out.println("<TR><TD
CLASS=\"CELL\">"+attInfo[i].getName()+"</TD>");
            out.println("<TD
CLASS=\"CELL\">"+attInfo[i].getType()+"</TD><TD CLASS=\"CELL\">"+
                        attInfo[i].isReadable()+"</TD>");
            out.println("<TD
CLASS=\"CELL\">"+attInfo[i].isWritable()+"</TD>");
            out.println("<TD
CLASS=\"CELL\">"+beanServer.getAttribute(beanObj,attInfo[i].getName())+"
</TD></TR>");
        }
%>
 <TR><TD CLASS="HEADING">Operation Name</TD><TD CLASS="HEADING">Return
Type</TD><TD CLASS="HEADING" COLSPAN="3"> </TD></TR>
<%

        MBeanOperationInfo opInfo[] = beanInfo.getOperations();

        for (int j=0;j<opInfo.length;j++){
            out.println("<TR><TD
CLASS=\"CELL\">"+opInfo[j].getName()+"</TD><TD CLASS=\"CELL\">"+
opInfo[j].getReturnType() + "</TD><TD CLASS=\"CELL\"
COLSPAN=\"3\"> </TD></TR>");
        }


    }
%>
</TABLE>

</BODY>
</HTML>
```

This JSP should be saved in a file named `viewmdbdetail.jsp`. This JSP operates almost identically to the detail page that was shown in the servlet example. The primary differences are that it obtains a handle to the MBean Server from the `JMXMessageDrivenBean` class and prints the current value of each attribute found in the management interface.

The client simulator application is next, and it is responsible for sending enough messages so that your example has some data to work with. Listing 15-12 shows the source for the application, which is just a simple Java application that uses JMS.

**Listing 15-12: Client simulator application**

```
package com.hmi.mdb;

/**
 *
```

```
     * This application will send several requests to an
     * MDB. Each request will consist of varying message types
     * that are defined in the javax.jms package.
     *
     **/

import javax.jms.*;
import javax.naming.*;

public class MDBClientSimulator {

        public static void main(String args[]){

            try{
                Context ctx = new InitialContext();
                QueueConnectionFactory qFactory =

(QueueConnectionFactory)ctx.lookup("jms/QueueConnectionFactory");
                QueueConnection qConnect =
qFactory.createQueueConnection();
                Queue theQueue = (Queue)ctx.lookup("jms/Queue");
                QueueSession qSession =

qConnect.createQueueSession(false,Session.AUTO_ACKNOWLEDGE);
                // Create Sender //
                QueueSender qSender = qSession.createSender(theQueue);
                TextMessage msg =
(TextMessage)qSession.createTextMessage();
                msg.setText("JMX Programming Guide");
                for (int i=0;i<20;i++)
                    qSender.send(msg);
                qConnect.close();
                System.exit(0);
            } catch (Exception ex){
                System.out.println("EXCEPTION: " + ex);
            }
        }
    }

}
```

The MDBClientSimulator is relatively straightforward. It operates by first creating a JMS queue using the default JMS queue. This queue is retrieved using JNDI and the name jms/Queue. Next, you create a session; and from this session, you create a QueueSender. This QueueSender is the object you will use to send the messages to the MDB.

For this example, you're going to create a text message and then send this message repeatedly in a simple for/loop. After all the messages have been sent, close the connection to the JMS service and exit the application. The application assumes that all messages have been delivered and does not check to see if any exceptions occurred while either creating the text message or sending it.

## Deploying the MDB example

Before you can use the MDB, you need to deploy it as you did with the servlet example earlier. The steps to deploy the MDB will be shorter because you are going to re-use the application JAR we created earlier.

> **NOTE:** If you have not gone through the servlet example, you may want to review the section titled "Packaging and deploying the servlet example." It explains how to create the initial Enterprise Application Archive and Web Application Archive.

For this example, you add the MDB and the new JSPs. The JSPs are added to the WAR file, and the MDBs are added to the EAR file. The steps shown here assume that you already have the deployment tool running.

1.  Select the JMX-Programming application in the navigation tree.

2.  Select New ⇨ Enterprise Bean from the File menu. This option launches the New Enterprise Bean Wizard.

3.  You will see an introduction screen. Read the introduction to get an idea of the type of information you will be requested to supply, and then click the Next button to continue.

4.  Select JMX-Programming from the drop-down list for the Create a New EJB File in Application option. (If you have more than one application defined, you will also see the others in the drop-down list.)

5.  Type **JMX-Programming** in the EJB Display Name text field.

6.  In the lower part of the dialog box is a section titled Contents. This is where you will select the class from the file system to be placed in the JAR. Click the Edit button at the middle-right. This launches a dialog box titled Edit contents of JMX-Programming.

7.  At the top of the dialog box, in the Available Files area, navigate using the tree until you see the class named ManagedMessageDrivenBean.class in the list. Highlight the class and click the Add button. The ManagedMessageDrivenBean.class is added to the lower pane titled Contents of JMX-Programming. Repeat this step for both the JMXMessageDrivenBean.class and the JMXMessageDrivenBeanMBean.class. Click the OK button when you are ready to proceed.

8.  Click the Next button to navigate to the dialog box in which you will select the type of bean you desire.

9.  Select the radio button labeled Message-Driven. Then select ManagedMessageDrivenBean from the drop-down list labeled Enterprise Bean Class. Type **ManagedMessageDrivenBean** in the text field labeled Enterprise Bean Name. Click the Next button to proceed.

10. In the next dialog box you will select the type of Transaction Management for the bean. For this example, select the radio button labeled Container-Managed. This causes a row to be added to the table below the radio buttons. You can leave the values of this row as is and click the Next button to proceed.

**11.**   In the next dialog box you will select the destination for messages that the bean is expecting. By default, the radio button labeled Queue is selected. You are going to use queues for this example, so leave that selection as is. Next, select the value `jms/Queue` from the drop-down list labeled Destination, and `jms/QueueConnectionFactory` from the drop-down list labeled Connection Factory. Click the Finish button.

Now you need to proceed with adding the JSP for this example.

**12.**   Select the File ⇨ New ⇨ Web Component menu option, which again displays the New Web Component Wizard dialog box. This time, you are going to add a Web component to the WAR that you created in the previous steps. Rather than selecting the Create a New WAR file in Application radio button, you need to select the Add to existing WAR in Application radio button.

**13.**   Follow Steps 7 and 8 to select the `monitormdb.jsp` JSP file and then click the Next button to continue. This will display the Choose Component Type dialog box, where you need to select the JSP radio button. Click the Next button to continue to the Component General Properties dialog box.

**14.**   Select the `monitormdb.jsp` file from the JSP drop-down list and type in a name for the JSP in the Web Component text field. For this example, I used the value `Monitor MDB JSP`. Repeat teps 13 and 14, but this time select `viewmdbdetail.jsp` from the JSP drop-down list. I used `viewmdb` for the JSP name. Click the Finish button when you are done.

**15.**   Click on the tree node labeled Monitor MDB JSP, select the Aliases tab in the right pane, and click the Add button. This will add to the list of aliases a row in which you can type in a value of **mdb** and enter Return. Repeat this step, but this time select the **viewmdb** JSP and type in a name of **viewmdb** for the alias. Now you are ready to add the JSP to the application.

**16.**   Click the Finish button. Several screens remain for this dialog box, but for this example you do not need to access them. You will be returned to the main dialog box of the `deploytool`.

**17.**   Next you need to add the `MDBClientSimulator` application to the EAR. To do this select the File ⇨ New ⇨ Application Client from the menu. This displays the New Application Client Wizard. Click the Next button to continue. This displays the New Application Client Wizard – JAR Contents dialog box.

**18.**   Make sure you have selected the JMX-Programming entry in the drop-down at the top. In the Contents page at the bottom, click the Edit button, which displays the Edit Contents of <Application Client> dialog box. Select the `com/hmi/mdb/MDBClientSimulator.class` class from the list of files and click the OK button to continue.

**19.**   The next dialog box is the New Application Client Wizard – General dialog box. You can leave all the fields at their default values and click the Next button. On the next dialog displayed, click on the Finish button and proceed to Step 20.

**20.**   Select the `JMX-Programming` node in the tree of the dialog box and then select Tools ⇨ Deploy. This brings up a dialog box in which you select the object you want to deploy. From the Object to Deploy drop-down list, select JMX-Programming. Select `localhost` from the Target Server drop-down list. You should already have a server added to the `deploytool`'s list of available J2EE servers. You must have a J2EE server running before you can add it to the list.

**21.** If you are writing a standalone client application, you should select the check box labeled Return Client Jar. The dialog box explains what this JAR is for. When ready to proceed, click the Next button. When the next dialog box is displayed, click Next again and then click the Finish button.

## Running the MDBClientSimulator

Before you can execute the client simulator, it needs to be compiled, of course. This can be done using the normal javac compiler. When you want to run the application, I recommend using the `runclient.bat` script that is provided with the J2EE SDK. Many libraries are involved with J2EE, and the client application makes use of a couple of them. In addition, many environment variables will be set up to make sure that things are in order before your application is run.

Rather than trying to keep track of all the required libraries, the `runclient.bat` application makes it easy for you by handling all the details. You can execute the client simulator by passing it as a parameter to the `runclient.bat` script:

```
runclient -client JMX-Programming.ear -name MDBClientSimulator
```

The `-client` argument is used to indicate the name of the JAR or EAR where the application resides, and the `-name` argument is the name of the class with the `main()` method that will be executed. When the application begins to execute, you are prompted for a username and password. You can use a value of `guest` for the username and `guest123` for the password. After you've entered the authentication information, click OK and the `MDBClientSimulator` application will begin to run.

After running the client simulator application a few times, you can launch your Web browser and point it at the URL `http://localhost:8000/jmx/mdb`. You should see output in the Web browser that looks like what is shown in Figure 15-5.

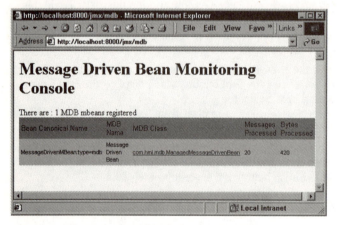

**Figure 15-5:** Monitoring a Message-Driven Bean with JMX.

From the output, you can see that several messages have been processed. You can also optionally launch the browser, run the MDBClientSimulator another time, and refresh the display of the browser. If you do, you will see the counts for Messages Processed, and Bytes Processed increase as the MDBClientSimulator runs.

You can see from the display that the MDB MBean was registered properly and has recorded some statistics! In this example, I ran the MDBClientSimulator twice before checking the state of the MDB. It recorded that twenty messages — with a total byte count of 420 — have been processed at this point. Of course, a refresh of this Web page could change those results; and you might even manage to catch the values increasing if the MDBClientSimulator is running. All the information you see in this display was derived from the management interface defined in the JMXMessageDrivenMBean interface.

Each MDB listed in the display has a link from the MDB class name to a detail page. This is the same navigation option that was used in the servlet example earlier. I have included some, but not all, of the detail information on this page as well. When you click on the link, you are taken to a detail page that lists all the attributes and operations. Each attribute that is listed includes detail information for that attribute. Figure 15-6 shows the detail page from this example after running the MDBClientSimulator application twice.

I have re-used the viewinterface.jsp JSP from the servlet example and changed it slightly to include some additional information about each attribute that is found. The detail for an attribute includes the Java type of the attribute, whether it is read-write, and the current value at the time this page was last displayed.

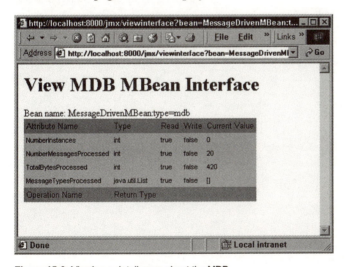

**Figure 15-6:** Viewing a detail page about the MDB.

The current values represent the last values of the fields, and they are printed using the toString() method of the various Java types. That is why in this example display, the current value of the MessageTypesProcessed attribute indicates two brackets []. If there were members in the list, they would show up here. When processing the return values of attributes, you can also check the Java type and do special processing before displaying the value. For this example, however, I've relied on the `toString()` method of each type to show the values.

## Summary

This chapter examined how to use JMX in a J2EE environment by monitoring servlets and Message-Driven Beans. Each example built on the concepts presented earlier in the book by building standard MBeans that represented the management interface for a servlet and an MDB.

The servlet example focused on viewing the management interface using a JSP, but the MDB example went a little further. It used the management MBean for the MDB to compile some statistics about the messages processed by the MDB. These statistics can later be viewed using a JSP. The detail page for the MDB not only showed the attributes of the management interface, but their current values as well.

With JMX you can develop a management interface for any Java, and in some cases non-Java, object or application. You can manage J2EE and non-J2EE applications as well as hardware devices. The JMX specification provides a solid foundation for management frameworks that, like the J2EE management specification, is being adopted in other areas of management. With the examples in this book and the coverage of the JMX specification, you will be well prepared to use JMX in your own applications.

# Appendix A

# JMX Resources

You can find a number of invaluable resources when working with JMX. These resources include, but are not limited to, reference implementations of the JMX specification. Some are related utilities for working with network protocols. Provided here is a list of addresses for the various specifications you might work with, and Web sites offering tools that may be of assistance to you.

## Reference Implementations

♦ Sun JMX reference implementation 1.0 /1.1 maintenance release

    http://java.sun.com/jmx

♦ Java Dynamic Management Kit

    www.sun.com/products-n-solutions/nep/software/java-dynamic

♦ Tivoli JMX reference implementation

    www.alphaworks.ibm.com/tech/TMX4J

♦ MX4J open-source reference implementation

    http://mx4j.sourceforge.net

## Networking APIs

♦ AdventNet Agent Toolkit / ManageEngine

    www.adventnet.com

♦ NET-SNMP

    www.net-snmp.org

# Products That Use JMX and Network Management Products

- ◆ JBoss Application Server

  `www.jboss.org`

- ◆ BEA Weblogic Application Server

  `www.beasys.com`

- ◆ Lutris Enhydra Application Server

  `www.lutris.com/enhydra`

- ◆ CA Unicenter

  `www.cai.com/unicenter`

- ◆ Hewlett Packard OpenView

  `www.openview.hp.com`

- ◆ Tivoli Netview

  `www.tivoli.com/products/index/netview/`

- ◆ Hewlett Packard Application Server

  `www.hpmiddleware.com`

- ◆ Macromedia JRUN 4

  `http://www.macromedia.com/jrun`

- ◆ Pramati Application Server

  `www.pramati.com`

- ◆ Sun ONE Application Server

  `wwws.sun.com/software/products/appsrvr/home_appsrvr.html`

# Standards and Organizations

- ◆ Internet Engineering Task Force

  `www.ietf.org`

- ◆ Distributed Management Task Force

  `www.dmtf.org`

- ◆ Web Based Enterprise Management

  `www.dmtf.org/wbem`

- ◆ Common Information Model

  `www.dmtf.org`
- ◆ Simple Network Management Protocol (SNMPv1)

  `www.ietf.org/rfc/rfc1157.txt`
- ◆ Simple Network Management Protocol (SNMPv2)

  `www.ietf.org`
- ◆ Simple Network Management Protocol (SNMPv3)

  `www.ietf.org`
- ◆ Hypertext Transfer Protocol (HTTP)

  `www.w3.org/Protocols/rfc2616/rfc2616.html`

# Web Sites:

- ◆ SNMP Web general XSNMP tools

  `www.simpleweb.org`
- ◆ Open NMS

  `www.opennms.com`
- ◆ SNPM products

  `www.snmp-products.com`
- ◆ SNMP utilitites

  `www.snmp.com`
- ◆ SNMP FAQ Part 1

  `www.faqs.org/faqs/snmp-faq/part1/`
- ◆ SNMP FAQ Part 2

  `www.faqs.org/faqs/snmp-faq/part2/`

# *Appendix B*

# **JMX Exceptions**

The exceptions defined in the JMX specification cover a wide range of problems. The exceptions can result from user-defined modules or the JMX implementation itself. The JMX specifications provide some standard exception classes, and developers can also create user-defined exceptions.

User-defined modules can include services or MBeans that you write yourself. The exceptions that can result from user-defined modules can be ones that you define yourself or those that represent runtime exceptions. This appendix describes the different exceptions, most of which are covered in various chapters of this book.

## javax.management.*

 - ◆ AttributeNotFoundException

   When attempting to get or set the value of an attribute, the attribute could not be found in the MBean with the object name you specified. This could be because you have specified the wrong MBean object name, you have the wrong attribute name, or you have misspelled the attribute name. Another possibility is that you used the wrong case for the attribute. For example, if you have an attribute named "QueueSize" and you try to access that attribute using "queueSize" this exception will be thrown.

 - ◆ BadAttributeValueExpException

   This exception is thrown during construction of a query expression involving an `AttributeValueExp` object. The `AttributeValueExp` object must be a valid attribute.

 - ◆ BadBinaryOpValueExpException

   This exception is thrown when an invalid expression is passed to one of the methods while constructing a query expression.

 - ◆ BadStringOperationException

   This exception is thrown when constructing a query and an invalid `StringValueExp` is passed to one of the methods while constructing a query expression.

 - ◆ InstanceAlreadyExistsException

   An instance of the MBean that is being registered is already registered in the MBean Server you are using. You must unregister the first MBean before another MBean with the same object name can be registered in the MBean Server.

◆ InstanceNotFoundException

The MBean with the object name specified is not registered in the MBean Server you are using. The object name you specify must match exactly in order for the MBean to be located. You can optionally use either the `queryNames()` or `queryMBeans()` methods of the `MBeanServer` interface to find MBeans using pattern matching on the object name.

◆ IntrospectionException

While an MBean was being introspected, an exception was thrown. Chapter 5 described dynamic MBeans and how to build the management interface using the reflection API. Using this API can result in exceptions of this type being thrown. The introspection of an MBean occurs when the MBean Server is examining its management interface. Because introspection is a dynamic process, exceptions that only occur at runtime might be exposed as an `IntrospectionException`.

◆ InvalidApplicationException

This exception occurs when attempting to apply a query or attribute value expression to an MBean of the wrong class.

◆ InvalidAttributeValueException

This exception is thrown as a result of using an invalid value when setting the value of an attribute. For example, if you have an attribute that is defined as type `java.lang.String` and you try to set its value as `java.util.Set`, this exception will be thrown.

◆ JMException

This class represents exceptions thrown by JMX implementations, except for runtime exceptions. For runtime exceptions, see the `JMRuntimeException` class.

◆ JMRuntimeException

This class acts as the superclass for runtime exceptions that occur in JMX implementations. Instances of `java.lang.RuntimeException` that are thrown from JMX implementation methods, such as those that invoke methods and get or set attributes on MBeans, will be caught and rethrown as a `JMRuntimeException`.

◆ ListenerNotFoundException

This exception occurs when an attempt is made to send a notification to a listener that is no longer registered or never was registered. Notifications are usually sent to classes that implement the `NotificationListener` interface, but it is possible to send notifications to a registered MBean. MBeans can be dynamically loaded and unloaded, which might lead to the possibility of this exception being thrown.

To reduce the chances of this exception occuring, notification broadcasters might want to register interest in the registration and unregistration of MBeans that act as notification listeners.

♦ MalformedObjectNameException

When constructing an object name string, the `ObjectName` class must be able to parse the string into a valid object name representation. Chapter 8 covers the format of the object name. The object name can consist of a domain and one or more key/value pairs.

♦ MBeanException

This class acts as a wrapper for user-defined unknown exceptions that occur while performing operations on an MBean. For example, if a `NullPointerException` is thrown while in a method of an MBean, this will be caught and rethrown as an `MBeanException`. You can also utilize this exception class to catch and rethrow your own exceptions so that problems with your MBean can be dealt with in a standard way.

♦ MBeanRegistrationException

This exception wraps exceptions that are thrown during the registration phase of an MBean. This exception will be thrown from the `preRegister()` and `preDeregister()` methods of the `MBeanRegistration` interface. These methods are called immediately before an MBean is registered and immediately before an MBean is unregistered from the MBean Server.

♦ NotCompliantMBeanException

The MBean you are attempting to register in an MBean Server is not compliant with the JMX specification standards. This might happen if you specify a class for a standard MBean that does not implement an interface that matches the standard naming convention for MBean interfaces. The JMXGrinder utility can help you ensure that MBeans you design and implement are compliant with the specification.

♦ OperationsException

This class acts as the superclass for exceptions that occur when performing operations on an MBean. Subclasses of this exception include MBean `AttributeNotFoundException`, `InstanceAlreadyExistsException`, and `NotCompliantMBeanException`.

♦ ReflectionException

This exception represents exceptions thrown in the MBean Server while using the Java Reflection API to invoke methods of MBeans.

♦ RuntimeErrorException

This exception should be used by JMX agents when a `java.lang.Error` occurs. JMX agents should catch the `java.lang.Error` and re-throw it as a `RuntimeErrorException`.

♦ RuntimeMBeanException

This exception is thrown by an MBean Server when a `java.lang.RuntimeException` is thrown by a method of an MBean. The MBean Server will build an instance of the `RuntimeMBeanException` and wrap the original MBean runtime exception.

♦ RuntimeOperationsException

This exception is thrown by an MBean Server when a
`java.lang.RuntimeException` is thrown by a method of an MBean while
performing operations on an MBean. The MBean Server will build an instance of the
`RuntimeOperationException` and wrap the original MBean runtime exception.

♦ ServiceNotFoundException

This exception is thrown when attempting to use a service that is not supported. The
supported services are those that are considered core components of the JMX
implementation, such as M-Let or monitor.

## javax.management.modelmbean.*

♦ InvalidTargetObjectTypeException

This exception is thrown when an invalid target object is specified while setting the
managed resource of a model MBean, or when an operation is attempted against a model
MBean and the target object in the descriptor specifies an invalid object type. When
using model MBeans, a specific set of object types can be managed.

♦ XMLParseException

This exception is thrown while creating an instance of a model MBean from an XML
string, or while creating an XML string from an MBean instance. This is also intended
for use with XML parser exceptions that are being used in an MBean implementation.

## javax.management.monitor.*

♦ MonitorSettingException

This exception is thrown if a monitored attribute becomes invalid during monitoring.
Each time an attribute is monitored, it is checked for validity before its value is retrieved
and returned to listeners.

## javax.management.relation.*

♦ InvalidRelationIdException

This exception is thrown when trying to define a relation ID that has already been used.

♦ InvalidRelationServiceException

This exception is thrown when an operation is attempted against an invalid relation
service.

♦ InvalidRelationTypeException

This exception can occur during definition of a relation type and is caused because a
relation type with the same name already exists; the same relation type has been used for
two different `RoleInfo` objects; or when creating the relation type, a null or non-
existent `RoleInfo` object was provided.

♦ InvalidRoleInfoException

This exception occurs when the minimum defined number of MBeans exceeds the maximum defined number of MBeans. This exception is similar to the `InvalidRoleValueException` but it does not cover as many causes.

♦ InvalidRoleValueException

This exception occurs when the value of a role conflicts with the constraints defined in its `RoleInfo` object. The `RoleInfo` object defines the cardinality, which indicates the minimum and maximum number of MBeans that can be in a role value at one time. This exception can also occur if one of the MBeans in a role is not of the same type as all the others. Role values must consist of MBeans that share the same class.

♦ RelationException

This class represents the superclass of all exceptions that can be raised by the relation service.

♦ RelationNotFoundException

This exception occurs when an attempt is made to use a relation that does not exist or has not been defined in the relation service.

♦ RelationServiceNotRegisteredException

This exception occurs when an action is attempted against the relation service and a relation service MBean has not been registered in the MBean Server you are using. The relation service is one of the agent services defined in the JMX specification, and is implemented as an MBean.

♦ RelationTypeNotFoundException

This exception occurs when an attempt is made to use a relation type that does not exist or has not been defined in the relation service.

♦ RoleInfoNotFoundException

This exception occurs when an attempt is made to use a `RoleInfo` object that does not exist or has not been defined in the relation service.

♦ RoleNotFoundException

This exception occurs when an attempt is made to use a role that has not been defined, or is not readable or writable.

# Appendix C

# JMX Tracing and Debugging

In Chapter 8, you learned how to use the MBean Server and the dynamic loading agent service. Chapter 8 also briefly introduced you to debugging M-Let tags, and provided a class that utilizes some of the debugging and tracing facilities built into the Sun JMX reference implementation.

> **NOTE:** The examples in this appendix make use of the `SimpleObject` class that was introduced in Chapter 8, Listing 8-10. You can substitute a class of your own design here if you wish, however the output from the examples will be slightly different.

This appendix describes the debugging and tracing facilities available in the Sun JMX reference implementation. As described in Chapter 8, the debugging and tracing facilities are not considered part of the official JMX specification, so the information provided applies only to the Sun JMX reference implementation. For instance, the Tivoli JMX reference implementation does not include similar tracing classes. From this appendix you'll learn how to do the following tasks:

- ◆ Identify the classes used for tracing and debugging
- ◆ Set up a `TraceListener` to listen for trace and debug events
- ◆ Filter the trace and debug events to identify those you are interested in
- ◆ Create your own custom `TraceListener` subclass

Even though the trace and debug facilities are not defined in the JMX specification, you can utilize some other aspects of JMX to provide similar capabilities. For instance, you can utilize the notification facilities to provide runtime diagnostics regarding when events are occurring, such as registration or changes in the values of an MBean. The debug and tracing facilities give you some insight into what the various components and agent services are doing while executing requests on your behalf. This appendix also examines the `Introspector` class that the Sun JMX reference implementation provides to check MBean compliance.

## Tracing and Debugging

The terms trace and debug as used in this appendix do not indicate implementations of classes for tracing and debugging. Rather, they indicate one set of classes that are used to establish a class as a listener for events related to debugging. These events can represent operations taking place in the different components of the Sun JMX reference implementation. The level of detail in the information that you can receive differs in the DEBUG and TRACE levels, as you'll see later in this appendix.

The tracing classes you'll be looking at are in the com.sun.jdmk package found in the jmxri.jar archive. Table C-1 describes the classes that you use to enable tracing in your JMX applications.

### Table C-1    Trace Classes

| Class Name | Description |
| --- | --- |
| Trace | The primary class for establishing notification listeners and filters. It also contains the static fields for the types of trace events that can be sent. |
| TraceListener | Represents a class that wants to receive trace events |
| TraceFilter | Represents a filter on the types of trace events you want to receive |
| TraceNotification | Represents a notification representing a trace event |

The trace facilities work in a manner similar to other notifications in the JMX architecture. You set up the options and types of events that you want to listen for, establish a listener, and add the listener to the component that will generate the events. In fact, the TraceListener, TraceFilter, and TraceNotification classes are based on the NotificationListener, NotificationFilter, and Notification classes, respectively, from the JMX specification.

## Trace event types

The types of trace events are determined by the static fields defined in the Trace class. The event types correspond to the different modules that exist in the Sun JMX reference implementation. For example, you can specify that you want to receive trace level events for the MBean Server, the timer service, or for the M-Let service.

Trace events come in two basic varieties, trace and debug, and each variety can be used for different situations. The trace level messages can be used by developers who need relatively detailed information about what is going on in the JMX implementation for writing JMX applications. The debug level messages can also help provide a developer with information about what is going on in the JMX implementation. You'll learn how to set up the event types you want in a moment. Table C-2 describes the different event types defined in the Trace class. This table is a subset of those defined in the Trace class that are specific to JMX. The others you'll see defined are related to the Java Dynamic Management Kit (JDMK) reference implementation. These fields are inherited from the com.sun.jdmk.trace.TraceTags interface.

## Table C-2    Subset of Trace Event Types

| Field Name | Description |
|---|---|
| INFO_ADAPTOR_HTML | Provides information about the HTML adapter in the Sun JMX reference implementation |
| INFO_ALL | Provides information about all event types |
| INFO_MBEAN_SERVER | Provides information about events in an MBean Server |
| INFO_MISC | Provides miscellaneous information about other classes |
| INFO_MLET | Provides information about the dynamic loading service |
| INFO_MODELMBEAN | Provides information about model MBeans |
| INFO_MONITOR | Provides information about the monitor service |
| INFO_RELATION | Provides information about the relation service |
| INFO_TIMER | Provides information about the timer service |
| LEVEL_DEBUG | Enables you to specify information at the debug level |
| LEVEL_TRACE | Enables you to specify information at the trace level |
| UNKNOWN_TYPE | Indicates that an unknown event type has occurred |

The Trace class includes two fields; LEVEL_DEBUG and LEVEL_TRACE, which are technically not event types, but fields that enable you to specify how much detail you want in your messages. How do these actually differ? The following code snippet represents output from an application that uses the MBean Server to load an MBean. The snippet shows some example output at LEVEL_TRACE level:

```
(MBeanServer createMBean) ClassName = SimpleObject,ObjectName =
SimpleObject:the
name=simple
(MBeanServer internal_addObject) Name= SimpleObject:thename=simple
(Repository addMBean) name=SimpleObject:thename=simple
(MBeanServer addObject) Send create notification of object
SimpleObject:thename=
simple
(MBeanServer sendNotification) Incr sequenceNumber = 2
```

The same example output at LEVEL_DEBUG looks identical. This is because debug messages are used to diagnose problems with the JMX implementation. In the case of a successful run, you would not see debug level messages. You would see messages at the LEVEL_DEBUG level emitted when an exception is thrown in some component of the JMX reference implementation, such as the MBean Server, whereas LEVEL_TRACE is used to diagnose problems that exist in a JMX application that may not necessarily be a JMX reference implementation component. The format of the LEVEL DEBUG is the same as that of the LEVEL_TRACE, meaning that messages at both levels have the same content.

In this particular case, the output results are the same. You can also control the formatting of the output, which you'll see shortly. In these two output snippets, you can see the flow of execution in some detail, as the MBean named `SimpleObject` is created using `createMBean` with the object name `SimpleObject:thename=simple;` and then some internal methods are called by the MBean Server to keep track of the MBean. You can also see from the output that some notifications are created and sent in response in to the MBean being created.

This particular example also used the `INFO_MBEANSERVER` event type in the `TraceFilter` object it created. The "Setting up a trace filter" section in this chapter describes how to construct a `TraceFilter`, which is used to control the types of trace events you'll receive and the level of detail emitted.

## Format of trace messages

The example trace messages shown in the previous section have a format specified by the Sun JMX reference implementation. The example messages are in the *default* format, which follows this syntax:

```
(ClassName MethodName) Message
```

The class name specified in the message is the MBean class that emitted the trace message. The method name specified in the message is the method of the class that was executing when the trace message was emitted, and the message part is the text that describes the trace event. The message portion does not have a format or syntax. In the next section, you'll learn how to control the format of trace messages.

## Setting up a trace filter

You can set up the filtering of trace event types using the `TraceFilter` class. This class defines a small set of methods that are used to retrieve information about the types of events it will filter. The `TraceFilter` class implements the `NotificationFilter` interface; therefore, it implements the method of that interface.

`TraceFilter` object instances are constructed using the single constructor, which takes two arguments. The first argument specifies the level of events, which is either `LEVEL_TRACE` or `LEVEL_DEBUG`. The second argument enables you to specify which trace events you want your filter to see. You must specify that you want to see trace events from either all modules or a specific set of modules, using the Java `or` operator. The values you specify for the second argument are taken from Table C-2. The following code snippet shows a `TraceFilter` object that will process trace level events for the MBean Server and timer service:

```
TraceFilter filter = new TraceFilter(Trace.LEVEL_TRACE,
                              Trace.INFO_MBEANSERVER |
                              Trace.INFO_TIMER)
```

In this snippet, the second argument has two values: `Trace.INFO_MBEANSERVER` and `Trace.INFO_TIMER`, which are separated by the `or` operator.

Constructing a new instance of a `TraceFilter` class does not enable or disable a filter. You must pass the new instance to the `addNotificationListener()` method of the `Trace` class. The `TraceFilter` class declares two methods, `getLevels()` and `getType()`, which return the level and types of events, respectively.

## Setting up a trace listener

The `TraceListener` class is where trace event notifications are sent. This is similar to other types of notification listeners that you can register with components to receive events. There are a couple of differences between this class and other notification listener components, however. First, this is a class, whereas others are interfaces.

The `TraceListener` class acts as an implementation of the `NotificationListener` interface as sort of a helper class. With other notification listener components, such as a `TimerNotification`, you must implement the `NotificationListener` interface yourself and cast the `Notification` class instance that is passed in to get at the notification of the appropriate subtype.

Another difference is that you can control the formatting and style of the output produced by the `TraceListener` class. You can also configure the `TraceListener` class to send the output to a file or to an instance of the `java.io.PrintStream` class. If you don't specify a file or `PrintStream`, the output goes to standard output. Therefore, if you run an application that uses a `TraceListener` from a console or command prompt, you'll see the trace messages printed there.

Table C-3 lists the methods of the `TraceListener` class and provides a brief description of each.

### Table C-3    TraceListener Class Methods

| Method Name | Description |
|---|---|
| `handleNotification(javax.management` `.Notificatoin notif,` `java.lang.Object handback)` | Called by the `Trace` class when a notification arrives |
| `setFile(java.lang.String formatted)` | Sets the name of a file to which trace information can be sent. The name of the file is passed as a `java.lang.String`. |
| `setFormated(boolean f)` | Sets the style and formatting of the trace messages |

The formatting of trace and debug level messages can be controlled somewhat by the `setFormated()` method. This useful feature can provide an easy-to-read listing of the trace events as they happen. Earlier in this appendix, you saw a snippet of code that showed what the output from a trace might look like. Now you'll create a simple application that loads the MBean and enables tracing to produce the same output from that earlier snippet. Listing C-1 shows the source for this application.

**Listing C-1: The ExampleJMXTrace application**

```
import javax.management.InstanceNotFoundException;
import javax.management.IntrospectionException;
import javax.management.MalformedObjectNameException;
import javax.management.ReflectionException;
import javax.management.ObjectName;
import javax.management.MBeanServer;
import javax.management.MBeanServerFactory;
import com.sun.jdmk.Trace;
import com.sun.jdmk.TraceListener;

public class ExampleJMXTrace {

    private static MBeanServer server = null;

    public ExampleJMXTrace() {
        server = MBeanServerFactory.createMBeanServer();
    }

    public static void main(String[] args) {

        try {

            ExampleJMXTrace agent = new ExampleJMXTrace();

            Trace.addNotificationListener(new TraceListener(),
                                          null,
                                          agent);

            ObjectName simpleObject = agent.loadBean("SimpleObject",
                              "SimpleObject:thename=simple");

        } catch (Exception ex){System.out.println(ex);}

    }

    private ObjectName loadBean(String className,String objectName) {

        ObjectName mbeanObjectName = null;
        String domain = server.getDefaultDomain();
        String mbeanName = className;
        try {
            mbeanObjectName = new ObjectName(objectName);
        } catch(MalformedObjectNameException e) {
          e.printStackTrace();
          System.exit(1);
        }
            // Create our simple object to manage //
```

```
        try {
           server.createMBean(mbeanName,mbeanObjectName);
        }catch(Exception ex){
              ex.printStackTrace();
              System.exit(1);
        }


        return mbeanObjectName;

    }


}
```

In this example, you set up the `TraceListener` using the `addNotificationListener()` method, which takes a `TraceListener` as the first argument. The remaining arguments are for the `TraceFilter` and the handback object, which for this example are the values of null and agent, respectively. The latter is a reference to the `ExampleJMXTrace` application itself. The output from this application looks like the following:

```
(MBeanServer createMBean) ClassName = SimpleObject,ObjectName =
SimpleObject:the
name=simple
(MBeanServer internal_addObject) Name= SimpleObject:thename=simple
(Repository addMBean) name=SimpleObject:thename=simple
(MBeanServer addObject) Send create notification of object
SimpleObject:thename=
simple
(MBeanServer sendNotification) Incr sequenceNumber = 2
```

If you compare this output to the example output in the "Trace event types" section, you'll see they are the same. The format of this output was described in the same section. This example showed the default formatting, in which the trace output is unformatted. When formatted, that same code snippet is a little more readable. To alter the format of the listing, you can use the `setFormated()` method of the `TraceListener` class. By default, you don't have control over the exact format and style; rather, the output will be formatted into a more readable form. To use the `setFormated()` method, you need to alter the `ExampleJMXTrace` application to look like the following snippet:

```
TraceListener listener = new TraceListener();
listener.setFormated(true);

Trace.addNotificationListener(listener,
                             null,
                             agent);
```

If you run the `ExampleJMXTrace` application again with the aforementioned changes, the output will look like the following:

```
Global sequence number: 1      Sequence number: 1
Level: LEVEL_TRACE      Type: INFO_MBEANSERVER
```

```
Class  Name: MBeanServer
Method Name: createMBean
Information: ClassName = SimpleObject,ObjectName =
SimpleObject:thename=simple

Global sequence number: 2     Sequence number: 2
Level: LEVEL_TRACE      Type: INFO_MBEANSERVER
Class  Name: MBeanServer
Method Name: internal_addObject
Information: Name= SimpleObject:thename=simple

Global sequence number: 3     Sequence number: 3
Level: LEVEL_TRACE      Type: INFO_MBEANSERVER
Class  Name: Repository
Method Name: addMBean
Information: name=SimpleObject:thename=simple

Global sequence number: 4     Sequence number: 4
Level: LEVEL_TRACE      Type: INFO_MBEANSERVER
Class  Name: MBeanServer
Method Name: addObject
Information: Send create notification of object
SimpleObject:thename=simple

Global sequence number: 5     Sequence number: 5
Level: LEVEL_TRACE      Type: INFO_MBEANSERVER
Class  Name: MBeanServer
Method Name: sendNotification
Information: Incr sequenceNumber = 2
```

The content of this message is very similar to that of the default output you saw earlier. It does include some additional information that provides extra details about the message. The information included in the formatted version of trace output is as follows:

```
Global Sequence Number     Sequence Number
Trace Level                Trace Event Type
Class Name
Method Name
Information
```

The global sequence number portion of the message represents the sequence number of this trace event message among all trace event messages. The sequence number portion represents the sequence of this message among all trace event messages of the same type; in this case, INFO_MBEANSERVER. The trace level and trace event type represent the level of detail and type of trace events, respectively, that you want to receive.

The class name, method name, and information portions represent the same information that the unformatted version does. A helpful exercise might be to write your own TraceListener and format the output in a way that is more useful to your needs. For example, you could write a TraceListener that outputs the trace information as an XML document. Before you do this, though, you need a little more information about the notifications themselves. Trace notifications are represented as instances of the `TraceNotification` class, which is a subclass of the `Notification` class.

The `TraceNotification` class presents all its information in public fields, unlike other notification subtypes such as `TimerNotification` and `RelationNotification`, which use accessor methods to retrieve information about the notification. Table C-4 describes each of the public fields.

### Table C-4    TraceNotification Public Fields

| Field Name | Description |
| --- | --- |
| className | Represents the name of the class from which the trace information comes |
| exception | Represents any exception information associated with the trace |
| globalSequenceNumber | Represents the sequence number of this notification within all notifications |
| info | Represents the information or message associated with this notification |
| level | Represents the level of information |
| methodName | Represents the method that sent out the notification |
| sequenceNumber | Represents the sequence of this notification within all notifications of the same type |
| type | Represents the type of notification, such as INFO_MBEANSERVER |

With these descriptions of each field, you can use this information to build your trace listener. You can even tailor the information to be more or less specific than what is available in the `TraceListener` class. In fact, you can write any type of `NotificationListener` you want for use with the `Trace` class. The `Trace` class provides two methods for adding a listener: one takes an instance of the `NotificationListener` interface, and the other takes an instance of the `TraceListener` interface. Therefore, you have some level of flexibility regarding how you approach writing your own `TraceListener`.

If you write a listener that implements the `NotificationListener` interface, you might be able to re-use the class in other cases for notification handling. For this next example, however, it will be useful only for tracing, as your `TraceListener` class needs to check for instances of the `TraceNotification` class being passed in. In addition, you might recall that the tracing facilities are not an official part of the JMX specification. Therefore, this example extends the `TraceListener` class and overrides the `handleNotification()` method to provide custom formatting.

# The CustomTraceListener class

The CustomTraceListener class extends the TraceListener class and overrides the handleNotification() method to achieve the custom formatting in XML of your trace messages. Formatting the trace data in XML does not improve its readability, but it does provide the capability to present the trace information in different markup languages. This is useful if you plan to share debug information or want to provide debugging information to different types of devices such as Web browsers and handheld machines. Listing C-2 shows the source code of the CustomTraceListener class.

**Listing C-2: The CustomTraceListener class**

```
import javax.management.Notification;
import com.sun.jdmk.TraceNotification;
import com.sun.jdmk.TraceListener;


public class CustomTraceListener extends TraceListener{

        public static String CRLF = "\r\n";

        public void handleNotification(Notification notif,
                                        Object handBack){
                if (notif instanceof TraceNotification) {
                        TraceNotification traceNotify =
                                        (TraceNotification)notif;

                        StringBuffer msg = new StringBuffer();
                        msg.append("<TRACE-MESSAGES>"+CRLF);
                        msg.append("<TRACE-MESSAGE>"+CRLF);
                        msg.append("<CLASS-NAME
NAME=\""+traceNotify.className+"\"/>"+CRLF);

msg.append("<EXCEPTION>"+traceNotify.exception+"</EXCEPTION>"+CRLF);
                        msg.append("<GLOBAL-SEQUENCE-NUMBER
VALUE=\""+traceNotify.globalSequenceNumber+"\"/>"+CRLF);
                        msg.append("<INFO>"+traceNotify.info+"</INFO>"+CRLF);
                        msg.append("<LEVEL
VALUE=\""+traceNotify.level+"\"/>"+CRLF);
                        msg.append("<METHOD-NAME
VALUE=\""+traceNotify.methodName+"\"/>"+CRLF);
                        msg.append("<SEQUENCE-NUMBER
VALUE=\""+traceNotify.sequenceNumber+"\"/>"+CRLF);
                        msg.append("<TYPE
VALUE=\""+traceNotify.type+"\"/>"+CRLF);
                        msg.append("</TRACE-MESSAGE>"+CRLF);
                        msg.append("</TRACE-MESSAGES>"+CRLF);

                        out.println(msg.toString());
```

```
            }
        }
}
```

As you can see, this class is relatively straightforward. You first need to make sure that the notification is the correct type. Using the Java `instanceof` operator, cast it to the `TraceNotification` type, take the fields of the `TraceNotification` class and wrap each value in an XML element. You then specify the actual values of the XML elements as either an attribute or text node. Once you've put together the output, it's time to write it out. You can use the variable named `out` that is defined in the `TraceListener` class and it will represent whatever the you have defined as an instance of the `java.util.PrintStream` class, the default being standard output. At the end of each XML element, you add a carriage-return and line-feed to make the output more readable.

While an XML format is certainly more verbose than the previous examples, it does lend itself to more flexibility, as anyone familiar with XML would probably agree. Listing C-3 shows the source code of the application that used this custom trace listener.

**Listing C-3: Using the CustomTraceListener class in an application**

```java
import javax.management.InstanceNotFoundException;
import javax.management.IntrospectionException;
import javax.management.MalformedObjectNameException;
import javax.management.ReflectionException;
import javax.management.ObjectName;
import javax.management.MBeanServer;
import javax.management.MBeanServerFactory;
import com.sun.jdmk.Trace;
import com.sun.jdmk.TraceListener;

public class ExampleJMXTrace {

    private static MBeanServer server = null;

    public ExampleJMXTrace() {
        server = MBeanServerFactory.createMBeanServer();
    }

    public static void main(String[] args) {

        try {

            ExampleJMXTrace agent = new ExampleJMXTrace();

            JMXDebug debug = new JMXDebug(agent);

            ObjectName simpleObject = agent.loadBean("SimpleObject",
                            "SimpleObject:thename=simple");
```

```
        } catch (Exception ex){System.out.println(ex);}

    }

    private ObjectName loadBean(String className,String objectName) {

        ObjectName mbeanObjectName = null;
        String domain = server.getDefaultDomain();
        String mbeanName = className;
        try {
            mbeanObjectName = new ObjectName(objectName);
        } catch(MalformedObjectNameException e) {
          e.printStackTrace();
          System.exit(1);
        }
          // Create our simple object to manage //
          try {
             server.createMBean(mbeanName,mbeanObjectName);
          }catch(Exception ex){
              ex.printStackTrace();
              System.exit(1);
          }

          return mbeanObjectName;
    }

}
```

The `ExampleJMXTrace` application works much like many of the other examples you've seen in this book. It creates an MBean Server and loads an MBean. The difference, of course, is that this class uses the `JMXDebug` class to set up the `CustomTraceListener`. The source code for the `JMXDebug` class is shown in Listing C-4.

**Listing C-4: Source code of the JMXDebug class**

```
import com.sun.jdmk.Trace;
import com.sun.jdmk.TraceFilter;
import com.sun.jdmk.TraceListener;


public class JMXDebug {

    public JMXDebug(Object callback) {

            TraceFilter filter =

            new TraceFilter(Trace.LEVEL_DEBUG,Trace.INFO_MBEANSERVER);

            Trace.addNotificationListener(new CustomTraceListener(),
```

```
                                                filter,
                                                callback);

        }

}
```

The callback object that is passed in is passed as the last argument to the method `addNotificationListener()`. This will be passed around by the JMX runtime, and you should not try to modify it. The `CustomTraceListener` object is created as the first argument to this method.

Running the `ExampleJMXTrace` application with your new `CustomTraceListener` class yields output that looks like the following:

```
<TRACE-MESSAGES>
<TRACE-MESSAGE>
<CLASS-NAME NAME="DefaultMBeanAccessor"/>
<EXCEPTION>null</EXCEPTION>
<GLOBAL-SEQUENCE-NUMBER VALUE="1"/>
<INFO>ClassName = SimpleObject,ObjectName =
SimpleObject:thename=simple</IN
<LEVEL VALUE="1"/>
<METHOD-NAME VALUE="createMBean"/>
<SEQUENCE-NUMBER VALUE="1"/>
<TYPE VALUE="1"/>
</TRACE-MESSAGE>
</TRACE-MESSAGES>

<TRACE-MESSAGES>
<TRACE-MESSAGE>
<CLASS-NAME NAME="ClassLoaderRepositorySupport"/>
<EXCEPTION>null</EXCEPTION>
<GLOBAL-SEQUENCE-NUMBER VALUE="2"/>
<INFO>trying loader = sun.misc.Launcher$AppClassLoader@71732b</INFO>
<LEVEL VALUE="1"/>
<METHOD-NAME VALUE="loadClass"/>
<SEQUENCE-NUMBER VALUE="2"/>
<TYPE VALUE="1"/>
</TRACE-MESSAGE>
</TRACE-MESSAGES>

<TRACE-MESSAGES>
<TRACE-MESSAGE>
<CLASS-NAME NAME="DefaultMBeanAccessor"/>
<EXCEPTION>null</EXCEPTION>
<GLOBAL-SEQUENCE-NUMBER VALUE="3"/>
<INFO>ObjectName = SimpleObject:thename=simple</INFO>
<LEVEL VALUE="1"/>
<METHOD-NAME VALUE="registerMBean"/>
<SEQUENCE-NUMBER VALUE="3"/>
```

```
<TYPE VALUE="1"/>
</TRACE-MESSAGE>
</TRACE-MESSAGES>

<TRACE-MESSAGES>
<TRACE-MESSAGE>
<CLASS-NAME NAME="Repository"/>
<EXCEPTION>null</EXCEPTION>
<GLOBAL-SEQUENCE-NUMBER VALUE="4"/>
<INFO>name=SimpleObject:thename=simple</INFO>
<LEVEL VALUE="1"/>
<METHOD-NAME VALUE="addMBean"/>
<SEQUENCE-NUMBER VALUE="4"/>
<TYPE VALUE="1"/>
</TRACE-MESSAGE>
</TRACE-MESSAGES>

<TRACE-MESSAGES>
<TRACE-MESSAGE>
<CLASS-NAME NAME="DefaultMBeanAccessor"/>
<EXCEPTION>null</EXCEPTION>
<GLOBAL-SEQUENCE-NUMBER VALUE="5"/>
<INFO>Send create notification of object
SimpleObject:thename=simple</INFO>
<LEVEL VALUE="1"/>
<METHOD-NAME VALUE="addObject"/>
<SEQUENCE-NUMBER VALUE="5"/>
<TYPE VALUE="1"/>
</TRACE-MESSAGE>
</TRACE-MESSAGES>

<TRACE-MESSAGES>
<TRACE-MESSAGE>
<CLASS-NAME NAME="DefaultMBeanAccessor"/>
<EXCEPTION>null</EXCEPTION>
<GLOBAL-SEQUENCE-NUMBER VALUE="6"/>
<INFO>Incr sequenceNumber = 2</INFO>
<LEVEL VALUE="1"/>
<METHOD-NAME VALUE="sendNotification"/>
<SEQUENCE-NUMBER VALUE="6"/>
<TYPE VALUE="1"/>
</TRACE-MESSAGE>
</TRACE-MESSAGES>
```

The examples so far have demonstrated the use of a single `TraceListener`; however, because the `Trace` class defines the `addNotificationListener()` method, you can add multiple listeners, each with a different filter. For example, you could have all MBean-related trace information go to one file, and all timer service–related traces go to another. Alternatively, you could have each filter go to a different output type, such as logging traces to the console versus logging to a file. You could create listeners set up with defaults specific to each type of trace message.

For example, you could use subtypes named `FileTraceListener` or `SocketTraceListener`. The latter could be used for remotely monitoring trace messages by sending trace messages to a network location specified. The former, of course, would be defined to send trace messages to a file specified in the constructor. Using subtypes is more understandable than trying to set up a single type to do multiple functions.

The `Trace` class also includes a method named `addNotificationListener()`, which takes two arguments: a `TraceListener` instance and the handback object. This creates a listener with default settings of all event types set at `LEVEL_TRACE`.

## Setting up tracing via the command line

In addition to all the classes described here, you have yet another option for enabling tracing. This method enables you to set up tracing and change trace options on the fly without recompiling. The tracing facilities enable you to specify trace information via the command line of the Java interpreter. All you need to do is add a single call to your application, which sets up a default trace listener with the options you specify via the command line.

You can modify the `ExampleJMXTrace` application in Listing C-2 slightly to use the command-line specification of trace options. The following code snippet shows the `main()` method of the updated application:

```
public static void main(String[] args) {

        try {

            Trace.parseTraceProperties();

            ExampleJMXTrace agent = new ExampleJMXTrace();

            ObjectName simpleObject = agent.loadBean("SimpleObject",
                            "SimpleObject:thename=simple");

        } catch (Exception ex){System.out.println(ex);}

    }
```

The change to this method involves the boldfaced line that reads `Trace.parseTraceProperties()`. The `main()` method begins by calling the `parseTraceProperties()` method, which causes the `Trace` class to read the system properties that were passed in on the command line, and then create a default notification listener and trace filter using those options. An example using the `ExampleJMXTrace` class with this update looks like the following:

```
java -DLEVEL_DEBUG -DINFO_MBEANSERVER ExampleJMXTrace
```

This command line executes the `ExampleJMXTrace` application and passes in two system properties: `LEVEL_DEBUG` and `INFO_MBEANSERVER`. It doesn't matter how you specify the properties, as the `Trace` class will treat them appropriately. You can also specify the name of an output file using the TRACE_OUTPUT system property. By default, the output goes to standard output, which in the case of this example means the screen. The output from this command looks like the following:

```
(MBeanServer new) Initializing domain DefaultDomain
(MBeanServer registerMBean) ObjectName =
JMImplementation:type=MBeanServerDelega
te
(MBeanServer internal_addObject) Name=
JMImplementation:type=MBeanServerDelegate

(Repository addMBean) name=JMImplementation:type=MBeanServerDelegate
(MBeanServer addObject) Send create notification of object
JMImplementation:type
=MBeanServerDelegate
(MBeanServer sendNotification) Incr sequenceNumber = 1
(DefaultLoaderRepository addClassLoader)
sun.misc.Launcher$AppClassLoader@71732b

(DefaultLoaderRepository addClassLoader)
sun.misc.Launcher$AppClassLoader@71732b

(MBeanServer createMBean) ClassName = SimpleObject,ObjectName =
SimpleObject:the
name=simple
(MBeanServer internal_addObject) Name= SimpleObject:thename=simple
(Repository addMBean) name=SimpleObject:thename=simple
(MBeanServer addObject) Send create notification of object
SimpleObject:thename=
simple
(MBeanServer sendNotification) Incr sequenceNumber = 2
```

In the preceding output, first the MBeanServerDelegate MBean is registered, and then a notification is sent to any listeners who are interested in this registration. The same sequence of events occurs with the SimpleObject MBean; it is registered and a notification is issued.

# Summary

In this appendix, you've learned how to use the tracing and debug facilities in the Sun JMX reference implementation. You've identified the classes and created a TraceListener that receives trace and debug-level events. You also learned how to filter the types of events you want to receive using the TraceFilter class. Although the trace and debug classes are not defined in the JMX specification, their inclusion in the JMX API enables you to save time and avoid frustration when writing your own JMX applications.

# *Appendix D*
# UML Quick Reference

In this appendix, you'll find UML diagrams that describe the various JMX classes and interfaces. These diagrams present a quick view of the makeup of these classes and interfaces, and in some cases, the relationships between them. You'll also find UML diagrams throughout the book that further describe the relationships between these classes and interfaces.

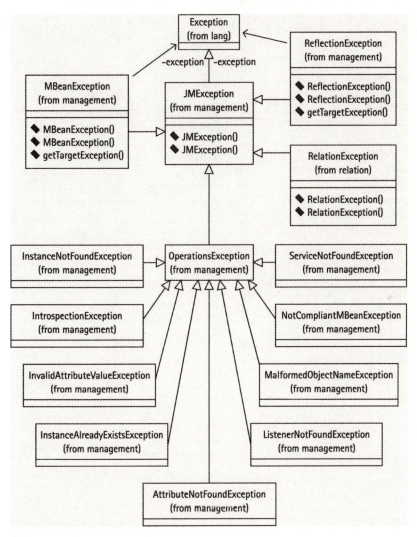

**Figure D-1:** JMX runtime exceptions.

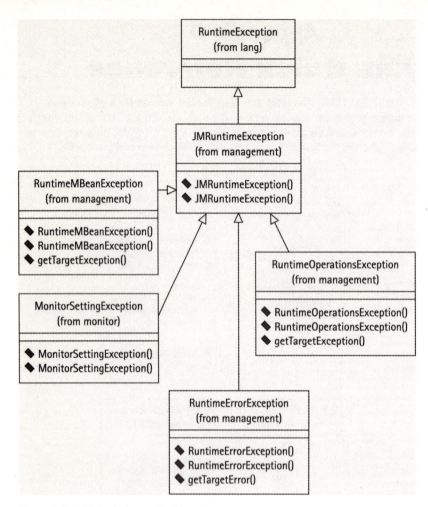

**Figure D-2:** JMX checked exception hierarchy.

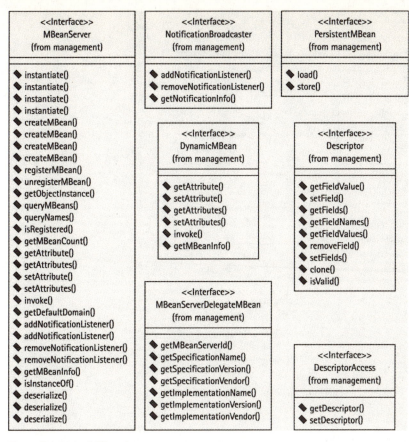

**Figure D-3:** Main JMX interfaces.

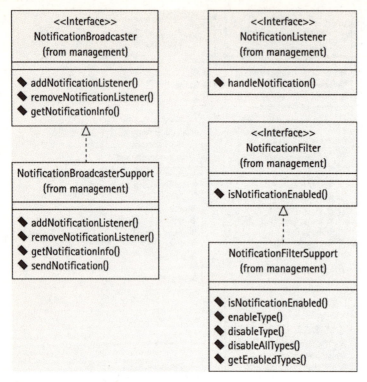

**Figure D-4:** JMX Notification interfaces and classes.

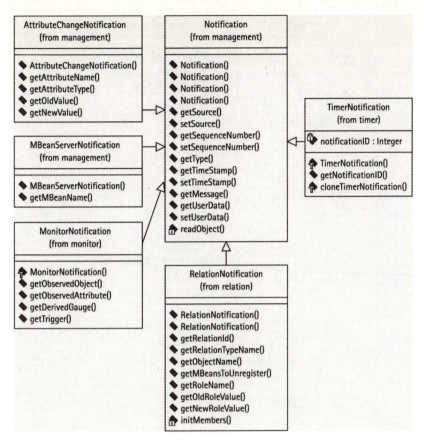

**Figure D-5:** JMX Notification classes.

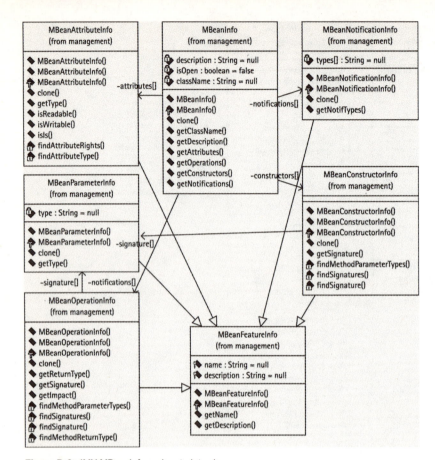

**Figure D-6:** JMX MBeanInfo and metadata classes.

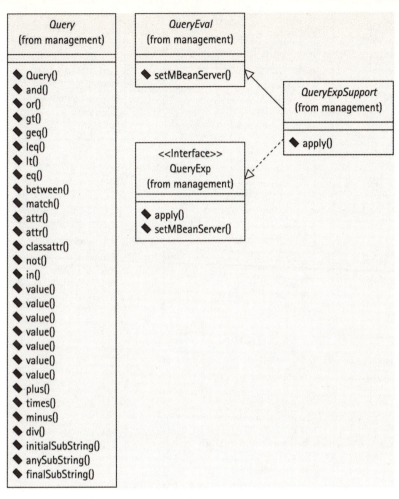

**Figure D-7:** JMX query interfaces and classes.

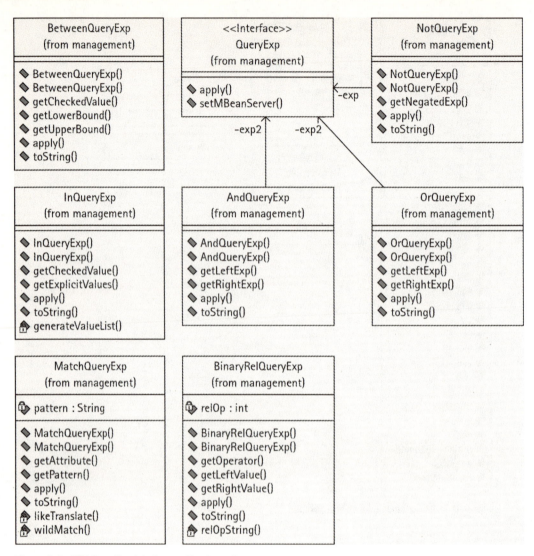

**Figure D-8:** JMX QueryExp interface and implementors.

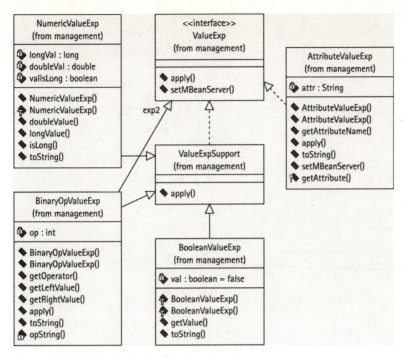

**Figure D-9:** JMX ValueExp interface and implementors.

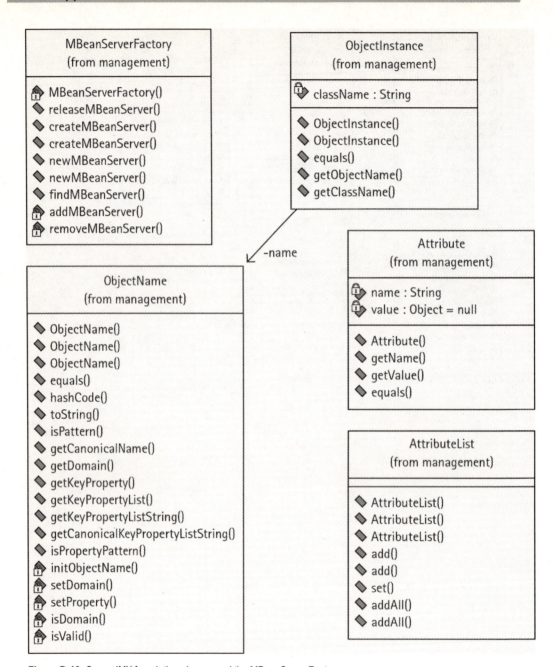

**Figure D-10:** Some JMX foundation classes and the MBeanServerFactory.

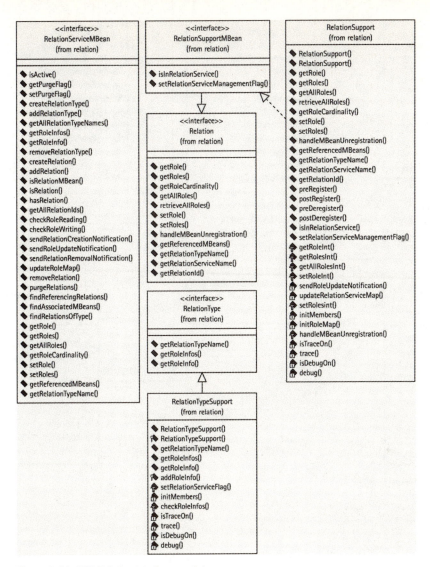

**Figure D-11:** JMX Relation interfaces and classes.

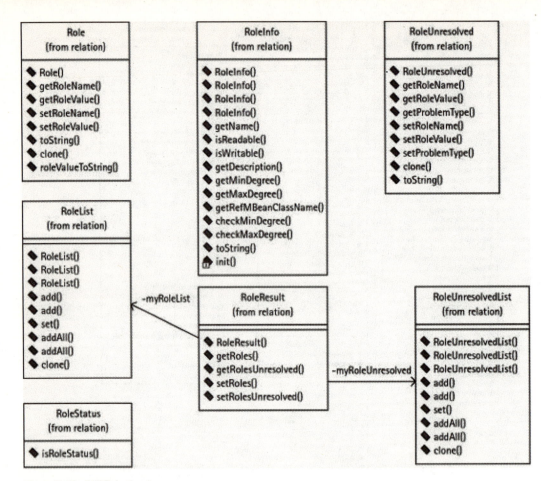

**Figure D-12:** JMX Role classes.

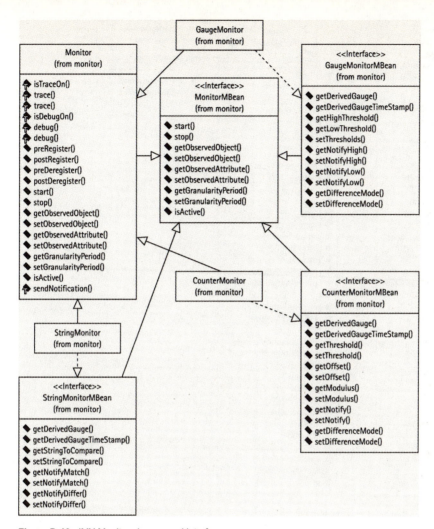

**Figure D-13:** JMX Monitor classes and interfaces.

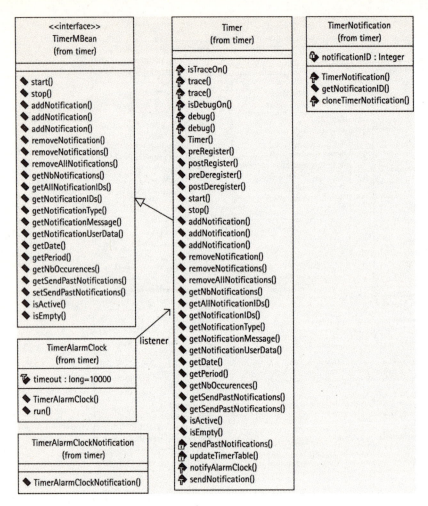

**Figure D-14:** JMX Timer classes and interfaces.

# Index

## X-Y-Z